FROM YALTA TO THE IRON CURTAIN

Le Temps Mondial/World Time Series

Edited by Zaki Laïdi, *Centre National de la Recherche Scientifique (Centre d'Etudes et de Recherches Internationales), Paris*

Previously published title in the Series:

Power and Purpose after the Cold War
Edited by Zaki Laïdi

Le Temps Mondial/World Time Series

FROM YALTA TO THE IRON CURTAIN

The Great Powers and the Origins of the Cold War

Pierre de Senarclens

Translated from the French by
Amanda Pingree

BERG

Oxford/Washington D.C., USA

English edition
first published in 1995 by

Berg Publishers Limited

Editorial offices:
150 Cowley Road, Oxford, OX4 1JJ, UK
13590 Park Center Road, Herndon, VA 22071, USA

English edition © Berg Publishers 1995
Originally published as *De Yalta au rideau de fer: Les grandes puissances et les origines de la guerre froide*
Translated from the French by permission of the publishers
© Presses de la Fondation nationale des sciences politiques
Translated by Amanda Pingree

Library of Congress Cataloging-in-Publication Data

A catalogue record for this book is available from the Library of Congress.

British Library Cataloguing in Publication Data

A catalogue record for this book is available from the British Library.

ISBN 0 85496 809 1

Printed in the United Kingdom by WBC Book Manufacturers, Mid Glamorgan.

CONTENTS

FOREWORD

The destruction of the Berlin wall in 1989 symbolized the end of the "iron curtain" that had divided Europe into two hostile camps. This event brought a definitive close to the Cold War, a conflict between the USSR and Western countries that had influenced the course of world politics for more than forty years. Statesmen, diplomats and specialists in international affairs had not predicted this rapid turn of events in history, and the governments of the former occupying powers in Germany – the United States, France, Great Britain, and the USSR – were totally unprepared to reopen the peace negotiations their foreign ministers had left off in 1948 in the winter of the Cold War. Today, the diplomatic stage set in 1990 by the former Second World War Allies to legitimate German reunification has lost all its meaning; for the collapse of the Soviet regime has erased in one fell swoop the prevailing circumstances in which the two German states were created.

Since the Berlin Wall was torn down, history's course has accelerated so sharply, and the nature of international politics has changed so rapidly, that today it is difficult to fully comprehend what the Cold War actually was. The aim of this work is to recapitulate the origins of that conflict in order both to explain Europe's division in the years following the Second World War, and to bring to light the ideological and political foundations of the East–West opposition that marked the structures of international society for so long. It examines the rapid disintegration of the wartime alliance against the Third Reich subsequent to the conference at Yalta, then describes the main issues of the Potsdam conference, where the plans were laid for Germany's dismemberment. It then studies the laborious process and the impasses in the peace negotiations between the former Allied powers, and the confrontation that arose among the victors as the USSR built its ascendancy over Eastern Europe, while Great Britain, France and the United States sought to restore their imperial hegemony or to extend their spheres of influence throughout the world. It also explains how the United States came to take over Great Britain's position in the Mediterranean, the Middle East, and Europe in order to defend the political and strategic interests of the West.

The antagonism between East and West that developed after the Yalta conference was not an ordinary international conflict, and its explanation cannot be reduced to a typical confrontation among great powers seeking hegemony. The outburst of the Cold War is generally associated with the "Truman Doctrine," introduced in March 1947 when the president of the United States declared his country's will to defend the "free world" against the advance of Soviet totalitarian designs; but Stalin, too, had a decisive role in the emergence of this conflict. At the end of the Second World War, he made clear his intention to extend the Soviet Union's empire to Central Europe, the Balkans and Asia. He then relentlessly pushed the borders under his hegemony farther west, and backed Communist party action in the rest of the world. By undermining the peace negotiations, blocking the construction of a new international order to replace the defeated fascist regimes, and propagating his will to destroy the capitalist world and to pursue Lenin's revolutionary program, Stalin opened the way to a global confrontation with the Western countries the ideological virulence of which bears some resemblance to the religious wars of the seventeenth century. The Cold War was hence much more than a political standoff between states. From its very origins, it compromised stability in all national societies, compelling them by means of force and propaganda to choose between different economic systems and irreconcilable historical philosophies and regimes.

This work is not the first of its type. In Britain, and especially in the United States, there are many studies of the origins of the Cold War. In France and the Francophone countries, however, the question has been neglected, as though historians of international relations were uninspired by this period of European history, which is overshadowed by relations between Washington and Moscow. This shortfall, due in part to the abundant American historiography of the Cold War, which generally focuses exclusively on United States policy, has certainly lent to the myriad of simplistic myths about the Yalta conference and the policies which the great powers adopted after the Second World War. It has also preserved the notion that the Western European countries were merely powerless victims of the Cold War, as if they had taken no part in the decisions that led to the emergence of the conflict. Nothing could be farther from the truth. An examination of British foreign policy and French diplomacy during this crucial period, which dates from the Yalta conference to the Berlin blockade, based on Foreign Office analyses and the French government archives, shows clearly that these states were important actors in the origins of the Cold War.

ACKNOWLEDGMENTS

I wish to thank the Swiss National Science Foundation for its help in completing this work. With its support, I was able to collaborate with Pascale Schaller, whose work was concentrated, among others, on the French National Archives, before her tragic death in an automobile accident in August 1987. The memory of her youthfulness and radiance have remained with me as I finished this project. I also thank Madame Garcés-Fisher for the research she conducted at the National Archives, Washington, in 1988. I also extend my gratitude to Jean-Christophe Graz and Yohan Ariffin, assistants at the University of Lausanne, for having read the final manuscript of this work.

ABBREVIATIONS

DBPO	*Documents on British Policy Overseas*
FRUS	*Foreign Policy Relations of the United States*

THE "GRAND ALLIANCE"

In early 1945, the Second World War was coming to an end. Hitler's army was opposed with stubborn resistance on all fronts, including Poland, Silesia, Hungary, west of the Rhine – from Switzerland to the North Sea – and Italy. Japanese troops controlled Manchuria and the principal urban and industrial centers of China. They also occupied Indochina, Indonesia, and the Philippines. The Allied advance in Europe and the American advance in the Pacific steadily reduced the economic and military capacity of the Axis. The hostilities were still fierce, but there was no longer any doubt about what their outcome would be. Great Britain, and later the USSR and the United States, had mustered the most formidable armies in the history of war. Their "grand alliance" never gave way, but the coalition's ideological and political stability was fragile.

A Heterogeneous Coalition

Great Britain was forced to declare war on the Third Reich to honor its commitment to France and to protect Poland's independence. Since the seventeenth century, Great Britain had striven to maintain a measure of political balance on the continent in order to prevent a large hegemonic power from rising up in Europe, and to control the access corridors to its dominions and colonies. Its objective in once again taking up arms against Germany was similar to that which it had fought for in the First World War. Now its aim was to prevent Hitler from controlling Europe, and thus to defend its liberal political and ideological concepts while protecting the Empire's essential interests. Winston Churchill was the symbol of this policy. In contrast to the Third Reich's totalitarian ideology, Churchill, more than anyone else, symbolized the defense of liberal democratic values. Nonetheless, he was determined to preserve the British Empire, whose civilizing principles were incontestable in his view.

Well before the attack on Pearl Harbor, President Franklin D. Roosevelt and his staff were convinced that the United States should aid the democracies warring against Nazi Germany so that Europe would not fall under the domination of that tyrannical power. They were aware that isolationist policy was a dangerous illusion in a world marked by growing socioeconomic interdependency and communication networks. The president was able to win the approval of Congress for substantial economic and military aid to Great Britain, and later the USSR, under the terms of the famous "Lend–Lease Act." Over the summer of 1941, it became clear to him that the United States would have to enter the war against the Third Reich; but, to avoid making the same mistakes as his illustrious predecessor, President Woodrow Wilson, he tried to dissuade his allies from accepting political compromise and secret agreements that would put a price on the future peace. The Atlantic Declaration of 12 August 1941, which concluded Churchill and Roosevelt's meeting aboard a ship sailing off the shores of Newfoundland, neatly sums up his program for the international society:

> The President of the United States of America and the Prime Minister, Mr. Churchill, representing His Majesty's Government in the United Kingdom, being met together to resolve and concert the means of providing for the safety of their respective countries in face of Nazi and German aggression and of the dangers to all peoples arising therefrom, deem it right to make known certain principles which they both accept for guidance in the framing of their policy and on which they base their hopes for a better future of the world.
>
> First, their countries seek no aggrandisement, territorial or other.
>
> Second, they desire to see no territorial changes that do not accord with the freely expressed wishes of the peoples concerned.
>
> Third, they respect the right of all peoples to choose the form of government under which they will live. They are only concerned to defend the rights of freedom of speech and thought, without which such choice must be illusory.
>
> Fourth, they will strive to bring about fair and equitable distribution of essential produce, not only within their territorial boundaries, but between the nations of the world.
>
> Fifth, they seek a peace which will not only cast down for ever the Nazi tyranny, but by effective international organisation will afford to all States and peoples the means of dwelling in security without fear of lawless assault of the need of maintaining burdensome armaments.[1]

The declaration, which was later entitled the Atlantic Charter, affirms Woodrow Wilson's conception in its return to an image of the international society based on democracy, the right of self-determination, and liberal economics. The world was becoming the new frontier of American policy.

This global project gained new strength when the United States entered the war in December 1941. Having established a link between the breakdown of free trade in the 1930s and the rise of fascism, United States

1. Winston S. Churchill, *The Second World War*, vol. 3, *The Grand Alliance*, Cassel, London, 1954, pp. 385–6.

leadership was convinced that the origins of the Second World War were determined by socioeconomic conditions. The reasoning was sound: the 1929 crash, the rise of protectionism, restrictive trade practices, and monetary disorder had indeed played a decisive role in the advent of Hitler's regime and the rise of Japanese imperialism. Roosevelt and his staff were aware that the United States was to some extent accountable for the crystallization of these economic disorders. They were intent on doing their best to structure the world economy on liberal foundations. They also wished to re-create a system of collective security similar to the League of Nations but based on understanding among the big powers. It was to this end that the United States government played a decisive role during the war of creating international institutions parallel to the collective security system whose functions were to stabilize monetary fluctuations, prevent financial crises, and promote trade. Maintaining a peaceful international order meant first bringing about the economic and social conditions of peace. In 1943, Henry Dexter White, the United States Treasury representative, and Lord Keynes negotiated to create a new monetary and financial system. One year later, the Bretton Woods Agreement brought their institutional plans into effect. Concurrently, the economic and social provisions of the Charter of the United Nations, drawn up at Dumbarton Oaks, were similar in their neoliberal principles.

Great Britain had upheld similar concepts in the nineteenth century, when it was at the pinnacle of its economic and political power. Its government was still a proponent of free trade, but, in the immediate future, it did not plan to dismantle the system of imperial preferences it exercised under the Ottawa Agreement of 1932. It was, however, forced to commit to do so when it signed the Lend–Lease Act with the United States in 1942. Article 7 of the act provides for the elimination of all forms of discriminatory treatment in international trade and the reduction of tariffs and other forms of trade barriers.[2] Furthermore, Churchill did not envisage granting the right of self-determination as it is defined in the Atlantic Charter to all peoples of the British Empire. In their loyalty to the founding myth of the American nation, Roosevelt and his staff generally disapproved of perpetuating European imperialist structures. The president made his desire for India's independence known. He favored the restitution of Hong Kong to China, and was particularly critical of French colonialism. In 1942, he encouraged the king of Morocco to declare the country's independence. Moreover, he invariably took France to task for its policies in Indochina. His commitment to the emancipation of the colonial peoples was a constant source of irritation

2. See, notably, *Documents on British Policy Overseas (DBPO)*, Series I (1945–1950), vol. 3, "Memorandum by Mr. Hall-Patch," pp. 1–5.

for the prime minister.[3]

In the days preceding the Yalta conference, the Red Army had already advanced to the heart of East Prussia and Central Europe, yet the USSR had still not clearly expressed its views on the postwar international order. In September 1941, the Soviet ambassador in London voiced his support of the Atlantic Charter, though he suggested that its application be adapted "to the circumstances, needs and historic peculiarities of particular countries."[4] Stalin, however, never made a mystery of his intent to recover the territorial gains he had won in 1939 when, after the hostilities had ended, he made an alliance with Hitler. Under the Ribbentrop–Molotov pact, the USSR was awarded the eastern part of Poland. It occupied the Baltic States of Estonia, Latvia and Lithuania, then annexed them in June 1940. It took Bessarabia and North Bukovina, which previously had belonged to Romania. In his first letter to Churchill after Hitler's army invaded, Stalin mentioned the strategic advantages the USSR's new western borders had provided early on in the invasion. When British Foreign Minister Anthony Eden arrived in Moscow in December 1941, Stalin immediately asked him to sign a secret agreement guaranteeing that his former conquests would be returned to him. As the German army was still several kilometers from the Soviet capital, Stalin's request did not appear to be a burning issue, and in fact, the British minister could not honor it without violating the principles of the Atlantic Charter and the trust of the Polish government in exile in London. Yet Stalin would never relinquish these territorial claims, and his persistence poisoned relations between the Allied forces throughout the war.

Strategy and Conflict

These divergences in policy were not, however, the greatest problem of the "grand alliance." Since 22 June 1941, the USSR had shouldered the brunt of the war against Hitler, and Stalin incessantly demanded that his allies participate more actively in military operations. Directly after the German invasion, he urged Churchill to open a second front, and his request became more pressing when the United States entered the war.

3. See, notably, William Roger Louis, *Imperialism at Bay, The United States and the Decolonization of the British Empire, 1941–1945*, New York, Oxford University Press, 1978; Christopher Thorne, *Allies of a Kind. The United States, Britain and the War against Japan, 1941–1945*, London, Hamish Hamilton, 1978; Richard N. Gardner, *Sterling–Dollar Diplomacy in Current Perspective: The Origins and Prospects of Our International Economic Order*, New York, Columbia University Press, 1980.
4. Quoted by Vojtech Mastny, *Russia's Road to the Cold War. Diplomacy, Warfare, and the Politics of Communism, 1941–1945*, New York, Columbia University Press, 1979, p. 41.

Roosevelt and the United States military began to question the Red Army's ability to resist; they intended to comply as best they could with Soviet demands by giving priority to the European theater of operations and opening a second European front as early as possible. When Molotov arrived in Washington in the spring of 1942, the president promised to dispatch Anglo–American troops to France in the coming months. But would this be possible? The British doubted it. Memories of the bloodshed at the Somme and Dunkirk plagued them, and they were terrified by Germany's strength and the formidable efficiency of its submarines. Churchill and his chiefs of staff conceived a strategy directed at the edges, which reflected their desire both to avoid another defeat on the continent and to protect communications with the Empire. After the British troops were defeated at Tobruk in Cyrenaica, Churchill managed to convince Roosevelt to postpone opening a second front in Europe and to organize a landing in North Africa. Stalin was intensely bitter over the decision.

In early 1943, strategic debates between the United States and Great Britain recommenced. Again, Churchill and the British chiefs of staff made their opinions prevail. The British and American troops were to advance toward Tunis, and then to invade Sicily. The landing in France was planned for early 1944. When he learned of the decision, Stalin was again greatly disappointed in his allies. In response to Churchill's attempt to justify the strategic choices, he wrote:

> You say that you "quite understand" my disappointment. I must tell you that the point here is not just the disappointment of the Soviet Government, but the preservation of its confidence in its Allies, a confidence which is being subjected to severe stress. One should not forget that it is a question of saving millions of lives in the occupied areas of Western Europe and Russia and of reducing the enormous sacrifices of the Soviet armies, compared with which the sacrifices of the Anglo–American armies are insignificant.[5]

The war changed its course on the Russian front, however. On 2 February 1943, the German army commanded by General Friedrich von Paulus surrendered at Stalingrad, and in the early summer the Red Army contained the last German heavy offensive on the Russian front. Thereafter, Stalin had no cause to moderate the policy requests he had made in the winter of his defeat. This is apparent in his decision on 25 April 1943 to break relations with the Polish government in London

5. *Correspondence between the Chairman of the Council of Ministers of the USSR and the Presidents of the United States of America and the Prime Ministers of Great Britain during the Great Patriotic Wars of 1941–1945*, vol. 1, p. 138, Moscow, Foreign Languages Publishing House, 1957.

following its appeal to the International Committee of the Red Cross to investigate the discovery of a mass grave in Katyn, near Smolensk, containing the remains of thousands of Polish officers whose assassination Stalin had ordered by the National Commissariat of Domestic Affairs (NKVD, a precursor of the KGB) in early March 1940, when he was colluding with Hitler. At the conference of Teheran, the first summit meeting between Churchill, Roosevelt, and Stalin (28 November to 1 December 1943), the Soviet leader forcefully restated his territorial claims on Poland. The Foreign Office knew it would have to make concessions, for the Soviet claims conformed to Lord Curzon's partition plan, proposed after the First World War to delineate ethnic borders between Poland, Ukraine, Belorussia, and Lithuania. Furthermore, Great Britain and the United States had no way of opposing Russian ambitions in Poland. It was Churchill who first accepted Stalin's claim on Poland's eastern border: he recognized Stalin's right to annex the territories east of the former Curzon line, a border that granted the Kremlin the same advantages it had enjoyed under the Ribbentrop–Molotov pact. In return, Stalin suggested that in due time Poland should be offered territorial compensation at Germany's expense. Roosevelt also seemed to recognize that this arrangement was sensible, but in his apprehension over Congress's reaction, he refused to commit himself on the matter. His main concern at the time was to win Stalin's trust to maintain cohesion in the "grand alliance," and to obtain his support as the post-War world was organized, notably in designing a system of collective security. In a long letter of 29 January, William Bullitt, the former United States ambassador in Moscow (1933 to 1936), sent a warning to the president: Stalin had not come around to the ideals of the Atlantic Charter, nor had he foregone his plans for revolution; his political and territorial objectives remained unchanged. He would attempt to annex Bessarabia, North Bukovina, an undefined part of East Poland, and the Baltic States. When he could, he would install Soviet governments in Romania, Bulgaria, Poland, and Germany. Bullitt also predicted that Communist "partisans" in Yugoslavia would install a Soviet-style government, and that Edvard Benes would play into Stalin's hands. "There is only one sure guarantee that the Red Army will not cross Europe – the prior arrival of American and British Armies in the eastern frontiers of Europe."[6]

On 6 June 1944, the British–American troops commanded by General Dwight Eisenhower landed in Normandy. In Italy, Rome had just been liberated. At this point, the Americans wanted to thin out the Italian front so that they could land in the south of France as they had promised Stalin

6. Orville H. Bullitt (ed.), *For the President, Personal and Secret. Correspondence between Franklin D. Roosevelt and William Bullitt*, London, A. Deutsch, 1973, p. 588.

at the Teheran conference. Winston Churchill was fiercely opposed, and resubmitted his plan to land at Istria with a view to reaching Central Europe as rapidly as possible; but his protests were in vain. The United States, which now carried a decisive weight in the conduct of military operations, discounted the "peripheral" strategy, which might slow their main offensive toward the Rhine.

At the same time, the Soviet troops were advancing in Poland and the Balkans. As the war's end was near, Stalin had no reason to abandon the territorial claims he had made in 1941, when the troops of the Reich were only kilometers from Moscow. Polish General Tadeusz Bor-Komorowski's Polish Home Army, which pledged allegiance to the Polish government in exile in London, attempted to assist in the liberation of the German-occupied cities and regions, and notably those that lay east of the Curzon line. But the Soviet forces rejected their aid. They had already created their own Polish army, and on 22 July 1944 they recognized de facto the Polish national liberation committee headed by Boleslaw Bierut, a Communist. Polish resistance fighters were arrested, deported, and some were sent before the firing squad. When the Red Army reached the fringes of Warsaw, the Polish government in exile in London and the Polish Home Army planned an insurrection in Warsaw in the hope of liberating the city before the Soviet forces arrived. Hitler ordered his soldiers to remain in Warsaw, however. Rapidly, the insurrection took a tragic turn. The Red Army did not budge, despite appeals for aid from the Polish government in London and pressing appeals from Churchill and Roosevelt.

On 19 September 1944, Averell Harriman, the United States ambassador in Moscow, wrote a pessimistic letter on developments in the USSR to the president's closest assistant, Harry Hopkins: "Since the end of the war is in sight our relations with the Soviets have evidenced a startling turn during the last two months. They have shown an unwillingness to discuss pressing problems and have held up our requests with complete indifference to our interests." The USSR's demands on its allies were growing incessantly, and the United States' generosity was now interpreted as a sign of weakness. The United States had to change its policy by demanding reciprocal concessions in diplomatic negotiations. Harriman believed that opinions were divided among Stalin's advisers on the chances of cooperating with the United States, and that the opponents among them were gaining the upper hand. The letter was transmitted to President Roosevelt, who sent it on to the British prime minister.[7]

Polish independence was now at stake, as was that of the Baltic States,

7. PREM 3/396/4.

where Soviet troops were deploying. The Western Allies had limited means to redirect the political fate of these countries, for their armies carried no weight in this part of Europe. Churchill was worried. He was particularly concerned about Greece, which had been in the British sphere of influence since the nineteenth century; for, because of its proximity to the Middle East and the Suez Canal, its strategic position in the Mediterranean made it very important. In 1941, Churchill had dispatched 70,000 men to help in the country's defense. After their defeat, he backed the Greek resistance movements. As the end of the war approached, he was gravely worried over political developments in Greece, for the main Greek resistance movement, the EAM (National Liberation Front), and its military arm, ELAS (National People's Liberation Army), pledged allegiance to the Communists.

The Prime Minister decided to meet Stalin in Moscow in October 1944 to settle the Polish problem, which was weighing upon the anti-Hitler coalition's future, and to broach the issue of the Balkans. The head of the Polish government in exile in London, Stanislaw Mikolajczyk, attended the negotiations. Little progress was made, as Mikolajczyk's cabinet had not authorized him to accept Stalin's claims on the Curzon line, and certainly not to make any agreements with the pro-Soviet government that the USSR had helped to set up in Lublin. On the question of the Balkans, however, Churchill proposed his famous "percentage agreement," which laid out in arithmetical terms Soviet Russia's and the Western Allies' respective future spheres of influence in this region and in Hungary. Churchill submitted his proposal to Stalin in these terms:

"Your armies are in Roumania and Bulgaria. We have interests, missions, and agents there. Don't let us get at cross-purposes in small ways. So far as Great Britain and Russia are concerned, how would it do for you to have ninety per cent. predominance in Roumania, for us to have ninety per cent. of the say in Greece, and go fifty-fifty about Yugoslavia?" While this was being translated, I wrote out on a half sheet of paper:

Roumania	
Russia	90%
The others	10%
Greece	
Great Britain	90%
(in accord with U.S.A.)	
Russia	10%
Yugoslavia	50–50%
Hungary	50–50%

Bulgaria	
Russia	75%
The others	25%

I pushed this across to Stalin, who had by then heard the translation. There was a slight pause. Then he took his blue pencil and made a large tick upon it, and passed it back to us.[8]

For Churchill, the agreement might have prevented "civil war breaking out in several countries." The Prime Minister stated that it would be valid only for the duration of the hostilities against the Third Reich. He was realistic enough to foresee its harmful consequences, although he certainly must not have anticipated Stalin's brutal repression of the countries he handed over to the Soviet sphere. This appears to account for his unease when the time came to finalize the agreement, particularly because he had not consulted his own cabinet, and because the United States was not directly involved in the negotiation. During the Moscow talks, Stalin requested a revision of the Montreux convention regulating navigation of the Bosphorus. According to him, the 1936 instrument was a hindrance to Soviet Russia's freedom of navigation of the Mediterranean. Churchill acknowledged the Soviet claim was valid, but suggested that in return Stalin restrain communist fervor in Italy.[9]

The percentage agreement, to which the United States was not a party, had no effect on political developments in Yugoslavia, for Tito was determined to carry through the Communist revolution he had begun. In Greece, however, the British were able to tilt the scales in favor of George Papandreou's government of national unity after the EAM ministers broke off ties with it and the Communists instigated heavy rioting in Athens. On 5 December, Churchill sent these peremptory instructions to General Robert Scobie: "Do not however hesitate to act as if you were in a conquered city where a local rebellion is in progress. [. . .] We have to hold and dominate Athens."[10] His resolution aroused broad criticism from both the House of Commons and United States public opinion. The United States Department of State, from which Churchill's instructions to Scobie had leaked, was visibly displeased.

---

8. Churchill, *The Second Word War*, vol. 6, *Triumph and Tragedy*, p. 227.
9. FO 371/64202; see also Graham Ross (ed.), *The Foreign Office and the Kremlin. British Documents on Anglo–Soviet Relations, 1941–1945*, Cambridge, Cambridge University Press, 1984, pp. 175–83.
10. Churchill, *The Second Word War*, vol. 6, *Triumph and Tragedy*, p. 252.

The Yalta Conference

On 4 February 1945, as the Yalta conference among Churchill, Roosevelt, and Stalin was getting underway, Roger Garreau, who was posted in the USSR as a delegate of the French Republic's provisional government, warned the French Ministry of Foreign Affairs that "The Soviet Union [had] renounced none of the principles that [had] motivated its actions thus far." He wrote, "whenever a problem arises, it should be recalled that the men leading the Soviet Union are party members, and are still immersed in Marxist–Leninist doctrine whose increased spread they will constantly attempt to ensure among the Union's peoples." Garreau predicted that the USSR would try to create a buffer zone in neighboring countries, thus protecting itself from a new cordon sanitaire. But he also predicted that it would try to transform these states by introducing new principles of democratic legitimacy and gaining support not so much from the popular majority as "from its most socially advanced elements." The USSR would not, however, lose interest in the domestic affairs of Western countries, where it would do its best to fend off influence from Great Britain and the US. If either country used economic aid as a means of political pressure, the USSR would rather delay its own reconstruction than give in to such pressure. Finally, he predicted that the problems of Germany and the Far East would soon become stumbling blocks for the big powers.[11]

At the time, no Soviet affairs expert would have argued with this analysis. The Western Allies, however, had no choice but to cooperate with Stalin. In early 1945, as the Yalta negotiations were opening in Crimea, the Allied troops were in no position to turn Central Europe's fate around. In December, the Germans had launched a violent counteroffensive in the Ardennes, and General Eisenhower did not think it possible to cross the Rhine before early March. Roosevelt's strongest hope was that he could convince Stalin to accept the principles of the United Nations Organization, an institution that would be set up after the war to uphold the principle of collective security. The project had already been the subject of lengthy Allied negotiations in 1944 at the Dumbarton Oaks conference. He also hoped, for reasons he shared with the British prime minister, to find a solution to the Polish problem and to form the basis for a policy agreement on Germany and the Third Reich's former satellites, or the countries that were being liberated from Nazi administration. Finally, the president hoped Stalin would confirm his commitment to enter the war against Japan.

11. Z Series, Europe 1944–1948, "URSS, politique intérieure," Dossier Général January 1945–March 1946, vol. 18.

The conference proceeded slowly. Stalin, after some evasive talk, accepted the project for the United Nations Organization that Roosevelt and Secretary of State Edward Stettinius had vigorously advanced. In exchange for his involvement in the war in Japan after the victory in Europe, he requested and obtained permission to place the Kurile Islands and the southern half of Sakhalin under USSR administration. The president also granted him control of Manchuria's railways and of the naval bases in Dairen and Port Arthur. The Western Allies had more difficulty reaching an agreement with him on Germany. Stalin asked them to accept its dismemberment, despite Churchill's objections. He strongly resisted the idea of France's receiving a zone of occupation, as the British prime minister had requested. The financial reparations he calculated – 20 billion dollars, half of which would accrue to the USSR – alarmed the British and the Americans, who both remembered how damaging reparations had been under the Treaty of Versailles; and Churchill remained firm in his disagreement with the amount the Soviet side demanded.

The Polish settlement gave rise to many difficulties, and its discussion took up most of the conference. Churchill and Roosevelt made an immediate concession to Stalin by accepting the Curzon line as the new border between Poland and the USSR; but it still remained to define the political regime that would govern the martyred country's fate. In late 1944, Stalin formally recognized the Lublin Committee in Warsaw as the legal Polish government. The Americans and the British, however, continued to support the Polish government in exile in London, as did the Polish resistance and the Polish people. After days of sour discussions, Roosevelt and Churchill conceded an ambiguous agreement on the Polish regime:

A new situation has been created in Poland as a result of her complete liberation by the Red Army. This calls for the establishment of a Polish Provisional Government which can be more broadly based than was possible before the recent liberation of western Poland. The Provisional Government which is now functioning in Poland should therefore be reorganized on a broader democratic basis with the inclusion of democratic leaders from Poland itself and from Poles abroad. This new Government should then be called the Polish Provisional Government of National Unity.

Mr. Molotov, Mr. Harriman and Sir A. Clark Kerr are authorized as a Commission to consult in the first instance in Moscow with members of the present Provisional Government and with other Polish democratic leaders from within Poland and from abroad, with a view to the reorganization of the present Government along the above lines. This Polish Provisional Government of National Unity shall be pledged to the holding of free and unfettered elections

2

THE DISINTEGRATION OF THE "GRAND ALLIANCE"

Hopes and Concerns

The Yalta conference marked a high point in Allied cooperation. Stalin appeared to have accepted Roosevelt's idea of a world order. He supported the United Nations Organization, which was the American president's most cherished project. He promised he would send in his army against Japan three months after the hostilities had ended in Europe, thus repeating the promise he had made at the Teheran conference. He recognized Poland's independence and held respect for its democratic aspirations, making similar promises for the Central European and Balkan countries that the Red Army had liberated. The Allies allowed the German dismemberment plan to pass, and Stalin finally approved a revised version of the 12 September 1944 agreement on the Allied sectors awarding a sector to France.

Of course, nothing was certain. The negotiations on Poland had been laborious, and the compromise on the country's government allowed for divergent interpretations. The Declaration on Liberated Europe, made at the end of the conference as a demonstration of the Allies' desire to uphold the right of all peoples to choose their own form of government, comprised a set of abstract principles modeled after the Atlantic Charter. Would they be enforced? The declaration, a United States proposal, had hardly been discussed. Its true scope was uncertain, especially because Churchill and Stalin had defined their respective spheres of influence in the Balkans and Hungary shortly before, in October 1944. In fact, the British and the Americans were hardly concerned about the conditions in which the Soviet forces would liberate Bulgaria and Romania. They had accepted the fact that their representatives on the Allied Control Council would have no role in implementing the armistice agreements, and this left the Soviet side in charge of the political situation in the countries liberated by the Red Army. The Yalta agreements were also imprecise about Germany's future; the question of war reparations was far from being resolved, for Roosevelt and Churchill especially had made their opposition to Stalin's compensation claims known.

Yet the United States president and his principal advisers said they were satisfied with the results of the conference. Roosevelt was particularly pleased that Stalin had been persuaded to support the Security Council system. He hoped that the United Nations Organization would prolong the alliance among the great powers, giving them common responsibilities in building the international order and keeping the peace. In a report to Congress, he appeared optimistic, emphasizing the Allies' unity and the perfect congruity of their war aims and peace projects. The Yalta agreements signified, in his opinion, the "end of the system of unilateral action, exclusive alliances, and spheres of influence, and balances of power and all the other expedients which have been tried for centuries and have always failed." United States public opinion did not criticize the results of the conference; on the contrary, it hailed them.[1]

The British prime minister had a mixed impression of the summit meeting, and was still wary of Soviet ambitions. In his report to the War Office, he nonetheless said that he was confident that Stalin's intentions were good. As he explained, the Soviet leader acknowledged that Russia had committed grave wrongs against Poland by dividing it and subjecting it to cruel oppression. Stalin had appeared to him sincere in stating that the Soviet government did not intend to resume this policy. The Russians were anxious to maintain harmonious cooperation with the British and US democracies. Churchill was clearly gratified by the position Stalin had taken on the unrest in Athens shortly before the Yalta conference. He pointed out that Stalin had not criticized British policy in the slightest. When the question was raised, he had been amiable, even "facetious"; he had respected his commitments scrupulously. This was proof that he kept his word. Stalin had considerable power. During his lifetime, Russia certainly made good use of it.[2]

The debate in the House of Commons, however, revealed unease among British leaders and public opinion over the Yalta agreements. The decisions on Poland brought sharp criticism from the Conservative Party. Arthur Greenwood, Labour Party leader and a former member of the War Office, and William Beveridge, a high-ranking member of the parliamentary Liberal Party, also expressed strong reservations.[3] The prime minister appeared troubled by this criticism.[4] He underscored the results the conference had produced, defending in particular the provisions made for Poland. What else could he do? Yet it was clear that he was worried and doubtful. He even seemed unsure about the true meaning of Stalin's commitments, and this was reflected in his promise to the House of Commons to offer British nationality to Polish soldiers who refused to

---

1. Roy Douglas, *From War to Cold War, 1942–1948,* London, Macmillan, 1987, p. 72.
2. CAB 6/51.
3. Douglas, *From War to Cold War,* p. 74.
4. Martin Gilbert, *Winston Churchill, 1874–1945, Road to Victory, 1941–1945,* London, Heinemann, 1986, p. 1241.

return to their country.

It was not long before the spirit of understanding and cordiality at Yalta dissipated. In the weeks following, relations between the Soviet government and its allies deteriorated briskly, taking a highly unpleasant turn. Disagreement centered around apparently insignificant matters, such as that of American and British prisoners of war released with the advance of Red Army, but also, more fundamentally, on the interpretation of commitments made at Yalta on the Balkans and Poland.

After the Nazi forces' retreat, thousands of British and American soldiers were found in East Prussia and Poland. The United States and British embassies in Moscow received orders to repatriate them as quickly as possible: they requested Allied missions to facilitate the return, in conformity with the Yalta agreements. Yet despite repeated requests, the Soviet chief of staff turned a deaf ear. US aircraft were not allowed to enter Poland to rescue the freed soldiers and bring them home. This attitude gave rise to incomprehension and annoyance in London and Washington. Ambassador Averell Harriman finally asked the president to put the matter to Stalin. Roosevelt wrote to him on 4 March to report on the difficulties in regrouping and resupplying the former POWs. He asked him immediately to authorize ten US planes to land near the locations in Poland where the Americans might be. He specified that he attached the greatest importance to the request.

Stalin's reply was hardly obliging. He said that a special body had been created to take care of this problem. Furthermore, aside from a few sick men, there were barely any American POWs left in the regions the Red Army had freed, as they had all been sent to Odessa. These assertions were inconsistent with the United States authorities' information. A number of former prisoners had made their own way to Moscow and taken refuge in the United States embassy. They alleged that hundreds of fellow servicemen had been abandoned in Poland and were often mistreated by the Soviet forces.[5] Roosevelt tackled the matter again, repeating his request in pressing terms: "I cannot, in all frankness, understand your reluctance to permit American contact officers, with the necessary means, to assist their own people in this matter. This Government has done everything to meet each of your requests. I now request you to meet mine in this particular matter."[6]

Stalin then became abusive. Soviet commanders had other things to do than host American officers. He added that the POWs the Red Army

5. Averell W. Harriman and Elie Abel, *Special Envoy to Churchill and Stalin, 1941–1946,* New York, Random House, 1975, pp. 419–22.
6. *Stalin's Correspondence with Churchill, Attlee, Roosevelt and Truman 1941–1945,* vol. 2, London, Lawrence and Wishart, 1958, p. 196.

had freed were enjoying good conditions, "better conditions than those
afforded Soviet ex-prisoners of war in US camps, where some of them
were lodged with German war prisoners and were subjected to unfair
treatment and unlawful persecutions, including beating."[7] He sent a
similar reply to Churchill.

This pugnacious insolence angered Washington. It was not understood
why repatriating soldiers abandoned in Eastern Europe should be
contingent upon Soviet goodwill. In this and similar cases, it was difficult
to know whether the Soviet reaction was the result of bureaucratic
carelessness, or a deliberate policy. It is plausible that the action was
intentional. From Stalin's perspective, the matter was not as insignificant
as it may seem. The Soviet authorities feared that the United States and
Britain might use their presence in Poland to glean information of public
interest. They may have considered using the affair to haggle for the rapid
repatriation of Soviet soldiers who had been freed by their allies. The
Western powers were overwhelmed by the number of Soviet prisoners
who refused to return to the USSR, typically soldiers belonging to
minority ethnic groups and in particular Latvians, Estonians, and
Ukrainians. The Soviet Union demanded their return. The Yalta agreements provided for repatriation, but failed to address the delicate issue
of the nations the USSR had annexed in 1940.[8]

These apparently absurd contentions were made in the midst of growing
divergence over the nature of the political regimes in the countries
liberated by the Red Army. In Romania and Bulgaria, the Soviet Union
favored the creation of patriotic-front governments, alliances that would
group together the antifascist parties, but within which the Communists
would have a privileged position. The Communists, who had no real
popular support, were working hard to infiltrate state institutions. They
had been applying a policy of antigovernment agitation for some months.[9]
In January, Ana Pauker and Gheorghe Gheorghiu-Dej, two principal
leaders in the Romanian Communist party, arrived in Moscow for
instructions on how to gain control of their government. The Soviet Union
did not intend to maintain the country's conservative-leaning rule, which
still had close ties with the leaders who had brought Romania into the
war against the USSR.

On 24 February the Communists organized a demonstration in
Bucharest, demanding the resignation of the coalition cabinet King
Michael had just appointed. The affair took a bad turn, probably at the

7. Ibid., p. 197.
8. Warren F. Kimball, *Churchill and Roosevelt. The Complete Correspondence,* vol.
2, *Alliance Declining,* Princeton, Princeton University Press, 1984, p. 539.
9. Robert L. Wolff, *The Balkans in Our Time,* Cambridge, Harvard University Press,
1974, pp. 280 et seq.

instigation of Communist agents provocateurs, and there were a number of deaths. On 27 February, Andrei Vyshinskii, the USSR deputy foreign commissar, arrived in the Romanian capital. He was a sinister character, who had come into the limelight internationally in the 1930s, when, as prosecutor-general, he orchestrated the famous Moscow show trials. Now, he demanded that King Michael procure Nicolai Radescu's resignation. The next day, he gave him two hours and five minutes to announce the name of the new government leader. When the king suggested Prince Stirbey, Vyshinskii refused and gave an order to name Petru Groza, a troublemaker and the leader of an obscure "peasant front" that the Communists had infiltrated. If the king refused, explained Stalin's envoy, Romania would cease to exist as an independent state. Soviet troops were occupying Romanian army headquarters, disarming military units, and patrolling Bucharest. On 28 February, Radescu resigned and a new government was formed on 6 March. It was made up of Communists, their sympathizers, and persons close to or in allegiance with them. The Communists controlled, notably, the Ministries of the Interior and of Justice. The new government began purging the administration and the army of persons associated with the former regime. With the consent of the Soviet Union, it announced that North Transylvania was to come under Romanian sovereignty. It also began a land redistribution campaign.[10]

Churchill was worried about the Soviet attitude in Romania. On 8 March, he wrote to Roosevelt:

I feel sure that you will be as distressed as I am by recent events in Roumania. The Russians have succeeded in establishing a rule of a Communist minority by force and misrepresentation. We have been hampered in our protests against these developments by the fact that, in order to have freedom to save Greece, Eden and I at Moscow in October recognised that Russia should have a largely preponderant voice in Roumania and Bulgaria while we took the lead in Greece. Stalin adhered very strictly to this understanding during the thirty days fighting against the Communists and ELAS in the city of Athens, in spite of the fact that all this was most disagreeable to him and those around him.

Churchill added that he intended to restore democracy in Greece and hoped that elections could take place there in the next months, preferably to be jointly monitored by Great Britain, the United States, and the USSR. At the time, Stalin's policy in Romania and Bulgaria was contrary to democratic ideals, notwithstanding the commitments he had made at

10. Barbara Jelavich, *History of the Balkans*, vol. 2, *Twentieth Century*, Cambridge, Cambridge University Press, 1984, pp. 288 et seq.

Yalta. The prime minister therefore asked Roosevelt to intervene, invoking the Declaration on Liberated Europe made at Yalta.[11]

Roosevelt reacted with discretion, though he voiced his desire for Stalin to respect the Yalta agreements. He did not wish to intervene personally, preferring to have his ambassador in Moscow take up the affair with Molotov. Harriman had already called upon the Soviet minister, reminding him of his country's obligations under the Declaration on Liberated Europe and suggesting a tripartite discussion of the matter. Roosevelt knew that the Soviet Union had installed a minority government in Bucharest. He felt, however, that Romania was not an ideal place in which to contest Soviet policy. The country lay on the Red Army's access corridors, and the Kremlin could invoke strategic considerations in defense of its policy. The president probably had the precedent of Italy's occupation by the Western Allies in mind. He added, however: "I am fully determined, as I know you are, not to let the good decisions we reached at the Crimea slip through our hands and will certainly do everything I can to hold Stalin to their honest fulfillment."[12]

The Disagreement about Poland

During this period, Poland was a major preoccupation for Great Britain and the United States. The hopes awakened by the Red Army's liberation of the country were short-lived. As in all the countries to which they had spread, the Soviet forces behaved poorly, and rapidly excited the enduring hostility of the civilian population. This was exacerbated by their protection of a Polish Communist party that had no real popular support and which imposed itself with the occupant's help. Terror raged. General Kazimierz Okulicki, the commander in chief of the prestigious Polish Home Army, ordered his units to be dismantled on 19 January 1945. The Polish government in London approved the decision on 8 February. But the order had yet to be put into effect. Resistance against the Soviet occupier and the pro-Soviet government continued. With the Red Army's aid, the Warsaw government adopted a policy of repression against members of the resistance movement.[13] The situation was crueler still as Poland had been left crushed and battered by its years of war, occupation, and resistance. Its population, more than decimated, had dropped from 35 to 24 million. Warsaw lay in ruins and the country had lost 65% of its

11. Kimball, *Churchill and Roosevelt,* p. 547.
12. Ibid., p. 562.
13. John Coutouvidis and Jaime Reynolds, *Poland, 1939–1947,* Leicester, Leicester University Press, 1986, pp. 170–5.

Berg.

Aredo, D. (1991), *The Potentials of the IQQUB as an Indigenous Institution Financing Small- and Micro-Scale Enterprises in Ethiopia*, The Hague: Conference Paper.

Besley, T., Coate, S. and Loury, G. (1990), *The Economics of Rotating Savings and Credit Associations*, Harvard: John F. Kennedy School of Government.

—— and Levenson, A. (1993), *The Role of Informal Finance in Household Capital Accumulation: Evidence from Taiwan*, Princeton: Woodrow Wilson School of Public and International Affairs. Discussion Paper.

Bouman, F.J.A. (1979), 'The ROSCA. Financial Technology of an Informal Savings and Credit Institution in Developing Countries', *Savings and Development*, 3:253–76.

Carsten, J. (1990), '"Cooking Money", Money, Morality and Exchange', in M. Bloch and J. Parry, (eds) pp. 117–141.

Chapman, M. (1992a), *Social Anthropology and International Business – Some Suggestions*, Brussels: Academy of International Business Annual World Conference. Conference Paper.

—— (1992b), *Patronage and Corruption, Honour and Shame*, Reading: European International Business Association Annual Conference. Conference Paper.

Chipeta, C. and Mkandawire, M.L.C. (1991), 'The Informal Financial Sector and Macroeconomic Adjustment in Malawi', *African Economic Research Consortium*, Paper 4, Initiatives Publishers, Nairobi.

Davis, J. (1992), *Exchange*, Milton Keynes: Open University.

Geertz, C. (1962), 'The Rotating Credit Association: a "Middle-Rung" in Development', *Economic Development and Cultural Change*, I (3).

Guyer, J.I. and Peters, P.E. (1987), 'Conceptualizing the Household: Issues of Theory and Policy in Africa' *Development and Change*, vol. 18, no. 2, pp. 197–215.

Hamalian, A. (1974), 'The Shirkets: Visiting Patterns of Armenians in Lebanon', *Anthropological Quarterly*, vol. 47, pp. 71–92.

Koufopoulou, S. (1992), Unpublished paper presented at CCCRW workshop, Oxford.

Madge, C. (1991), *Intra-household Use of Income Revenue and Informal Credit Schemes in the Gambia* (mimeo).

Messerschmidt, D.A. (1973), 'Dikhurs: Rotating Credit Associations in Nepal', in *The Himalayan Interface*, J. Fisher (ed.), Amsterdam. pp. 141–65.

Nzemen, M. (1993), *Tontine et développement ou le défi financier de l'Afrique*, Cameroon: Presses Universitaires du Cameroun.

Pignede, B. (1966), *Les Gurungs: une population himalayenne du Nepal*, Paris: Mouton.

Pischke, von J.D. (1991), *Finance at the Frontier*, Washington: The World Bank.

Wainaina, N. (1990), *Indigenous Savings and Credit Schemes for Women in Kenya* (cyclostyled), Nairobi: Swedish Development Authority.

PART I

Africa

2

Building New Realities: African Women and ROSCAs in Urban South Africa[1]

Sandra Burman and
Nozipho Lembete

Our interest in investigating specifically women's rotating savings and credit associations (ROSCAs) arose from work Sandra Burman conducted on the support networks of single mothers in urban areas, using Cape Town as her sampling area. As interviews progressed, it became evident that ROSCAs were not only widespread throughout the African townships but much used by single mothers. As a result, we conducted a set of interviews specifically on ROSCAs both in Cape Town and in the highly urbanized triangle formed by Pretoria, the Witwatersrand and Vereeniging (the 'PWV'), to help us evaluate their importance to such women, and this dictated the framework of our research. However, our interviews revealed women's use of ROSCA's to be so varied and vital that to describe them as support groups fails to convey more than a part – albeit a major one – of their multi-faceted functions. This paper is therefore a discussion of the roles ROSCAs play in the lives of women who use them, and their possible importance for women in a future South Africa.

Background

ROSCAs are known by various names in South Africa, many regional. The more common ones include *stokvel*, *gooi-gooi*, *umgalelo*, *mahodisana*, and *umshayelwano*, though most of the terms are also used to cover burial societies, non-rotating savings clubs, and various other types of mutual aid societies.[2] We are, however, confining our discussion below to associations 'formed upon a core of participants who agree to make regular contributions to a fund which is given, in whole or in part, to each contributor in rotation' (Ardener, 1964:201).

Although ROSCAs have operated in South Africa since at least early this century, there is very little detailed anthropological work on them, and what there is was generally done several decades ago (notably Kuper and Kaplan, 1944; Hellman,1934,1948; Brandel-Syrier, 1962, 1971; Wilson and Mafeje, 1963; Mayer and Mayer, 1971). More recently work by Cross (1986; 1987) on rural ROSCAs, and by Kokoali (1987) on religious organizations in the little town of Paarl, includes some discussion of ROSCAs. While the investigation described in this paper was in progress, reports on four small studies of urban ROSCAs appeared (Thomas, 1989a and 1989b; Webb, 1989; Lukhele, 1990; Ross, 1990), but of these only the study by Ross, which was formulated in conjunction with our investigation and used the same questionnaire, concentrated on women. Data therefore tends to be regional and sparse. However, a market research survey of 1,300 African adults in the main metropolitan areas except Cape Town and the squatter areas, undertaken in October 1989 by Markinor, the largest independent South African-owned market research organization, provides an indication of the size of the phenomenon in urban areas – although it must be borne in mind that ROSCAs also exist in rural areas, where some 60 per cent of Africans in South Africa still live. Markinor concluded that a quarter of the African adult population in metropolitan areas were members of ROSCAs, burial societies, or communal buying groups, with ROSCA members constituting less than a sixth of this total (Scott-Wilson and Mailoane, 1990). By 1991 a subsequent Markinor survey, which included Cape Town and squatter areas, showed a membership of 28 per cent, a result of both expanded survey coverage and a general increase in the size of ROSCAs (*Business Day*, 1992). Some 60 per cent of ROSCA members are women (Lukhele, 1990), and according to the Markinor study are likely to be aged between 24 and 49, in the higher monthly income groups, and working. This prosperous profile is, however, somewhat misleading when applied to Cape Town's ROSCAs.[3]

Kokoali (1987) suggests that ROSCAs began as savings clubs among contract labourers, especially on the mines, and Lukhele (1990) writes that women have been intimately involved in ROSCAs since at least early this century, when their traditional role as the brewers of beer evolved into that of running shebeens – places where beer (and later other alcoholic drinks) was sold and 'parties' organized as vehicles for ROSCAs. In those days 'respectable' Africans did not usually belong, but as Lukhele (1990:8) explains, African women running shebeens 'began to use the stokvel as a means of protection from police harassment [for selling illicit liquor]. When a stokvel member was arrested, the others would help with the home and children until the member came out of jail. In this way stokvels became more than just organisations for circulation of money and evolved into comprehensive support systems for members in time of hardship.'

Nowadays some ROSCAs have members of both sexes; others of only one. They vary greatly in size and to a lesser extent in mode of operation. Thomas (1989b), on the basis of fieldwork in Cape Town, tentatively divides ROSCAs into three categories. First, those with small membership, dealing in relatively small amounts of cash, which usually do not lend out money and operate primarily as savings groups. Second, those which save with a specific goal in mind, such as the purchase of some expensive item. These have variable membership size and may have an additional fund to lend on interest. Many of this type of club do not have rotating payouts, but some do in the sense that, for example, a special deal is struck with a shop to buy the required items (such as, for example, a fridge), and as enough money is saved for one to be bought the person with the first turn will receive one, and then saving will resume for the second, and so on. Thomas's third category is 'high-budget rotating credit associations (HBRCAs), which may have over 100 members, deal in very large amounts of money, and whose main function is lending of funds, often at high interest rates, to members' (p.6). Our research indicated that this last category of ROSCAs is dominated by men, although women may be members.[4] In Cape Town, groups composed entirely of women largely fall into the first category – that of small groups operating primarily as general savings and credit clubs. In Johannesburg, however, women's groups are also found more frequently in the second category – that of clubs which save with a specific expensive purchase in view and which more frequently lend money on interest.

Recently the potential of ROSCAs as vehicles for the financial betterment of Africans in South Africa has become increasingly evident. As far back as 1984 a study by the Perm Building Society drew attention to this huge untapped savings market in the African community. A special account was designed to suit the needs of non-rotating savings groups and ROSCAs which operated a lending fund – a book-based account with no charges, elected office-bearers authorized to sign for withdrawals, a better-than-average rate of interest paid monthly and rising as the balance increased, and no minimum balance imposed to keep the account open. After piloting, this Club Account was formally launched in 1988, and proved so successful that it has been copied by other financial institutions, which are competing vigorously for group savings and have introduced such additions as training schemes in meeting and money-management skills for *stokvel* chairpersons.

Meanwhile, in 1987 the community development organization Get Ahead (financed by US Aid, fifteen foreign governments, and a wide range of South African corporations) set up a Stokvel Loans programme, on the basis that peer pressure and group involvement would ensure debt repayment. The aim of the programme was to put emerging African entrepreneurs on the first step up the economic ladder, and most of the programme finances informal ventures. Get Ahead lends an initial R500 a member to a group with a minimum of five members and a maximum of ten. All members must know one another, and not more than two family members are allowed in a *stokvel*. The group has to function as a conventional *stokvel* for a month before receiving the loan and throughout the loan repayment period. The leader of the group is expected to collect the *stokvel* savings and the loan repayments each month and hand the latter to Get Ahead. If the loan is paid back in full and on time, the *stokvel* group may apply for a second loan of about R800, and after that a third of R1,000 – the maximum given by Get Ahead at the time of writing (1992). Interest on the loan is set at 32 per cent, but 10 per cent of this is set aside for the customer and given back after a year, when the loan is repaid. The group is encouraged to use this 10 per cent as a deposit on its next loan. Thus the interest paid on the loan is effectively 22 per cent. Get Ahead has branches throughout the country except in Cape Town, where it was forced to suspend its branch because loans were not secure in the squatter camps (*Business Day*, 1992).

In 1988 the National Stokvel Association of South Africa (NASASA) was created by the man who became its president, Andrew Lukhele, to fight for the rights of *stokvel* members and promote recognition of *stokvels*, especially by formal financial institutions, as a source of informal credit. NASASA has been very active in Johannesburg, the financial centre of South Africa, where most of its membership is based, with the result that various imaginative schemes are currently being implemented to tap the considerable funds collected by *stokvels* (R84 million in metropolitan areas, according to Markinor's 1991 survey, and R1.6 billion nationally, according to preliminary research by the National Building Society) (*Business Day*, 1992).

The aim of several schemes which have NASASA's backing is to increase the stock of much-needed housing for the African community, both for ownership and renting. In a bid to overcome the difficulty that *stokvel* members do not qualify for loans, NASASA and specialist financial services group Syfrets have clinched an agreement enabling *stokvels* to invest money in Syfrets-administered unit trusts. The aim is to divert the millions in *stokvel* savings from banks and building societies to unit trusts, which can then serve as collateral for home loans. This has the added advantage of ploughing African savings back into the African community which generated them. The scheme also, very importantly, removes the eroding effect of inflation on *stokvel* savings, and can be used for raising loans for African businesses too. Again, other financial organizations are enthusiastically starting to market unit trusts to the African community; the Old Mutual insurance company, for example, uses a comic paper format, featuring an imaginary township savings group as characters, as a marketing tool.

Another brainchild of NASASA is the Stokvel City Housing Project, focusing on building informal homes in site-and-service areas or upgrading the ubiquitous backyard shacks that house many township dwellers in formal housing areas. The strategy is to provide access to cheap, convenient building materials through the creation of depots selling these on a cash-and-carry basis in the townships, where training in building skills is available. Loans, generated by the NASASA Unit Trust and the Independent Development Trust (IDT), are to be made to men and women who form housing *stokvels* to buy materials, with NASASA as a financial intermediary. At the time of writing the Development Bank of South Africa is also involved in discussions with NASASA on providing additional financing in the housing market.

With all this evidence of recognition by the formal sector of *stokvels* as an important unit in South Africa's financial system, the South African Reserve Bank has embarked on a campaign to define the role of the informal financial sector within present deposit-taking institution legislation. The bank has made it clear that it wants to act not as a regulator of *stokvels* but rather as a facilitator of their development, adding legitimacy to a market already functioning efficiently. The bank therefore proposes that while *stokvels* should remain largely self-regulatory and exempted from the Deposit Taking Institutions Act, they should be registered with NASASA and comply with all the self-regulatory guidelines, while NASASA should work in co-operation with the bank's supervisory department.

It is against this background of the growing strength of ROSCAs as the formal sector awakens to their importance in South Africa's financial future that the role of women in ROSCAs must be viewed.

Fieldwork

The primary research on which this paper is based is, first, detailed interviews with nineteen women, belonging to ten different ROSCAs in Cape Town and six in the PWV area (five in Johannesburg and one in Pretoria) – comprising two metropolitan areas with rather different economic and demographic profiles in their African populations. The PWV is the largest metropolitan area in South Africa, with Africans from all parts of the country congregating there. They constitute the greatest concentration, from all over South Africa, of well-to-do Africans, although the area also contains many who are very poor. Cape Town's African population, in contrast, is mainly Xhosa-speaking and is probably still the poorest African population of South Africa's major cities, as already explained.

Our sample of women members of ROSCAs reflected something of this wide range of demographic and economic backgrounds: *inter alia* they included not only Xhosa-speakers but also those whose home languages were Zulu, Tswana, and Northern Sotho. However, as single women they were probably not representative, in the sense that they were usually poorer than women of similar occupational and family background but different marital status. Our broader study dictated a focus on unwed mothers, who constitute a very high proportion of mothers in urban areas but who are in general a disadvantaged group compared with other single mothers, and even more so when compared with married women.[5] Moreover, obtaining a statistically random sample was impossible, given the financial constraints of our research funding, which forced us to choose interviewees on grounds of availability and access rather than representativeness. We have, however, been able to draw on a further four detailed interviews with women (not selected on grounds of marital status) in two ROSCAs, undertaken by Fiona Ross using our questionnaire, and her research findings are included in our figures.

Our and Ross's detailed interviews on ROSCAs produced data on groups which varied considerably in size, type of membership, length of time in existence, and mode of operation. Since our primary interest was in discovering the roles ROSCAs could play in the economic and social arrangements for single mothers, we needed such a varied sample. Our questions set out to investigate the importance of ROSCAs to women from different backgrounds and with different experiences of such associations, rather than to estimate women's importance within the range of ROSCAs operating in urban areas.

In addition to the interviews specifically on ROSCAs, the paper draws on detailed life histories of divorcees, wives married by customary law only, and unmarried mothers. All were interviewed in Cape Town over the past twelve years as part of various investigations by Sandra Burman into socio-legal aspects of divorce and illegitimacy. Seventeen interviewees provided some information on their membership of ROSCAs. They came from a wide range of economic backgrounds, but again economic constraints prevented any attempt at statistically random selection, so that it would be misleading to draw conclusions from the percentage of interviewees who were members of ROSCAs.

Finally, to place our interviewees' ROSCAs in the contexts of other alternatives offered by social and economic credit- and aid-giving bodies, interviews were conducted with three single mothers belonging to non-rotating savings clubs, as well as a number of organizers of, and researchers on, various institutions involved in forming mutual assistance groups and/or giving credit in the townships. These covered such organizations as the Cape Credit Union League, the National Stokvel Association of South Africa (NASASA), non-profit-making companies operating loan schemes for informal sector entrepreneurs, and *manyanos* (Christian women's church groups).

Profile of the ROSCA Interviewees and Composition of their Clubs

Interviewees

All fifteen of our interviewees were single mothers, three being divorced and the remainder never having married. In four cases their children lived with maternal relatives, not their mothers, but the mothers all contributed to their expenses. The additional four women interviewed by Ross were all mothers, three of them living on their own: one was married, two were separated and one had never married. The total sample thus consists of nineteen women, eighteen of whom were in effect single mothers and one married mother. It should be noted that the fact that a woman's offspring have reached adulthood does not usually mean that the woman is relieved of duties of child-care and support; on the contrary, her obligations frequently increase with the addition to her household of grandchildren, often without much or any financial support from their parents. Of the nineteen women in the sample, only one was no longer responsible for children: her offspring were adults caring for their own children, and no longer lived with her.

The Cape Town women ranged in age from 24 to 45, most being in their late twenties or early thirties. The majority had not completed the possible twelve years of schooling before leaving school, two remaining only till passing standard five (seven years of schooling) and others for varying extra numbers of years. Three of the women had full- or part-time domestic jobs, two were cleaners (at a station and in a restaurant), one was a bakery attendant, one a saleslady in a shop and one an 'unskilled' crèche worker; but most (eleven) had trained as nurses, teachers, or secretaries and were using their qualifications in such posts. This last group claimed in general not to earn money outside their jobs, but information from the less skilled workers indicated various additional sources of income – as is to be expected, given the very high rate of participation by women in the flourishing informal economy in African townships. Of the eleven who revealed their earnings in the formal economy, only one earned over R1,000 per month (R1,700 per month gross), and at least seven earned less than R400 per month, one single mother earning only R120 from a part-time charring job. However, in at least one case additional earnings from the informal economy usually more than doubled the interviewee's meagre earnings, raising her income to R1,000 in good months.

The six PWV women interviewed were aged between 26 and 39, half being in their twenties. At least three had completed school, and two had degrees in social work. The two latter were working as social workers, two others were clerks (one with a jewellery firm, the other with a clinic), one a teacher, and the sixth the branch manageress of a small up-market shop. Two reported additional sources of income outside their jobs: the senior social worker sold beauty products on a part-time basis, and one of the clerks received frequent financial assistance from her mother. Five of the six told us their monthly earnings: all earned R1,000 or over, the highest being R1,760.

The ROSCAs

Our and Ross's detailed interviews on ROSCAs produced data on sixteen clubs, which varied in size from five to forty-five members, three being of twenty or more. All six PWV ROSCAs had only women members, in most cases by deliberate choice of the members: and at least three specifically excluded men. As one group expressed it, they preferred it that way simply because they felt that 'men can find it difficult to work with ladies. They may feel they are being controlled'. Another group told us that they had only women members as they felt women understood one another better. In contrast, most of the ten Cape Town clubs did not in principle exclude members on grounds of gender, but three had only one male member and in one other case the only male in a club of forty-five had left after one rotation, as 'he just didn't seem to feel comfortable with the ladies only.' In practice, therefore, five clubs had only women members, and two – each a club of six close friends – said that they preferred to keep it that way, the explanation offered being in one case that a man might feel uncomfortable as the sole male. One well-established club of twenty-two women was specifically a women's club. At least two Johannesburg and one Cape Town club had only unattached members, the Cape Town club (of six) including both men and women.

Apart from gender, criteria for membership were many and varied, influenced primarily by the requirements of trustworthiness and an ability to pay – or at least an inability to vanish into thin air. Thus some clubs specified that people should be over (or under) certain ages. In one case it was stated that members must be employed, and in others that members must receive a constant income – an important qualification, given the present very high rates of unemployment in the African community and the uncertainties of such informal sector trading. Several clubs were composed largely or exclusively of people in the same occupations at the same places – nurses, clinic workers or cleaners. Others were from different occupations but the same workplace. One was composed exclusively of members of the same church, while membership of another one was limited to the same block of flats. Some clubs were formed by a small band of close friends, others specifically admitted members of the same family. In one case six of the eleven members were from the same nuclear family – a mother and her five daughters. One club of both men and women co-workers, all single, said that they preferred people who were not married as they felt marriage led to decreased reliability: married people were more likely to default on a contribution, pleading family problems, whereas single people had fewer responsibilities. (In contrast, however, two interviewees told us that married people were viewed as desirable members, as marriage made for responsible behaviour.) All the clubs required that new members be recommended by an existing member, a process in some cases reinforced by a semi-formal ceremony of introduction to the group and explanation of the constitution. No interviewee reported formal references being required, beyond that of the introducer.

The length of time those interviewed had been members of their clubs also varied. Two had been members for some three years, two for between two years and thirty months and three for between twelve and twenty-four months, but most had joined within the preceding year.

Operation of the Clubs

The Formalities and Social Arrangements at Meetings
We were interested in how often clubs met, how formal the meetings
were, what effect this had on knitting the club together, and how much
social life they provided for their members. It transpired that three of
the clubs did not have any meetings, although two were hoping to
introduce them. Of the remaining thirteen clubs, eleven met monthly
and two fortnightly.

Clubs that did not have meetings had various features in common.
All were small – one of seven members, the other two of five each. One
of the latter did not have meetings because four of the members were
nurses who worked different shifts and also lived in different parts of
the Cape Town metropolitan area. The club therefore revolved round
the organizer (there was no formal executive), who was the only member
who had met all the others, three of whom were her friends. (The fifth
member was the boyfriend of one of the others.) However, it was a
requirement of membership that each member should have at least one
close friend in the group, and the operation of the club depended on close
friends taking responsibility for contacting each other when necessary.
The constitution laid down that the member who was to be paid must
receive the money by at least the fifth day of the calendar month, and
members took the time limit very seriously. If there were any delays or
other problems, they tended to telephone the organizer. How the money
was actually transmitted was left to the discretion of individuals.
Although no formal records of payment were kept, the organizer kept
her own. Similarly, the other club of five had a fixed payment date of
the first day of the calendar month and members either paid in person
or gave their contributions to the unofficial organizer, who was one of
the three co-founders and the person who had recommended the other
two members. Members either worked together or lived near other
members, so there was contact between them even without formal
meetings. The organizer kept a list of the order of rotation, but no receipts
were issued. In contrast, the third group had no person who acted as
organizer, since all members worked at the same clinic and merely ticked
the rotation list, which hung in the office of the founder of the club,
who had recruited the others. Payment in kind (at the time of interview,
in soap powder) had to occur within the first week of the month.

Not only did some of the clubs not have meetings, but only five had
a name – there was no correlation between this and the size of the clubs.
Only one club – a relatively long-standing one of twenty-two members

– had a formal uniform, but two others, both in Johannesburg, explicitly expected members to dress smartly for meetings. Although all clubs had some basic rules, the constitutions of some were much more formal than others. Almost half had no formal executive officers. Meetings generally took place at members' houses (often that of the recipient of the payout) except where the group revolved round a place of work or a church, in which case meetings at these venues were more appropriate. In the case of some big clubs, meetings had to be held in larger venues, such as schools. The most affluent clubs in Johannesburg sometimes held meetings in hotels.

Procedure at meetings varied in degree of formality, several beginning with a prayer and then regularly following the same agenda. Most clubs which had meetings appeared to operate on the basis of group decisions, but with two exceptions – one being a small club of six where the secretary made most of the decisions but where group pressure no doubt curtailed any autocratic tendencies. The other exception was one of the two clubs composed of both men and women (we were not told the exact composition but there were twenty-four members), where the chairman had an unusual degree of power. The five-person executive did not include a treasurer, the chairman doubling as both. He was responsible for all banking; with other executive members he decided the order of rotation, making the decision one week in advance of payment, with no safeguards against favouritism beyond the secretary's records to show that nobody was paid twice in a rotation. However, we were assured that all the executive members were elected by the ROSCA at the beginning of each rotation, with an eye to leadership qualities that included an ability to listen to other people's views and problems.

A feature of all ROSCA meetings in our sample was of course the receipt of contributions from members and the handing over of money to the person whose turn it was to receive it; this will be discussed in detail below, together with loan schemes. But in addition some clubs operated a system of fines for various offences, either using the money for refreshments or banking it and dividing it – and the interest it generated – between members at the end of the year. Two clubs levied a fine of R10 (that is, 10 per cent and 20 per cent of the contribution respectively) for non-attendance (even if the contribution were sent). It was felt that attendance at meetings was essential to reinforce group relationships of trust and unity. The former club also fined a member an additional 20 per cent of the contribution if payment was late, while the latter (a club of twenty-two members) imposed a sizeable fine for talking during meetings, and fined members wearing the club uniform improperly. An unusual feature in a society not noted for its punctuality was that several clubs placed considerable emphasis on members arriving on time, and fined latecomers. Of the nine Cape Town clubs which had meetings, two fined members R1 and R3 (enough to hurt) if they were late – though we were not told what counted as late – while of the four PWV clubs which had meetings, one stressed that punctual attendance was important – on the dot of 2 p.m. – and two others fined latecomers heavily: in one case, R5 if late by half an hour; in the other, 'R2 if late, even if by a minute'. While not all of these punctual clubs paid particularly high contributions, most had other features compatible with an upwardly-mobile membership.

Such features could also be seen in the type of socializing at the meetings of the more affluent clubs. The largest group in the sample (with forty-five members) served no refreshments at meetings, although it provided a useful forum for members to meet and make friends; but this lack of food was unusual. The normal pattern was for refreshments to play an important role at meetings. In some cases in our Cape Town sample the person who was about to be paid out served light refreshments and cool drinks; in others the club provided, either from small set refreshment contributions by members or from the fines-kitty. One Cape Town group of which we were told (outside our sample) had a membership of sixty-six men and women, organized in six groups of eleven, with one from each of the six groups receiving payment at each meeting.[6] Meetings were considerable occasions, with impressive party fare and photographs of the six recipients dressed in their most elegant clothes, while other members wore either smart suits and ties, if men, or the club uniform of black skirt, white shirt and black tie, if women.

The PWV clubs were even more lavish: two provided three-course meals, usually at the home of the person who was to be paid but sometimes at hotels; and a third planned to do so the following year. In at least two cases members made a sizeable set contribution towards this. In another club – the Ladies Elegance Society – members contributed even more towards a party with music and dancing, again sometimes at a hotel. Items discussed over the three-course meals included in one case 'marital problems, children and beauty tips', in another 'general matters, relationships, politics and dresses'. One of these clubs had, as an official on the four-member executive, a Public Relations Officer, whose function it was to organize social occasions, including trips to such places as Sun City (South Africa's most lavish casino at the time of writing) or to the adjoining state of Swaziland. Interestingly, this club of eleven had two 'half members', who belonged for purely social reasons, contributing towards meals and the compulsory gifts but not the basic contribution, and receiving no payout.

As can be seen, therefore, socializing of various types played an important role in all the clubs that had meetings. However, none of the ROSCAs in our sample – nor any other women's ROSCA of which we were told – had anything approaching the lavish two-day parties described by Lukhele (1990) of mixed-gender ROSCAs on the PWV, where the payouts and receipts from the parties were so large that one recipient used his to buy a farm, and another 'six buses and nine small businesses'. While it is not unknown for the parties of women's clubs to include outsiders (whose contributions and gifts on such occasion can be of sizeable economic importance), in Cape Town these are usually other women and the parties are generally smaller and more sober occasions than those of men's, or many mixed-gender, ROSCAs. However, in Johannesburg, where NASASA is based and is most active, it serves as a network for information on parties, to which all members are often invited. Women's clubs which belong to NASASA are therefore more likely to have men at their parties as guests, in which case the party takes on a different nature.

Contribution, Payouts and Loans
In the Cape Town ROSCAs in the sample, the average contribution per month (whether paid monthly or fortnightly) was conspicuously lower than in the PWV sample. Members paid less than R100 in half the clubs, the two lowest being R25 and R30 and the highest R200. In contrast, only one Johannesburg club paid less than R100 (and paid only in kind), while the highest contribution was R250. At least seven of the sixteen clubs definitely allowed some form of doubling (payment of more than the minimum contribution when the payer had money to spare, on the understanding that the recipient would repay the amount when the payer's turn came round for receiving the kitty).

Most allowed members to swop payout turns between themselves, though several stressed that this was discouraged except in emergency situations. It was apparently feared that allowing swops could cause squabbling.[7] We were told of at least two clubs which prohibited all swopping. Most clubs paid out the entire kitty each time, to only one person, and entirely in cash – though the most affluent club accepted payment by cheque. Four clubs also accepted payment in kind as part – or, in one case, all – of the contribution: one club was currently paying entirely in soap powder; one Johannesburg club paid R100 in cash and R50 in either groceries (from a list supplied by the recipient) or cash, if this was requested a week in advance; another paid R100 in cash and R20 in the form of a compulsory gift of some small household item; and one Cape Town club paid R50 in cash and R10 in the form of a gift of the payee's choice (the payee making up the difference in price if it exceeded R10).

The exceptions to the general rule that clubs paid out the full amount were all connected to loan schemes. In one case less than two-fifths of the R50 contribution (from each of the twenty-four members) was paid out to the person whose turn it was, the rest being banked by the treasurer and used as a loan fund for members at a spectacular interest rate of 20 per cent per fortnight. The banked funds were then divided between all members at the end of the annual rotation. In another case the member was paid out in full but then required to put R300 (half the payout) into the club's loan account. Recipients of loans (to members, or through them in the case of non-members) were charged interest of 10 per cent over a three-month period; in the event of non-payment a further 10 per cent per month was charged for each month the debt was outstanding, failing a satisfactory arrangement with the executive. None of the PWV clubs in the sample had loan schemes, but one (of eleven members) would contribute towards a member's expenses in a crisis: the example was cited of a member involved in a strike, who had not been paid one month. The member was expected, when her turn for the kitty money came round, to pay back the amount advanced to her, but there was no mention of interest. (The supportive ethos of that club is illustrated by the fact that members automatically contributed R5 each in the event of the death of a member's close kin; similarly in another PWV club members each contributed R50 in similar circumstances as 'a sign of sisterhood, since death is unplanned'. In neither case was the ROSCA seen as doubling as a burial society.)

One Cape Town club merits special mention, in that it was exceptional in several ways. It meets the Ardener definition cited above, but the payout, although made according to a rota, was viewed as a compulsory loan on which the member had to pay interest. The rota was compiled by all members placing their names on it in advance, and each was obliged in her turn to borrow a minimum amount. If the person at the head of the list did not want to borrow the entire kitty, loans would proceed down the list until the entire amount from contributions and loan repayments for the month had been paid out. The club had been in existence for many years, and past experience had led it to decide that a rota was necessary to avoid favouritism.[8] Interest was charged at 20 per cent per month, but was not compounded unless the borrower failed either to make repayment within three or four months or to report a difficulty to the group. As the entire fund was lent at every meeting, the club did not use banks and obtained a higher rate of interest than the bank would have given. The composition of the club had dictated its mode of operation: originally its membership comprised mainly uneducated women, but the difficulties of record-keeping and interest calculations led to the recruitment of better-educated members, and by the time of the interview it was composed of forty-five women from a wide variety of backgrounds including teachers, domestic workers, hawkers and nurses.

Logically, record-keeping would appear to be important for the running of ROSCAs, but we found that in fact some of the smaller ones kept no records at all except whatever notes members (or an organizing member) might have made for themselves. In others the executive kept a record of contributions and payouts, or else had a minute book – in which, presumably, this information was recorded. Most did not issue receipts. (This was in marked contrast to Thomas's report (1989a) on the immaculate record-keeping in the mainly larger ROSCAs he investigated.) Where a club had a building society or bank account as well, that would of course provide a partial record of club finances, but it could necessitate checks on the scrupulousness of the treasurer. We were told of the solution adopted by one club (not in the sample) which was given a plastic card for access to their account via a machine. The club decided to give two office-holders each half of the machine number needed for access to the account, while a third held the card. All three thus had to visit the machine together to withdraw money from it: one to insert the card and the other two each to punch in half the number, retreating some distance after doing so to ensure the secrecy of the number. Presumably the three could have colluded to cheat the club but this arrangement provided some safeguard against temptation overcoming one member – a modern version of the three-lock trunks used by some early English Friendly Societies.

Disputes within Clubs
Given these somewhat scanty arrangements, we investigated whether there was much dispute over payments, absconding of members, people leaving before the end of a rotation, or executive corruption. None of the sixteen clubs had ever had anyone abscond, and only one reported having to evict a member for defaulting on her payments. Several said that they had never had anyone leave even at the end of a rotation, and the rule seemed to be fairly general that nobody would be allowed to

leave during a rotation. Some women were bemused when asked what would happen if someone did not pay her contribution: it was clearly unthinkable, given the basis of trust on which the clubs were formed and the strength of public opinion in the townships – in some cases reinforced by a high level of violence. (One woman from an Informal Housing Area, for example, when asked about potential enforcement of payments, spoke of the group beating the person into submission.) Of our seventeen interviewees outside the survey sample who told us about their ROSCA membership, only one reported having left a ROSCA, in that case because she no longer had an income with which to pay her contribution; and the mother of one of our ROSCA interviewees had also been forced by financial problems to withdraw from (another) ROSCA the preceding year.

Nor could any woman interviewed tell us of disputes with office holders; this probably results largely from the limited power of executive members in clubs where none of the kitty is banked or where members' turns are largely decided by consensus within the group. In the club with twenty-four members and a powerful executive, mentioned above, problems were potentially more likely; but mismanagement of funds was controlled by publicly counting at every meeting the money collected from contributions and loan repayments. Deductions to pay officials were not permissible. Our interviewee could not tell us whether there were disagreements over the chairman's decisions about the order of rotation and, if so, what happened.

How much of this apparently trouble-free organization was a result of the relatively small size and weak executives of women's ROSCAs, and how much a consequence of the way women, compared to men, operate in a club, is difficult to judge. Certainly large ROSCAs, which invariably have a high percentage of male members, are by all accounts much more troubled by disputes and corruption.[9] To place the scale of our fieldwork clubs in perspective, it may be helpful to contrast them with a large ROSCA of which an interviewee for a different study in Cape Town supplied details in 1985. That club, which was both a burial society and savings club, had 200 members, although we were not given the details according to gender. She paid R80 per month, which was equivalent to more than R200 in 1991 and higher than any contribution paid in our Cape Town sample for this study. The payout was between R20,000 and R40,000 (enough at the time to buy a house, a car and a business) depending how many branches one joined: our interviewee belonged to three. (A number of branches would all be present at a meeting.) The organizers took R1,000 of each payout to a member and placed it in a savings account (from which the member received the interest) until it was ascertained that all the member's debts within the ROSCA – from other members having 'doubled' during the rotation – had been paid. Given the size of the ROSCA and the correspondingly weaker social pressures, this was presumably a cheaper and less time-consuming option for the executive than possibly having to resort to lawyers to recover debts from the payee. However, despite a powerful executive, the club had an unusual feature which, if it indeed operated as promised, would serve to curb executive corruption to some extent. This was an arrangement whereby one could 'insure' one's investment by 'signing for one's children'; the list of their names was then sent to a lawyer, so that if one died before one's turn came round, the children benefited from the payout instead of the organizers. This particularly appealed to our interviewee, given her divorced status and the fact that a rotation took several years, but unfortunately we did not discover whether non-executive members, especially women, were in fact protected by this measure.

Members' Uses and Perceptions of Their Clubs

To assist us in assessing the financial importance of ROSCAs to their women members, we asked the women interviewed how they had used or intended to use their payouts. This revealed a variety of needs, pressures and aspirations, few of which appeared to be frivolous. Some were of a universal nature: for example, the safeguarding of children's futures by depositing the money in savings accounts or buying insurance policies, payment of crèche charges, payment towards building an extension to a home, payment of accounts, or the purchase of large items (such as a fridge or a room divider) or luxuries such as clothes or a bicycle for a child. Other goals had a very South African ring to them. One woman planned to save the money towards her aim of giving up her job as a crèche worker so that she could spend more time with her own child (who was not allowed to attend the affluent crèche); another had used her payout to buy a cow for a feast to introduce her child to the ancestors. A woman from Natal used her payout for a visit home – an expensive undertaking, as the visit was for a housewarming party to which she was required to contribute after the family had bought and extended a house. Another woman used her payout to build herself a shack in the back yard of her home, to obtain more privacy than was possible in her crowded four-roomed house. An enterprising entrepreneur used a payout to buy a dilapidated van, which at the time of interview she hoped a relative would repair so that it could be used to fetch produce from the Transkei for sale. She planned to save her next payout towards the conversion of the shack at the back of their home into a restaurant and bar, which would in turn generate more money. Another wanted to buy a house for her trips back to the Ciskei, her rural area of origin, but family demands were such that, when she arrived at her aunt's house there and found the family in dire need, she felt obliged to spend the money on supplying the household and having the leaking roof fixed. For her next payout she had lowered her sights to the building of an extra room on to her aunt's house, but a house of her own in the Ciskei remained a long-term goal.

From the earlier interviews outside the sample we gleaned examples such as the installation of electricity in a home, or in one case contributing to a father's business in the Transkei and helping him to expand it. One woman, who had already had two other payouts, had used the first to renovate her home, the second to put the finishing touches, and planned to use the third to buy a car. But sometimes the money had merely fended off disaster, as in the case of a woman who used it to pay her rent arrears.

A few clubs had clearly enunciated views on how the payouts should be spent, or even imposed actual restrictions. Thus a six-member ROSCA encouraged members to buy expensive household items they could not otherwise afford, or to extend their houses. We were told that members, when visiting the payee's house, liked to see how the money had been spent – 'it pleases them'. Another group of six, all single and working together, as a policy decision urged each other to bank at least 60 per cent of their payouts and show the others proof of this, although their work was not well paid. Yet another group of six, all women living in the same block of flats, decide at the beginning of each rotation how the money should be spent. For their first rotation members were restricted to purchases of underwear or nightwear; for their second (the current one at the time of interview), they had decided that everyone should buy curtains.

As it is very difficult to leave a ROSCA during a rotation, which in the case of larger clubs may continue for several years, we asked, at the end of each interview, whether in the light of her experience the interviewee still thought ROSCAs useful institutions, and if so why. All without exception still approved of them, some volunteering such enthusiastic comments as 'everyone should join one'; at least one interviewee hoped to join a second one as soon as her salary increased.

(Two others already belonged to a second but non-rotating savings group.) All were very decided that the clubs were of great importance for single mothers.

Reasons for this support proved to be quite varied. Naturally, financial considerations loomed large, though frequently linked with social ones. Some interviewees thought ROSCAs 'the best way to save money', because the social pressures imposed by a club made it virtually impossible to default on payments. Moreover one could not withdraw money on impulse, as could be done from a bank or building society account. Some mentioned that savings made the purchase of larger items possible without resort to hire purchase: one told us, for example, that her desire to join a club dated back to a visit to a friend who had invited her to see what the payout had bought: 'she had a new, beautiful bedroom suite'. Others, who had already used their payouts for such purposes, indicated that not only their lifestyles but their self-esteem had been augmented. As one woman – a cleaner at the railway station – told us, after she had bought linen from her pay-out she felt very proud of herself; as her ROSCA usually liked to hear what members used their payouts for, she had happily shared this with them. Some women saw payouts as a way of supplementing their regular salaries, for example for end-of-year payments for Christmas, and school uniforms for their children's new school year. One interviewee explained that she belonged to get more money than she put in, since her club had additional income from both fines and loan interest, which was split between members at the end of each rotation. Another woman, whose club had an additional system of compulsory gifts, spoke of the extra motivation to belong which it provided, enabling her to collect household items that she would probably never buy for herself. Above all, interviewees stressed that the savings themselves, the possibility of loans from the ROSCA or of swopping turns in emergencies, and the close friendships resulting from the club, all gave additional security in times of unexpected financial demands. (Most would probably have had difficulties in obtaining a bank loan.) Many stressed the usefulness of ROSCA money in freeing them from reliance on frequently unreliable or uncooperative men who had fathered their children, a major concern given the serious deficiencies of the South African maintenance system (Burman and Berger, 1988). Several spoke glowingly of how their payouts enabled them to save for their children's education, as well as to buy their children toys and clothes which they could not afford on their earnings.

Given the lack of interest payments in the majority of ROSCAs in the sample, an obvious question was whether the women were aware of the interest most were forfeiting by putting their money into their ROSCAs rather than a bank or building society. However, investigation of their additional savings methods showed that they were aware that banks, for example, paid interest. We obtained information on this point from eleven of the nineteen interviewees: only one (from an Informal Housing Area) did not have a bank account, and she was planning to open one in order to save at least R20 per month. She said she had realized that she could not do without a savings account book. Others also told us of separate savings accounts, and in two cases fixed deposit accounts; whether these were with banks or building societies was not always clear. Some had their salaries paid into the bank, and at least one mentioned the interest gained from the bank as a motive for this, although her ROSCA operated without interest payments.

Undoubtedly an important reason why women ROSCA members were prepared to forego interest from their savings, where applicable, was the social role of the clubs, which loomed large in a number of answers and often had financial implications too. Some interviewees emphasized that they valued their clubs as forums in which to collect advice from other members on how to save and use money constructively. At the upper end of the income scale, a member of one of the most prosperous clubs explained that the club had a number of professional members who acted as a resource for the others; she, as a social worker, found that she also had much to contribute to the group – which no doubt increased both her status and her self-esteem. In common with several others interviewed, she indicated that as a single mother she could be lonely at weekends and over holidays; her membership of the club gave a sense of belonging. It was also helpful to share information with other divorcees, and led to a productive use of leisure time. Her club actually organized excursions for its members and had ambitious travel plans for the future, including trips to Botswana, Mauritius and even further afield overseas. She found it a highly stimulating group. Similarly, another told us that she had joined to make friends from other backgrounds, occupations and townships outside her usual circle, but this obviously was less of a motive in the case of small clubs. Typically in such cases membership was viewed as a way to see friends regularly. One woman from the PWV told us that members of her ROSCA had mostly been at school together, but until the formation of the club no longer saw much of each other. She regarded the club as a way of having fun which was also productive. Another PWV club had been founded by four friends, who had been at university together but subsequently found that their busy careers prevented them from seeing each other, although working in the same city. Several of those interviewed had been founding members of their clubs: at least two were the main instigators of their respective ROSCAs, one choosing to form a new club rather than join an existing one so as to operate only with close friends. Interestingly, Ross's informants, who came from lower income groups, stressed to her that membership of a ROSCA carried with it prestige in the community. A number of other interviewees probably indicated much the same, though they expressed this in a more personal way, several of the poorer telling of their desire to join a ROSCA after seeing how friends, by saving together, could buy expensive things. Among the more affluent, entertainments such as lavish dinners and expensive travel no doubt had a similar effect – an interesting change from Brandel-Syrier's (1971:47) findings in Johannesburg in the early 1960s that the educated considered ROSCAs primitive.

Conclusions

In the light of the information supplied by the women in our survey, we found various erroneous ideas prevalent among some of the researchers we interviewed who did not actually work in the townships. It was thought that as banks became more accessible, both geographically and culturally, ROSCAs would fall away, and that this was indeed happening. However, this expectation was based on an assumption that ROSCAs were continuations of some earlier 'traditional', communal life style, less strange and hostile than banks (an expectation also found in the literature: see e.g. Geertz, 1962). Such ideas have been under fire recently (Boonzaier and Spiegel, 1988; Thomas, 1989a), and all our evidence supported these criticisms. Moreover, what became abundantly clear was that, far from being the resort of the poorest in the community, ROSCAs were available only to those who had a job or a regular source of income to meet contributions without fail, unless (as in one case from outside our sample) a relative – in this case a son – could be found to pay for the woman instead. The very poorest in need of credit would usually be obliged to resort to township loan sharks, who charge interest of 50 per cent or more; indeed, our earlier interviews provided an illustration of a divorced woman who was obliged to do just this because her income had been too uncertain for her to join a ROSCA.

It was, however, the flexibility and resulting variety of the institution that led us to regard it as a possible portent of the future. From our sample of ROSCAs it was evident that, rather than acting as support groups for those in need of a crutch, the clubs were vehicles for the upwardly mobile from *every* income group who could afford to belong to them. This is borne out by Lukhele (1990:32), who reports that ROSCAs 'are becoming increasingly popular among young upper-income Africans, whose clubs are fashion-orientated'. He reports that ROSCAs with members of one or both sexes adopt the name of some famous make of clothing and use payouts to patronize their favourite stores: among his examples is that of a women's group which named itself after an expensive Johannesburg shoe store. Moreover our data show that, as needs changed, so did the clubs, adopting new modes of socializing and enforcing new values such as punctuality. In addition, although the clubs often consciously retained long-standing systems of communal support in times of crisis, such as donations to express sympathy on a close relative's death, the motivation for these old institutions might be described in a new terminology of 'sisterhood', highlighting a new feminist consciousness. It was noteworthy that both PWV clubs which presented club donations to bereaved members 'as a sign of sisterhood' contained a high percentage of well-educated professional members. While we would not suggest that women in 'traditional' African society did not consciously rely on other women for support and assistance, the connotations of that interdependence are changing as women's place in urban society changes yet again and finds new expression.

Given the strong interdependence between members of ROSCAs, it is hardly surprising that they – and particularly women's ROSCAs – should serve as vehicles for women's support for each other. Nor is this a phenomenon peculiar to ROSCAs with only single women as members: in our sample a number of groups which included married women displayed it too, even if not expressing it in feminist terminology. The reasons given for excluding male members, such as feeling more comfortable with women and being able to work better with them, were examples of this. Seeing that the clubs also empower women by helping them to become to some extent economically independent of their husbands, families and boyfriends, and to create social standing for themselves within the community, it becomes obvious that they are a natural vehicle for liberating and strengthening women in a very patriarchal society. With the increasing economic power that current developments are making possible for ROSCAs, even the generally smaller women's ROSCAs are likely soon to be able to increase women's financial strength considerably too. Moreover, there seems every likelihood that as African affluence increases with the current political adjustments, women's ROSCAs will grow in number and influence.

While this may well provoke a backlash from those who feel threatened by women's increasing power, this is unlikely to be strong enough to prevent the ROSCAs from having notable consequences for the role of women in the new South Africa.

Notes

1. Our thanks go to our interviewees for their co-operation and help, and to Ms Ann Turner and Ms Amanda Tiltman for their research assistance. The research would not have been possible without the sponsorship of the Human Sciences Research Council, the UK Save the Children Fund, the Research Committee of the University of Cape Town, the UCT Foundation and the Wingate Foundation, to all of whom we are most grateful.
2. ROSCAs also exist among the Indian population in Natal, where the very sparse literature on them records the use of the names *chita* (Hindi) or *chitu* (Tamil) (Kuper, 1960).
3. The economic situation of Africans in Cape Town is still adversely affected by the consequences of the Coloured Labour Preference Area policy instituted in 1955 and abolished only in 1985. Under it, no job could be given to an African unless there was nobody classified as Coloured to take it. Training facilities for Africans, particularly women in Cape Town, were very limited. This, together with the legislation requiring suitable passes and aimed at excluding women and children from urban areas, generally left Africans, particularly women, in only the most poorly paid work (Burman, 1985). The effects of this are still visible in the economic profile of Cape Town's African population, compared with that of other major South African metropolitan areas.
4. In this kind of ROSCA a woman often contributes along with her husband, the contributions being in her husband's name. While doing research in the Southern Divorce Court, Sandra Burman encountered several cases of women bitterly (and inevitably unsuccessfully) opposing their husbands' divorce petitions, although no children, housing, or other property were involved. Investigations revealed that in these cases the woman had usually contributed to her husband's long-term ROSCA, which was due for payment soon and would in effect have provided both partners with a large lump sum, equivalent to a pension in the case of older spouses. While arrangements can be made in South African divorces for the future sharing of regular pensions, ROSCA payouts are not subject to them.
5. In 1989/90, the latest year for which statistics are available, 69.8 per cent

of African babies born in Cape Town were classified as illegitimate, and our research shows that these would have been born to women unmarried by civil *or* customary law, who would probably not have been living with the father, and who were unlikely to be receiving child support from him (see Burman and Berger, 1988; Burman, 1992).

6. Membership covered a wide range of occupations, from domestic workers to nurses and a (male) university professor.

7. Even where turn-swopping was not allowed, the expectation of a payout soon sometimes enabled women to cope with an emergency. Thus one was able to borrow the expected amount interest-free from her employer shortly before her turn, enabling her to reroof her mother's house in the Transkei immediately after the roof blew off in a storm.

8. Interestingly, this procedure had not been followed by a very similar club that we found had been formed a year before our interview and modelled on the long-established one. Regrettably, therefore, we were obliged to exclude the newer club from our sample as it did not rotate the order of loans. It preferred to invite members to apply at each meeting, though urging those who had not yet borrowed at least the minimum amount to do so within the 'rotation' or face exclusion without repayment of contributions.

9. One woman told us of her mixed-gender ROSCA, outside our sample, from which an office-holder had recently disappeared with a large sum of money. Members were scouring South Africa for him. However, his girlfriend (who did not know where he was) had not been obliged to withdraw from the club, and our informant was adamant that they had a lawyer (rather than more informal methods) ready to deal with him when he was found.

References

Ardener, S. (1964), 'The Comparative Study of Rotating Credit Associations', *Journal of the Royal Anthropological Institute*, XCIV, pp. 201–29.

Boonzaier, E. and Spiegel, A. (1988), 'Promoting Tradition: Images of the South African Past', *South African Keywords*, E. Boonzaier and J. Sharp (eds), pp. 40–57.

Brandel-Syrier, M. (1962), *Black Woman in Search of God*, London: Lutterworth Press.

—— (1971), *Reeftown Elite*, London: Routledge and Kegan Paul.

Burman, S. (1985), 'The Interaction of Legislation relating to Urban Africans and the Laws regulating Family Relationships', *Acta Juridica 1984*, pp. 89–104.

—— (1992), 'The Category of Illegitimate in South Africa: Its Size and Significance', *Questionable Issue: Illegitimacy in South Africa*, Cape Town: Oxford University Press.

—— and Berger, S. (1988), 'When Family Support Fails: The Problems of

Maintenance Payments in Apartheid South Africa', *South African Journal on Human Rights*, 4: pp. 194–203 and 334–54.

—— *Business Day*, 11 March 1992, Survey on Stokvels, pp. 12–15.

Cross, C. (1986), *Informal Credit – Or, How Does a Rural Community Capitalize Itself?*, paper presented at the Seventeenth Annual Congress of the Association for Sociology in Southern Africa, University of Natal, 30 June–4 July 1986.

—— (1987), 'Informal Lending: Do-it-Yourself Credit for Black Rural Areas' *Indicator SA* 4 (3): 87–92.

Geertz, C. (1962), 'The Rotating Credit Association: A "Middle Rung" in Development', *Economic Development and Cultural Change* 1(3): pp. 241–63.

Hellman, E. (1934), 'The Importance of Beer-Brewing in an Urban Native Yard', *Bantu Studies* VIII: pp. 34–60.

—— (1948 [1935]), *Rooiyard: A Social Study of an Urban Native Slum Yard*, Cape Town: Oxford University Press.

Kokoali, C. (1987), 'Umgalelo and the Failure of the Church? A Study in Voluntary Associations in Mbekweni Paarl', Unpublished M.A. Thesis, University of Cape Town.

Kuper, H. (1960), *Indian People in Natal*, Durban: University Press.

—— and Kaplan, S. (1944), 'Voluntary Associations in an Urban Township', *African Studies*, 3(4): pp. 178–86.

Lukhele, A. (1990), *Stokvels in South Africa: Informal Savings Schemes by Blacks for the Black Community*, Johannesburg: Amagi Books.

Mayer, P. and Mayer, I. (1971 [1961]), *Townsmen and Tribesmen: Conservatism and the Process of Urbanization in a South African City*, Cape Town: Oxford University Press.

Ross, F. (1990), *Strategies against Patriarchy: Women and Rotating Credit Associations*, Unpublished B.Sc. Hons. Thesis, University of Cape Town.

Scott-Wilson, P. and Mailoane, M. (1990), *Developments in the Informal Sector*, Unpublished seminar paper.

Thomas, E. (1989a), *Rotating Credit Associations in Cape Town: A View from Anthropology*, Preliminary Report to the Small Business Development Corporation.

—— (1989b), *Rotating Credit Associations in Cape Town*, paper presented at the Annual Conference of the Association for Anthropologists in Southern Africa, University of the Western Cape, 13–16 September 1989.

Webb, N. (1989), *Informal Credit Markets in Cape Town, Guguletu – A Case Study*, Unpublished B.A. Hons. Thesis, University of Cape Town.

Wilson, M. and Mafeje, A. (1963), *Langa: A Study of Social Groups in an African Township*, Cape Town: Oxford University Press.

3

The Kiambu Group: A Successful Women's ROSCA in Mathare Valley, Nairobi (1971 to 1990)

Nici Nelson

> *'Women in Groups can Solve their Problems Together'*

Introduction

This is the tale of a successful Rotating Savings and Credit Association in a large squatter area of Nairobi known as Mathare Valley. The group, which will be referred to in this paper as the Kiambu Group (not its real name, for obvious reasons) has been successful for the following reasons. First, it has had a continuous existence (if not an exactly continuous membership) from 1971 to the present, a period of twenty-one years. Second, it is a ROSCA which evolved gradually over the years from an informal association to a formal, registered co-operative plus ROSCA and finally to a very successful land-buying co-operative. I question whether one can describe a ROSCA as successful when it has evolved into another form of economic association.

In this paper I give a brief background of Mathare Valley and the women who lived there and describe my twenty-year contact with the community of Mathare and the Kiambu Group. After a brief discussion of ROSCAs in general and the Gikuyu of Kenya in particular, I will give a history of the Kiambu group from 1971 to 1990 (the period of my last visit). I will then analyse why I think that consolidation and expansion of the Kiambu Group has been successful, discussing whether or not it can be called a successful ROSCA, and end with a discussion of Geertz's contention that ROSCAs were the product of a shift from a traditional agrarian social formation to a commercial one.

Mathare Valley, Then and Now

When I arrived there early in 1971, prepared to do fieldwork on the migratory and economic strategies of female heads of household residing there, the area had 60,000 people living in scattered 'villages' which had developed after the ending of the Mau Mau Emergency along the irregular valley of the Mathare River. In the ten years since the ending of the Emergency, poor rural–urban migrants (mainly Gikuyu) had spontaneously created housing on this piece of marginal urban land. Indigenous leaders, both men and women, had arisen from within the community, allying themselves with the then leading (and subsequently only) political party. They constituted themselves a KANU committee, cultivated patron–client links with the local MP, established their loyalty to the President (mainly through women's dancing groups which sang loyalty songs to the President at his country house) and eventually set up 'local' party elections to legitimate their leadership roles. By the late 1960s these KANU committees operated in each of the Mathare 'villages' much as the village elders used to in the rural Gikuyu context, dealing with local disputes and acting as a conduit of local opinion to the adminstrative Chief of the area. The major difference was that the Mathare committees included women as well as men, something that did not happen in the village (see Ross, 1973). This reflected the large number of female heads of household in Mathare, and women's relatively more independent economic position in the urban informal economy compared with the women farmers of rural Gikuyuland, who did not have access to land except through a father or a husband. These community leaders had weathered a serious confrontation with Nairobi City Council in the late 1960s, and the community had won the *de facto* right to continue to exist. For this reason community spirits in the early to mid-1970s were running high and the KANU political party leaders who had spearheaded the fight for existence were active and highly respected. Due to the ecological position of Mathare Valley, it was ideally sited for what Ross (1973) referred to as the 'entertainment industry'. Many women were attracted to the area by its economic opportunities for women, such as brewing local maize-millet beer (called *buzaa*) and/or 'sex work' (the exchange of sexual services for payment). It was on this category of women that I concentrated my research efforts.

Many changes have taken place in and around Mathare Valley and the areas to the north-east of the centre of Nairobi. In 1973 a small but significant area of 'rehousing' development was created further to the east, out along the Juja road extension. Several hundred low-cost housing

seek maximum security. Stalin would not necessarily apply his policy through territorial conquest; he might be content with "ideological Lebensraum" in the countries he considered crucial to the Soviet Union's defense. To counter this tendency, Sargeant recommended an active policy. Soviet Russia had been weakened by the war. It certainly was impressed by the United States' power and the Western air forces. It had been relatively cooperative, especially in the affairs of Greece and Venezia Giulia, and even on the issue of Poland. Sargeant believed that Great Britain was not in a position to prevent Soviet penetration in Romania and Hungary, but he felt it must try to maintain its positions in Finland, Poland, Czechoslovakia, Austria, Yugoslavia, and Bulgaria, so as to prevent the USSR from extending its sphere of influence. If Great Britain refused to resort to diplomatic pressure, Soviet Russia would threaten southern Germany, Italy, Greece, and Turkey. Economic and social conditions created by the war could facilitate Russian penetration.

The diplomat was well aware that to counter Soviet expansion, Great Britain needed the United States, especially its financial help. Unfortunately, United States policy was ill-defined, its diplomacy lacked cohesion and continued to waver with public opinion. Sargeant seemed worried that Washington would refuse to come to Great Britain's side by continuing to act as the arbitrator between London and Moscow. He therefore proposed an alliance with the dominions, France, and the other European states to counterbalance US and Soviet influence. Great Britain must prevent economic crisis from developing in Europe. He also suggested that Britain should become a leader for the smaller colonial powers, such as France, the Netherlands, and Australia. Great Britain's policy must be based on liberal principles; hence, it must oppose all forms of totalitarianism, be they from the left or the right. It must adhere to this policy even if the United States adopted a policy of appeasement toward the USSR. His analysis met with very positive response from the Foreign Office. Anthony Eden approved it.[22]

France Weakened

Great Britain's position in Europe was even more difficult to uphold since a return to a balance of power on the continent was not foreseeable in the near future. France, although it came out of the war on the winning side, was very weak. Its defeat in 1940, the deep humiliation of its premature capitulation, the Occupation, collaboration with the Germans,

22. Memorandum by Sir Orme Sargeant of 11 July 1945 (*DBPO,* Series I, vol. 1, 1945, document number 102, pp. 181–92).

and internal political fractures excluded it from important strategic and diplomatic decision-making during the war. Its economy was drained, and its national revenue was not half what it had been in 1938. It had no more exports to speak of, and did not have the means to import goods needed for its own reconstruction.[23]

Thanks to General de Gaulle's government and the Resistance, France was finally able to take part in combat against Germany; but its role was modest, and insufficient to constitute a reasonable claim to participate with the great powers. De Gaulle was intent upon ensuring his country's return to center stage in international affairs, but he could do nothing without help from the United States and Britain. Churchill, although exasperated by the General's capricious, prickly disposition, attempted to include France in the peace negotiations, hoping thus to gain its support in Europe and the rest of the world. Since early 1945, the United States had been working toward the same goal.[24] Unfortunately, General de Gaulle's policy was in all respects counter to history's current trend and managed by a fragile, divided political class of young, inexperienced members of the resistance movement and former Third Republic politicians. Such was the state of French imperial policy. De Gaulle had made it his personal mission to restore to France the full sovereignty it had enjoyed before the war. Abandoning the French Empire was therefore out of the question. De Gaulle attended the Brazzaville conference of 1944, the objective of which was to redefine French colonial policy, and the conference affirmed the ideology that France had a "civilizing mission." René Pleven, who was in charge of the French colonies under the French National Liberation Committee, was explicit:

We say from time to time that this war must end in what is called the emancipation of the colonial peoples. In France's great colonies, there are neither peoples to emancipate nor racial discrimination to abolish. [...] There are populations we intend to lead, step by step, to legal personality, the most mature to political enfranchisement, but who wish for no other independence than France's independence.[25]

The conference's final statement was just as unequivocal: "The aims of the civilizing work France has accomplished in the colonies bars all thought of autonomy, all possibility of evolution outside the French bloc of the Empire; the eventual constitution of 'self-governments' [sic] in

23. Kennedy, *The Rise and Fall of the Great Powers*, p. 366.
24. *FRUS 1945*, vol. 2, *The Conference of Berlin*, pp. 251–3.
25. Quoted by Denise Bouche, *Histoire de la colonisation française*, vol. 2, Paris, Fayard, 1991, p. 390.

the colonies, even in the distant future, should be ruled out."[26] This vision, and the myths surrounding it about the Empire's republican tradition, were not realistic. It was true that no one dreamt of rushing into independence the African peoples deemed "backward," whose nationalist elites were still weak. In North Africa, the Middle East, and especially in Asia, however, colonialism's days were numbered. France's shameful defeat had been a shock, particularly as soldiers from the colonies had been decisive in combat against the Germans, especially in Italy. The United States forces deployed in North Africa were hostile to French colonialism. President Roosevelt had encouraged the king of Morocco to reclaim his independence, and in Tunisia, United States authorities had given hope to the Néo-Destour nationalist movement's leaders. The creation of the Arab League in Egypt in March 1945, and later the United Nations conference in San Francisco, gave a new legitimacy to the political movements militating for decolonization.

Algeria, whose economy had suffered gravely from breaking ties with France in 1942, was going through a period of great nationalist agitation. Violent demonstrations erupted in Algiers and Oran on 1 May 1945. One week later, as victory was being celebrated, the Sétif riots broke out, and Europeans were massacred. French repression was merciless: the French razed villages and wiped out entire populations with artillery and air strikes. The death toll was in the thousands.[27] French influence was threatened in the Middle East as well. During the war, the United States and Great Britain had formally recognized the independence of Lebanon and Syria. In January, unrest broke out in Damascus and Beirut. De Gaulle, convinced that "Anglo–Saxon intrigue" had stirred the agitation, sent reinforcements to Beirut. He hoped to force the Lebanese and Syrian governments to sign treaties, with guaranties to France that it could maintain its military bases and preserve its interests. In late May, French troops opened fire on a crowd in Damascus and shelled the parliament building, causing over a thousand deaths. This affair was the start of a grave crisis between France and its allies. London would not stand for French forces firing on the Lebanese and Syrian nationalist movements. Anxious to preserve its own political influence in the Middle East, the British government sent an ultimatum to General de Gaulle, and dispatched troops to coerce the French forces to return to their barracks. In Paris, the tragedy took a ridiculous turn when the General told British Ambassador Duff Cooper, "We are not, I admit, in a state to war with you at present. But you have outraged France and betrayed the West. This

26. Jean Lacouture, *De Gaulle*, vol. 1, *Le rebelle*, Paris, Le Seuil, 1984, p. 751.
27. Jean Lacouture, *De Gaulle*, vol. 2, *Le politique*, Paris, Le Seuil, 1984, pp. 178–83.

cannot be forgotten."[28]

General de Gaulle's initiatives in Italy irritated the United States profoundly. Despite United States protest, French troops refused to pull out of the Valle d'Aosta at the end of the war, and tried to create a fait accompli so that France could annex the region. In early June, the affair spurred a new crisis in relations between Paris and Washington. The president threatened to cut off all arms and military equipment shipments to France, and did not rule out a test of strength. On 11 June, the French troops were forced to withdraw.[29] In a very firm response to French initiatives in the Near East and Italy, President Truman postponed the General's scheduled visit to Washington.

To compensate for his weak position, de Gaulle tried to establish ties with the USSR by endorsing a European policy that was independent of the Anglo–American Allies. It was with this policy in mind that he visited Moscow in early December 1944. He signed a Franco–Soviet treaty in Russia, under which he acceded to recognizing the pro-Soviet Lublin government de facto by sending a diplomatic mission to Warsaw. He refused to adhere to the principles of the Declaration on Liberated Europe, and made no attempt to dispute the representative character of the ruling governments. In reality, General de Gaulle's policy with regard to Soviet Russia proved disappointing. Stalin did not have a great regard for the leader of the Free French, and poked fun at his claims. As in Teheran and Yalta, his treatment of de Gaulle was invariably cavalier, and he rubbed in his refusal to include him in the concert of great powers. General Georges Catroux, France's representative in Moscow, was unable to obtain an envoy of representatives to Poland and the USSR to speed the repatriation of French prisoners. He received very little consideration in Moscow. He noted bitterly that on victory day, the Soviet press attributed "only the most modest role" to his country. Pictures and statements by Marshal Stalin, President Harry Truman, and Prime Minister Winston Churchill appeared on the front page of the Soviet papers, but General de Gaulle's picture was not among them, and his statement was printed on the inside, with no congratulatory messages from the principal heads of state.[30]

Furthermore, the French government in Paris complained that the

28. Charles de Gaulle, *Mémoires de guerre,* vol. 3, *Le salut, 1944–1946,* Paris, Plon, 1959; Livre de Poche, 1959, pp. 227–8. See also Lacouture, *De Gaulle,* vol. 2, pp. 171–5; François Kersaudy, *Churchill and De Gaulle,* London, Fontana Press, 1990, pp. 339 et seq.

29. Irwin M. Wall, *The United States and the Making of Postwar France, 1945–1954,* Cambridge, Cambridge University Press, 1991, pp. 31–2.

30. Georges Catroux to the Minister of Foreign Affairs on 12 May 1945 (Z Series, *Europe 1944–1949,* "Relations bilatérales France–URSS," vol. 51).

Soviet government was creating all sorts of obstacles for French representatives and diplomats posted in Moscow and the countries freed by the Red Army.[31] Stalin opposed France's attendance at the Potsdam conference, and repudiated its seat on the reparations committee. Molotov refused to back the French request to take part in the Japanese surrender. Thus, General de Gaulle was ill-rewarded for his efforts since the autumn of 1944 to obtain political support from the USSR, which had culminated in the Franco–Soviet alliance treaty.

Divergence over the International Order

The armies had fallen silent in Europe, and diplomacy must now necessarily resume its predominant role in the victors' efforts to restore peace and define the framework of a new world order. The art of diplomacy proved complicated, even more so than that of the military strategy that had so recently secured the victory over the Axis powers. The victors' intentions toward Germany and its former allied and satellite states were still uncertain. European reconstruction and, on a broader scale, the restoration of international order required that the winners attune their occupation policies and define the procedure and direction of the peace talks. These problems were to be the subject of negotiations at Potsdam.

By seeing their demands for unconditional surrender carried through, the Allies had brought an end to a total and merciless war, the last months of which had been terrible. Germany lay devastated. On 12 February, Great Britain and the United States had bombed the city of Dresden into ruins, killing some 200,000 persons, most of whom were civilians, including many refugees from the East. In the month of March alone, the United States and British air forces rained 206,000 metric tons of bombs on German cities, about three times as much explosive as had been dropped on the Reich since the beginning of the war.[32] The victors had entered cities and villages that "smelled of death and destruction."[33] All reports concurred: the war had caused dire material damage, subjecting the population to poverty, starvation, and social collapse. When they arrived in Berlin, the Western delegations were shocked by the magnitude of the tragedy. Admiral William Leahy speaks in his memoirs of the "long procession of old men, women and children, presumably evacuated from

31. Ibid., 4 May 1945.
32. War Cabinet meeting of 3 April 1945, CAB 65/50.
33. John Gimbel, *The American Occupation of Germany: Politics and the Military, 1945–1949,* Stanford, Stanford University Press, 1968, p. 6.

their homes by their Russian conquerors. They were marching in great numbers, along the country roads, carrying their pitifully small belongings and their infants, probably to an unknown destination, and probably without hope."[34]

In their sector, the Soviet Union was seizing as war booty anything that could serve the Soviet economy or hinder Germany's reconstruction. Soviet soldiers subjected the civilian populations to the worst hardship, avenging the suffering they had endured and the Nazis' cruelty against their own country. The former SS camps at Buchenwald and Sachsenhausen and the Bautzen prison were filled with Nazis and other persons the Soviet occupiers wished to repress.[35] Yet on 9 June, the Soviet military administration authorized "antifascist-democratic" worker's parties and unions, and two days later Walter Ulbricht and Communists who had been wartime refugees in Moscow founded the German Communist party, the SED.[36]

The Western military commanders' instructions also exacted a "Carthaginian" peace. The US military government's orders were particularly harsh. Germany was to be treated like a vanquished nation, and the military administration had orders not to fraternize with the population. The United States had no economic recovery plan for its sector – on the contrary. Agricultural production had to be stepped up and an agrarian reform implemented; the war industries were to be dismantled immediately and, while waiting for the Allied Control Council's agreement, output of iron, steel, machinery, radios, electrical equipment, automobiles, heavy machinery, and chemical products was to be stopped. Industrial output was to serve no other purpose than to meet the occupation forces' needs and provide the vital minimum to avoid epidemic and social unrest.[37]

These instructions were laid out by Secretary of the Treasury Henry Morgenthau in his 1944 plan for Germany's "pastoralization"; they proved impracticable and detrimental, for they did not take into account the local situations faced by the Allied sectors' commanders in chief. General Lucius Clay realized this immediately, and attempted to bring about a change in the orders, which restrained him from exercising his economic responsibilities. A new policy for Germany was in order. The Department of State was aware of this: "Reports from Germany indicate

34. William D. Leahy, *I Was There*, New York, New York, Whittlesey House, 1950, p. 396.

35. Dennis L. Bark and David R. Gress, *Histoire de l'Allemagne depuis 1945*, Paris, Robert Laffont, p. 1146.

36. Peter Rassow, *Histoire de l'Allemagne des origines à nos jours*, vol. 2, Stuttgart, Ed. Horwarth, 1969, p. 286.

37. J.E. Smith (ed.), *The Papers of General Lucius D. Clay: Germany 1945–1949*, vol. 2, Bloomington, Indiana University Press, 1974, pp. 17–19.

that it is impossible to maintain the political vacuum created by defeat."[38]
More fundamentally, Washington was beginning to fathom the problems
posed by the ruin of the European economies. On 8 June, US Under-
Secretary of State Joseph Grew wrote to Henry Stimson, the war secretary:
"I am deeply concerned over conditions in Western Europe and the
possibility that serious disorders may develop during the coming
months."[39] In the same vein, President Truman wrote to Churchill on 24
June, insisting that German coal production must be raised: "From all
the reports which reach me, I believe that without immediate
concentration on the production of German coal we will have turmoil
and unrest in the very areas of Western Europe on which the whole
stability of the continent depends."[40]

The United States occupation policy was intended to de-Nazify and
rehabilitate the German people; the project also called for certain
economic and social conditions to be restored. "The soul of man abhors
a vacuum quite as much as nature abhors one," wrote Under-Secretary
of State Archibald MacLeish in a memorandum he sent to James Byrnes
during the Potsdam conference. Spreading ideals of liberty, justice, and
human dignity, all part of the US occupation leaders' relief program, was
all the more urgent since the USSR most certainly intended to convert
Germany to communism.[41] The war secretary shared this point of view.
He wrote to the president, warning him that restoring European stability
required that the United States promote a liberal regime in Europe. In
Germany's prevailing conditions of famine, sickness, and distress,
however, it was impossible to nurture budding liberal principles.[42]

For the same reasons, the United States was poised to change its
position on reparations. The sum calculated at Yalta seemed too high. The
British had never accepted the figure, though Roosevelt had finally
allowed it at the Yalta conference as a "basis for discussion." Meanwhile,
the reparations committee had met for discussion in Moscow. This proved
unproductive. Since the meeting, the Allied armies had continued their
advance and destruction of the German economy. The Russians had
spread over Germany and its satellites like the locusts of biblical Egypt,
grabbing an enormous war booty haphazardly and without consulting
their allies. Washington and London hoped to avoid having to cover the
German balance-of-payments deficit and hence indirectly subsidizing
reparations. The United States was therefore hostile to internationalizing
the Ruhr, or attaching it to France as General de Gaulle proposed. In their

38. *FRUS 1945, The Conference of Berlin,* vol. 2, p. 438.
39. Ibid., p. 524, n.3.
40. Ibid., p. 612.
41. *FRUS 1945, The Conference of Berlin,* vol. 2, p. 783.
42. Ibid., p. 808.

opinion, this industrial region should play a vital role in the European and world economies. By severing it from Germany, the Allies would set the scene for the country's dismemberment, which would culminate in nationalist retaliation. In certain circles, fears were cropping up that Germany would disintegrate, hence allowing the USSR to move in to the center of Western Europe.[43] There was less certainty, however, about what position to take on France's request about the Rhineland, for Washington knew how much importance France attached to this issue.[44] Before Potsdam, President Truman still had in mind the idea of Germany's dismemberment, which Roosevelt had advocated at Teheran and Yalta. The Department of State agreed that it would be premature to recreate a German central government, but it wished to revive the local administrations rapidly. It was concerned that German unity be maintained. It worried that political and administrative fracturing would lead to "the creation of partite states having diverging political philosophies and the termination of inter-zonal commerce." It feared that the US and British sectors would pay dearly for this division, which would thrust upon them enormous economic and social problems that "would mean either a poor-house standard of living in the West with Communism the probable end-result or an elaborate relief program at American and British expense."[45]

The Department of State examined the possibility of proposing a four-power treaty among the occupying powers to the Allies, which would provide for German demilitarization and make the United States accountable for repressing any emergence of German military activity. If it was carried through, the project would likely convince the USSR to adopt a more liberal policy in its sector, and might dissuade it from creating a sphere of influence in Eastern Europe. The Department of State was, however, aware that the initiative might be perceived as a show of defiance toward the United Nations, which could draw criticism from the Senate. Nonetheless, it encouraged the president to sound out Stalin and Churchill informally.[46]

The British were also troubled by Germany's economic and social situation, notably by supply problems in its cities. In May, Winston Churchill told General Eisenhower that he was concerned they "might well be faced with Buchenwald conditions on a vast scale" in Germany.[47] On 6 July, Marshal Montgomery, the commander in chief of the British

---

43. *FRUS 1945, The Conference of Berlin*, vol. 1, pp. 586–9.
44. Ibid., pp. 592–5.
45. Ibid., p. 439.
46. Ibid., pp. 450–2.
47. Martin Gilbert, *Winston S. Churchill, 1874–1945, Never Despair*, London, Heinemann, 1988, p. 17.

army, sent an alarming report to Anthony Eden: "Two months have now passed since Germany surrendered and the country passed to the control of the Allied Nations. During these two months the full extent of the debacle has become apparent; we now know the magnitude of the problem that confronts us in the rebuilding of Germany." He predicted that the coming winter would be critical, anticipating shortages of food, coal, and lodgings, and the breakdown of transportation and distribution channels in the British sector. The British sector had twenty million civilians and hundreds of thousands of displaced persons. Montgomery was also responsible for two million German soldiers, who were waiting to be discharged. He was apprehensive about the emergence of political and social unrest, and noted the development of Communist propaganda.[48] Therefore, he felt it necessary to instill new hope in the German population by bettering their living conditions. His goal was not only to win "the battle of the winter," but also to plan for Germany's long-term economic recovery. The process required a return to a minimum of political activity. Consequently, he wished to lift the ban on the Germans' right of assembly and suggested authorizing unions and political parties. "We cannot resuscitate Germany without the help the people themselves; we cannot re-educate 20 million people if we are never to speak to them." Furthermore, if Germany's economy was to recover, persons must have the right to circulate from one sector to the next. This freedom did not exist in the Soviet sector.[49]

Foreign Secretary Anthony Eden shared Mongomery's concerns, for he saw the European dimensions of the problem: "The whole of Western Europe is in desperate straits for coal and Germany is the only important source on which to draw. It is not going to be easy to reconcile the minimum requirements of the Western Allies in this respect with the minimum requirements of Germany."[50] He hoped also that the Potsdam conference would allow certain government departments to reopen and hence to manage the administrative bodies that could revive economic activity.[51] The British did not intend to increase the cost of their military occupation, but their sector, which was essentially urban and industrial, could not meet its population's food supply needs. Therefore, they felt that reestablishing inter-German economic trade channels was important, particularly so that the Russian-occupied regions could supply agricultural products to the Western sectors' markets. The British feared that disagreement over the matter would lead to artificial insularity among

48. *DBPO,* Series I, vol. 1, document number 43, p. 69.
49. Ibid., pp. 69–72.
50. Eden to Montgomery on 12 July 1945 (*DBPO,* Series I, vol. 1, document number 112, p. 214).
51. Ibid., p. 214.

the sectors. If each sector was to become independent, the cost of the occupation would be very high indeed. Furthermore, it would be difficult to define a coherent reparations program. Consequently, the British government wished to set up a coordinated import program for the whole of Germany. It also envisaged cooperative policies for wages, rations, and the standard of living. This would entail appointing an administration capable of managing both a common currency and a fiscal program for all four sectors. The British were well aware that the Allies would never agree on Germany's economic organization if they disagreed on its political system. A consensus in the matter therefore seemed highly unlikely. The Foreign Office had a valuable bargaining chip, however: Great Britain occupied the Ruhr, which was still Germany's most economically powerful region.[52]

Finally, the question of Germany's economic organization could not be separated from the problem of defining its borders, especially its Polish border. The Russians had authorized the Warsaw government to set up a Polish administration in East Prussia, Silesia, Brandenburg, and Pomerania up to the shores of the Oder and the Neisse. This startled the British, who asked for an explanation. The Soviet Union had in fact unilaterally created a fifth sector, making the final decision on their frontier with Poland without the Western Allies' consent. The measure amputated about one-fifth of Germany's territory. The annexed region was inhabited by more than ten million persons of indisputable German origin. It was true that a good number of them had fled, but the problems raised by their exodus were far from being solved. Furthermore, by wresting a part of Germany from the Allied Control Council's authority, the Soviet Union had exacerbated the problems of reparations payments and supplies in the other sectors. The USSR's unilateral act, a breach of the Yalta agreements, was clearly inadmissible, but if the US and Britain challenged it, they might reinforce the Warsaw government's dependence on the Kremlin.

After Hopkins's visit to Moscow, the problem of the Polish government had taken second place in United States concerns. The Communist Polish Worker party, which was propped up by the USSR, made no secret of its hegemonic ambitions. It wanted to keep Mikolajczyk's Peasant party in a subordinate position by forcing it to join a common front and thus limiting its autonomy and political role. Immediately after its legalization, however, the Peasant party enjoyed a considerable expansion.

52. See "Brief for the United Kingdom Delegation to the Conference at Potsdam," Foreign Office, 12 July 1945, *DBPO,* document number 114, pp. 217–18, signed E.L. Hall-Patch; see also "Brief for the United Kingdom Delegation to the Conference n. 58," Foreign Office, July 1945, *DBPO,* document number 125, pp. 256–60.

Mikolajczyk was a realist. He knew that his room for maneuver was slim. He understood that Poland would remain in the Soviet sphere of influence, but he hoped to resist Communist control by spearheading a party that had a large audience in Poland and the West, capable of restoring domestic order, contributing to renewed production, and obtaining financial resources from the United States. He knew that the Communist party did not have the means to impose itself in any country without the use of sweeping repression and massive aid from the Soviet army.[53]

Directly after the Potsdam conference, the United States leaders planned to insist that free elections be held rapidly and somehow to monitor the electoral process. They wished to create the conditions for a return to democratic activity and renewed ties between Poland and the Western countries. Knowing that the Polish government would need credit, they hoped in return to secure a liberal economic Polish policy for investment and trade. The Foreign Office, which had been reticent about the Hopkins–Stalin agreement, wished nonetheless to keep a low profile on the Polish issue, and refused to give open support to the opposition. In the Foreign Office's opinion, Great Britain had no way of countering Soviet policy in this country.[54]

Before the Potsdam conference, Italy, too, drew the attention of Great Britain and the United States. It was under occupation. Its economy was in ruins, and its political autonomy was still limited. The Allies planned to force it to pay war reparations. Clearly, it would be unable to play a political role in international affairs for a long time to come. The United States, however, was determined to facilitate its economic recovery and consolidate its frail liberal institutions. Washington was worried about the Italian Communist party's ambitions, and the Department of State made it an objective to help Italy "withstand the forces that threaten to sweep her into a new totalitarianism."[55] Italy must once again become an agent of stability in Europe.

The Potsdam conference was intended, among others, to shed light on the differences that had cropped up since Yalta over the liberation of, and occupation policies in, the other Central European countries and the Balkan States. Faithful to Roosevelt's legacy, the Department of State remained opposed in principle to spheres of influence. Nonetheless, it could not ignore the reality of the existing situation, and was perfectly aware that the "Russians [had] taken steps to solidify their control over

53. John Coutouvidis and Jaime Reynolds, *Poland, 1939–1947,* Leicester, Leicester University Press, 1986, pp. 208 et seq.

54. See Sir Orme Sargeant's instructions to Mr. Hankey, the British chargé d'affaires in Warsaw (*DBPO,* Series I, vol. 1, document number 73, pp. 126–32).

55. *FRUS 1945, The Conference of Berlin,* vol. 1, p. 681.

Eastern Europe."[56] The USSR had signed trade agreements with Bulgaria (March 1945) and Romania (May 1945). These agreements displayed the Kremlin's intent to broaden its sphere of influence in the Balkan States. That signed with the Bucharest government authorized, notably, a broad control over Romanian mining resources and industry. It allowed the Soviet Union virtually to ban all trade between Romania and the Western countries. On 30 May 1945, E. Dubrow, head of the Eastern European Affairs Division, wrote a memorandum to his chief, Freeman Matthews, head of the European Affairs Bureau, stressing the highly restrictive nature of these agreements. They were, according to him, bartering agreements, which imparted preponderance to the USSR and tended to prevent all forms of trade liberalization with the other countries.[57] "Eastern Europe is in fact a Soviet sphere of influence," stated another State Department memorandum.[58]

The Americans and the British knew that the USSR was encouraging the expansion of pro-Soviet regimes in Bulgaria, Romania, and Hungary, supporting local Communist parties and the political forces it could manipulate as its interests dictated. "Information received from our representatives in Rumania and Bulgaria indicates that the Soviet authorities and the local Communist parties are actively engaged in establishing regimes based on the one-party or 'one-front' system, thus excluding from political life all democratic elements which do not subordinate themselves to the 'popular front' organizations which now hold governmental power."[59] These organizations included several parties and groups, many of which bore the names of established popular parties, but they were dominated by the Communists and excluded important democratic groups which had a consistent record of opposition to the Nazis. A similar situation appeared to be developing in Hungary although the government there was still a fairly representative coalition. In July, a Foreign Office study pointed out the violent repression administered by the new leaders of Bulgaria, Romania, and Hungary, and their encouragement by the Soviet Union.

The situation in Bulgaria was particularly distressing. The Soviet occupier's tactic in this country was to encourage the formation of a "patriotic front," a leftist coalition led by the Communist party despite its very weak social support. A pyramidal structure of "patriotic front committees" was set up to control and administer the cities and rural areas. Noncommunist parties were infiltrated. Political figures who could

56. Ibid., p. 258.
57. *FRUS 1945*, vol. 5, pp. 852–3.
58. *FRUS 1945, The Conference of Berlin*, vol. 1, p. 259.
59. *FRUS 1945*, vol. 1, p. 357.

impose their authority were removed and replaced by quislings. The secretary-general of the Peasant party, Georgi Dimitrov, who shared the same name with the Communist leader, was attempting to pursue an independent policy, and was forced to step down. In May 1945, fearing for his life, he took refuge at the United States mission. The United States representative's residence was under siege by the Bulgarian police for several weeks. Dimitrov's successor, Nicolai Petkov, also was removed by the Peasant party congress, now infiltrated by Communists. His secretary was arrested, and died under torture.

Purges of the former regime's supporters were very harsh. The Foreign Office report of July 1945 related the forced resignation of all army officers, the entire administrative service, the diplomatic service, and all teachers. It quoted the figure of 10,000 arrests, many instances of cruelty, and repression resembling a reign of terror. In late April 1945, the people's tribunals had already delivered 2,850 death sentences, but official Bulgarian sources report 30,000 to 40,000 executions without trial. A militia composed of Communists and the dissident minority was set up to handle security and do the bidding of the occupier.[60]

Hungary was equally marked by Soviet influence. The last months of the war had been brutal and industrial infrastructure, communications networks, and agriculture had been hit hard. Budapest got the worst of it. The Red Army had snatched a huge amount of war booty. It was making massive arrests and deportations. The occupier answered to no one, but relied essentially on the Hungarian Communist party, which had held a decisive place in political activity since the Horthy regime had crumbled. In the early summer of 1945, the Soviet Union had authorized no foreign diplomatic representation, and the British and United States military missions, which were part of the Allied Control Council, were isolated, unable to influence Hungarian political activity. The Soviet authorities pulled an even greater weight because they held the strings of the Hungarian economy. Under the armistice agreement, Hungary owed the USSR huge reparations payments: 200 million dollars over six years. The debt was made more grievous as the Red Army proceeded to dismantle factories and impound industrial plants. During the summer, the Soviet Union imposed a trade agreement that laid the foundations of Hungary's economic integration with the USSR, notably by establishing Soviet–Hungarian joint ventures.[61] The Communist party was an important

60. FO 371/47987, "Political Developments in Certain Soviet-Occupied and Soviet-Controlled Territories."

61. See A. Toynbee and Veronica Toynbee (eds.), *Survey of International Affairs 1939–1946. The Realignment of Europe*, London, Oxford University Press, 1955, pp. 323–4; Jörg K. Hoensch, *A History of Modern Hungary, 1867–1986*, London, Longman, 1988, pp. 161 et seq.

element in the coalition that formed the interim government. Its members won key positions in the country's economic and social reconstruction by controlling the Ministries of Agriculture, Industry, Transportation, and Social Welfare. To crown the situation, the Ministry of the Interior was infiltrated by Communists. From a political point of view, however, the country's fate had not yet been sealed.

In Yugoslavia, Marshal Tito, who had played a decisive role in liberating his country and could manage without Soviet aid, did not show the slightest intention of playing by democratic rules in Yugoslavia. The coalition government formed in 1945 under the terms of the Yalta agreements, reflected the complete hegemony of the Communists and the security forces they controlled. Opposition leaders were unable to reconstitute their parties.

After the Yalta conference, Roosevelt had seemed to hesitate over how to enforce the Declaration on Liberated Europe. However, the increasing number of dismal reports on political developments in the countries occupied by the Red Army had since convinced the Department of State that it must act to change the course of Soviet policy in the Balkan States, and especially in Romania and Bulgaria. It did not wish to recognize these countries' governments, for this might legitimate them undeservedly and thus consolidate their power. Abandoning the principles of the Yalta agreements would be tantamount to tacitly endorsing the USSR's action of installing unrepresentative Communist regimes in these countries, which would turn fully to the East and reduce their contact with the United States to a minimum. Such a move would discourage the forces of democracy, and lead to their elimination from the political stage. The Department of State feared that signing hasty peace treaties with these countries would give their regimes unmerited prestige, and that the USSR would insist on keeping troops in Romania until the last reparations payments had been made.[62]

The Department of State's reaction was based on ideological criteria. United States interests in Bulgaria were negligible. They were hardly larger in Romania. The American population originating from these countries was small, and was not a potential factor of internal political pressure. Maynard Barnes, the United States representative to Bulgaria, and his counterpart in Bucharest, constantly stressed the brutality of repression, the need to support the liberal democratic elements that relied on the United States, and the danger of an appeasement policy.[63] US representatives in Sofia and Bucharest emphasized the strategic dimension of the problem, pointing out in particular the Soviet will to control Turkey

62. *FRUS 1945, The Conference of Berlin*, vol. 1, pp. 359–60.
63. Ibid., p. 403.

and the eastern Mediterranean.

Before the Potsdam conference, the Foreign Office, contrary to the Department of State, had begun to think that it was useless to contest Soviet policy in Romania and Bulgaria based on the Declaration on Liberated Europe. It was convinced that the USSR would neither accept representative governments in these countries nor grant the Western countries further sway in the control commissions. It saw protest as worthless, and reckoned that it was preferable to speed the conclusion of peace treaties, which naturally rested on the diplomatic recognition of the governments concerned.[64] This tactical diversion was perhaps not unrelated to the British government's desire to maintain a sphere of influence in Greece according to the terms of the "percentage agreement." Great Britain was supporting the conservative regime in Greece, which, although its legitimacy was flimsy and questionable to say the least, was leading a determined struggle against ELAS, the former Communist-led national liberation army. In Greece, as in most East European countries, political splits were rooted in antiquated sociocultural circumstances from which great fervor was fueled, though this was cloaked in the liberal or Marxist ideologies their supporters invoked in self-legitimation.

The British were, however, worried about Soviet policy in Persia. On 11 July, the British ambassador in Teheran cabled Anthony Eden: "There are many signs that the Russians are making a tremendous effort to obtain virtual mastery over this country before the moment of evacuation arrives." He quoted *Pravda* articles that attempted to justify the plan. He also mentioned the actions of the Soviet-backed Communist party in Tudeh, which was sparking disturbances in industry and causing unrest to flare up in the northern and northwestern regions. He mentioned the separatist tendencies that were cropping up in northern Kurdistan, which were abetted by the Soviet military forces preventing Teheran from advancing its troops. Furthermore, the Soviet Union was using Radio Teheran to serve up anti-Western propaganda.[65] On 19 July, Eden noted to Churchill: "The presence of the Soviet forces in Persia is an excellent example of their methods of penetration and is causing me much concern." He suggested to the prime minister that this affair be settled in Potsdam.[66] London was equally worried about the pressure the USSR was exerting on the Ankara government to obtain a Soviet naval base in the Bosphorus and detach Kars and Ardahan – two provinces Russia had claimed from the Ottoman Empire in 1878, only to have Turkey reclaim them in 1920 – from eastern Anatolia.

The Americans went to Potsdam set on securing the Soviet Union's

64. *DBPO*, Series I, vol. 1, document number 82, p. 152.
65. Ibid., document number 91, p. 166.
66. Ibid., p. 413.

promise to enter the war against Japan. Was their help really necessary? Opinion was divided, but the chief of staff wanted it. In any case, this Allied collaboration effort was not being challenged. The Soviet armies would concentrate around Manchuria, and Stalin was determined to gather the territorial and political advantages laid down in the Yalta agreements' secret provisions. Shortly before the conference, the Chinese foreign secretary, M.T.V. Soong, had gone to Moscow to negotiate on the basis of the agreements. For the Chiang Kai-shek government, as for the United States, Soviet support had more than a military value. Stalin could play a decisive role in the civil war between the nationalist government and Mao Tse-tung's Communists. The Yalta agreements also stipulated that the Soviet Union must support Chiang Kai-shek.

The Potsdam Conference

1945

The Potsdam conference was held at Cecilienhof castle, the old residence of the Kronprinz in Berlin, the former capital city of the Third Reich which had recently liberated by the Soviet forces. It opened on 17 July and rose on 2 August.

Diplomacy has its constraints, and for it to be effective, certain rules of procedure must be enforced, in particular those of defining and following a precise agenda. This formality is necessary in maintaining a favorable forum for negotiating problems and solving or managing disagreements. It is designed to mask the power play and the conflicts of interest that prevail in international relations. But at the conferences of Teheran and Yalta, Roosevelt had refused to be tied down to a precise agenda, believing that he would thus create an informal, relaxed climate in which he could win Stalin's trust. He also had refused to prepare for the conferences with Churchill or to meet with him beforehand, fearing that the Soviet leader would interpret this as a US–British attempt to join forces against him. This deliberate nonchalance would leave its mark on the outcome of the meetings, and those of the Yalta conference in particular, for issues were examined in a disorderly and often premature way. The Potsdam conference would also suffer from serious procedural failings. Before the meeting, Churchill asked Truman to London, hoping to prepare with him, but also to use the visit to serve his electoral aims. Truman refused, saying he feared Stalin would read anti-Soviet collusion into a preliminary meeting, as if the Soviet leader had the slightest doubt about the fundamental congruity of British and US interests.[67] Hence, despite their deteriorating relations with Stalin and

67. *FRUS 1945, The Conference of Berlin,* vol. 1, p. 8.

the gravity of the problems these disagreements engendered, Churchill and Truman arrived in Berlin without an agreed common position on European affairs, allowing their advisers only a brief meeting the day before the conference.[68] Although they did not diverge on essential matters, the United States and Great Britain adopted distinct, if not contradictory, positions on many important issues as the negotiations unfolded.

Furthermore, the Allies had not reached a prior agreement on the final agenda. They were therefore ill-prepared to lay down their priorities and the methods for negotiating their differences. The sheer number of the problems slated for discussion at the conference, as well as their complexity, made orderly debates and coherent, rigorous discussion very difficult. The Foreign Office and the Department of State had suggested which issues should be debated, but the Soviet side had abstained. The United States' list was short. It included: setting up a council of foreign ministers, whose function it would be to prepare the peace treaties; the treatment of Germany; the Declaration on Liberated Europe; the treatment of Italy; German reparations payments. The British proposed a similar but more detailed agenda. In addition to the problems of Germany and Italy, it included certain highly contentious issues: authorization for press agents to work unhindered in the East European countries; the problem of Poland's western border; the peace treaties with the former German satellites; United States and British representatives' status on control committees; and the removal – by the Soviet Union, it was implied – of Allied industrial equipment, notably from Romania. On their list of proposals, the British also included problems relating to the Declaration on Liberated Europe. Thus they made it clear that they intended to open discussions on the domestic situation in former satellites and in Yugoslavia, and on an "assurance of free elections in the Balkan countries." These proposals were surprising, since the Foreign Office was reluctant to continue debating with the Soviet side over how the Declaration on Liberated Europe was to be implemented.[69] The British also requested an examination of the Dardanelles, Russo–Turkish relations, and the withdrawal of Allied troops from Persia.

At Stalin and Truman's first interview on 17 July, Molotov intervened to state his proposals for the agenda.[70] The Soviet Union wanted to discuss the problems of dividing the German fleet, and reparations. It proposed

68. *DBPO*, Series I, vol. 1, document number 142, pp. 284–8.
69. *DBPO*, document number 170, p. 346; see, on British reluctance, "Brief for the United Kingdom Delegation to the Conference at Potsdam," 9 July 1945 (*DBPO*, Series I, vol. 1, document number 62, pp. 109–12).
70. See Bohlen's report of the conversation between Stalin and Truman in *FRUS 1945, The Conference of Berlin*, vol. 2, p. 1583.

examining the status of the former Polish government in exile. As in San Francisco, Molotov once again raised the issue of mandates, revealing the Soviet Union's desire to gain similar rights over the former Italian colonies. He also touched on relations with Germany's former satellites, comparing them to the Franco regime.[71] At the first plenary session, Stalin reiterated his proposals, adding the problem of Tangiers.[72] Molotov repeated to the British foreign secretary that the Soviet side planned to discuss Syria and Lebanon at Potsdam.[73]

The lack of prior agreement on the agenda affected the dynamics of the conference. The first sessions set the tone for a disorderly meeting, where the number and complexity of matters to be treated, the opposing points of view, and the various priorities and interests, created a climate of confusion, delay, and profound differences of opinion. Off to a poor start, the conference went on to dawdle over marginally important issues.

Of course, in Potsdam as in Yalta, the foreign ministers were charged with preparing the plenary session debates, untangling complicated issues, and reaching compromise solutions. Churchill, Stalin, and Truman tended to foist problems they were unable to solve on their ministers. Yet discussion within this body also proved difficult, as the subjects raised were too numerous and too sensitive. Moreover, Molotov had no room for maneuver in carrying out Stalin's orders, which restricted him from taking initiatives that might have advanced the negotiations.

After one week of deliberations, Churchill complained that negotiations were stalled as the days rushed by.[74] The conference was suspended when the prime minister left for London to hear the electoral results and was further postponed by his defeat and the change of government in England. When Clement Attlee returned to Potsdam accompanied by Ernest Bevin, the new foreign secretary, Stalin was indisposed. Time marched on . . . As one can imagine, the sheer lengthiness of the work was unbearable, especially as the heads of state and government were already harried by domestic problems. Truman, who could not remain away from the United States for long periods of time, grew impatient. Sir Alexander Cadogan noted in his diary on 28 July: "Jimmy B. (Byrnes) told me the President wanted to get away tomorrow (Sunday) night, so was in rather a hurry to finish the business! I think that it will be quite impossible; however, I'm all for hurrying things up as much as possible."[75] It would have been

71. See memorandum by Charles Bohlen of 28 March 1960 in *FRUS 1945, The Conference of Berlin*, vol. 2, pp. 1582–7.
72. *DBPO*, document number 170, pp. 342–3.
73. *DBPO*, document number 158, p. 313.
74. *FRUS 1945, The Conference of Berlin*, vol. 2, p. 207.
75. Davis Dilks, *The Diaries of Sir Alexander Cadogan, O.M., 1938–1945*, London, Cassel, 1971, p. 775.

inconceivable to end the Potsdam conference in failure. Compromise, albeit clumsy, must be reached to put a mask of formality on profound disagreement over the quadripartite occupation procedure, the peace conditions, and the framework of international post-War society. The Potsdam decisions on Germany would bear the stamp of this mismanagement.

Winston Churchill did not facilitate the negotiation proceedings. He had keenly wished for this new summit meeting, but it came at a bad time for him. He was exhausted and no longer had the resilience of his war years. Shortly before his arrival in Berlin, he had gone to rest in Hendaye, in the south of France, setting aside all his political activity. Clearly, he was going through a depressive phase. Tension, and the tremendous efforts he had exerted during the war were obviously responsible for his disarray. The state of world affairs troubled him, and worry crystallized his intuitions into visions of gloom. Whether consciously or not, he appeared to harbor feelings of personal failure. Accounts of the matter seem to agree: the prime minister had reached his limit.

In Potsdam, he was also preoccupied by the elections and unable to concentrate on negotiations. He appeared addled, verbose, maladroit. Leahy sensed that Churchill had not studied his files and was improvising. Cadogan had the same feeling, and was harsh in his judgment of Churchill's early statements at Potsdam:

> The P.M., since he left London, has refused to do any work or read anything. That is probably quite right, but then he can't have it both ways: if he knows nothing about the subject under discussion, he should keep quiet, or ask that his Foreign Secretary be heard. Instead of that, he butts in on every occasion and talks the most irrelevant rubbish, and risks giving away our case at every point.[76]

Churchill was inconsistent in his dealings with Stalin. Prior to the conference, he had singled himself out for the firmness of his position on the USSR. Shortly before Potsdam, his foreign secretary, Anthony Eden, wrote to him: "I find world outlook gloomy and signs of Russian penetration everywhere."[77] Yet the prime minister was conciliatory in private interviews with Stalin, again appearing to be completely subjugated by the dictator. Cadogan noted in his diary: "[H]e is again under Stalin's spell. He kept repeating 'I like that man.' I am full of admiration of Stalin's handling of him. I told him I was, hoping it would

76. Ibid., p. 765.
77. *DBPO*, Series I, vol. 1, document number 111, p. 212.

move him. It did a little."[78]

When, in a conversation on 18 July, Stalin asked him what he thought of the situation in Hungary, Churchill was evasive and said that he did not have enough information on the matter. He did not react when Stalin stated that the USSR was moving ahead with its plan to install strong, independent, sovereign states in all the regions the Red Army had liberated, and that he was against a policy aimed at Sovietizing these countries. Churchill had cause to be skeptical about this claim, but simply noted that certain persons were concerned about Russia's intentions. He then spoke of the boundary that split Europe from the northern coast to Albania, and named the capital cities to the east of the dividing line. Russia was giving the impression that it was on a westward advance, he added.[79] In the following plenary sessions, he happily resumed his polemical tone, disputing Soviet policy.

These failings slowed the conference down, especially as the United States did not have a very coherent policy. Truman was retiring and did not always seem at ease, though he had reviewed his files thoroughly. His secretary of state, James Byrnes, had just taken office. Byrnes's experience in international affairs was limited. He was a man of modest beginnings whose political ascent had been rapid, and he had carved himself a solid reputation for his ability to strike compromise in the Senate. Roosevelt had brought him to the Yalta conference but had kept him apart from delicate negotiations, and his role there was negligible.

Once again, Marshal Stalin played a domineering role as the summit meeting took shape, primarily because he kept his aims a secret. By revealing his intentions parsimoniously and leaving it to the United States and Great Britain to set the items on the agenda, he was able to determine how the negotiations would unfold. He had arrived late in Potsdam, postponing the opening day of the conference. He gave the China treaty negotiations as an excuse and recalled that his doctors forbade him to fly, owing to the condition of his lungs. Stalin's true intent was clearly to underscore his authority over the coalition of victors and his dominant role in the negotiations at hand. It was true that his state of health was deplorable. In Berlin, he had looked worn out by five years of war and the terrible strain of political power and military command. He was rumored to be ill. Just a few weeks after interpreting for Hopkins and the Soviet leader, Charles Bohlen was struck upon seeing Stalin again to find him suddenly aged and tired.[80] Dmitrii Volkogonov acknowledged that over the war years Stalin had accumulated a "leaden weariness, which it

78. Dilks, *The Diaries*, p. 764.
79. *DBPO*, Series I, vol. 1, document number 185, pp. 386–90.
80. Charles Bohlen, *Witness to History, 1929–1969*, New York, Norton, 1973, p. 230.

was increasingly difficult for him to overcome."[81] During the conference, negotiations had to be suspended for two days because Stalin was unwell. Admittedly, this coincided with a particularly delicate stage in the negotiations. In October, Stalin took several weeks of vacation, which was apparently unprecedented in the history of his rule. Despite his failing health, he was in Potsdam, as he had been in Yalta, an unparalleled negotiator. He never made a superficial statement and he knew his files inside-out. He was clear, precise, consistent, and handled his adversaries' arguments with agility. In reality, time was on his side. His armies were camped in the heart of Europe and, within the framework of the Soviet regime, their demobilization was sure to go slowly.

Disagreement and Compromise

The conference stumbled immediately over the issue of political regimes, which, as was evident, were to determin the political and economic structures of Europe and the post-War world. Churchill and Truman's positions on the matter were inconsistent, starting with their positions on Poland. The United States and Britain knew perfectly well that the Moscow compromise between Hopkins and Stalin authorizing the new Polish interim government had resolved nothing and had at the most given London and Washington a chance to save face by conceding to the Kremlin. They were aware that the chances for a democracy in Poland were very slim, and that the Red Army and the NKVD were not loosening their grip on the country. Nonetheless, they refrained from opening the debate on this delicate issue once again. When he had a chance to recall the Yalta agreements' provisions for free elections, Churchill said he was pleased about the improvement in Poland's situation. He would have liked to make further headway in the constitution of the new government, "but the progress made was a splendid example of the collaboration of the great powers." When questioned about the problems surrounding the former Polish government's dissolution, he explained the difficulties involved at length, asking for Stalin's patience on the matter. His tone was most conciliatory. At the end of the meeting, Truman repeated his own interest in enforcing the Yalta agreements and the principle of free elections.[82]

During the foreign ministers' meeting, Molotov immediately squeezed Eden to transfer the former Polish government in exile's assets to Warsaw. Again, discussion of this issue monopolized most of the deliberations on

81. Dmitrii Volkogonov, *Staline, triomphe et tragédie*, p. 410.
82. *FRUS 1945, The Conference of Berlin*, vol. 2, pp. 92 et seq.

Poland. Moreover, by invoking the principle of noninterference in the affairs of an independent state, the Soviet minister attempted to dilute the Anglo–American side's proposed recommendations to the Warsaw authorities for freedom of the press and elections. This issue was discussed again briefly in the plenary session. The final communiqué reflected the Soviet opinion, noting simply that the Polish interim government had accepted the Yalta agreements' provisions for elections, and that the Allied powers' press agents would be at full liberty to cover the pre-election situation in Poland as it unfolded. By refraining from further discussion of Poland's government, Churchill and Roosevelt in fact appeared to have rallied to Stalin's view of the matter.

Paradoxically, the United States was much more tenacious on the issue of government in Romania and Bulgaria. At the first plenary session, the Americans submitted a paper demanding that the Declaration on Liberated Europe be implemented. The text read: "Since the Yalta Conference, the obligations assumed under this declaration have not been carried out." Entente and the big powers' credibility were in the balance. Consequently, the United States asked for an agreement on the immediate reorganization of the Romanian and Bulgarian governments. It also proposed assistance measures for free, democratic elections in the Balkan States, including Greece.[83]

The Soviet riposte was not lacking in subtlety. Adroitly, Stalin inquired at the first plenary session about his allies' intentions for fascist Spain. He was able to keep this topic of discussion going for several plenary sessions, and to force the foreign ministers to fit it in to their meetings. The Soviet side submitted a paper recalling that the Franco regime, which maintained its power through terror, had been imposed upon the Spanish people by Nazi Germany and fascist Italy. They stated that it was a menace to all European and Latin American countries that valued their freedom. Consequently, they asked for an Allied recommendation to the United Nations to break off relations with the government and support Spanish democratic forces.

This proposal was an embarrassment for a number of reasons, for it brought to light the inconsistency in Western positions on democracy, while implicitly alluding to the US sphere of influence in Latin America. Truman refused to accept Stalin's proposal, on the pretext that it would be an interference in the domestic affairs of another state. Churchill, who had been regarded as a pro-Franco sympathizer before the war, took the same position, explaining in great detail that intervention might reinforce Franco's position and wake the dogs of civil war. A good part of the third plenary session was spent discussing Spain. The affair was of course only

83. Ibid., pp. 643–4.

marginally important, and Stalin's maneuver had nipped the scheduled discussion of the Declaration on Liberated Europe in the bud.

The British submitted a paper expressing their regret that the Yalta agreement on Yugoslavia had not been put into effect. When Churchill intervened shortly after the discussion on Spain to request that the Tito–Subacic agreement be enforced, it was easy for Stalin to counter that this would be an interference in Yugoslav domestic affairs. At the plenary session of 19 July, the prime minister pointed out that there had been no elections in Yugoslavia, that the antifascist national liberation assembly (AVNOJ) had not been reorganized, and that the legal and judiciary systems had not been restored. Tito had imposed a one-party system under police surveillance and censorship similar to that in the fascist countries. Curiously, Truman did not pursue the argument further. When Stalin suggested inviting Yugoslav government representatives to Potsdam, the United States president became impatient: he recalled that he was attending the conference as a US representative to discuss world affairs, not to debate issues that the UN could resolve. He did not mean to waste his time hearing complaints and attempting to solve every political difficulty; rather, he wished to attend to the large problems, which it was the three heads of state's mission to settle in Potsdam.[84] Truman's reaction closed the debate on Yugoslavia, but it also further discredited the United States' position on enforcing the Yalta agreements. Furthermore, it revealed differences between London and Washington on the matter.

During the discussions on Italy, Stalin had another chance to impose his views about spheres of influence, and to put the Western Allies in an awkward position. At the first session, Truman asked his allies to admit the Italian state to the United Nations Organization. He also suggested alleviating Italy's armistice terms so as to improve its economic situation and political position. The United States was appropriating massive financial aid to improve living conditions in Italy. It had already lent Italy 200 million dollars, and planned to double the figure.[85]

Curiously, it was Churchill who expressed doubt about the proposal in the plenary session. He recalled the casualties the British navy and armed forces had sustained in the Mediterranean and Africa, the bombings of London, and Italy's disloyal acts against Greece and Albania. He was, as he explained lengthily and confusedly, prepared to make a gesture to alleviate the Italian people's suffering, in line with the president's proposal. Drawing up a peace treaty with Italy would, however, take time, and one could not escape the fact that the groundwork of democracy was not yet in place in Italy.

84. Ibid., pp. 128–9.
85. Ibid., p. 148.

Stalin's position was more guarded. It was true that Italy had committed "great sins," but the Allies would be wrong to be guided by the memory of past injuries. The feeling of revenge, hatred, or the desire for redress was a bad adviser in politics. He said it was not for him to teach, but he thought he should be guided in politics by the weighing of forces.[86] It was therefore right for the Allies to do all they could to include Italy in the United Nations, but the same principle must apply to all of Germany's former satellites.

This was precisely what Stalin had been getting at. During the war, he recalled, Romania and Hungary had mobilized twenty-two and twenty-six divisions, respectively, against the USSR. Without Finland's aid, Germany could not have maintained its blockade of Leningrad. Bulgaria had also done considerable wrong to the Allies. The armistice with these countries stipulated that they pay reparations, and they could rest assured that the USSR would enforce payment of the damages. Stalin therefore supported the president's proposal on Italy. Notwithstanding, he asked the Allies to normalize their relations with all the satellite states, in other words, he wanted the United States and Great Britain to establish diplomatic relations with them. In Stalin's point of view, the issue of political regimes should not apply at this stage. The Italian government had not been elected democratically, nor had the French and Belgian governments; and yet the Allies had established diplomatic relations with these states. Thus, Stalin made it clear that he would not make the slightest concession to the United States on Italy if the United States maintained its position on Romania and Bulgaria. Negotiations on the issue reached a stalemate, for President Truman refused to recognize the other satellite states before they were reorganized on a democratic basis.[87] The Council of Foreign Ministers continued the negotiations, which were once again submitted to the plenary session. The United States still insisted that the Bulgarian and Romanian governments must be reorganized in accordance with the Yalta agreements. Truman stated that only in this way would they be recognized and admitted to the United Nations. Stalin retorted that these countries' governments were more democratic than Italy's, and recalled that Argentina's fascist government was represented in the United Nations; but he did not get his way.[88] Stalin called this an attempt to turn Romania, Bulgaria, Hungary, and Finland into "leper states" in order to discredit the USSR.[89]

Churchill supported Truman unreservedly, and his support was heightened by Stalin and Molotov's denunciation of the prevailing

86. Ibid., p. 172.
87. Ibid., p. 207.
88. Ibid., pp. 359–60.
89. Ibid., p. 358.

situation in Greece in retaliation to criticism of the Romanian and Bulgarian governments. The Soviet side was proposing a draft resolution to denounce escalating terrorism against democratic forces, which had borne the entire burden in the struggle against the German invasion; the Soviet Union reproached the Greek government for breaking the peace with its Albanian and Bulgarian neighbors. The Soviet protest sparked their old quarrel with the British. Eden objected to this "complete travesty of fact." Press agents from the world over could circulate freely in Greece and report events without the least censorship. The Greek government had announced that the upcoming elections would be open to all parties. It had invited foreign observers to attend.[90] The Western Allies had no way of knowing what was happening in Bulgaria or Romania, Churchill said at the 24 July plenary session. "An iron fence had come down around these countries." "All fairy tales," Stalin replied.[91]

During the conference, Truman was informed that the United States' first nuclear test explosion had been successful. It has often been said that President Truman, clearly withdrawn during the conference's early deliberations, took a much firmer tone with the Soviet side that day. Churchill said that when Truman learned of the atomic explosion, he had suddenly appeared more self-assured. He had been surprised to see the president talk back to the Russians so energetically and decisively.[92] One must not forget, however, that by 21 July, the conference had been dragging on for a week. Following its poor start, it had centered, as we have seen, on marginally important issues. On that day, however, Stalin made his first formal request to the Allies to recognize the Romanian, Bulgarian, and Hungarian governments, knowing that the United States had no intention of doing so. He also tried to gain approval to transfer part of the Soviet sector to Poland, although Truman did not intend to recognize the Soviet initiative.[93]

Stalin exacted full recognition of the USSR as a great world power at Potsdam. This was reflected in his claim on part of the German fleet. When Churchill started to object by speechifying on the fact that the arms of war were "horrible things," the Marshal cut him off: "Let's divide it [the German fleet]. If Mr. Churchill wishes, he can sink his share."[94] He also said that he intended to gain an open channel to the Mediterranean. The British prime minister did not seem opposed. At the meeting Churchill had arranged with Stalin before the conference opened, he had reminded

90. Ibid., p. 150.
91. Ibid., p. 362.
92. Ibid., p. 225.
93. *DBPO*, Series I, vol. 1, pp. 505–12.
94. *FRUS 1945, The Conference of Berlin*, vol. 2, p. 59.

Stalin that he looked forward to the day when Russia would become a
great sea power, and hoped to see Russian ships on all the world's oceans.
He repeated, "Russia had been like a giant with his nostrils pinched." He
liked this image, which he had already used at the conferences of Teheran
and Yalta, referring of course to the narrow straits of the Baltic and the
Black Sea. Hence, he was favorable to a revision of the Montreux
agreement. He did not, however, appreciate in the least the Soviet requests
to the Turkish government, particularly their demand for a base in the
Dardanelles and their claims on Kars and Ardahan in eastern Turkey.
During the conference, he expressed concern over the clusters of troops
fronted at Turkey in Bulgaria, and denounced Soviet press and radio
criticism of Ankara.[95] Nonetheless, Stalin still insisted that there must be
a Soviet base in the Dardanelles. Turkey was a weak country, he explained,
and the USSR must be able to guarantee free passage to its ships by force
if complications arose. After all, the United States navy protected the
Panama Canal, and the British did the same on the Suez Canal.

It was during this discussion that the United States president submitted
his plan for freedom of navigation on all straits, oceans, and rivers. A
lengthy study of history, he said, had led him to conclude that every war
in the past two centuries had broken out in the area connecting the Black
Sea to the Baltic, between France's eastern border and Russia's western
border. One way of avoiding the resurgence of conflict would be to make
provisions ensuring free passage for goods and ships through the straits,
as was the case on the United States' waters. He proposed, therefore, to
declare freedom of navigation on all international waters, and in particular
on rivers that flowed through more than one state. The plan provided for
international committees to regulate navigation on the Danube and the
Rhine.[96] The United States' goal, he continued, was to restore healthy
economic conditions all over Europe and create prosperity to ensure the
welfare of Russia, England, France, and other European countries while
contributing to the expansion of US trade and to its economic welfare.

When he was presented with the plan, which was quite blatantly
contrary to Soviet ambitions in Eastern Europe, Stalin asked for time to
reflect. He was reserved when Truman brought up the issue a few days
later, and asked for an answer to his claims on the Black Sea straits.
Churchill seized the moment to suggest that the straits be placed under
international control. "If it was such a good rule, why not apply it to the
Suez?" asked Molotov. Stalin made it clear that he would pursue the
matter directly with Turkey.[97]

95. *DBPO,* Series I, vol. 1, pp. 387–8.
96. *FRUS 1945, The Conference of Berlin,* vol. 2, p. 303, p. 304, p. 654.
97. Ibid., p. 365.

At the same time, the Soviet side repeated its desire to have a mandate over one of the former Italian colonies or to participate with the United States and Great Britain in their administration. It was also interested in the status of Tangiers, and wished to join in the discussions of the matter. These requests were another reflection of Stalin's determination to see the USSR fully recognized as a world power, on a par with the United States and Great Britain.

Stalin's requests worried Churchill. In 1945, the Mediterranean was still a British sea. Though he saluted Stalin's desire to obtain a channel to the ocean, Churchill did not propose to share control with the Soviet Union of the key areas that had built the grandeur of the British Empire. Visible in this more than any other domain were Churchill's traditional political concepts, which he based on both a respect of spheres of influence and his own imperial ambitions. After the plenary session where the Soviet side had made its claims, Eden shared his concerns with Churchill: "You mentioned in conversation yesterday that the Russian policy was now one of aggrandisement. This is undoubtedly true [...]. The truth is that on any and every point, Russia tries to seize all that she can and she uses these meetings to grab as much as she can get."[98] Eden was worried about Russia's ambitions in the Mediterranean: first the straits, Tangiers, and Lebanon, but why not some day Egypt, which it could penetrate by exacerbating social conflicts that were merely waiting to explode?

The mandates were discussed at more length at the sixth plenary session, on 22 July. Churchill was quick to become emotional, as he had been each time the problems of the Empire's structures were broached. He recalled the casualties the British army had suffered in their conquest of the Italian colonies, and the hard-won victories with no help from abroad. "Berlin [was] conquered by the Red Army," Molotov pointed out, to put things back into perspective! But Churchill would not be shaken. The British, he explained, had suffered bitterly in this war. Admittedly, British casualties were less than those of their victorious Soviet allies, but by the end of the war Great Britain had amassed an enormous financial debt to the rest of the world. Its navy no longer equaled that of the United States. Yet despite all this, the British had made no territorial claims, "no Königsberg – no Baltic States – nothing." Churchill did not want the Italian colonies, but he was visibly worried that the USSR might acquire a large strip of the African coastline.[99] Finally, it was agreed that the issue would be laid aside until the peace treaty with Italy was drawn up.[100]

98. *DBPO*, document number 176, pp. 352–3.
99. *FRUS 1945, The Conference of Berlin*, vol. 2, pp. 253–5.
100. Ibid., p. 1458.

[margin notes: Persia; Stalin agreed to pull out; Germany was at the centre of Potsdam]

Churchill brought up the problem of Allied withdrawal from Persia. Stalin asked for time to think: under the treaty he had signed with Persia, he had the right to maintain troops there for six months after the end of hostilities. Nevertheless, he agreed to pull out of the country.

Germany was at the heart of Allied concerns at Potsdam, and the Western leaders were eager to commence negotiations to define the structure and general objectives of their joint occupation policy. From the beginning, the United States had made proposals on the matter, as had the British. The dynamics of the conference, however, did not allow for a thorough examination of the German problem, as secondary issues forced its negotiation to be postponed. Notwithstanding, the Allies were able to agree on occupation policy principles without too much difficulty. The Soviet Union accepted the United States' proposals, which were general and lent themselves to different interpretations. The Allied Control Commission was named as the governing body, while commanders in chief were given authority in affairs that concerned their own sectors exclusively. The terms of the agreement called for the German political structure to be decentralized, and it expanded local responsibility, notably of community councils. They also provided for non-Nazi political parties and the freedoms of assembly and public discussion to be restored. Finally, they stipulated that democratic principles must be defined and thereafter applied by the regional, provincial, and *Länder* administrations. The Soviet side accepted the program to establish community councils, but its application came second to considerations of military security.[101]

In contrast, it was much more difficult to agree on how the German economy was to be run, for this issue was tied in with reparations and borders, whose role would be decisive in the Allied occupation policy for Germany and the future of Europe. Indeed, how could one calculate reparations and redesign the economy without first knowing the precise lay of the Polish–German border? Throughout the entire debate, the question of Germany's eastern border further complicated the issues of the German economy and reparations payments. It put the United States and Great Britain in an extremely awkward position, for the outcome might further push the Polish government into the Soviet Union's lap. Truman stood firm on the matter: the three governments, he explained, had laid out their sectors and their established borders. Now it appeared that yet another occupying power was to receive a sector. This had been done without consultation, and the Western Allies had not agreed to the concession of German territory. Truman did not see how the issues of reparations or other economic and political questions could be resolved

101. Ibid., pp. 1149–51.

if Germany was thus partitioned.[102] Churchill took the same stance. He observed that the transfer would alienate a quarter of the arable land Germany had possessed in 1937; yet foodstuffs and reparations could be reaped from the region. Further, he stressed that more than eight million Germans would have to be transferred, creating a heavy burden for the rest of Germany. Stalin retorted that almost all of the populations in these regions had already fled, and he refused to go back on the decisions he had already taken in the matter. The Poles were invited to defend their position in Potsdam, but they failed to persuade Truman and Churchill.

For the rest, the Soviet side appeared a priori to favor German economic unity, but it refused to define common principles for the German people's treatment. Nor would it recognize the Allies' right to circulate freely from one sector to the next. The Soviet Union's main concern was the reparations program it had defended since Yalta: Germany must pay 20 billion dollars, half of which would be drawn over the next two years, the remainder over ten years. The bulk of the reparations would be levied from German production infrastructures and output. The Soviet side was resolutely opposed to the plan submitted by the United States and Britain, which held that reparations payments should be second to paying for imports necessary for the German people's subsistence. The Western Allies' constant appeals not to inflate the financial charge of their occupation made no difference. Unlike its allies, the Soviet Union had experienced the German occupation: it felt that it had a right to demand substantial reparations.

The negotiating parties were at loggerheads, for the Americans and the British refused to concede. The United States secretary stated this clearly at the 23 July session: "It is the position of the United States that there will be no reparations until imports in the American zone are paid."[103] Stalin and Molotov would not hear any of it. The discussion seemed hopeless. To get around the situation, the secretary of state made a proposal to Molotov on 23 July, without consulting the British, that each occupying power collect the bulk of its reparations in its own sector.[104] The Soviet sector held about 50% of Germany's national wealth. The USSR could therefore levy the reparations it wished. It could obtain equipment or goods from the United States and British sectors in exchange for food and coal. In all other respects, Germany would be treated as a single economy.

The proposal was attractive, and it was apparently the sole way of unblocking negotiations of the affair. One could, however, already

102. Ibid., p. 208.
103. Ibid., p. 279.
104. Ibid., p. 275.

anticipate its political consequences. As a high-ranking official at the Foreign Office, Sir John Troutbeck, noted: "It is difficult to believe that such a system would not divide Germany completely into two parts, however much we might try to avoid that result."[105] The Soviet and the American officials were seemingly aware of what the proposal implied. On 27 July, in another private meeting with the secretary of state, Molotov asked if the United States suggestion was not in fact tantamount to giving each occupying power total freedom of maneuver in its own sector and the right to act independently. Byrnes said that the interpretation was correct in substance, but that they would have to make further agreements for the trade of goods among the sectors.[106]

The Foreign Office was reticent. The British position had been weakened, initially by Churchill's departure, and further by the change in government. When the new prime minister, Clement Attlee, arrived in Potsdam with his foreign secretary, Ernest Bevin, it appeared a new solution would prove impossible to find. It would have been inconceivable to disavow the US secretary of state's initiative. Bevin was openly skeptical about any agreement that went against the principle of German economic unity. He did not see how one could possibly evaluate the trading of goods that were as incomparable as chemical industry and potatoes.[107]

Despite concessions by the United States, the negotiations progressed with difficulty. The Soviet side fought grimly to obtain a higher percentage of reparations from the Western occupied sectors. At last, a compromise was struck by which the USSR would receive 15% of the industrial equipment in the Western sectors that was considered nonessential for Germany's peacetime economy in return for shipments of food and raw materials. In addition, the USSR would receive 10% of the Western sectors' industrial products without anything in return.[108]

James Byrnes also found a provisory solution for Germany's eastern border. While awaiting "the final determination of Poland's western frontier" under the peace treaty, Poland would rightfully administer the former Germany's eastern part up to the Oder and the western Neisse. Secretary of State Byrnes thus gave partial satisfaction to the Soviet Union and the Warsaw government.[109] The foreseeable outcome of this concession was undeniable. The agreement amputated a large part of Germany's territory, a region rich in coal, industry, and farmland. Under its terms, millions of Germans were condemned to flee

105. *DBPO*, Series I, vol. 1, p. 920.
106. *FRUS 1945, The Conference of Berlin,* vol. 2, p. 450.
107. Ibid., p. 485.
108. *FRUS 1945, The Conference of Potsdam,* vol. 2, pp. 1485–6.
109. Ibid., pp. 1150–1.

the regions Poland would appropriate in exchange for territory lost to the USSR in the East, and as compensation for the crimes and devastation the Third Reich had committed.[110] The British were not in favor of this: if the border was accepted, the Foreign Office estimated that between ten and twelve million Germans would have to be transferred.[111] The decision's economic consequences would weigh heavily on German recovery, and might aggravate the occupying powers' financial difficulties.[112]

As consideration for his concessions on Poland's western border and the reparations, Byrnes had demanded an automatic agreement on Italy's membership in the United Nations. The Council of Foreign Ministers was to give priority to the peace treaties with Italy, Bulgaria, Finland, Hungary, and Romania. Byrnes and Molotov found a compromise solution for these countries also: "the conclusion of Peace Treaties with recognized democratic Governments in these States" would make it possible for the big powers to endorse these states when they applied for United Nations membership. Furthermore, the three Allied powers would examine separately and "in the light of the conditions then prevailing," the chances of establishing diplomatic relations with Finland, Romania, Bulgaria, and Hungary, if possible before the peace treaties were ratified. These measures allowed them to bypass the differences that had arisen over the nondemocratic character of the Romanian and Bulgarian governments.[113]

110. Alfred de Zayas, *Nemesis at Potsdam. The Anglo–Americans and the Expulsion of the Germans. Background, Execution, Consequences,* London, Routledge and Kegan Paul, 1977.

111. *FRUS 1945,* vol. 2, *The Conference of Berlin,* p. 781.

112. Ibid., p. 1459.

113. Ibid., p. 1457.

4

SPHERES OF INFLUENCE

Toward the Division of Europe

The Potsdam conference lasted two weeks, without making any real progress in the main matters of the European peace settlement. It began on a bad footing, and was subsequently thwarted by incessant harsh opposition between diverging interests and antagonistic worldviews. Stalin and Molotov proved unreceptive to compromise, and hence the Americans and the British were forced to lower their ambitions. They accepted the Soviet claim on Poland's western border implicitly, and this arrangement increased Poland's dependence on the Kremlin while singularly complicating Germany's problems. They had resigned themselves to Germany's dismemberment under diverging, even antagonistic occupation policies. Allied disagreement over the defeated country's borders, its economic management, and methods of collecting reparations augured particularly badly for the peace negotiations.

This, at least, was how the South African prime minister, Jan Smuts, who still enjoyed great influence in London, saw things. After the Potsdam conference, he wrote to Prime Minister Clement Attlee on 10 August to voice his apprehension about Europe's future. Germany clearly stood to lose one quarter of its territory; moreover, it would have to bear the weight of millions of refugees fleeing the Russian, Polish, and French occupied regions. Its industrial capacity would be cut back and severely limited. Smuts predicted that Germany would become an impoverished nation, and that its poverty would have a contagious effect on its European neighbors. Furthermore, Poland was potentially the next Soviet republic, and the other Central European and Balkan countries would also fall into Russia's economic and political sphere. Smuts was concerned that none of the remaining forces in Europe could offset Soviet power.[1]

The conference had not only revealed the victors' disunity over Germany, it had confirmed that their interpretations of the Yalta agreements did not concur. Stalin had been unbending on the nature of the Romanian and Bulgarian governments. The Americans were committed to uphold the Declaration on Liberated Europe, under which

---

1. FO 800/443.

the Allies had a common responsibility to aid in the restoration of governments broadly representative of democratic elements. On returning from Potsdam, Truman had repeated this clearly to the American people on 9 August in his report of the conference. Romania, Bulgaria, and Hungary, he stated, "[were] not to be spheres of influence of any one power."[2] Stalin also had rejected the United States president's proposal to internationalize European waters, which made it clear that he was far from subscribing to a conception of European peace and economic stability based on liberal economic principles.

Of course, the peace talks must go on, and the Council of Foreign Ministers had been set up at the conference to oversee the drafting of peace treaties with Germany's former allies and satellites. The first Council of Foreign Ministers was to convene in London in September. There was some likelihood of complications owing to the ideological and political disagreements that had arisen at Potsdam, but also because the Big Three had resolved to open the peace talks to French and Chinese participation. France did not consider itself bound by the decisions taken at Yalta and Potsdam. Its position on Germany was quite singular, and in many ways contrary to United States, British and Soviet ideas. General de Gaulle and Georges Bidault, his foreign minister in the interim government, arrived in Washington in late August. There was a good climate at the meetings. Truman promised financial support for French recovery. General de Gaulle, however, was hardly able to rally the president or Secretary of State Byrnes to his plans for Germany. De Gaulle demanded that several states "attached economically and strategically to the West" be created in the Rhineland. He also asked that the Ruhr be placed under an international trusteeship.[3]

Shortly after the Potsdam conference, the Bulgarian Communists struck out against political forces that were standing in the way of their hegemonic ambitions. The Peasant party was the main target of their intimidation tactics, but they also attempted to divide the Social Democratic party, forcing its leader, Kosta Lulchev, to resign. In August, Nicolai Petkov, the Peasant party leader, resigned from the government to protest continued persecution of noncommunist forces through acts of intimidation and repression. Conceding to heavy pressure from the United States representative in Sofia, however, the government finally decided to postpone the elections that had been slated for late August.

In Romania, Communists supported by the Red Army continued to

2. *Department of State Bulletin,* 12 August 1945, p. 211.
3. Charles de Gaulle, *Mémoires, 1940–1946,* vol. 3, *Le salut,* Paris, Plon, 1959, pp. 462 et seq.

Romania + Communism

extend their grip on the machinery of government and political activity. On 21 August, United States and British representatives sent a memorandum to King Michael communicating their refusal to recognize the Groza government. The king demanded the prime minister's resignation, and asked the three Allied powers to aid him in forming a new government. After consulting with the Soviet Union, Petru Groza refused, however, to step down. In turn, the king refused to ratify government decrees or to approve its appointments.[4]

Yugoslavia + Communism

Yugoslavia was feverishly preparing to install a Communist government. After the Potsdam conference, an electoral law was passed by the interim assembly in August. This law allowed the Communists to silence the views of their opponents on the grounds that they were "reactionaries" or "collaborators." In September, the foreign minister, Dr. Subacic, was placed under house arrest. He handed in his resignation a few weeks later. Opposition newspapers were censored or banned. It was

Albania + Communism

already becoming clear that Tito would use the upcoming elections as a chance to consolidate his dictatorship, and that Albania, too, would adopt a Soviet-type regime.

Poland + communism

The Soviet Union was consolidating its own sphere of influence in Poland. The British chargé d'affaires in Warsaw, R.M.A. Hankey, wrote to the Foreign Office on 17 August: "The Russians really control nearly everything. This is essentially a *polizeistaat*."[5] Ernest Bevin entertained no illusions in this matter. On 23 August, he wrote to Victor Cavendish-Benthinck, his new ambassador in Warsaw: "I am by no means convinced that it is the real intention of M. Bierut and his followers in the Polish government to establish a truly representative regime. On the contrary, my impression is that, no doubt with Soviet support if not on Soviet instructions, they are aiming at a regime much nearer to the Soviet model."[6] The United States ambassador in Warsaw also sent pessimistic reports to Secretary James Byrnes on the Polish government's direction, and the chances of holding free elections.[7] In reality, the government and administration were almost entirely in the hands of the Communists, who, with Soviet aid, were gaining control of all major government bodies as evidenced by their increasing hold over the army, the security forces, the justice system, and the press.

4. Arnold Toynbee, *The Realignment of Europe,* London, Oxford University Press, 1955, pp. 292–3.
5. *DBPO,* Series I, vol. 6, document number 4, p. 15.
6. *DBPO,* Series I, vol. 6, document number 8, p. 28.
7. Arthur Bliss Lane, *I Saw Freedom Betrayed,* London, 1949. See also *DBPO,* Series I, vol. 6, p. 81.

The End of the War in Asia

The Asian peace settlement, which could not be treated at Potsdam, became another source of political complications. By dropping the atom bomb on Hiroshima and Nagasaki on 6 and 9 August 1945, the United States had brought an early end to the fighting in Asia, while precipitating Soviet intervention in Manchuria and Korea. The USSR declared war on Japan on 8 August. Japan surrendered one week later, on 14 August, but definitive disarmament of the Japanese forces in Asia remained a highly important political and strategic issue.

Japanese surrender might exacerbate the conflict in China between Chiang Kai-shek's nationalist government and Mao Tse-tung's Communists. General Patrick Hurley, whom President Roosevelt had sent to Chungking in November 1944 as the United States ambassador to the nationalist government, was trying to end the civil war. How would the Soviet Union stand on the issue? Shortly before Potsdam, Chinese Foreign Secretary M.T.V. Soong had gone to Moscow to negotiate on the basis of the Yalta agreements. The Sino–Soviet treaty, signed in Moscow on 14 August, confirmed the USSR's advantage in Manchuria, but also Stalin's commitment to the nationalist government. This event generated hope for the constitution of a government of national unity. In late August, General Hurley's efforts brought Mao Tse-tung, accompanied by Chou En-lai, to Chungking to negotiate the new government's formation. The Nationalist armed forces were in a weak position, because the Japanese offensive of 1944 in southwestern China had forced them to retreat. The Communists, on the other hand, held an advantageous strategic position, for their armies were at the gates of the major cities: Peking, Tientsin, Nanking, Shanghai, Hankow, Canton, Tsinan, and Loyang. They were poised to enter Manchuria, which was under Red Army occupation.[8] The United States could not ignore the struggle, for its outcome would determine China's future, and this immense country would one day become a great power with a leading economic and political role in Asia and the rest of the world. American business had a vested interest in an open Chinese market.[9] Consequently, General Douglas MacArthur, commander in chief of the US forces in Asia, ordered the Japanese troops to surrender to the Nationalist authorities. Also, American units stationed in China were reinforced rapidly, and they launched a huge airlift to transport Chiang Kai-shek's army to the coastal cities and northern China. Meanwhile, General Chu Teh's Communist troops were advancing in

---

8. Tang Tsou, *America's Failure in China, 1947–1950*, Chicago, University of Chicago Press, 1963, pp. 300 et seq.
9. FO 800/513.

Manchuria, where they demanded to participate in the Japanese withdrawal alongside the Red Army. The Soviet forces did not block the move, quite the contrary.[10]

The United States did not intend to involve the Allies in the occupation of Japan. On 16 August, Stalin requested that the Japanese forces surrender to Soviet troops in the Kurile Islands in accordance with the Yalta agreements, and proposed that the Red Army participate in the occupation of Hokkaido Island. He explained that Soviet public opinion would be deeply offended if the USSR's troops did not receive a zone of occupation somewhere in the exclusively Japanese territory.[11] President Truman answered immediately that General MacArthur would be responsible for the enemy troops' withdrawal in Japan, but that he could use symbolic Allied forces, which might include Soviet troops.[12] The United States leaders planned to manage Japan's occupation and political development single-handedly. The USSR had not contributed to the war effort in the Pacific, and its conduct in Eastern Europe did little to encourage the United States to change its tack.

The United States policy caused some uneasiness in the Foreign Office. On 20 August, the British government firmly voiced its desire that an allied control council be set up to assist General MacArthur in the "exercise of his responsibilities" in Japan's political, economic, and financial affairs.[13] The United States proposed to create a consultative body: the Far East Consultative Committee. It would comprise not only the four Allied powers and China, but also France, the Philippines, Australia, Canada, New Zealand, and the Netherlands.[14]

The United States was also modifying its Korean strategy. Initially, it had not intended to enter the peninsula. General Marshall had told his Soviet counterparts on 24 July at Potsdam that the Americans would not land in Korea before Kyushu, a large west Japanese island, was taken.[15] But the United States representative to the reparations committee, Edwin Pauley, warned Truman that to gain the advantage, the US forces must occupy the industrial regions of Korea and Manchuria as quickly as possible.[16] The War Department felt that it must prevent a situation similar to that which had developed in Poland from emerging in Korea. The

10. Ibid.
11. *FRUS 1945*, vol. 6, p. 668.
12. Ibid., p. 670.
13. Ibid., p. 678.
14. Ibid., p. 648; John L. Gaddis, "Korea and American Politics, Strategy and Diplomacy, 1945–1950," in Yonosuke Nagai and Akira Iriye (eds.), *The Origins of the Cold War in Asia,* New York, Columbia University Press, 1977.
15. *FRUS 1945*, vol. 2, *The Conference of Potsdam*, pp. 351–2.
16. Harry S. Truman, *Memoirs of Harry S. Truman*, New York, Doubleday, 1955, p. 433.

United States and the USSR finally agreed to set the 38th. parallel as the dividing line between their respective armies in Korea.[17]

The Joint Chiefs of Staff (JCS) asked the British forces commanding the Southeast Asian theater of operations to free the Dutch islands and southern Indochina. With symbolic forces, they should regain their hold in their former colonies of Burma, Singapore, Malaya, and Borneo. The British also received orders to land in Siam, Java, Sumatra and the rest of the East Indies, and in Indochina south of the 16th. parallel to take over the withdrawal of some 750,000 Japanese troops and liberate some 123,000 Allied POWs scattered over an immense region, where communications were rudimentary and the population numbered 160 million. This military operation would have inevitable political consequences.

The end of the war in Asia ushered in the collapse of European imperial structures. Japanese expansion dealt a heavy blow to European hegemony, debilitating colonial power with its own spectacular victories, and spurring national independence movements. In Burma, as in Malaya, the British must necessarily come to terms with the nationalist leaders, and these countries seemed well on their way toward independence, especially since there was no opposition from the Labour government. In Indonesia as well, the Japanese defeat precipitated the move toward decolonization. On 17 August, the Indonesian nationalist leaders, Sukarno and Hatta, who had been negotiating with the Japanese occupying forces since the spring, hastened to declare their republic's independence.[18]

France's position in Indochina appeared to be seriously compromised. In March 1945, the Japanese had launched an attack on the French colonial administration and its army led by Admiral Jean Decoux, a Vichy supporter. They then handed power over to the Vietnamese nationalists. In the summer, Communists led by Ho Chi Minh spearheaded the move toward national independence. Shortly after, the interim French government repeated that it firmly intended to win back its sovereignty over Indochina, claiming it would reform colonial structures and guarantee both equal access to public office and the individual and collective exercise of republican rights and liberties.[19]

The French government, however, could not restore its hegemony in Indochina without allied collaboration. In Potsdam, the Allies had decided that the Chinese armies would intervene in Northern Indochina against the Japanese army, while British General Douglas Gracey's Indian troops

17. *FRUS 1945*, vol. 6, p. 1039.

18. François Joyaux, *La nouvelle question d'Extrême–Orient,* vol. 1, Paris, Payot, 1985, pp. 36–9.

19. Jacques Dalloz, *La guerre d'Indochine, 1945–1954,* Paris, Le Seuil, 1987, pp. 76 et seq.

would land in the south. After the Japanese capitulation, de Gaulle appointed Admiral d'Argenlieu high commissioner of Indochina. It was his mission to reestablish French sovereignty in the Indochinese Union. The situation there was turbulent, however, and the French reconquest seemed very uncertain. Nonetheless, when General de Gaulle went to Washington in late August, President Truman assured him that the United States would not stand in France's way in Indochina. The threat the USSR posed in Europe and the leverage it was gaining at the end of the war in Asia encouraged the United States and France to strengthen their ties and eased the antiimperialist sentiment that had prevailed in Washington under President Franklin D. Roosevelt.

The Labour Government's Ideas

Great Britain's change of government after the summer elections hardly altered the direction of its foreign policy. The new prime minister, Clement Attlee, had entered the coalition government under Winston Churchill in 1940. He had been a member of the War Cabinet, and later Lord President. He had also sat on the British delegation in Potsdam. His ideas on foreign policy expressed more idealism than those of his illustrious predecessor. He had attended in the conference in San Francisco, and believed sincerely in the universalistic project of the United Nations. He was a sensible man, modest and intelligent. In the area of foreign policy, he gave Bevin more room for maneuver, but intervened with authority in important strategic debates. He meant to play a decisive role in accelerating Asia's decolonization.

Clement Attlee was one of the first statesmen to reflect upon the consequences of the atomic bomb in world politics. On 8 August 1945, he wrote to Harry Truman to express his concern over the weapon's further development. He suggested a declaration stating the two governments' mutual will to take responsibility for this new source of power in the interest of justice and peace, and in the name of all humanity.[20] In late August, he wrote a long memorandum on the matter to his cabinet. In his opinion, the new weapon called for a complete review of British strategy:

> Nothing can alter the fact that the geographical situation of Britain offers to a continental Power such targets as London and the other great cities. [...] Again it would appear that the provision of bombproof basements in factories and

20. *DBPO*, Series I, vol. 2, document number 187, pp. 520–1.

offices and the retention of A.R.P. & Fire Services is just futile waste. [...] I
noticed at Potsdam that people still talked of the Western Neisse although rivers
as strategic frontiers have been obsolete since the advent of air power. It is
infinitely harder for people to realise that even the modern conception of war
to which in my lifetime we have become accustomed is now completely out
of date.

The Berlin and Magdeburg bombings had been led in retaliation against
the London and Coventry bombings. An atomic bombing of London
would be answered with similar attacks on other enemy cities. "Duelling
with swords and inefficient pistols was bearable. Duelling had to go with
the advent of weapons of precision. What is to be done about the atomic
bomb?" Attlee put no faith in written agreements in this matter. Had
Germany invaded England, it would have used gas. He also knew that
the secret of the weapon could not be kept forever. Warfare must therefore
be renounced. All nations must abandon their expansionist dreams.
Previously, this vision of things had seemed utopian; now, it was the
condition for the survival of civilization as a whole.[21]

On 25 September, he wrote again to President Truman about his
concerns, and proposed they discuss the matter: "Never before has there
been a weapon which can suddenly and without warning be employed
to destroy utterly the nerve center of a great nation." Attlee doubted it
would be possible to limit the production of atomic bombs. He was
equally convinced that Anglo–Saxon superiority in atomic weaponry
would be temporary. How could they meet the challenge? "Now we have
to restart our industries and rebuild our wrecked homes. Am I to plan for
a peaceful or a warlike world? If the latter I ought to direct all our people
to live like troglodytes underground as being the only hope of survival,
and that by no means certain." Attlee felt that the collective security
mechanism created in San Francisco must now be advanced at all costs.[22]

These new strategic considerations affected the Empire's defense and
made the preservation of colonial structures illusory in the long term. The
prime minister was convinced of this. On 1 September 1945, he wrote a
memorandum to contest the traditional positions upheld for the Foreign
Office and the Colonial Office:

Quite apart from the advent of the atomic bomb which should affect all
considerations of strategic area, the British Commonwealth and Empire is not
a unit that can be defended by itself. It was the creation of sea power. With the

21. Ibid., document number 192, pp. 529–31.
22. Ibid., document number 196, pp. 544–7.

advent of air warfare the conditions which made it possible to defend a string of possessions scattered over five continents by means of a Fleet based on island fortresses have gone. In the 19th century the passage of the Mediterranean could be secured by sea power with Gibraltar, Malta and Egypt as its bases. In the air age the neutrality, if not the support, of all countries contiguous to the route are needed.[23]

The British Empire's defense depended on compliance with the principles of the Charter of the United Nations and support of its collective security mechanism. If the United Nations became a reality, it would make no difference who controlled Cyrenaica, Somalia, or the Suez Canal. If it did not, the government would have to concentrate on protecting the British Isles, for no foreign possession could guarantee their defense. Attlee saw no economic advantage in preserving the Empire. The colonies would become a financial burden. Expenditure on their behalf would only hasten their demands for autonomy or independence. "Why should it be assumed that only a few great Powers can be entrusted with backward peoples? Why should not one or other of the Scandinavian countries have a try?"[24]

His foreign secretary, Ernest Bevin, had also been a member of the War Cabinet as minister of labor. The illegitimate child of a very poor family, self-taught, this colorful personality had exercised great influence in the British unions and the Labour Party before becoming minister of labor in 1940. In this office, he had played a central role in organizing war production; he made his reputation with his organizational talents, imagination, and industriousness. He enjoyed British leadership's highest respect, and immediately became a central figure in the new Labour government, for the prime minister trusted him entirely, and gave him broad freedom to act in foreign policy. The Foreign Office remained immutable while Bevin dynamically secured the defense of Great Britain's traditional interests.

The foreign secretary knew that Indian independence was inevitable. Contrary to the prime minister, however, he remained faithful to the Victorian tradition and believed in the value of the Empire, although he was convinced that imperial relations must be changed profoundly. He observed that his era was marked by the rise of nationalism, and that economic and social development were becoming major factors in global relations. In his opinion, Great Britain must draw upon new resources to ensure progress in its colonies and the perpetuation of its imperial hegemony. He lent particular strategic value to the Middle East. This,

23. Ibid., pp. 42–3.
24. Ibid.

notably, was the cause of his deep concern over Soviet claims in the Mediterranean, especially as they were combined with pressures on Iran. Great Britain, he said, must take an interest in the Italian colonies' future. These territories lay along imperial routes to India, Australia and New Zealand. They constituted bases from which Egypt, Sudan, and Kenya could be attacked. Great Britain's potential enemies must therefore be prevented from gaining a toehold in these regions. Furthermore, the states that took over their trusteeships must be capable of maintaining order and defending key points: "The maintenance of our position in the Middle East remains a cardinal feature of British policy and in consequence we must be prepared to undertake the commitments and expenditure inherent in maintaining that position." Therefore, it was his plan to propose that Italy keep its mandate over Tripolitania, and that Great Britain obtain a new mandate over Cyrenaica, Italian Somalia, and Ogaden. Eritrea would be returned to Ethiopia, with the exception of a northwestern region, which would be attached to Sudan.

In September 1945, Bevin called a meeting in London of His Majesty's principal diplomats and representatives to the Middle East and Egypt. Knowing that British hegemony over the region could no longer rest upon essentially military and political foundations, he intended to promote measures to improve the quality of life of its peoples.[25] The conference supported his point of view, concluding that Great Britain should help develop economic and social progress in the Middle East and Egypt with technical assistance programs, by raising its investment and trade quotas there. Agricultural development would be a priority for these countries' governments. The project would entail developing irrigation systems, veterinary services, reforestation programs, road construction, and improved living and infrastructure conditions in general. It also emphasized the need to improve sanitation services and the education system, the importance of constitutional reform, the promotion of union activity, and the urgency of land redistribution.[26] London was wary of the US businesses that were seeking a place in the region, notably in the Gulf countries, but its greatest fear was of Soviet penetration and Communist influence.[27]

The Labour government's Middle East policy and strategy were hampered by the conflict between the Zionists and the Arabs. In the First World War, Great Britain had promised the Zionists a "Jewish national home" in Palestine, whilst vowing it would give independence to the Arabs and split the region into spheres of influence with France and

25. See Minutes of Foreign Office Meeting, 5 September 1945 (FO 371/45252).
26. CAB 129/2, C.P. (45) 174, 17 September 1945.
27. CAB 129/2, 17 September 1945.

Russia. In 1920, Palestine was placed under British mandate, and Great Britain was forced to suffer the consequences of its contradictory commitments. There had been occasional rioting in the beginning, which developed into full-scale unrest between 1936 and 1939. Before the Second World War, Great Britain had responded to Arab grievances by drastically curtailing both Jewish immigration in to Palestine and the Zionists' right to acquire new land, in hopes of quieting their revolt. The war and the Holocaust steeled the Zionists' determination, as did the support they garnered in Western opinion, especially in the United States. Hence, Great Britain faced inextricable problems in Palestine. Jewish terrorism had been rampant since 1944, notably in the assassination of Lord Walter Moyne, the British high commissioner to Cairo. Some 50,000 refugees who had escaped extermination were waiting in camps. They were soon joined by tens of thousands of Jews trying to emigrate from Eastern Europe who were urged on to Palestine by clandestine Zionist organizations.

The Labour government was favorable to the Zionist cause in principle; but how, with its power hanging in the balance, was it to maintain Great Britain's hegemony in the Middle East? Truman pressured Churchill and Attlee at Potsdam to lift the restrictions on Jewish immigration to Palestine. Yet how could the government satisfy his request without losing the whole of the Arab world and the 90 million Muslims in the Indian Empire? At a press conference shortly after he returned from Berlin, President Truman stated that he had appealed to the British leaders to authorize the largest possible number of Jews to enter Palestine. He specified, however, that the project would be contingent upon British–Arab agreement, for he did not want to have to send half a million US servicemen to Palestine to keep the peace.[28] The Department of State understood the political and strategic problems raised by Zionist ambitions; the War Department did as well. When questioned about the possible consequences of free Jewish immigration to Palestine, the War Department answered that it would take some 400,000 men to keep order if unrest broke out in the country. United States demobilization would be slowed as a consequence.[29] In spite of these warnings and pressing appeals from Prime Minister Attlee, on 29 September the White House revealed to the press the substance of its pressures on the British government to allow 100,000 Jewish immigrants into Palestine.

The conflict between London and Washington was awkward, for, in the Middle East and elsewhere, Great Britain could not maintain its

28. *FRUS 1945*, vol. 8, p. 722.
29. Michael J. Cohen, *Palestine and the Great Powers, 1945–1948*, Princeton, Princeton University Press, 1982, pp. 55–6.

position without United States assistance. The war had created tight political and economic ties with the United States, and maintaining these privileged relations was fundamentally important to Bevin. He knew above all that Great Britain would be powerless to act without US financial aid. On 13 August 1945, Hugh Dalton circulated a memorandum on Great Britain's financial situation, which Lord Keynes had written during the final days of the war in Europe. It was catastrophic: Great Britain had fought the war on credit and accumulated a considerable debt. "The conclusion is inescapable that there is no source from which we can raise sufficient funds to enable us to live and spend on the scale we contemplate except the United States." He suggested asking the United States for aid in the form of a gift of three to five billion dollars. Without this financial support, Keynes predicted true financial disaster.[30]

The British foreign secretary hoped to strengthen relations with the European countries, and with France in particular.[31] He also hoped to facilitate Italy's economic and political recovery, knowing the country's continued presence in the Western sphere was contingent upon it. The military suggested a policy aimed at incorporating Italy into the Western sphere. An unduly harsh peace settlement, Field Marshal Alexander explained in a memorandum on 15 August, would "inevitably precipitate conditions of anarchy in the country which would reduce Italy to the level of a Balkan country under Russian influence."[32] Obviously, this program leaned toward stronger British control in the Mediterranean, though it did not completely eliminate Italian influence: "The general aim of our policy towards Italy, is, however, to build her up into a useful member of society, to encourage her to look to the West rather than to the East and to make use of her for our own purposes as a 'bastion of democracy' in the Mediterranean."[33]

The issues of Central Europe and the Balkans were another source of concern in London. Although the Labour government intended to preserve Great Britain's influence in Greece, it was troubled by the Soviet grip on Bulgaria and Romania. The Foreign Office thought that a strict enforcement of the principles in the Declaration on Liberated Europe would be unrealistic. Ernest Bevin sensed that a new modus vivendi must be found with the Soviet government on this issue, or it might become a source of grave political conflict. He was irked that the United States government had adopted an offensive, rigid position on the Groza

30. *DBPO,* Series I, vol. 3, document number 6, pp. 33 and 36.
31. See the report of a meeting on 13 August between Bevin and Foreign Office officials (*DBPO,* Series I, vol. 5, pp. 15–21).
32. *DBPO,* Series I, vol. 2, p. 7.
33. "Memorandum from Mr. Bevin and Mr. Hall for the Overseas Reconstruction Committee," 25 August 1945 (*DBPO,* Series I, vol. 2, p. 27).

government in Romania without consulting him. Prudence was essential if one planned to question Soviet policy in that country, he felt. He knew that hopes of holding free elections in Yugoslavia and Albania were slim, and he was pessimistic about Hungary's political future. Developments in Czechoslovakia appeared to be improving, but the country was cut off from the West and was subjected to constant USSR propaganda. The two countries were vitally important to Central Europe's economy: Czechoslovakia for its industrial assets, Hungary for its agricultural resources. In fact, the region as a whole could, in a sense, constitute a separate economy. It could be largely autonomous if its countries pooled their resources and lifted tariff barriers in their trade relations. Of course, the Soviet Union had already imposed restrictive trade agreements on Romania and Bulgaria. They would look suspiciously on efforts to encourage these countries to collaborate among themselves.[34] Was there an alternative? Could a Russian sphere of influence be allowed? Bevin was well aware that the West had very little room for maneuver. He hoped to define a coherent Western policy for the Balkans and Central Europe, and he made this known to the Department of State.[35]

Disagreement over the Peace Treaties

The Council of Foreign Ministers opened on 11 September in London in the majestic halls of Lancaster House, a beautiful building with Victorian architecture. In accordance with the Potsdam decisions, the ministers were to draw up peace treaties for Italy, Bulgaria, Romania, and Finland. They were also to continue their study of the items that their heads of state and government had left unresolved, such as the withdrawal of Allied troops from Persia, trusteeships over Italy's former colonies, and the status of international waters. The French and Chinese foreign ministers had been invited to take part in the deliberations, but their negotiating position was ill-defined. It had been stipulated at Potsdam that only the states that had signed the armistice agreements would be authorized to draft peace treaties. As France had been involved in the Italian armistice, it would be on an equal footing with the Big Three in negotiating the peace treaty with Italy. But France and China's roles in discussions of other affairs were as yet unknown.

The conference started under unfavorable auspices. Molotov began by explaining that, as long as it did not have a democratic government, he refused to give Greece any say in the peace treaty with Italy. He circulated

34. Ibid., pp. 15–18.
35. Ibid.

a memorandum on this point, stating that the country's domestic situation was still extremely tense, and that the Greek government terrorized its people and threatened its neighbors to the north with its aggressive policy. Under these circumstances, it was impossible to organize democratic elections. Furthermore, the USSR opposed sending observers to Greece to monitor elections, because they could not possibly ensure the free expression of popular will; rather, their presence would be an endorsement of the regime, which was violating the Varkiza agreements of February between the Greek government and representatives of the democratic movements.[36]

This initial salvo, though directed against British policy in Greece, was intended to temper the British and Americans' insistence on enforcing the Yalta agreements, or at least to force the Western ministers to acknowledge existing ties between spheres of influence and political regimes. Molotov knew that the United States planned to invoke the Declaration on Liberated Europe during the conference to demand an overhaul of the Romanian and Bulgarian governments. The draft peace treaties he submitted to his colleagues for Romania, Bulgaria, and Hungary, clearly showed the Kremlin's intention to integrate these countries into the USSR's economic, political, and military sphere of influence.[37] The United States would not accept a violation of the commitments made at Yalta under the Declaration on Liberated Europe. The Byrnes resolution was based in part on his conviction that the United States could use its possession of the atomic bomb as a trump card in the peace treaty negotiations.[38]

The secretary of state preferred to examine the problem of the Romanian and Bulgarian governments informally, outside of the plenary sessions, and, on 16 September, a few days after the conference began, he tried to explain the basis of the US position to Molotov. The United States wished to maintain cooperation with the USSR. It understood the USSR's desire to share its borders with "friendly" states; however, it could not accept the governments in power in Sofia and Bucharest because they were not democratic. The Senate opposed them, and American public opinion did as well.

Byrnes's arguments did not daunt the Soviet minister, and the interview quickly turned into a dialogue of the deaf. Molotov recalled that the United States had supported the Radescu government, which was hostile to the USSR; yet now it challenged the Groza government, with which the

---

36. *DBPO*, Series I (1945–1950), vol. 2, document number 45, p. 135.
37. *FRUS 1945*, vol. 2, pp. 147–50; see also the American comments, pp. 182–5.
38. John L. Gaddis, *The United States and the Origins of the Cold War, 1941–1947*, New York, Columbia University Press, 1972, p. 264.

*Some of the problem was that the U.S was making one
rule for the British + another for Russia.*

Soviet Union enjoyed friendly relations. Moreover, the United States supported the Greek government, which was in no respects democratic. If the United States had been invaded or occupied for two years by Mexico, it would not tolerate a hostile government there. Byrnes had difficulty countering this logic. To circumvent it, he suggested a compromise similar to the one they had made on Poland, entailing an enlargement of the Groza government.

By referring to this precedent, invoking the constraints he was under from Congress and public opinion, and articulating his request to change the Romanian government in rather vague terms, Byrnes made it clear that he was trying to find an amiable solution with the Soviet Union. But Molotov refused to be flexible, and consequently Byrnes had to repeat his refusal to recognize the Romanian and Bulgarian governments. The Soviet minister made it clear that his position on Italy would be similar. On Molotov's initiative, the two men again exchanged their views on the question, but by all accounts, they did not have the same conception of democracy: they could not agree on what constituted a government that was "friendly" to the USSR. The same arguments were repeated on both sides, in almost the same terms. Molotov held that his government would not sign a peace treaty with the Italian government, which he considered more undemocratic than the Romanian regime.

The affair was examined formally on 21 September at the fifth plenary session. Molotov asked the secretary of state rather baldly what the United States was attempting to cover up with its position:

> The United States Delegation did not regard the present Government of Roumania as truly democratic, Molotov exclaimed. Could it be said that the present Government of Italy was more democratic? [...] The present Governments in Spain and Argentina were certainly more Fascist than democratic, yet the United States Government maintained diplomatic relations with them. [...] In Greece the present Governments were suppressing by terrorist methods democratic elements with whom they had previously concluded an agreement. There, however, the United States Government proposed that elections should be held. [...] Was not the true reason for the American dislike of the present Roumanian Government that it had adopted a friendly attitude to the Soviet Union?[39]

Byrnes objected vigorously to Molotov's accusations, notably by reminding him that the United States had recognized the Finnish and Polish governments, and that it would soon be recognizing Hungary's. It

39. *DBPO*, Series I, vol. 2, pp. 274–5.

Byrnes compared the different situations between Greece + Romania

was, however, bound by the Yalta Declaration. The Groza government had been imposed by Vyshinskii, who had given the king two and one half hours to install it, whereas the Greek government had invited foreign observers to its elections. The argument dragged on, with no end in sight. It continued into the next day. Bevin joined in to defend Greece and press for a reasonable solution. Georges Bidault implicitly took sides with the Americans and the British, voicing his support of the Declaration on Liberated Europe and echoing the importance of free elections.

To all appearances, the Soviet Union was reasoning in terms of spheres of influence, and was not mistaken in thinking that its British and US allies were doing the same. Therefore, it was no surprise when Molotov mentioned Mexico and Argentina in his argument with Byrnes over the Balkans. In his view, Bulgaria and Romania should be under USSR control, which implied that Soviet-type regimes must govern them. This principle was no more refutable than the principle of United States hegemony in Latin America. The Soviet Union had a realistic enough view of politics to understand the ambitions lurking behind Anglo–American universalism.

While Molotov made his unbending, obstinate defense of the Soviet sphere of influence in the Balkans, Bevin was repeating Britain's desire to maintain control in the Mediterranean. This was further reflected in the debates over the Italian colonies. During the fourth plenary session, Byrnes, who had taken the precaution of consulting Molotov first, opposed Italy's recovery of its former possessions in Africa. He recalled that Italy had failed to fulfill its role as a colonial power in a productive manner, and that it had not led its colonial populations to autonomy. These peoples would not have aided the United Nations war effort had they not harbored hopes of freedom. He recalled the principles of the Atlantic Charter. He proposed, consequently, that Libya should be placed under international trusteeship and governed by a United Nations-appointed administrator.[40]

The proposal thwarted British interests. It was equally distressing for French ambitions in North Africa. Bidault said that it would be neither equitable nor sound to take away Italy's colonial territories. The French minister wanted to maintain the political status quo, which protected France's position in North Africa.[41] Molotov refused to allow the colonies' return to Italy, and repeated that the Soviet Union expected to have the trusteeship over Tripolitania. He based his request on the destruction the USSR had suffered at the hands of the Italians, while recalling the extensive experience his country had in establishing good relations with

40. Ibid., p. 161.
41. Ibid., p. 162.

diverse nationalities.[42] The next day, Bevin pointedly announced his government's opposition to Soviet trusteeship in Tripolitania. He said he was very surprised by the proposal, recalling Great Britain's vital interests in North Africa: "The British claims in that area had been put forward on the same basis as had Russian claims in Eastern Europe, namely security – a perfectly legitimate basis." Molotov's promises that the USSR would never obstruct Great Britain's access channels to its Empire, nor set up a Soviet regime in Tripolitania, made no difference.

Discussion of the peace treaties advanced but little. The Soviet side backed Yugoslavia's claims on Trieste. They denied Italy an exemption from reparations payments. They also pleaded against a reduction of Finnish, Romanian, and Bulgarian armed forces. They acted as Romania's protectors, defending its claim to Transylvania under the Treaty of Trianon, an overture aimed at facilitating the USSR's annexation of Bessarabia.

On 23 September, Bevin met Molotov in private. "Our relationship with the Russians about the whole European problem is drifting into the same condition as that which we had found ourselves in with Hitler," Bevin said. Bevin continued, saying in substance:

> He was most anxious to avoid any trouble about their respective policies in Europe. He wanted to get into a position in which there was not the slightest room for suspicion about each other's motives. [...] Everyone who spoke to the Secretary of State about the West suggested that the Soviet Union was suspicious about a *bloc* directed against Russia. [...] His Majesty's Government would do nothing secret or enter into any arrangement against the USSR with any defensive design of any kind. [...T]he Secretary of State [...] wanted to know precisely what was the Soviet policy in Europe. [He] then turned to the question of *Tripolitania* and said that he had been told by Mr. Churchill that Marshal Stalin had said that Russia had no interest in the Mediterranean.[43]

Bevin asked Molotov to state the Soviet Union's intentions frankly, and said they should "lay all [their] cards on the table."

The allusion to Hitler was not in very good taste. Molotov seized upon it: "Hitler had looked on the USSR as an inferior country, as no more than a geographical conception. The Russians took a different view. They thought themselves as good as anyone else. They did not wish to be regarded as an inferior race."[44] The Soviet minister reminded Bevin that relations with the USSR must be based on principles of equality. He also

42. Ibid., p. 163.
43. Ibid., p. 316 et seq.
44. Ibid., p. 317.

submitted that the British government had changed its attitude now that it no longer needed the USSR. Then he repeated the Soviet claims on the Dardanelles. The Turks could not defend the maritime passage alone, and the British were blocking a Soviet–Turkish agreement. As for the United Kingdom's Balkans policy, it seemed to be based on a desire to launch an attack on the USSR. He also brought up the problem of repatriating the Belorussians and Ukrainians living east of the former Curzon line.

Bevin suggested that he could modify his position on the straits, but firmly repeated British security ambitions in the Italian colonies. He also tried to appease Molotov's suspicions about British intentions in Romania and Bulgaria. Molotov felt sure they could reach an "agreement." He did not specify which one, but perhaps he was thinking of renewing the commitments Churchill and Stalin had made in October 1944 concerning their respective spheres of influence. Bevin may have been tempted to accept, because he thought that openly challenging Soviet policy in the Balkans would be futile, and that Byrnes's position was unrealistic. Molotov's negotiating tactics did not, however, win his confidence, and the days of secret agreements on the spheres of influence were over. The negotiations took place in full public view. Moreover, Great Britain was dependent on the United States, with whom it had entered important negotiations for a new financial loan.

Shortly before the interview, after ten days of tough discussions, Molotov created a new obstacle by questioning whether France and China should participate in the peace treaty negotiations for Romania, Bulgaria, Hungary, and Finland. Suddenly, Molotov refused to allow states that had not waged war on Germany's former satellites to help draft their treaties. In Soviet opinion, London and Washington wanted to bring France and China into discussions on Romania and Bulgaria for no other purpose than to strengthen their influence in the European peace settlement. In addition, the United States clearly intended to define the occupation policy for Japan unilaterally.

Formally, Molotov was not in the wrong in invoking this procedural snag. However, when Bevin suggested at the first plenary session on 11 September that the French and Chinese foreign ministers be included in the discussions – though not in the final vote – of all the peace treaties, he had not objected. To justify his about-face, he spun out the arguments Stalin had used in Yalta, stating that it would be a long time before France returned to its former status as a great power. Thus, once again, the Kremlin showed its intention to exclude France from the European peace settlement and to minimize the French role in restoring world order. According to this reasoning, Molotov could not allow China, which had not sent "a single soldier to Europe," had failed to make an earnest contribution to the war against Japan, and whose regime was fragile to say the least, to participate in the European peace settlement on an equal footing with the big powers.

It is revealing that Molotov challenged the five-way negotiation procedure after Bidault, rather demure in his previous statements, made it clear that he wished to discuss the peace treaty with Finland and then offered an interpretation of the Balkans situation that approached that of the United States and Britain. The French minister also opposed Soviet ambitions in North Africa. Shortly before the conference opened in London, General de Gaulle had made an equivocal statement in *The Times* on England and France – "Western European powers" that were "democratic" – expressing his wish to form some association with the other countries in the region. He had also spoken of "West Germany."[45] The Soviet press had loosed itself upon the "Western bloc" plan, challenging General de Gaulle and his government's "reactionary" policy.[46] The press campaign coincided with the conference in London.

By suddenly demanding that France and China be excluded from the negotiations already underway, Molotov placed Byrnes and Bevin in an awkward diplomatic position with their allies, in particular with France. As Molotov conceived them, tripartite negotiations worked in favor of spheres of influence, for they led to political haggling and hence to the exclusion of other countries. His tactic was an open affront to American universalism. It undermined the United Nations' authority before the new organization had even begun to function, because it diminished the roles of two permanent members of the Security Council – France and China – in the peace talks and contradicted the democratic principles on which the General Assembly was founded. Bevin could not allow France to be excluded from European affairs, especially now that it was a participant in the negotiations. He was worried about the Soviet Union's desire to keep the European countries out of the talks. The British dominions, which had played an important part in the war, would not accept exclusion from the diplomatic process.

The Foreign Office knew that Molotov's unwillingness to compromise on the peace treaty negotiation procedure was a bargaining tactic to force the United States to modify its position on the democratization of the Romanian and Bulgarian regimes. As Dixon, Bevin's private secretary, pointed out, the Soviet expedient of blocking procedure was part of a scheme to obtain satisfaction in fundamental matters. This method was typical of Soviet negotiation. It had served the Soviet Union often in inducing the United States to find compromise solutions favorable to the

45. Charles de Gaulle, *Discours et messages,* Paris, Plon, 1970, pp. 652–8.
46. Georges-Albert Catroux, *J'ai vu tomber le rideau de fer. Moscou, 1945–1948,* Paris, Hachette, 1952, p. 109.

former's ambitions. Moreover, the Soviet Union knew that time was on its side. The Western Allies were under pressure to conclude the negotiation. Dixon thought that the Soviet Union hoped thus to satisfy its ambitions in the Mediterranean, and that it was trying to create a rift between England and France to prevent a Western bloc from forming. Sargeant thought, however, that the Soviet claims on Tripolitania were not serious, but that they had been advanced to force the United States and Britain to recognize the Soviet sphere of influence in the Balkans.[47]

The last week of the conference was essentially given over to seeking a compromise on the negotiation procedure. Truman and Attlee appealed to Stalin, urging him to resolve the matter, but to no avail. On a number of occasions, Molotov made it clear to Byrnes and Bevin that this problem of form was directly related to Soviet–US disagreement over the Balkans. He forcefully repeated Soviet claims on Tripolitania. As a bargaining tactic, he refused to grant the Dodecanese islands to Greece. The conference dragged on through increasingly laborious discussions, interspersed with bitter-sweet exchanges.

In the midst of the huckstering, Molotov raised the issue of the Far East. At the very first session, Molotov had expressed interest in deliberating on Far East matters. On 24 September, he raised the issue again, submitting a Soviet memorandum requesting an allied control commission in Japan, which was to include the United States, Great Britain, the Soviet Union, and China. Now, he asked that this item be included on the conference agenda, openly defying General Douglas MacArthur's policy in Japan. He proposed that the allied control commission immediately be instated in Tokyo. Two days earlier, President Truman had publicly outlined the United States' Japan policy, without consulting the Allies first. Impertinently, Molotov asked what would happen if Clement Attlee, General de Gaulle, Chiang Kai-shek, or Marshal Stalin began to make their own declarations on the matter. He further accused the United States of doing nothing to demobilize the Japanese forces, and of maintaining Japanese industrial capacity intact.

Byrnes refused to discuss this item on the pretext that it was not on the agenda, invoking his lack of preparation in the matter, and the absence of US experts to counsel him. Formally, this was true. Yet his dilatory behavior, which was understandable in light of the Soviet attitude in Poland and the Balkans, was as much a reflection of the United States' intention to exercise an independent policy. Although they denied it, the Americans acted as if Japan and China should belong to their sphere of influence from now on.

47. *DBPO*, Series I, vol. 2, document number 120, pp. 349–50.

On 27 September during a private interview with Byrnes, the Soviet minister linked his refusal to let the negotiations move forward to the United States' obstruction of Japan.[48] Byrnes finally suggested a compromise solution for the treaty negotiation procedure that was largely in line with the Soviet position.[49] He accepted France and China's exclusion from the preliminary peace treaty negotiations for those countries with which they had not signed an armistice agreement. Following these proceedings, an international conference would be convened representing the five permanent members of the United Nations, as well as all of the organization's European members and the other states that had made a substantial contribution to the war against the Axis. Despite the concession, the interminable, repetitive discussions continued hopelessly for several days, ultimately pervading every area of the talks. During Bevin and Molotov's meeting on 1 October, the Soviet minister made it clear that his position was dictated by a desire to obtain recognition of a Russian sphere of influence in the Balkans and advantages in the Mediterranean.[50]

Bevin and Byrnes therefore had to resign themselves to the conference's failure. The great powers had elaborated on their disagreement over peace treaty negotiation procedures while debate of the essential issues had not advanced and the German problem, which was decisive for Europe's future, had not been examined. The ministers were not even able to agree on a final statement. The failure in London revealed that the alliance which had prevailed in the war against the Axis was breaking down. The disagreements that had cropped up among the great powers in Potsdam over the boundaries of their spheres of ideological influence, and hence over international post-War structures, were intensifying. The Kremlin seemed to prefer an isolationist policy over continued Allied cooperation, which would oblige it to temper its expansionist will. Molotov's attitude revealed that the Soviet leaders did not intend to relinquish their war spoils to satisfy Western political conceptions. Soviet Russia held a strong position in London. It had instated itself in the East European countries. Its only claims outside the vast territorial domain controlled by its army were in the Mediterranean and Japan.

This was also a failure of the normal rules of diplomacy. Molotov made no concessions in London. He possessed an extraordinary mastery of negotiation procedures, which inevitably won admiration from his

48. *FRUS 1945*, vol. 2, p. 426.
49. Ibid., p. 438.
50. Ibid., p. 488.

audience.[51] His obstinacy and inflexibility, his endurance, his tireless, monotonous repetition of the same arguments, his delaying tactics, and his hedging unnerved his negotiation partners. He could be belligerent, constantly invoking questions of procedure to defer debates of the real issues. His attitude seemed to indicate that his room for manoeuver was limited, for surely he had no authority to soften his position. Molotov was simply carrying out the Kremlin's orders: no one had remained in Stalin's service by taking the initiative. It appears that on 22 September Stalin told him to challenge the procedure rules, which had been approved early in the conference, and thus to exclude France and China from the German satellite peace treaty discussions. Stalin had made no concessions in Potsdam when it came to protecting his sphere of influence in Eastern Europe, and the Potsdam experience seemed to indicate that tenacity in discussions with the Western leaders paid off. Hence, Molotov tried the patience and occasionally the sang froid of his British and American partners, and thus undermined the diplomatic process.

Byrnes and Bevin had long-standing political careers. They had, however, hardly any experience in international affairs. The US secretary of state was not up to his task. He was inconsistent with Bevin and Molotov. His proposals were indecisive. Near the end of the conference, he grew sarcastic and condescending. Finally, he took the initiative to suspend the conference, despite lack of progress on the main items. Byrnes's position was all the weaker as he had declined to define a common stance with the British. To speed the negotiations, Byrnes insisted that the Council of Foreign Ministers meet twice a day. This was a mistake. As Harriman remarks in his memoirs, the long council sessions were tiring. They were a grueling test of the negotiators' nerves and left hardly any room for informal discussion. After the conference, in a conversation with Harriman in Moscow, Molotov bemoaned the negotiation procedure, in particular because the three big powers had not had the chance to attune their points of view prior to the plenary sessions.[52]

Shortly after the conference in London, the Foreign Office intelligence sub-committee reported on Soviet negotiation methods, based notably on experience during the Second World War. According to the report, the Russians were characterized in negotiations by their wariness, which could be explained by their generations-old attitude toward outsiders. The isolationist and xenophobic tendencies of the Politburo and Communist party reinforced the tradition. Furthermore, their decision-making process was extremely centralized, notably in all affairs treating foreign policy.

51. Memorandum by Boyd Shannon (Dominions Office) (*DBPO*, Series I, vol. 2, document number 164, p. 474).
52. *FRUS 1945*, vol. 2, p. 560.

Soviet negotiators had no room for maneuver, and acted under the NKVD's constant control. Their tactic was to adopt the most inflexible positions when negotiating the most insignificant issues, in such a way as to force the adversary to concede on affairs they deemed important. The report went on to say that the refusal of the United States and Great Britain to accept the Soviet sphere of influence in Eastern Europe had dug in the USSR's already hardened position, as had Soviet insecurity about the atomic bomb, and England's refusal, combined with the United States' hesitation, to grant them the financial means to speed their reconstruction. The sub-committee advised that no further concessions be made to the Soviet Union without due consideration.[53]

Stalin's Isolationist Policy

The failure of the London conference did not bode well for the peace talks and cloaked relations between the big powers in gloom. As the Council of Foreign Ministers had reached an impasse, there was a threat that disagreement on Germany's future would reappear and hinder European reconstruction. This was also a bad omen for the United Nations Organization, as the Security Council clearly could not function if its permanent members failed to agree on Europe's future or the framework of international relations. In early November, the French ambassador in London, René Massigli, reported to Georges Bidault on the sessions of the United Nations preparatory committee:

> The UN is based on a postulate of agreement between the five powers. Without agreement, the machine cannot work. It is only too obvious that, today, agreement does not exist. On important issues, no basis for understanding has been reached. There is good cause to fear that the "United Nations" shall make quite a deplorable spectacle of slowness, if not impotence.[54]

The Red Army was a heavy burden on the economic and political outlook in the countries it occupied. Moreover, the United States and British governments had to maintain forces in Italy, although they wanted to speed demobilization and curtail military spending. The Foreign Office wondered now if Great Britain and the United States should not resolve unilaterally to end the state of war with Italy by negotiating with the Italian government for diplomatic relations and continued US–British military

---

53. *DBPO*, Series I, vol. 6, document number 41, pp. 151–6.
54. Z Series, Europe 1944–1948, "Organisation des Nations unies," dossier général.

presence in the country, with a view to occupying Austria, protecting Venezia Giulia, and securing communications in the Mediterranean. There was, however, some fear that the USSR would take advantage of the initiative to consolidate its sphere of influence in Eastern Europe further.[55]

Molotov's position on France at the London conference had caused some disarray in the French Ministry of Foreign Affairs in Paris, for it seemed to indicate that General de Gaulle's pro-Soviet policy had failed. Molotov had not in the slightest supported Bidault's efforts to detach the Ruhr from Germany in return for France's recognition of "the USSR's special interests in Eastern and South Eastern Europe."[56] On 28 October 1945, a memorandum from the French Ministry of Foreign Affairs reported bitterly that "Soviet support" had failed France since the new year, notably when France had asked to attend the Potsdam conference and sit on the reparations committee; yet French policy had backed the Soviet Union's efforts in Eastern Europe, especially in Poland, the Baltic States, and the Balkans.[57]

The State Department hesitated over what line of conduct to take. In a memorandum on 18 October, Bohlen acknowledged that the USSR was aiming to gain complete control of the countries it occupied. This policy was incompatible with the principles of international cooperation defined and adopted during the war. It would meet with growing opposition from Western democracies, he stated, ultimately leading to the world's division into spheres of influence. It would mean abandoning the United Nations Organization, and forming armed camps to prepare for the next world war. What could stop this disastrous development? The United States could, of course, recognize the USSR's interests in Eastern Europe as legitimate, owing to geographic proximity. Consequently, it would have to allow the USSR to establish a sphere of influence similar to the current ties between the United States and Latin America. In conformity with the Monroe Doctrine, the USSR would have the right to oppose military and political alliances in this part of Eastern Europe. It could not, however, impede trade and cultural relations between the countries in the region and the rest of the world by creating a rigorously controlled bloc, closed to foreign influence.[58] Cloyce K. Huston, head of the South-Eastern European Affairs Division, was convinced that Soviet policy was geared toward preventing a cordon sanitaire from being formed around Russia.

55. CAB 129/5, C.P. (45), 351, 28 December 1945.
56. Catroux, *J'ai vu tomber*, p. 138.
57. Z Series, Europe 1944–1948, "URSS, politique extérieure; relations bilatérales avec la France," dossier général, vol. 52.
58. Edward Mark, "Charles Bohlen and the Acceptable Limits of Soviet Hegemony in Eastern Europe: A Memorandum of 18 October 1945," *Diplomatic History,* n. 3, 1979, pp. 201–13.

In a memorandum on 24 October, he suggested that the United States might make a public approval of the USSR's desire to cultivate friendly governments in this region of Europe.[59]

The US secretary of state tended to interpret the failure in London as a misunderstanding. To prove the United States' good faith, he sent Mark Etheridge to the Balkans on 10 October. The journalist from the *Louisville Courier-Journal* had as his mission to investigate the situation in the countries of the region. Byrnes reckoned that Stalin was ill-informed of US intentions, and thought that it would be useful to approach him directly to explain the United States' position clearly and restore trust. He instructed Ambassador Harriman personally to transmit a letter to Stalin from President Truman laying out the latest United States proposals on peace treaty negotiation procedure, which the secretary of state had already tried to get Molotov to accept and which were essentially in line with Soviet ideas.

The mission turned out to be complicated, for Stalin was away from Moscow. For the first time in the history of his rule, the press announced, Stalin had gone on vacation. Rumors spread in diplomatic circles that the "Generalissimo" was gravely ill, and even that he was dead. It appears that he had in fact had a stroke.[60] Harriman was finally authorized to meet with Stalin. The dictator was staying at Gagra in Crimea, where he was resting near the Black Sea on an estate cut off from the outside world by a high wooden fence flanked by an enormous security unit.

Stalin read the president's letter attentively. "The Japanese question is not touched upon here!" he said, raising his eyes to meet his guest's. It was a pertinent remark! For the Americans did not plan to involve the USSR in the occupation of Japan, nor in the occupation policy. The war in the Pacific had been their affair. The current experience in Eastern Europe and Germany was not encouraging for shared responsibility with the Soviet Union in Asia. During the summer, United States leaders had made it plain to Stalin that they did not need the Red Army's help to occupy the island of Hokkaido. Molotov's questions on this issue had gone unanswered. Stalin could only interpret Washington's dilatory attitude as a reflection of its plans to create a United States sphere of influence in Japan, and thus to spread its hegemony over most of Asia and the Pacific.

Harriman was in a tight spot. The object of the meeting was to find a way out of the impasse created by the failure in London. He had not been instructed to discuss this new issue with Stalin. The United States, Harriman replied, was undertaking Japan's disarmament alone. It might

59. Ibid., pp. 206–7.
60. Report by Ambassador Smith of 17 March 1948 (*FRUS 1948*, vol. 4, pp. 821–2).

consider inviting some Russian and British forces to participate in the country's occupation. It would not, however, approve the creation of sectors. On the other hand, there were plans for a military council which could discuss matters with General MacArthur, leaving him the final word in case of disagreement.

Stalin understood the reasoning behind this policy well. He compared it adroitly to prevailing policies in East European countries, for example in Romania and Hungary, where Soviet troops controlled the situation. There, the discussion seemed to come to a halt. During the second interview, however, using a ploy that had served him often in Allied negotiations, Stalin changed tack abruptly. He expressed great bitterness over the USSR's role in Japan's occupation. The Soviet government had never been consulted, nor even informed by the United States of its decisions in the matter. In fact, the USSR was nothing but an American satellite in the Pacific, for the United States leaders did not consider it one of the Allies. It could not accept this position. The Soviet Union, he added, would be better off leaving Japan than being treated like a chattel. Finally, as if thinking aloud, Stalin made it clear that from then on he would adopt an isolationist policy. He had never favored this direction before. "Perhaps, in fact, there is nothing wrong with it," he added.[61]

At the end of the meetings, Stalin accepted the United States' position on Japan. He also took note of its desire to recommence negotiations of the peace treaties by making large concessions to the Soviet position. Could an improvement in Soviet–US relations be hoped for? The United States ambassador remained skeptical. He was troubled by Stalin's "isolationist" statements, which he interpreted as the reflection of expansionist intentions in Europe. It was his understanding that these statements foretold a plan to control all of Eastern Europe and to use the Communist parties to spread the Russian sphere of influence farther still. Consequently, Stalin would not expect economic assistance from the United States or any other Western power. He would not rely on their future military cooperation. Nor would he agree to participate effectively in the collective security mechanism established with the creation of the United Nations. Harriman was convinced, therefore, that this new direction had been discussed by persons inside the Kremlin: it was their decision to opt for an independent, militant policy.[62]

Many indicators corroborated Averell Harriman's analysis. The United States mission in Moscow acknowledged that the USSR was increasingly closed to foreign contact. The Kremlin demurred at proposals to establish

61. Averell W. Harriman and Elie Abel, *Special Envoy to Churchill and Stalin, 1941–1946,* New York, Random House, 1975, pp. 512–14.
62. Ibid., p. 515.

aviation rights with the Western countries. The United States had been negotiating these privileges since 1943. In September, customs suddenly banned the entry of diplomatic pouches from the United States.[63] Western correspondents in Moscow were subjected to censorship that was as strict as it was arbitrary, as they had been during the war years. The Soviet press was preparing the break with the Western world by returning to its pre-War black-and-white portrayal of the United States and Britain. Isaiah Berlin, who was posted to the British embassy in Moscow, made the pithy observation: fascism was not dead. It could return in Japan, assuaging a desire for vengeance. In Persia, the masses were groaning under the arbitrary rule of a reactionary, anti-Soviet clique. The situation in Turkey was just as bleak. Worst off was Greece. The fascists and monarchists were repressing freedom and progress with British aid. France was in a highly troubled period, and public opinion was tiring of General de Gaulle's policies. Reactionary circles had a significant role in France and Great Britain. While the masses wished only to collaborate with the USSR, reactionary politicians were toying with the idea of a "Western bloc" to revive plans to surround the USSR with a cordon sanitaire. On the other hand, in such East European countries as Romania, Bulgaria, Hungary, Poland, Czechoslovakia, and even Austria, hopes of a new dawn were appearing. Land had been redistributed among farmers, and industrial activity was beginning again thanks to the efforts of workers and intellectuals, after its destruction by years of corruption, capitalist oppression, and German domination.[64]

All evidence indicated that the USSR was entrenching itself in ideological and political isolation. On 7 November 1945, during the October Revolution celebrations, Molotov made a long speech to the Soviet people in Moscow harking back to old themes of Bolshevik propaganda. He glorified the USSR's leading role in the victory, counting fascism's defeat among the achievements of the "Great Stalin's" regime. "The world has seen that the USSR is gloriously capable of defending its interests. [...] It was our army's offensive alone [...] that gave the oppressed nations their chance for liberation. [...] Other countries have learnt to struggle for their freedom by following the example of the USSR . . ." True democracy existed only in the USSR. In other countries, there were two categories of people: the oppressors and the oppressed. He denounced the Western powers' designs to form a bloc, recalling that similar plans had been undertaken against the USSR in the past. Vestiges of fascism in the capitalist states accounted for the difficulties the Soviet Union had encountered in international collaboration. Referring to the failure in London, he said

63. *FRUS 1945*, vol. 5, p. 886.
64. Telegram of 12 October 1946 (FO 371/47870).

that the United Nations must not become the instrument of a single big power. He added that the atomic bomb could not remain the exclusive property of a few states, nor could it serve as an instrument of diplomatic pressure. He also mentioned control of Japan, a problem that called for real cooperation among the three great powers. He concluded his speech by suggesting that the USSR's reconstruction and development would take place under the aegis of a "Bolshevik will" that would procure the atomic bomb and yet other assets for the Soviet Union.[65] For the first time since the war against Hitler, a top Soviet leader was launching attacks on the policies and even the domestic regimes of its allied nations.[66] In late November, Harriman met Maksim Litvinov, the former Soviet national commissar for foreign affairs, at the theater. "I [Harriman] asked him what we, for our part, could do about it [the international situation]. He replied 'Nothing.' I then asked 'What can you do about it?' [...] 'Nothing.' [...] I then said 'You are extremely pessimistic' to which he replied 'Frankly, between us, I am.'"[67]

The "Three Great Monroes"

The resurgence of antiimperialist themes in Soviet propaganda became a source of embarrassment for Western powers, because colonial problems were taking on an increasing tenor of immediacy. Great Britain backed General de Gaulle's imperial policy in Indochina, including the redeployment of French forces in Saigon. It was also involved in the Netherlands' plans to restore colonialism in Indonesia. British forces, mostly the formidable Gurkhas, had landed in Java to monitor the Japanese withdrawal. They were flanked by Dutch troops, who were unrelenting in their determination to shatter the Sukarno government's timid bid for independence. Admiral Louis Mountbatten, the Allied commander in chief for South East Asia, tried to keep his distance from the Dutch, and encouraged them to open discussions with the Indonesian Republic. But the Hague was obstinate. The British forces soon found themselves in an impossible position. Grave troubles broke out in late October, starting with massacres of Dutch civilians, and culminating in the death of a British general. The British forces reacted with uncharacteristic cruelty to the rebels' refusal to hand over the perpetrator of the assassination. The city of Surabaya was savagely

65. Catroux, *J'ai vu tomber,* pp. 128–9.
66. See the analysis of Molotov's speech by the French embassy in Moscow in Z Series, Europe 1944–1948, "URSS, politique intérieure," dossier général, January 1945–March 1946, vol. 18.
67. *FRUS 1945,* vol. 5, p. 921.

bombed and, after heavy fighting, 6,000 Indonesians were left dead or wounded. The British troops had also suffered heavy casualties. Liberals in the United States protested vigorously.[68]

Ernest Bevin was not satisfied with the developments in world affairs. USSR expansion worried him. On 6 November, he exclaimed before the House of Commons in a clear reference to the USSR: "One cannot help being a little suspicious if a great Power wants to come right across, shall I say, the throat of the British Commonwealth."[69] However, the direction of US foreign policy also caused him some unease. The negotiations underway in Washington for a US loan to Great Britain were complex. It was obvious that the United States leaders had little sympathy for the Labour government's economic problems. On 18 October, Lord Keynes sent a long dispatch taking stock of the negotiations he had been involved in since the summer, in which he openly voiced his disappointment over the United States' financial demands:

> We came here in the hope that we could persuade the U.S. to accept a broad and generous solution which took account of our financial sacrifices before the U.S. entered the war and of President Roosevelt's principle of equality of sacrifice as well as of the post-war advantages to the U.S. of a settlement with us which would enable us to share world responsibilities.[70]

The American negotiators, Fred Vinson and William Clayton, refused to approve the British request for a gift or an interest-free loan, fearing it would be unacceptable to Congress. Furthermore, in return for its financial aid, the United States demanded that the System of Imperial Preferences be eliminated. Finally, on 7 November 1945, Byrnes gave Bevin a list of the Atlantic and Pacific naval bases the United States wished to keep. The list was long. It included the Azores and Cape Verde, but also thirty-five islands in the Pacific, some on which the United States had long-standing claims, others it wished to control with Great Britain. The United States was also pressuring the Icelandic government for the right to maintain bases in Iceland which it had obtained during the war.[71]

On 8 November, Bevin drew up a long memorandum, in which he expressed regret over the widening rift between the principles of collective security established in San Francisco and the policies of the big powers. He discerned the rapid resurgence of a regime of spheres of influence,

68. A. Rose Lisle, *Roots of Tragedy. The United States and the Struggle for Asia, 1945–1953,* London, Greenwood Press, 1976, pp. 80 et seq.
69. Quoted in *DBPO,* Series I, vol. 4, p. 287, n. 3.
70. *DBPO,* Series I, vol. 3, document number 74, pp. 227–8.
71. Ibid., document number 90, pp. 280–1.

which he in his singular language called the "Three Great Monroes." The United States, he explained, with economic and financial power behind it, was extending its Monroe Doctrine toward the Far East, in such a way as to include China and Japan. The Russians seemed to be deploying their own sphere over a vast continental expanse stretching from Lübeck to the Adriatic in the west and as far as Port Arthur in the east. Great Britain was situated between these two expanses, in the middle of a Western world that lay completely divided, while the French and British Empires were breaking down.[72]

If these spheres of influence were consolidated, he explained, Great Britain would be almost alone, with only France to support it on the continent. Yet France was undecided: it oscillated between East and West, trying to play the moderator in conflicts among the great powers. The French government surely would be forced to fall back into the Western camp, but Great Britain would hold a difficult place in the world. For Britain would have to defend a large sphere of influence including Italy, Greece, Turkey, the dominions, India, and the colonial empire in Africa, whilst braving Russia's colossal military power in Europe, which, moreover, had the potential to mobilize support from Communist parties abroad. Furthermore, the German people would remain a source of continual insecurity, and the former Allies would stop at nothing to control or prevent a resurgence of its power. In the past, spheres of influence were, above all, systems of security. The new hegemonies would tend to control economic institutions and political regimes, and could hinder free trade. This was true of Soviet policy in Eastern Europe. Yet the United States' behavior was not any better: it defended multilateral trade principles, but attempted to control the markets of the Far East and Latin America with its economic and financial resources. There was a return in force to cynicism and relations based on the survival of the fittest.

The desire to protect the British sphere of influence in the Middle East tempted Bevin to come to an arrangement with the Soviet side on the Balkans. Given current setbacks in Greece, he knew that the political regimes in this part of Europe were a more complex matter than the opposition between democracy and totalitarianism. He was convinced that it was time to change "tactics" and that it was pointless to defer diplomatic recognition of the Romanian and Bulgarian regimes. Clearly, diplomatic pressure by the United States and Great Britain had no effect. Fraudulent elections had taken place in Bulgaria despite United States protest, and the Etheridge mission had not affected the course of events. As a memorandum from the Foreign Office pointed out, it would be unrealistic to think that the USSR would make concessions entailing even

72. *DBPO*, Series I, vol. 3, document number 99, pp. 310 et seq.

the slightest loss of prestige. On the other hand, the Kremlin might agree to negotiate a compromise for the mandatory symbolic enlargement of these countries' governments and some liberalization of their regimes, if in consideration for these concessions the United States and Britain would agree to ratify the peace treaties soon. The normalization process would make it possible for most of the Soviet forces stationed in Romania, Hungary, and Bulgaria to pull out.[73] On 26 November, Orme Sargeant reminded William Houston-Boswall, the British ambassador in Sofia, of the importance the Foreign Office lent to consolidating Bulgarian independence. "We are trying to put a limit on Russian expansion in the Middle East and in fact to build up a kind of 'Monroe' system in that area. [...] If Bulgaria remains a Russian satellite it will always be in the power of the Soviet Government to use Bulgaria in order to keep Turkey and Greece perpetually on tenterhooks." But the policy of nonrecognition hindered the peace talks and thus increased the USSR's chances of gaining control over Bulgaria.[74]

The Specter of the Atomic Bomb

During the conference in London, Molotov had alluded to the atomic bomb several times, insinuating that Byrnes was taking advantage of his military edge.[75] This was also a theme in the speech he delivered on 7 November. In conversations between Russian artists and writers and United States diplomats in Moscow, the subject of the atomic bomb came up often in connection with accusations of aggressive, anti-Soviet sentiment in US policy.[76]

Was this the reason for the Soviet attitude? Stalin had puzzled Truman in Potsdam by not showing the least surprise when the success of the first United States test explosion was announced. The Marshal was always in control of his emotions, especially in international conferences, but in fact he had no real cause for surprise: since 1944 at the latest, Soviet espionage, and the spy ring led by Klaus Fuchs in particular, had kept him abreast of the Manhattan Project's progress. In 1942, Stalin had been informed of the possibilities for development in nuclear energy, and work

---

73. *DBPO*, Series I, vol. 2, pp. 699–707.
74. *DBPO*, Series I, vol. 6, pp. 245–6.
75. Gregg F. Herken, "Stubborn, Obstinate, and They Don't Scare. The Russians, the Bomb, and James F. Byrnes," in A. Kendrick Clements (ed.), *James F. Byrnes and the Origins of the Cold War*, Durham, Carolina Academic Press, pp. 49–57.
76. Harriman and Abel, *Special Envoy*, pp. 518. "The crucial effect of the atomic bomb in creating a new siege mentality among the Soviet leaders." (Ibid., p. 520.)

on the atomic weapon had begun shortly after.[77]

Marshal Zhukov stated that, on hearing the news from Truman in Potsdam, Stalin had said: "We shall have to have a discussion with Kurchatov about speeding up our work." On returning to Moscow, he supposedly told Kurchatov: "[T]he balance has been destroyed. Provide the bomb – it will remove a great danger from us."[78] In his memoirs, Khrushchev writes that Stalin was terrorized by the bomb testing. Stalin's daughter has said that the day after Hiroshima, her father seemed to be very absorbed by the news.[79] He apparently ordered Lavrentii Beria to put the whole of Soviet technology to work to develop an atomic bomb.[80]

In the autumn, Western diplomatic circles pondered the weapon's role in Soviet policy's changing direction. In September, in one of the last memoranda he sent to the president, War Secretary H. Stimson, wrote: "[One should consider] the problem of our satisfactory relations with Russia as not merely connected with but as virtually dominated by the atomic bomb." Moreover: "Unless the Soviets are voluntarily invited into the partnership upon a basis of cooperation and trust, we are going to maintain the Anglo–Saxon bloc over against the Soviet in the possession of this weapon." He anticipated a terrible arms race, and warned United States leadership against the temptation of using the new weapon in diplomatic negotiations. It was his recommendation that they, together with the British, approach the Russians to reach a mutual agreement on controlling and limiting the atomic bomb's use as an instrument of war, and, insofar as it was possible, on directing and encouraging developments in atomic power to pacific, humanitarian ends.[81] On 21 September, the proposal was discussed at the White House.

Harriman, too, thought that the Kremlin's worry over nuclear arms partly explained the Soviet attitude. The Bolshevik leaders, he explained in a telegram on 27 November, had lived all their lives in a constant state of fear, tension, and suspicion, in a climate of violence and intrigue, never enjoying security. Initially during the tsarist period, then after their takeover, the threat of "capitalist encirclement" and German invasion had left a lasting mark on their worldview. In spite of everything, including weak popular support, they had successfully overcome the shock of invasion and defeat, and organized a victory. Near the end of the war, they thought that at last they would have some security; they appeared

77. Robin Edmonds, *Setting the Mould. The United States and Britain, 1945–1950,* Oxford, Clarendon Press, 1986, p. 69. See also David Holloway, *The Soviet Union and the Arms Race,* New Haven, Yale University Press, 1983.

78. Quoted by Edmonds, *Setting the Mould,* p. 70.

79. Hugh Thomas, *Armed Truce. The Beginnings of the Cold War, 1945–1946,* London, Hamish Hamilton, 1986, pp. 466–7.

80. Ibid., p. 466.

81. *FRUS 1945,* vol. 2, p. 42.

determined to maintain the Red Army's strength as well as the industry that had made the revolution complete. The atomic bomb seemed to have revived their congenital insecurity. This state of affairs explained the failure of the London conference, the resurgence of antiimperialist themes, and propaganda against the bomb.[82] On 3 December 1945, the British ambassador in Moscow, Sir A. Clark Kerr, wrote to Bevin on this very topic, his analysis of which was almost identical.

Over the autumn, the problem of atomic energy control was the subject of intense discussion between London and Washington. On 3 October 1945, in a special message to Congress, Truman recommended the creation of the United States Commission on Atomic Energy. He also announced that he intended to open preliminary discussions with Great Britain and Canada, the countries that had been involved with the United States in discovering atomic power, but that he wished to continue these discussions with other nations later. In an unscheduled press conference five days later, however, he stated that "only the United States had the combination of capacity and resources necessary to produce the atomic bomb; if other countries were to catch up with the United States, they would 'have to do it on their own hoots, just as we did.'"[83] Shortly after, the Senate set up its Special Committee on Atomic Energy. Brian McMahon became its chairman.

In a letter to Truman dated 11 October, Attlee proposed they have a discussion with the Russians. Bevin agreed: he considered giving information on atomic energy developments to the Russians a necessary risk. Churchill, whom the prime minister had consulted, made a great show of skepticism and warned him he was risking an exchange of US–British collaboration for a generous, but meaningless agreement that was bound to be breached.[84] Attlee arrived in Washington in early November hoping to define a common nuclear energy policy with the United States and the Canada. After five days of deliberations, to which the Americans submitted without conviction, the president announced the plan to set up the United Nations Commission on Atomic Energy.

The Search for Compromise

The US secretary of state was persuaded that the atomic bomb played an important role in the Soviet attitude. He therefore tried to alleviate Russian distrust by "playing his cards on the table." The report of Harriman and

82. *FRUS 1945*, vol. 5, pp. 922–3.
83. Quoted by Edmonds, *Setting the Mould*, p. 79.
84. Ibid., p. 80.

Stalin's discussion also led him to believe that the Kremlin leader saw the United States' Asia policy as a new threat of capitalist encirclement. He tried to reassure him by suggesting that there should be a control mechanism for Japan that would reconcile the United States' wish to maintain a predominant role in the defeated country's occupation with the Kremlin's sensitivity in the matter.[85]

On 23 November, without consulting the Foreign Office, he suggested to Molotov that they call a meeting of the Big Three foreign ministers. The move was indelicate: toward Bevin, because Byrnes had given him no prior notice of the initiative, which could have serious consequences, and toward France, because the conference would exclude it once again from deliberations among the big powers. Bevin was very irritated by the impromptu maneuver. He saw no sign of a change in the Soviet position, and feared that discussions of procedure would recommence at a standstill and go on for several days. The United States had given no indication that it intended to change its position on the Balkans or the occupation of Japan. The Kremlin did not seem prepared to redirect its policy on these contentious issues. Bevin predicted that the Soviet side, wagering on the British and Americans' desire to finish before Christmas, would attempt to drag out the negotiations in order to get last-minute concessions. Nevertheless, because he did not want to risk being left out of US–Soviet negotiations on the future of Europe and the world, he finally gave in to his advisers and agreed to attend the meeting.

The conference opened in Moscow on 16 December. It rose after Christmas, as Bevin had predicted. Although the prevailing atmosphere was in general better than that at London, Molotov did not change his negotiation tactics. Byrnes quickly grew fed up, complaining that they were making no real progress in the deliberations.[86] Once again the conference was obstructed by negotiation procedure for the peace treaties. In his discussions with Stalin, Harriman had made it clear that the Department of State was ready to make concessions on the matter; moreover, by proposing a three-way conference, Byrnes had implicitly rallied to Molotov's side, since France and China had been excluded from the deliberations. Despite these gestures of goodwill, it was hard to reach a final agreement. The Soviet minister created all sorts of difficulties for his fellow negotiators, going into lengthy discussions of the countries they might invite to give their point of view before the peace treaties were finally ratified. He also asked for the Baltic States to be included in the consultative process, which was a way of gaining recognition of their

85. John Balfour to Ernest Bevin, report of a discussion between James Byrnes and American journalists on 4 February 1946 (FO 800/513).
86. FO 800/501, p. 116.

annexation by the USSR. Again, he seemed to be using questions of procedure, which took up much of the conference, to drag out the negotiations and thereby obtain concessions in other matters, notably in the recognition of the Romanian and Bulgarian regimes. Nevertheless, the foreign ministers finally reached a compromise: the representatives of the powers that had signed the surrender would write the draft peace treaties, which they would then submit to a conference of all countries that had contributed to the war effort in Europe, before reviewing them for the final draft. China was practically excluded from these negotiations. France's status was unsure, because in principle it could take part only in discussions of the peace treaty with Italy.[87]

Negotiation of other contentious issues was also under way. Byrnes had proposed scheduling Manchuria's transfer to the Chinese government – in other words, the Soviet forces' evacuation from China – on the conference agenda. He also brought up the problem of Allied troops in Persia, hoping to obtain the Soviet Union's firm commitment to withdraw. He repeated that he hoped to strike an agreement on the Romanian and Bulgarian regimes that would allow Washington and London to recognize them. Molotov counterattacked by requesting a discussion of the United States troops' withdrawal from northern China and an examination of the situation in Indonesia, where British forces were grappling with nationalist rebellion. He also demanded that the Greek affair be placed on the agenda.

The United States did not think it timely to harmonize its position on these issues with the British. The secretary of state felt he could negotiate with the Soviet side without consulting Bevin, and his attitude created uneasiness, even within the United States delegation.[88] Bevin hoped to take advantage of the meeting to clarify Soviet policy on the Mediterranean and the Middle East. Since the conference in London, the USSR had intensified its pressure on Turkey. The British minister was convinced that the object of the "war of nerves" the USSR was waging with Turkey was to incorporate it into its sphere of influence. He thought that the Soviet team was attempting to undermine the British position in the Middle East. He gave as evidence their aggressive positions on Greece, Turkey, and Persia, three regions where the USSR "rubbed with the British Empire."[89] Byrnes, however, did not share British concerns

87. *DBPO*, Series I, vol. 2, pp. 905–6; see also Catroux, *J'ai vu tomber,* pp. 131–2.
88. See the report of a discussion between P. Dixon with Bohlen and Harriman of 21 December 1945 (FO 800/501, pp. 111–12).
89. Concern expressed by Bevin during a conversation at the American ambassador's residence in Moscow of 17 December 1945 (*DBPO,* Series I, vol. 2, document number 294, pp. 733 et seq.).

Conference
Moscow

over the Soviet ambitions in the Middle East.[90]

Ernest Bevin may have been tempted to seek an agreement with the Soviet Union over the spheres of influence. In a private meeting he asked Molotov why he had brought up the Greek affair. Molotov replied that the Greek prisons were full of persons who had fought against the Germans, while former collaborators sat in the government. He was surprised that the British supported such a regime and still maintained forces in an Allied country more than one year after its liberation.

In truth, the Soviet side brought up the Greek problem time and again to counter British and US attacks on Soviet policy in Romania and Bulgaria. Molotov probably could have accepted a bargain whereby both the British and the Soviet spheres of influence would be recognized. He may have been suggesting this when he mentioned British policy in Indonesia and recalled his government's "extreme discretion" about political problems in India.[91] Bevin was perhaps prepared to find a modus vivendi with the Soviet side, but such agreements were difficult, because Molotov was an inflexible negotiator. The Bulgarian armed forces must demobilize, Bevin explained. As a rule, all foreign troops must pull out of the Balkans. Occupation forces should be curtailed in Austria, Hungary, and Poland, and the Persian and Turkish problems must be solved.[92] In one of the interviews he granted Bevin, Stalin complained about British opposition to giving the trusteeship over Tripolitania to the USSR: "The United Kingdom had India and her possessions in the Indian Ocean in her sphere of interest: The United States had China and Japan, but the USSR had nothing." Bevin replied that the Russian sphere stretched from Lübeck to Port-Arthur.[93]

The United States Secretary of State tried once again to convince his fellow negotiators that his country was acting in good faith in the Balkans affair. The issue was the subject of lengthy discussion, both in the plenary sessions and in private interviews among Byrnes, Molotov, and Stalin. Near the end of the conference, the three foreign ministers reached a compromise solution similar to the proposed resolution of the Polish regime at Yalta. A committee composed of Vyshinskii and Ambassadors Clark Kerr and Harriman would meet King Michael in Bucharest to discuss the Romanian government's enlargement. The government, which had eighteen ministers, would have to include a representative from both the National Peasant party and the Liberal party, who would promise "loyally" to support the government in power. Molotov insisted, however,

90. FO 800/501, p. 115.
91. *DBPO*, Series I, vol. 2, p. 754.
92. Ibid., pp. 748–55.
93. *DBPO*, Series I, vol. 2, p. 868.

that these parties' leaders must be kept out of the government. The Moscow agreement called for "free, democratic" elections as soon as possible, however, and it required the reorganized government to guarantee freedom of the press, religion, and association. The United States and Great Britain had, moreover, promised to recognize this government. In addition, under the Moscow agreement, the USSR could give "friendly advice" to the Bulgarian government on which opposition party representatives would be "acceptable," and these representatives would in turn accept to work "loyally" with the established regime.[94] The compromise on the Balkans allowed the United States to save face; however, it changed nothing in the course of events. By authorizing the Romanian government's enlargement while excluding opposition party leaders and undertaking, in rather vague terms, to advise the Bulgarian parliament to make room for opposition members in the government, Stalin's concessions were minimal. Bohlen and Harriman, who were observing their secretary of state in negotiations, had seen this coming.[95]

Before coming to Moscow, Byrnes had convinced himself that the Soviet Union must be included in atomic energy control. Yet when he proposed a discussion of the issue, Molotov buried the item at the bottom of the agenda. Clearly, the Soviet side was not interested in seeking a common solution to the problems of atomic energy. When Byrnes proposed the creation of the United Nations Atomic Energy Commission, Molotov insisted the matter be submitted to the Security Council, a body which the Soviet Union could control with its veto.

In Moscow, the Soviet Union accepted Washington's program for Japan formally, confirming Harriman and Stalin's agreement. The final communiqué announced the constitution of the Far Eastern Commission in Washington, which comprised representatives from eleven nations, and whose function it was to define the Japanese occupation policy. It also announced that a consultative council of the four powers would be set up in Tokyo to advise the supreme Allied commander, General MacArthur. It was already clear, however, that these bodies would have a limited scope, and that the United States would be able to redirect Japan's political future at will.[96]

On the other hand, the Soviet Union's China policy remained unclear. At the beginning of the conference, Byrnes had hoped to clarify the problem of foreign troops in China and obtain the USSR's early withdrawal from Manchuria. Molotov and Stalin were clearly suspicious of United States intentions in China. Byrnes made it clear that the US

94. *DBPO*, Series I, vol. 2, pp. 911–12.
95. Harriman and Abel, *Special Envoy*, p. 525.
96. *DBPO*, Series I, vol. 2, pp. 908–9.

forces had been ordered to protect Chiang Kai-shek's nationalist government against the Communist armed forces and that Japanese withdrawal came second to fulfilling this objective. His explanations did not satisfy the Soviet side, which requested the simultaneous withdrawal of Allied forces from China. Byrnes, however, refused to commit his government to a date for the United States forces' withdrawal. The conference's final communiqué made the divergence between their policies clear. The decisions on Korea were equally ambiguous. Byrnes proposed that Korea should no longer be divided, and that the United States, USSR, United Kingdom, and China should hold a joint trusteeship over it for six years. Molotov requested that a joint committee of occupation army commanders be appointed. It would be their duty to facilitate the creation of an interim Korean government and to resolve the most urgent problems concerning the country's economic and social future. The Moscow agreement therefore provided for the establishment of a US–USSR military committee, which would make recommendations on the instatement of a democratic government. It also provided for a five-year trusteeship over Korea. It affirmed the intentions of the United States and the USSR to aid the Korean people's economic and social development, support the formation of a democratic government, and set Korea on the path to national independence. Given current affairs in Europe, however, it was feared that the two powers would not be able to agree on how this trusteeship would be run.[97]

The Moscow conference did not resolve the problem of foreign troops in Persia. This affair was a long-standing British preoccupation. The US secretary of state was also worried about it, because the Soviet Union showed no intention of honoring its promise to pull its troops out of Persia six months after the end of the war. They appeared to be supporting the secessionist movements in Azerbaijan, and were hindering the Persian army's attempts to scout out the insurrection. Bevin and Byrnes had appealed several times to Molotov and Stalin, but got no reassurance. Stalin had repeated incessantly that he had to protect Baku's oil fields from potential Persian saboteurs: he complained that the Persian government was hostile, and refused to clarify his position. To Byrnes, who was concerned that the affair might have to be taken before the United Nations, Stalin replied that the General Assembly did not frighten him.[98]

97. *DBPO*, Series I, vol. 2, pp. 909–10; see also Soon Sung Cho, *Korea in World Politics, 1945–1950. An Evaluation of American Responsibility,* Berkeley, University of California Press, 1967, pp. 101–2.
98. *FRUS 1945,* vol. 2, p. 750.

5

THE BEGINNING OF THE COLD WAR

Public Confrontation

Once again, the Council of Foreign Ministers meeting was hard work, and its results uncertain. On 3 January 1946, Ernest Bevin wrote to Canadian Prime Minister Mackenzie King: "The situation is very complicated and many features of it, I confess, leave me full of anxiety."[1] Stalin still had the same misgivings about his former Western allies. In early January, he told the British ambassador in rather blunt terms that he did not think back fondly on his meeting with Bevin. He said he was especially offended by way the British minister had presented the Turkish issue.[2] Byrnes, however, who had left Moscow satisfied, believed he had convinced his Soviet partners that their fear of capitalist encirclement was unfounded. He believed that the United States could relax its surveillance of Russia's policy in the Balkans.[3] Optimism was not unanimous in Washington, however, and President Harry Truman felt that the Council of Foreign Ministers had not made enough headway on pending problems. On 5 January, he put this plainly to his secretary of state, reproaching him for not having secured unconditional support of the atomic energy control project from the Soviet Union. He was also concerned because the Soviet Union had not confirmed its intention to withdraw from Persia. Above all, he would not accept the compromise on Romania and Bulgaria, so laboriously hammered out in Moscow. He had just read the Etheridge report, which heightened his irritation over Soviet policy in the Balkans. He said that he had resolved not to recognize these countries' governments until they had been changed completely.[4]

Byrnes was far from winning unanimous approval from Truman's close staff, or from the State Department. Truman's chief of staff, Admiral Leahy, and Navy Secretary James Forrestal had doubts about the direction of his diplomacy, especially given their alarm over Soviet expansionism, as did Ambassador Harriman, who was finishing his term in Moscow.

1. FO 800/443.
2. FO 800/501, pp. 127–9; 29 January 1946.
3. John Balfour to Ernest Bevin, report of a confidential discussion of 4 February 1946 between Secretary of State James Byrnes and several journalists (FO 800/513).
4. John L. Gaddis, *The United States and the Origins of the Cold War, 1941–1947*, New York, Columbia University Press, 1972, pp. 288–9.

The continual pursuit of compromise with the USSR, as part of the secretary of state's policy, was also encountering growing opposition from the Republican party. There was talk of "appeasement." The influential Republican Senator Arthur Vandenberg, a former isolationist and a conservative whose support President Truman relied on to guarantee bipartisanism in his foreign policy, was openly reluctant to accept Byrnes's position. On 24 January, in the company of John Foster Dulles, he spoke with Bevin about the results of the Moscow conference. The British minister clearly feared the USSR. He spoke of the "two arms of the bear" circling Turkey, entering Persia, threatening Mosul. The question of Persia seemed crucial to him: "The Russian technique, which was precisely the same as that followed with such success by Hitler, consisted in taking one position at a time." He urged the Americans to take this matter seriously. Appeasement must be avoided at all costs: he held that only by resisting Soviet pressure in Persia would Turkey be saved. Bevin's words fell on attentive, benevolent ears.[5]

The United States leaders' increasing distrust of Kremlin foreign policy was not unrelated to national developments. The USSR's image was deteriorating in public opinion, and this was reflected in major American newspapers and periodicals.[6] The slow pace of the peace treaty negotiations was a growing source of irritation, especially as deliberations now concerned Italy, which had regained solid support in various political circles, notably in large east coast cities where Catholics and minorities of Italian descent were influential.[7] Public opinion was shocked by the 18 February discovery of a vast Soviet spy ring in Canada that had been investigating atomic research in the United States. In Congress, mention was made of the threat of Communist plants infiltrating the administration.[8]

Furthermore, old ideological quarrels over the economic and social policies pursued by the Democrats were rearing up once again. Truman claimed he was continuing the New Deal tradition President Roosevelt had started in the 1930s. In his 1946 State of the Union address, he upheld a program that provided for a raise in the minimum wage, new housing, hospital building, comprehensive health insurance, modernization of the

5. *DBPO*, Series I, vol. 4, document number 18, pp. 67–70.
6. Fraser Harbutt, *The Iron Curtain, Churchill, America, and the Origins of the Cold War*, New York, Oxford University Press, 1986, pp. 155–6; Gaddis, *The United States*, pp. 282 et seq.
7. James Edward Miller, *The United States and Italy, 1940–1950. The Politics and Diplomacy of Stabilization*, London, University of North Carolina Press, 1986, p. 196.
8. Robert J. Donovan, *Conflict and Crisis. The Presidency of Harry S. Truman, 1945–1948*, New York, Norton, 1982, pp. 170–1.

welfare system, farm subsides, and aid to small business.[9] The Republicans had always hated these projects. Early in the year, the influential Senator Robert Taft characterized certain aspects of Truman's program as "communist."[10] The elections for the partial renewal of Congress were close at hand. At the same time, a wave of strikes was sweeping the United States, crippling all of its large industrial production centers. The abrupt decline of the social situation and worry in conservative circles over these developments – in which some saw the actions of the American Communist party – as well as a new rise in inflation, created a climate that cultivated the United States' changing opinion of the USSR.

The first meeting of the United Nations first General Assembly opened officially on 10 January 1946 in London without Molotov, the USSR foreign minister. Vyshinskii, his proxy, was also absent. This was a sign of how little the Kremlin cared about the new organization, on which the United States and Britain had based so many hopes for guaranteed collective security and international order. The Security Council began its work one week later and on 19 January the head of the Persian delegation, Sayid Hassan Taquizadeh, submitted the problem of continued Soviet military presence in Persia to the UN secretary-general, requesting an investigation of Russian interference in his country's domestic affairs. The request was valid, for despite repeated British and US efforts, the Red Army did not appear to be of a mind to leave the Persian territory. The Soviet Union used its military presence in the country to support secessionist tendencies among the Kurds and the Azeris, encouraging them to set up a Communist-type regime in Azerbaijan. It also continued to pressure the Persian government for oil concessions in the north of the country, the objective being to secure advantages comparable to those the British enjoyed in the south.[11]

When the Persian delegate submitted the affair to the Security Council, Bevin supported him. The Soviet reaction was immediate. On 21 January, Vyshinskii asked the Council to examine the situation in Greece. The Soviet delegate attacked British imperialism with unusual violence, stigmatizing the fascist forces which the British were protecting in the country. Bevin's response was no less scathing. He denounced the Soviet leaders' tactics, which consisted in raising the problem of Greece to counter legitimate criticism of the USSR's foreign policy:

9. Ibid., p. 168.
10. Ibid., p. 164.
11. Bruce R. Kuniholm, *The Origins of the Cold War in the Near East. Great Power Conflict and Diplomacy in Iran, Turkey, and Greece,* Princeton, Princeton University Press, 1980, pp. 304 et seq.

The danger to the peace of the world has been the incessant propaganda from Moscow against the British Commonwealth, and the incessant utilization of the Communist parties in every country of the world as a means to attack the British people and the British Government, as if no friendship existed between us. That is the danger to the peace of the world which sets us one against another. It is this suspicion which causes misunderstanding and makes one wonder what is the motive behind it.[12]

The polemics continued. One week later, Ukraine joined in to attack British intervention against the Indonesian people; and finally, the Soviet Union backed the Lebanese and Syrian representatives, who were protesting French and British occupation of their countries.

Hence, in its first session the Security Council was confronted with a serious crisis in which its permanent members were embroiled. Unable to resolve their conflicts within their own conclave, the big powers called upon public opinion to arbitrate in a polemical climate that hardly favored harmonious compromise. Before the "world tribunal" of the United Nations, violent diatribes among the former Allies brought back the bitter hatred of the interwar period.[13] The United Nations Organization also gave representatives of Asian countries a forum from which to denounce imperialist structures, and allowed them to draw on rivalries among the victors to affirm their desire for freedom.

As the former Allies' ideological and political confrontation was coming to the fore in the United Nations, Stalin curtly restated the Leninist view of international relations in his 9 February speech at an election rally in the district of Moscow, recalling that crisis and conflict were inevitable in an era of "monopolistic capitalism." In Stalin's view, the two world wars had been the outcome of crisis in the capitalist system. His speech, an apologia for the Soviet regime and a glorification of its role in the victory over the Third Reich, marked a desire to break with the propaganda themes of the "Great Patriotic War." It also tended to justify Stalin's demands on the Soviet people to renew their efforts to meet the latest five-year plan's objectives. In *Pravda*, Georgii Malenkov, a member of the Central Committee of the CPSU who at the time was considered a possible successor to Stalin, emphasized foreign threats and the need to reinforce the USSR's military strength, notably by developing heavy industry. Lavrentii Beria, chief of the secret police, said that the foremost issue in current affairs was the threat of a new imperialist war and more specifically, a war against the USSR. Molotov also stressed dangers from

12. *Official Minutes of the General Assembly,* first year, first series, 1946, p. 1988.
13. *Official Minutes of the Security Council,* first year, 1946, pp. 75–7.

abroad and the urgent need to reinforce the Soviet army.[14]

Stalin's speech received extensive press coverage in the United States. It shocked and worried United States leadership. If the Second World War was the result of contradictions in the capitalist system, and imperialism was a permanent threat to world peace, it was also becoming clear that the USSR could not coexist with the capitalist system for long, and that pursuing hopes of true international cooperation was futile. This political conception argued against the "grand alliance" and undermined the political and ideological foundations of collective security.[15]

The USSR Gains Strength in Eastern Europe

Soviet influence in the East European countries was growing stronger. A few days after the Moscow meetings, Harriman, who was accompanied by Vyshinskii, and Clark Kerr, went to Bucharest. The Western diplomats realized then that the die had been cast. Romanian Prime Minister Groza and Vyshinskii were amiable, adroit, and cunning. At the end of their negotiations to enlarge the Romanian government, the two opposition leaders, one from the National Liberal party, the other from the National Peasant party, had received ministries without portfolio.[16] Groza had promised to uphold democratic rights and organize free elections, but there was no indication at the time that he planned to respect these commitments. The king was skeptical and had requested monitors for the coming elections, but Harriman and Clark Kerr, knowing that the United States and Great Britain could hardly change the Sovietization process, advised moderation. Moreover, the Department of State recognized the enlarged government on 4 February 1946.[17]

In Bulgaria, however, the democratic parties refused to join the Communist-controlled government. Vyshinskii arrived in Sofia on 9 January hoping to win over the Agrarian and Social Democratic opposition leaders, Petkov and Lulchev. They resisted him courageously: in return for taking part in the Bulgarian government, they demanded that the Communist party be removed from the Department of the Interior, that the next parliament be dissolved, and that free elections be held. United States representative to Bulgaria Maynard Barnes, who had lent unflagging moral support to the leaders of these parties, urged the

14. Werner G. Hahn, *Postwar Soviet Politics. The Fall of Zhdanov and the Defeat of Moderation, 1946–1953,* Ithaca, Cornell University Press, 1982, pp. 21–2.
15. Gaddis, *The United States,* pp. 299–300.
16. Averell W. Harriman and Elie Abel, *Special Envoy to Churchill and Stalin, 1941–1946,* New York, Random House, 1975, pp. 527–8.
17. Vlad Georgescu, *The Romanians,* London, Tauris Publishers, 1991, p. 230.

Department of State to stand firm. "Any further concessions by us, he wrote on 30 January, would in my opinion constitute complete capitulation."[18] In his reports to Washington, he alluded to Munich. In his view, which he said was shared by all attentive observers of the Balkan peninsula, Russia was attempting to create a southern Slavic union, which it would control and use to "emasculate Turkey and Greece." This would afford Russia a passage to the seas and enable it to cut off Great Britain's access to its Empire, thus shifting the world balance of power. Bulgaria was not only an important strategic region, but a test of the United States' will to resist constant Soviet "nibbling." The United States had made solemn commitments during the war in the Atlantic Charter and the Declaration on Liberated Europe. It must honor its promises.[19] From Moscow, United States chargé d'affaires George Kennan corroborated Barnes's strategic analysis. He felt that Bulgaria had an essential place in Soviet plans. The USSR was prolonging its tsarist tradition and attempting to extend its sphere of influence to the straits and the Mediterranean by controlling Bulgaria with a totalitarian party.[20]

On 4 February, shortly before leaving his post because of illness, General Crane, the United States representative to the Armistice Committee in Bulgaria, sent his final report to the Joint Chiefs of Staff. It was a disastrous account of Soviet conduct that confirmed the analyses Barnes had been sending the Department of State for many months. "Ever since our arrival here we have been in most humiliating position." By submitting to this treatment, the United States mission, and through it the United States, had become a laughingstock for the Russians and Bulgarians. He said furthermore that he was very skeptical about the possibility of cooperating with the Russians, who respected strength alone. He ended his report by stating: "I am afraid we are following policy of appeasement of late Mr. Chamberlain."[21] The report gained influence in Washington, and George Kennan in Moscow sent a sharp note of protest to the Soviet government on 15 February. The United States refused to recognize the Bulgarian government.

The situation in Hungary was also deteriorating, for, regardless of the Soviet presence, social unrest brought on by inflation, agrarian reform, the Budapest municipal elections in October 1945, and the national elections the following month, had led to a strong right-wing majority. The Smallholders' party received 57% of the vote and the Communist party 17%, whereas the Social Democratic party, some of whose members

18. *FRUS 1946*, vol. 6, p. 63.
19. Ibid., p. 54.
20. Ibid., pp. 55–7.
21. Ibid., pp. 68–71.

were very close to the Communists, got 17.4%. Communist influence over the newly elected government remained very strong, however, especially since it had total control of the Department of the Interior.[22] The party also enjoyed material support from its Soviet occupiers, who supplied transport, printing presses, paper, and subsistence goods for distribution. Its tactics toward the coalition's other political groups were equivocal. It tended to discredit the Smallholders' party, a heterogeneous group that had some right-wing members, including a few nostalgic for the ancient regime; but it also pressured the Social Democrats, whose ministers generally espoused Communist positions. In early 1946, pressure against "reactionaries" gained new strength. Prime Minister Imre Nagy, acting on instructions from Moscow, advised the press to portray Soviet–Hungarian relations in a favorable light and to play down the role of the Western powers. The Communists nonetheless redoubled their attacks. Mátyás Rákosi, the secretary-general of the Communist party, threatened to leave the coalition if extreme right-wing elements were not purged from the Smallholders' party. The Social Democrats backed his claim. The Communists had launched this campaign in order to pass a bill For the defense of the Republic, which conferred considerable powers on the police, whom they controlled. Finally, the prime minister gave in. His concession only emboldened Communist-controlled political movements. In early March 1946, the Communists sparked social unrest once again: they demanded a purge of the Smallholders' party, the expulsion of reactionaries from government office, further agrarian reform, and nationalization. Again, the prime minister was forced to concede, for over this affair and others, his party was divided; moreover, it was already partly infiltrated by Communists.

Meanwhile, the peace treaty negotiations over these very countries, which were becoming Soviet satellites, continued to flounder. The acting foreign ministers had reconvened on 18 January 1946. Once again, the USSR delegate's policy seemed to be one of prevarication. On 27 February, Dunn, the United States representative, wrote to the director of the Office of European Affairs in the State Department: "We have spent literally days of consecutive sessions of talk about the same subject [procedure] in the same form, restating our same positions without making any advance whatever toward arriving at a real development of the subject at hand."[23] He was convinced that the USSR was seeking to keep its occupation troops in the Balkans to consolidate the puppet governments

22. See further Jörg K. Hoensch, *A History of Modern Hungary, 1867–1986,* London, Longman, 1988, pp. 161 et seq.
23. *FRUS 1946,* vol. 2, "The Assistant secretary of state (Dunn) to the Director, Office of European Affairs (Matthews)," p. 18.

in these countries, and that it was attempting to block Italy's economic
and political reconstruction by deferring ratification of the Italian peace
treaty. Consequently, he wondered if a return to stability in Europe, and
particularly in Italy, could be postponed indefinitely, and if the United
States should not rather adopt a separate peace policy.[24]

Domestic developments in Poland were no less distressing. The
Communists knew they would have no chance of governing Poland if
they accepted a verdict by free elections. Since late 1945, it had been
growing clear that the Polish government did not have the slightest
intention of respecting its commitments in this matter. The opposition
had been muzzled. The "security police" sowed terror, arresting or
assassinating activists of Deputy Prime Minister Mikolajczyk's Peasant
party and Socialist party militants. Bevin denounced these political
assassinations and the collusion among security bodies on 23 January
before the House of Commons.[25] Pressed to do so by Senator Vandenberg
of Michigan, a state where many residents were of Polish descent, Byrnes
made a similar statement. The Communists, however, offered
Mikolajczyk's party 20% of the seats in the next parliament, demanding
70% for themselves and the political forces under their control.
Mikolajczyk refused, requesting 75% of the seats for his own party and
the Socialists. On 22 February, the main political groups abandoned their
negotiations to form an "electoral bloc."[26] This coincided with the new
Soviet hard-line toward London and Washington. The Communists
decided to defer the elections and launched a massive campaign of slander
and repression against Mikolajczyk's supporters.

In spite of Bevin's speech in the Commons, the British government
remained only moderately supportive of Mikolajczyk. In February 1946,
Mikolajczyk dispatched his deputy W. Zaremba to London to sound out
the Foreign Office. G. Warner affirmed the British government's position
in favor of free elections, but refused to make further commitments. Bevin
was wary, and wondered if Great Britain had not demanded too much of
Mikolajczyk by forcing him to take an intransigent position.[27] The arrests
and assassinations continued. In late March, Mikolajczyk sent an anxious
report to United States Ambassador Arthur Lane. He denounced the
summary decisions of the "people's tribunals" and their ruthless treatment
of influential persons throughout Poland who were affiliated with the
Peasant party or the former resistance. He stressed the growing number

24. Ibid., p. 19.
25. *FRUS 1946*, vol. 6, p. 390.
26. John Coutouvidis and Jaime Reynolds, *Poland, 1939–1947*, Leicester, Leicester University Press, 1986, p. 229.
27. FO 371/56434, N/2154 and N/2624, quoted by Coutouvidis and Reynolds, *Poland, 1939–1947*, p. 350 n. 31.

of police, and the efforts to disgrace him publicly.[28] Repression also
targeted United States citizens who had kept their Polish nationality,[29]
and security forces harassed Poles working in the United States, French,
and British embassies.[30]

The Department of State was at a loss over what it should do in the
Polish affair, which threatened to become another obstacle in peace treaty
negotiations. Furthermore, its means of action were limited. Of course,
Poland needed economic aid. It received considerable assistance from
the United Nations Relief and Rehabilitation Administration (UNRRA)
and was requesting appropriations for economic recovery. Washington
laid down conditions and attempted to win concessions on the political
front, but got no satisfaction. Despite vigorous protest from its ambassador
in Warsaw, the United States government decided to grant Poland $50
million in credit.[31] This decision came shortly before a referendum on
the agrarian reform and the constitutional removal of the Senate: a
violently organized vote that was clearly arranged to exact endorsement
of Communist-inspired government action.

Kennan's Long Telegram

The situation developing in Asia in the first months of 1946 was also
disturbing. General Marshall's mediation mission in China had been a
partial success, and in late January negotiations between the Nationalists
and the Communists had ended in an agreement to organize a government
and a program for national rehabilitation. Nonetheless, the agreement was
fragile, and the Soviet-supported Communists continued to infiltrate
Manchuria. Molotov had made it clearly understood at the conference in
Moscow that the Red Army soldiers would withdraw at the same time as
the American troops. The United States, however, was still repatriating
Japanese troops and consolidating the Nationalist government's
stronghold in the north, although its numbers were decreasing steadily.
It did not wish to become involved militarily in the Chinese civil war.
The Soviet Union demanded that the Chinese government draw up an
agreement granting them economic privileges in Manchuria, after having
plundered part of the region's industrial resources as war booty. The
United States government protested on 7 February, for this demand went

28. *FRUS 1946*, vol. 6, pp. 417–18.
29. Ibid., pp. 441–3.
30. Ibid., p. 431.
31. See also Geir Lundestadt, *The American Non–Policy toward Eastern Europe,
1943–1947. Universalism in an Area not of Essential Interest to the United States,* Oslo,
Universitesforlaget, 1978, p. 214.

against the "open door" policy it had always upheld. Moreover, the Soviet Union seemed to be attempting to defer withdrawal of its troops.[32]

In Korea, the situation of the USSR and the United States sectors, north and south of the 38th. parallel, respectively, had created a completely artificial division of the country, as in Germany. The partition hindered economic revival. Industry and sources of energy and raw materials were essentially in the north, whereas the south had to absorb a considerable number of refugees from Japan, China, and the Soviet sector. The Russo–American joint committee set up at the Moscow conference was supposed to hear the political parties and the country's principal organizations with a view to establishing a provisional Korean government; but the idea of a trusteeship was resisted vigorously by the great majority of political forces in Korea, with the exception of the Communist party. Deliberations between the two sectors' commanders, which were required under the Moscow agreement, had got off to a bad start because the USSR opposed the United States in its plans to advance Korea's economic and social integration. The Soviet Union installed a Communist regime north of the 38th. parallel, and there was every indication that it hoped to spread the regime over the entire country.[33] United States leadership did not have a clearly defined policy for Korea, but intended nonetheless to promote its liberal institutions and refused to accept its becoming a USSR satellite.

In late February, George Kennan, the United States chargé d'affaires in Moscow, was asked by the Treasury Department to report on why the USSR had refused to join the World Bank and the International Monetary Fund. Kennan was surprised by the naivity of the request. The Department of State considered him to be one of the foremost USSR experts with Charles Bohlen, adviser and interpreter to former President Roosevelt. He had been posted in Moscow since 1944, but had also been there from 1933 to 1937 as an adviser to Ambassadors Bullitt and Davies in the darkest hours of the Stalinian repression. He detested the Soviet regime in power: he had incessantly denounced the Kremlin's hegemonic ambitions and criticized the United States' policy of collaboration with the USSR. The assignment from Washington was a chance to voice his predictions about Stalin's objectives and to iterate his defense of a new strategy vis-à-vis the Kremlin. Consequently, he wrote a long dispatch in response to the department's candid query.

According to the Kremlin's official propaganda, he explained, the USSR was being encircled by capitalist states whose fundamental

32. François Joyaux, *La nouvelle question d'Extrême–Orient,* Paris, Payot, 1985, pp. 72–3; Tang Tsou, *American Failure in China, 1941–1950,* Chicago, Chicago University Press, 1963, pp. 332 et seq.

33. Soon Sung Cho, *Korea in World Politics, 1945–1950. An Evaluation of American Responsibility,* Berkeley, University of California Press, 1967, pp. 114 et seq.

differences put them at constant risk of war with each other. Consequently, it must reinforce its own strength to weaken that of its class enemies. If another imperialist war was to break out, the USSR would transform the conflict into a revolutionary uprising in all of the capitalist countries. Kennan pointed out the global nature of the Soviet menace. The Kremlin would work hard to increase the USSR's strength and prestige. It would pursue military industrialization and seek to conceal its own weaknesses. In its foreign policy, it would start capitalizing on its strategic advantages by pressuring border regions such as northern Persia and Turkey. If it won the Persian government's "friendship," it would ask for a port in the Persian Gulf; and if Spain fell under Communist control, it would demand a base at Gibraltar. The USSR would undermine the Western nations' power and influence over "backward" or dependent peoples in the colonial regions. Its objective was to create a political vacuum for Soviet-Communist influence to fill. It was with this goal in mind that Stalin was claiming a part in the trusteeship regime. The USSR would also develop ties with states that were in a good position to oppose the Western powers, such as Argentina and the Middle Eastern countries. It would do all it could to pull Germany in to its sphere of influence. In the area of economics, its policy would be one of self-sufficiency.

Kennan strongly emphasized the USSR's subversive methods. The Communist parties, whatever their confessed objectives might be, were working clandestinely to realize the Kremlin's goals. They acted both overtly and covertly through a great variety of cultural, religious, social, and political organizations, whose task it was to undermine Western policy and strategy. They were mobilized to sap national defense, create social unrest, stir up the claims of dissident groups, and drag liberal forces into supporting independence movements in the colonies, all with the intent of weakening the Western powers. The Communists would fight for the destruction of all regimes that protected individual liberties.

Kennan said that the USSR was a "political force committed fanatically to the belief that with the U.S. there can be no permanent *modus vivendi*." In his opinion, the Soviet position was nothing but an ideological perversion. It was maintained by sick, ignorant, dishonest individuals whose view of things could only be erroneous. For the Kremlin's attitude stemmed less from a political program than from a pathology, and its action had no other basis than the "neurotic" vision of its leaders, reflecting their congenital insecurity. It had no support among the Soviet people, who were fundamentally peaceful.

The United States must face this strategic challenge with the same seriousness and severity with which it had resolved the greatest problems of the war. The USSR was impervious to reason, but not to force. It might stop its expansion when it encountered firm resistance. It was therefore necessary to ensure the Western world's cohesion and resoluteness. The first step in this direction was to comprehend the threat the USSR posed and to "study it with same courage, detachment, objectivity, and same determination not to be emotionally provoked or unseated by it, with which doctor studies unruly and unreasonable individual."[34]

In following weeks, Kennan elaborated on this theme to prove that the liberal American circles' current trend of "Lenifying" the USSR was absurd. The Soviet attitude in international affairs was not determined by "suspicions" which one could dispel. The thesis of a hostile environment that the Kremlin was propagating was instrumental. It tended to legitimate the regime and to justify the great weight of its bureaucracy, police, and security forces, which lived off the hard work and idealism of the Russian people. The USSR needed outside enemies. Germany and Japan having been destroyed, Great Britain and the United States had necessarily to replace them in the role of the scapegoat.[35]

Kennan's observations immediately gained a large audience in Washington. Freeman Matthews, the head of the Office of European Affairs in the Department of State, gave the "magnificent" telegram a broad distribution. Byrnes praised the "splendid analysis." Truman took cognizance of it, and Navy Secretary James Forrestal, an impassioned anticommunist, had hundreds of mimeographed copies of the "Long Telegram" made and distributed to higher officers.[36] Shortly afterward, Kennan was called back to the United States, where he was appointed to a teaching position at the prestigious National War College, from where he could communicate his theses broadly to public opinion, which was exactly what the Department of State and President Truman's staff hoped he would do.

Kennan's perspective on the Soviet threat was henceforth acknowledged as fact, and encountered no real further challenge in the Department of State or the Pentagon. What accounted for the United States chargé d'affaires's sudden influence? His analysis was not truly original, at least, its essential elements were not. Ambassador Harriman, as mentioned above, had long been worried about the course Stalin's policy was taking. Kennan's ideas on Soviet totalitarianism were widespread among diplomats posted in the USSR and the capital cities of the countries occupied by the Red Army. They had done the rounds among spheres of United States leadership, but without really taking hold. In early 1946, however, the climate of relations between the United States and the USSR

34. *FRUS 1946*, vol. 6, pp. 696–709.
35. Ibid., pp. 721–3.
36. Walter L. Hixson, *George F. Kennan. Cold War Iconoclast*, New York, Columbia University Press, 1989, p. 31.

had changed, and Kennan's analysis made sense of, and lent coherence to, a string of events that reflected Moscow's growing hostility toward the Western world. His telegram also had the merit of explaining Soviet foreign policy in terms that were in accord with the main concepts of American liberal ideology. It broke with Roosevelt's optimism, yet fell into the same idealistic and moral vein. Kennan used the same explanation that had justified the war against nazism, whilst redirecting United States foreign policy to meet new external threats. Communism was defined as a "malignant tumor" that fed only on unhealthy organisms, an image that bore a striking resemblance to Franklin Roosevelt's speech on the need to "quarantine" the Axis powers. The United States must guide the European nations, which were "tired and frightened by experiences the past." Kennan offered a view of the outside world that corresponded with the founding myths of the American nation.

Warnings from Winston Churchill

On 28 February 1946, Byrnes made an important speech in New York to the International Press Club. He defended the principles of the United Nations and recalled the great powers' international responsibilities. He recalled that they had no right to maintain troops on a sovereign nation's territory without its consent. Nor could they seize enemy possessions in the liberated countries or the former German satellites before the Allies had agreed upon methods of reparations payment. It was their duty not to pointlessly delay the peace settlements for weakened and poverty-stricken countries. They must not get embroiled in a "war of nerves" to attain their strategic objectives.[37]

This speech unambiguously reflected a new firmness in United States diplomacy. To all indications, the secretary of state, in keeping with the president's own ideas, had acquiesced to public opinion and Republican groups – Vandenberg's in particular – which were enjoining the administration to cease its USSR "appeasement" policy.[38] Secretary of the Navy James Forrestal suggested sending a fleet to the Mediterranean to show that the United States intended to support Greece and Turkey. Truman liked the idea. While waiting for it to be put into effect, the United States government decided to send a cruiser to Istanbul on the pretext of repatriating the body of the Turkish ambassador, who had died in Washington during the war.[39]

---

37. *Department of State Bulletin,* 19 March 1946, p. 358.
38. Donovan, *Conflict and Crisis,* New York, Norton, 1982, p. 189.
39. Ibid., pp. 189–90.

The Department of State had not wanted the Persian affair to go before the Security Council, fearing that this would intensify the USSR's distrust of the United Nations and weaken the new institution's authority in a single blow. However, Loy Henderson, director of the State Department Office of Near Eastern and African Affairs, had long been troubled by Soviet initiatives in Persia. He knew the Middle East well, since he had been posted in Iraq during the war, and was extremely distrustful of the USSR's ambitions of hegemony and its revolutionary plans. In early March, it seemed clear to him that the USSR was pressing its expansionist movement on toward Turkey and that, notwithstanding the disputes before the Security Council, the Red Army was not preparing to pull out of Persia. The United States vice-consul in Tabriz sent dispatches reporting large movements of troops, which seemed, on the contrary, to indicate Soviet military reinforcements in the north. On 7 March, Henderson alerted the secretary of state by submitting a map penciled with red arrows to show the Soviet army's movements, which were directed at Turkey, where they planned to control the Dardanelles, but especially at Teheran and the oil fields of the Persian Gulf. This geostrategy was apparently imaginary; nonetheless, it prompted Byrnes to demand an explanation from the Kremlin. The same day, the Department of State sent a strong note of protest to Moscow, stating that the United States could not remain indifferent to the Soviet troops' continued presence in northern Persia, and requesting their immediate withdrawal.

It was in these circumstances that Winston Churchill came to support the proponents of a firmer United States policy toward the USSR. The former prime minister had been on a private visit to the United States since 14 January 1946. He received an enthusiastic welcome nation-wide. On 10 February he met with the president for almost two hours and met also with Admiral Leahy. On 16 February, he received a visit from the secretary of state and Bernard Baruch, an influential financier and friend of former President Roosevelt whom the administration was counting on to pass the loan to Great Britain through Congress. Churchill strongly defended the Labour government's position, which relied on this economic support.

On 5 March, he went with President Truman to Fulton College in Missouri, where he received an honorary degree. This gave him the opportunity to deliver a long speech on world politics. In the great Churchillian tradition, stroking American messianism, he recommended keeping the technology of the atomic bomb a secret. He pointed out the threat that would ensue if a Communist country were to possess the weapon, and stressed its value as a deterrent. He proposed a grand alliance of the English-speaking peoples of the Commonwealth, Great Britain, and the United States. Most of all, he spoke of the threats from Soviet

Russia and the international Communist movement. "From Stettin in the
Baltic to Trieste in the Adriatic, an iron curtain has descended across the
Continent. Behind that line lie all the capitals of the ancient states of
Central and Eastern Europe. Warsaw, Berlin, Prague, Vienna, Budapest,
Belgrade, Bucharest and Sofia, all these famous cities and the populations
around them lie in what I must call the Soviet sphere." He also talked
about the peril of communism in Italy and France; he said that fifth
columnists were acting the world over on orders from the "Communist
centre." The Western powers would not preserve the peace if they allowed
these proselytizing and expansionist tendencies to run their course. "From
what I have seen of our Russian friends and Allies during the war, I am
convinced that there is nothing they admire so much as strength, and there
is nothing for which they have less respect than weakness, especially
military weakness." The United Nations was a great hope for peace, but
the world organization would be ineffective without a "fraternal
association of English-speaking peoples."[40]

The speech caused a tremendous sensation. It popularized the notion
of the "iron curtain," a premonitory image to which Churchill had taken
a liking near the end of the war. The "old lion's" rhetoric was made all
the more impressive by Truman's attendance at the ceremony. Of course,
Churchill took the precaution of stating that these were his personal views.
After Churchill had closed, the president and State Department officials
withheld from commentary, but no one could deny the complicity among
Churchill and his American hosts. The speech had gotten through to
Truman and Byrnes; moreover, it reflected their own concerns about
Soviet policy in Manchuria and Korea.

After his speech, Winston Churchill wrote to Prime Minister Clement
Attlee:

Having spent nearly three days in the most intimate friendly contact with the
President and his immediate circle and also having had a long talk with Mr.
Byrnes I have no doubt that executive forces here are deeply distressed at the
way they are being treated by Russia and that they do not intend to put up
with treaty breaches in Persia or encroachments in Manchuria and Korea or
pressure for Russian expansion at the expense of Turkey or Greece in the
Mediterranean. I am convinced that some show of strength and resisting power
is necessary to a good settlement with Russia. I predict that this will be
prevailing opinion in the United States in the near future.[41]

40. Randolf S. Churchill (ed.), *The Sinews of Peace. Post-War Speeches by Winston Churchill*, London, 1948, pp. 93–105.
41. *DBPO*, Series I, vol. 4, document number 48, pp. 151–2.

The president had in fact informed the former prime minister of his intention to send a large naval fleet to the Dardanelles as a warning to the Soviet Union.

Churchill's speech awoke strong feeling in the United States. Conservatives in the War and Navy Departments were convinced that a test of strength with the USSR was inevitable, and "the sooner, the better," as the British ambassador wrote in a report of US reaction. In his view, Churchill's position on the Soviet threat held considerable sway with United States public opinion, despite its rejection of his proposed alliance with Great Britain. On the other hand, left-wing liberals vigorously challenged the idea of a Communist threat and criticized Churchill's hostility toward the USSR. They denounced the plan for an Anglo–American alliance as a maneuver to preserve British imperialism. This opinion current was wary of any commitment that might undermine the credibility of the United Nations.

Pessimism reached the upper spheres of the State Department. Sir Orme Sargeant wrote to the Foreign Office:

> I lunched today with Doc Matthews and found him plunged in gloom. He says that the State has no suggestion to make for the moment about Iran beyond the ineluctable discussions at the Council. Unless there was some unexpected change in the situation, this might well lead to the withdrawal of the Soviet Union from the US as hitherto conceived. There would then presumably follow a drawing together of nations opposed to indefinite Soviet expansion with the grim possibility of war with the Soviet Union shaping itself. He was depressed at the extent to which the American military machine has been dismantled.[42]

US demobilization had indeed gone ahead rapidly, and the military and the Department of State were beginning to worry about the consequences of this move. In early March, Chief of Staff General Eisenhower created a stir by stating that the army would need more than one year to reach its level of efficiency in 1940, one year before Pearl Harbor. Navy officials were also making alarming statements.[43]

An interview with Stalin in the 14 March issue of *Pravda* set the tone of the Soviet response:

> I would point out that Mr. Churchill and his friends bear a striking resemblance to Hitler and his friends in this matter. Hitler began to spread war by professing

42. FO 371/51719.
43. The Earl of Halifax (Washington) to Mr. Bevin, 10 March 1946 (*DBPO*, Series I, vol. 4, document number 49, pp. 153–5).

a racial theory which held that only German-speaking persons could constitute a real nation. Mr. Churchill is also beginning to spread war with a racial theory which holds that only English-speaking nations are real nations, and that these nations must decide the fate of the rest of the world. [...] In fact, Mr. Churchill and his friends from England and the United States pose a sort of ultimatum to the nations that do not speak English: recognize our hegemony of your own volition, and everything will remain in order. If not, war is inevitable.

Molotov, Zhdanov, and the whole Soviet press picked up these propaganda themes, placing the Soviet people and the peoples of the world on their guard against the "Anglo–Saxon bloc" and the threats it was posing to peace.[44]

In late March, however, Andrei Gromyko announced to the United Nations that the Soviet forces would withdraw in the next six weeks. It is therefore likely that the United States' firm stance did indeed bear its fruits. Stalin, who was probably surprised by US reaction, seemed to acknowledge that he could not overtly risk a contest with the United States and Britain in Persia and the Persian Gulf. Loy Henderson feared that the Soviet Union would nonetheless pursue its objectives in the region by reverting to subversive strategy.[45]

British Concerns

The Fulton speech embarrassed the British government. Nevertheless, Bevin and his staff shared the former prime minster's concern about the USSR and were not closed to his views on strategy. The Foreign Office had long-standing worries about the USSR's territorial and political ambitions, and hardly entertained illusions about the Soviet regime. This was why the bitter peace negotiations, the alliance's rapid disintegration, the Soviet expansion in Eastern Europe, and the Kremlin's ambitions in Persia, Turkey, the Mediterranean and the Middle East did not cause the same shock and scandal they had in Washington in the spring of 1946.

Frank Roberts, the British chargé d'affaires in the USSR, taking advantage of his ambassador's absence, produced some political analyses that were uncannily close to Kennan's. The two men were in constant contact and held each other in high esteem. Roberts had heard about the "Long Telegram." In March, he sent a string of dispatches to London

44. Georges-Albert Catroux, *J'ai vu tomber le rideau de fer. Moscou, 1945–1948,* Paris, Hachette, 1952, pp. 180–2.

45. H.W. Brands, *Inside the Cold War. Loy Henderson and the Rise of the American Empire, 1918–1961,* Oxford, Oxford University Press, 1991, pp. 144–5.

explaining the foundations and goals of Soviet foreign policy, and his analyses made it clear that he shared Kennan's point of view.[46] On 17 March, he said that it was impossible to separate the USSR's security plan from Soviet imperialism. He wondered whether the Kremlin could conceive of placing a limit on its hegemonic ambitions.[47] Three days later, he wrote: "Unlike Germany, the Soviet Union will not consciously provoke a major clash on any single issue, but she will never abandon her aims and will revive them at the first convenient opportunity. On the other hand she is in a hurry to achieve as much as she can in the fluid post-War situation."[48] According to the British diplomat, the Russians saw relations in terms of a power struggle. They knew that the United States and Great Britain could not check their expansion in Central Europe and the Balkans. Consequently, they would take no account of Anglo–American interests in the region, but would act as they themselves saw fit. In Greece, they would attempt systematically to undermine Great Britain's interests. If the British forces pulled out, they would interpret the measure as an invitation to continue their advance. Furthermore, the USSR would stop at nothing to prevent Germany from slipping into the Western sphere and to establish its own hegemony over the country. It would pursue its revolutionary plans in Asia, channeling its efforts into securing a Communist triumph in China, controlling Korea, and supporting the "oppressed peoples" of Indochina and South East Asia. If it was able, it would spread its influence over all of Persia by encouraging the establishment of a regime under its orders. It aimed to control the oil fields in the Persian Gulf, for its oil consumption would increase significantly with its economic reconstruction. It would try to create a safety zone in the south, but would also pursue its expansionist policy in Turkey, the eastern Mediterranean, and the entire Middle East as far as Egypt. On 20 March, Roberts suggested that one of the USSR's priorities was to create a protective belt in the south. Historically, Russia had always sought to control the Dardanelles. Roberts was convinced – and his colleagues at the United States embassy shared his opinion – that Soviet policy in the Middle East followed a coherent plan: Russia would deploy as far as it could without meeting resistance. It would take hold progressively, "as [of] an artichoke whose leaves are to be eaten one by one."[49]

46. Sean Greenwood, "Frank Roberts and the 'Other' Long Telegram: The View from the British Embassy in Moscow, March 1946," *Journal of Contemporary History,* no. 25, pp. 103–22. See notably *DBPO,* Series I, vol. 6, document number 80, pp. 305–12; document number 82, pp. 315–26; document number 83, pp. 326–31.

47. FO 371/56763.

48. *DBPO,* Series I, vol. 6 (21 March), document number 85, p. 335.

49. FO 371/56831.

The USSR, he added, pursued its long-term objectives with a flexible strategy and changing tactical measures. It needed scapegoats abroad to justify its regime. It would continue to give top priority to the development of its armed forces, and thus to its industrial growth. And, Roberts pointed out,

> Basically, the Kremlin is now pursuing a Russian national policy, which does not differ except in degree from that pursued in the past by Ivan the Terrible, Peter the Great or Catherine the Great. But what would, in other lands, be naked imperialism or power politics, is covered by the more attractive garb of Marxist-Leninist ideology, which in its turn moulds the approach to world problems of statesmen whose belief in their own ideology is as profound as that of the Jesuits in their own faith during the Counter Reformation.[50]

Roberts was suggesting, as Kennan had suggested to the Department of State, that Anglo–Soviet relations should be approached in the same way as the major military problems of the war. He asked for a coherent strategic policy, and hence the creation of a team of experts that could gather and analyze various data on Soviet policy and the activity of Communist parties controlled from Moscow.[51]

The director of the Northern Department (USSR and Eastern Europe), Christopher Warner, wrote a memorandum on 2 April 1946, drawing on Roberts's ideas:

> [T]he Soviet Union has announced to the world that it proposes to play an aggressive political role, while making an intensive drive to increase its own military and industrial strength. We should be very unwise not to take the Russians at their word, just as we should have been wise to take *Mein Kampf* at its face value. All Russia's activities in the past few months confirm this picture. In Eastern Europe, in the Balkans, in Persia, in Manchuria, in Korea, in her zone in Germany, and in the Security Council; in her support of Communist parties and Communist efforts to infiltrate Socialist parties and to combine left-wing parties under Communist leadership . . .[52]

50. *DBPO*, Series I, vol. 6, "Mr. Roberts to Mr. Bevin (17 March)," document number 82, p. 324.
51. *DBPO*, Series I, vol. 6, "Mr. Roberts to Mr. Bevin (18 March)," document number 83, pp. 327–8.
52. FO 371/56832. Quoted by Julian Lewis, *Changing Direction. British Military Planning for Post-War Strategic Defense, 1942–1947*, London, Sherwood Press, 1988, pp. 359–60.

In the weeks following, on Warner's request, the Foreign Office appointed a "Russia Committee" composed of under-secretaries of state and principal experts on the USSR. Its assignment was to make weekly analyses of all aspects of Soviet policy, propaganda, and activity.[53]

Bevin now shared his experts' pessimistic views. In March, he stated that the aim of Soviet maneuvers was to integrate Germany's eastern half into a solidly controlled Soviet bloc stretching from Lübeck to Trieste. "Finland, Poland, Hungary, Romania, Yugoslavia, Bulgaria, and Albania are either in the bag already or very nearly so. The prospect of Czechoslovakia holding out is not too hopeful."[54] On 10 April, he wrote to the prime minster: "The Russians have decided upon aggressive policy based on militant Communism and Russian chauvinism [...] and seem determined to stick at nothing, short of war, to obtain [their] objectives." The USSR's main target was Great Britain, which it defied the world over; primarily, because Britain was the leader of social democracy in Europe, but also because it was the weaker of the two great powers which the Soviet Union was confronting.[55]

Bevin was particularly worried about Soviet attempts to penetrate the Mediterranean and the Middle East.[56] Civil war had been fermenting in Greece for a long time, and there had been sporadic outbursts during the German occupation. In late March 1946, Communist guerrillas struck again. The British claimed they could still reconcile Greek liberal democracy and their own strategic interests. The endeavor was risky. Greece had come out of the war ravaged. It had lost more than half a million inhabitants (8% of its population).[57] One-third of its villages had been destroyed or damaged. Its lines of communication and merchant fleet had also been severely impaired.[58] Its industry had disappeared and its trade was crippled; inflation reached tremendous rates, making the drachma practically worthless.

In this depressed socioeconomic climate, the liberal cause gradually became indefensible and the British desperately sought political figures and movements worth supporting that might restore some political

53. FO 371/56885, 12 April; see also Ray Merrick, "The Russia Committee of the British Foreign Office and the Cold War, 1946–1947," *Journal of Contemporary History,* no. 20, 1985, pp. 453–68.

54. GEN 121/1, annex to COS (46) 93 (0); quoted by Lewis, *Changing Direction,* pp. 261–2.

55. See Allan L. Bullock, *Ernest Bevin, Foreign Secretary, 1945–1951,* Oxford, Oxford University Press, 1985, p. 234.

56. Ibid., p. 235.

57. Robert A. Pollard, *Economic Security and the Origin of the Cold War: 1945–1950,* New York, Columbia University Press, 1985, p. 114.

58. Thomas G. Paterson, *Soviet–American Confrontation: Post–War Reconstruction and the Origins of the Cold War,* Baltimore, Johns Hopkins University Press, 1973.

stability. The parties had clannish tendencies, however, and the ministries they formed were short-lived. Harassed by the Communists and weakened by internal fractures, the government gave itself up to the traditional gravitational force in Greek politics and passed into the hands of corrupt, unscrupulous groups whose backers were the products of fascism and Nazi collaboration. Terror reigned over all forms of opposition. The elections, which the British had been able to hold ahead of schedule with aid from the United States, took place on 31 March 1946. The Communist party, despite injunctions from Moscow and their French and Italian comrades, advised abstention. The results of the vote further reinforced political and social division. The Right took power, giving full rein to its inclination for intolerance and vengeance. Continued civil war would aggravate existing conditions of poverty and famine, which were sustained by an incompetent leadership. Furthermore, Great Britain no longer had the means to fulfill its ambitions. Its grants of financial aid proved insufficient. Stationing its troops cost it dearly.[59]

Because of their geostrategic situation, enormous oil resources, and economic potential, the Middle East and Egypt had an essential role in Great Britain's security and in the defense of its Empire. Despite the prime minister's qualms, the Labour government planned to preserve its imperial hegemony over these countries, but Soviet propaganda directed at the Arab world further thwarted it in meeting this goal. In early April, the Foreign Office sent a memorandum stating that it had become obvious that the Russians were attempting to infiltrate and cripple Great Britain's positions in the Middle East, and that they had a similar strategy laid out for the rest of Asia, and notably for India.[60] Yet, the Foreign Office knew that nationalism had become a significant political force in all countries in the region. Great Britain had built its hegemony by backing traditional elites. In keeping with his socialist convictions, Bevin knew now that it must support other political forces. When he spoke of the Arab world, he invariably stigmatized the politics of "kings, princes, and pashas."[61] As the British representative to Beirut, Terrance Shone, explained:

> I would suggest that the most efficient way to keep the Russians out of any part of the Middle East is not by means of pressure on the local governments to suppress Communist activity but by means of constructive economic or technical assistance to that area, thus depriving the Russians of the chief

59. G.M. Alexander, *The Prelude to the Truman Doctrine. British Policy in Greece, 1944–1947,* Oxford, Clarendon Press, 1982, especially at pp. 140 et seq.

60. *DBPO,* Series I, vol. 4, document number 62, pp. 208–11.

61. FO 371/45381; quoted by Michael J. Cohen, *Palestine and the Great Powers, 1945–1948,* Princeton, Princeton University Press, 1982, p. 63.

weapon in their army, namely the blatant disparity between the standard of living of the working classes and that of the privileged, bureaucratic, commercial or allegedly aristocratic classes.[62]

Progress, alas, can be interpreted in many ways, and the Labour government's plan was late coming into effect. It was not substantial enough, but most of all, it was too close to imperialist tradition to quench the burning nationalist fervor in the Arab world. On 20 December 1945, the Egyptian government requested a revision of the 1936 treaty. This treaty recognized Egyptian independence; however, it also authorized Britain to keep military bases in Egypt to protect its lines of communication. It stipulated that in peacetime, British forces could station only in the Canal Zone, but that they could be deployed freely on the Egyptian territory in case of conflict. Furthermore, Great Britain could keep air bases in Egypt at all times, and could occupy the country's airspace at will. Since its ratification, the treaty had come up against staunch opposition from nationalist groups in Cairo.

Bevin thought that a revision maintaining the essential elements of the military provisions would be possible. On 2 April 1946, the British government announced that it was sending a delegation to Egypt to renegotiate the basis of relations between Great Britain and Egypt. During the preliminary discussions, British negotiator Lord Stansgate came up against the refusal of Egyptian Prime Minister Ismael Sidky to allow British forces to remain in Egypt. He requested their complete evacuation, including the dismantling of their air bases. The British cabinet soon had to acknowledge that Egypt's demands must be met. On 7 May 1946, the prime minister announced to the House of Commons that the government had decided to evacuate British forces from Egypt, and the news elicited a sharp reaction from Churchill and his Conservative friends. Soon after, negotiations for a new treaty failed over the issue of Sudan, a country claimed by Egypt, and thus delayed the solution of the military problem. It was obvious, however, that Great Britain's strategic advantages in Egypt had become very uncertain.[63]

Great Britain's position in Palestine had also become indefensible. The Jewish resistance organizations had launched a series of attacks on Palestinian communication systems and military facilities starting in October 1945. The British reinforced their military presence, but terrorist action continued and grew increasingly savage. The upheavals undermined Middle East strategy and created constant tension between

62. FO 371/56786, 20 July 1946.
63. William R. Louis, *Imperialism at Bay,* Oxford, Oxford University Press, 1978, pp. 226 et seq.

London and Washington. Bevin sought to involve the United States in the search for a solution. In the fall of 1945, his motion for an Anglo–American Committee of Inquiry was approved. After having heard testimony from many refugees who were being held in camps, from top leaders of the Jewish Agency, and from British High Commissioner General Alan Cunningham, the committee suggested allowing the entry of 100,000 Jewish immigrants into Palestine and the repeal of the 1939 *White Book,* which posed limitations on immigration and land ownership. It failed, however, to define a lasting institutional solution, for it predicted that grave turmoil would result from a decision to create one or several independent Palestinian states.

On 27 April 1946, Bevin met with the United States secretary of state over the problem of enforcing the committee's resolutions. Great Britain was willing to allow 100,000 Jews to immigrate to Palestine but not immediately. He protested that the Zionist leaders were procuring arms with aid from American Jews and that they selected immigrants based on military criteria. The British government, Bevin explained, was planning to abandon Palestine completely, because it could not sustain the cost of keeping four divisions in the country much longer. Its withdrawal would, however, leave the field open to the Russians, whose entry into the Middle East would affect the entire region. In other words, Great Britain could not maintain its presence in Palestine if the United States did not take a share of the responsibility.[64]

On 30 April, bowing once again to pressure from the Jewish lobby, President Truman made a careless statement hailing the decisions of the Anglo–American Committee of Inquiry; yet he was aware of the problems involved in implementing its recommendations. The military chiefs of staff opposed military involvement in Palestine, and the Pentagon and the State Department realized that sending troops to Palestine would weaken the United States position in the Arab world. It was also feared that unrest resulting from the affair would make room for the Russians to penetrate the region, and would ultimately create the conditions of a third world war.[65]

The British military chief of staff announced that implementing the committee's recommendations would set off a disastrous reaction in the Middle East. In early July, he stated: "All our defense requirements in the Middle East, including maintenance of our essential oil supplies and communications, demand that an essential of our policy should be to retain the co-operation of the Arab States, and to ensure that the Arab

64. *FRUS 1946,* vol. 7, pp. 587–8, p. 112.
65. Harry S. Truman, *Memoirs of Harry S. Truman,* New York, Doubleday, 1955, vol. 2, p. 149; Michael J. Cohen, *Palestine and the Great Powers, 1945–1948,* p. 122.

world does not gravitate toward the Russians."[66] Great Britain's position was further threatened as its was currently negotiating with Egypt to withdraw its forces from the Canal Zone.

Confronted with these demands, London attempted to define a policy that would be acceptable to the two Palestinian communities by reviving the plan for provincial autonomy. But how would they organize the partition, given the fact that the Jewish and Arab populations were interwoven, and that both communities rejected this solution? The British government was divided over which policy to adopt. The Colonial Office, the Foreign Office, and the military did not always share the same point of view, and some ministers openly encouraged Zionist attacks on the British forces in Palestine.[67]

The end of the war had left London conjecturing over Great Britain's role in the world and the nature of its political and strategic commitments. In early 1946, these reflections took on a tenor of immediacy. Great Britain still had many servicemen in Germany, Austria, and Italy (mainly in Trieste) to cover its responsibilities. It also maintained a large force in Greece, the Middle East, especially in Palestine, and Egypt. It continued to man its traditional bases in Gibraltar, Malta, and Aden, and had stationed troops in Asia, most of which were in India. Yet it was evident that Great Britain could no longer conduct a grand-scale imperial policy, and the resources available to it to counter Soviet expansion and defend the Empire were insufficient. This truth came out in its military budget, and notably in its estimates of how many men were needed to meet its objectives. The military felt that Great Britain should be able to command forces of 2,068,000 men until June 1946. It envisaged reducing conscripts to 1,440,000 by 31 March 1947. On 21 January 1946, the British Cabinet Defence Committee reviewed these estimates. The prime minister, backed by Chancellor of the Exchequer Hugh Dalton, asked for a cut in the figures. He stated plainly that Great Britain had neither the manpower nor the financial means to maintain such a military force. He requested and consequently obtained a reduction in the armed forces to 1,900,000 by 30 June 1946 and to 1,100,000 by 31 December 1946. Economic needs took priority over defense.[68] The debate was opened again in March, when the prime minister, with continued support from Dalton, requested a complete revision of imperial Mediterranean and Middle East strategy. The prime minister believed that it was impossible to preserve British predominance in Greece. He advocated a drastic cut in Great Britain's

66. "Military Implications of the Anglo–American Report," COS (46), 188, 10 July 1946, in PREM 8/627, pt. 3 (see Cohen, *Palestine and the Great Powers,* p. 123).
67. Cohen, *Palestine and the Great Powers,* p. 82.
68. Lewis, *Changing Direction,* pp. 250–1.

commitments in the Middle East and Egypt, notably by withdrawing the forces it had stationed in the region. In his opinion, Great Britain was not in a position to defend Turkey, Iraq, and Persia from Russia. He did not think it possible to ensure control of the Mediterranean in conditions of modern warfare, especially since the development of atomic weapons. India would soon attain its independence, possibly withdrawing from the Commonwealth. In any case, it would wish to provide for its own defense. If the USSR decided to take military action against Persia or Iraq, Great Britain would be unable to respond. Its resources were limited, and it needed them all for the defense of the British Isles, which were strategic outposts of the American continent.

This view ran into strong opposition from military leaders. The foreign secretary also contested it. If Great Britain was to reduce its commitments in the Middle East, thus abandoning its dominant strategic position there, Russian influence would surely spread to the region. A strategy limited to defending the British Isles would result in the USSR's domination of Western Europe, North Africa, the Middle East, and East Africa. The USSR would also become a potential threat to India and South Africa. This would allow it to increase its industrial and human resources considerably and to broaden its strategic range.

British military leaders were aware of the problems raised by the development of new weaponry and the relative weakening of British power. The war had revealed Great Britain's extreme vulnerability to attacks by modern long-range weapons. Nevertheless, they believed that if Great Britain could keep its lead over the USSR in scientific and technical advances, it would deter the Kremlin. They also hoped to surpass the USSR in air and sea strength. To deter the USSR from attacking Europe, Great Britain must have bases in the Near East. Near East bases were also necessary to protect communications in the Mediterranean and to ensure the oil supply.[69] Therefore, control of communications in the Atlantic and the Mediterranean was indispensable, and hence the USSR must be prevented from gaining a toehold in the Middle East, North Africa, and the Iberian peninsula. If it adopted a strictly defensive strategy for the sole protection of national territory, the British government would be taking a heavy risk. The USSR would be positioned to concentrate all of its forces against Great Britain, which would remain vulnerable to USSR air and rocket attack. By holding the Middle East and thereby defending communications with both the East and South Africa, Great Britain would have a much broader strategic range. Egypt and Palestine were essential in this defense plan. In any case, if the Middle East was

69. Memorandum by Clement Attlee on Near East policy, 5 January 1947, (FO 800/ 476).

left undefended, Russia would continue to spread over the region.[70]

Ernest Bevin gave unqalified support to the military's position. The Russians respected strong nations only, and Britain's presence in the Mediterranean not only served a military function, but heightened Great Britain's prestige as a great power. It was via the Mediterranean that Great Britain could hope to influence South East Europe, Italy, Yugoslavia, Greece, and Turkey. Abandoning the Mediterranean would invite Russian penetration and force the British economy to forfeit an important trade route.[71] Bevin insisted especially that Great Britain maintain its military presence in Greece until the Balkan situation was cleared up. He was also counting on the Russian troops to withdraw from Bulgaria. Great Britain was the last bastion of social democracy between United States capitalism and Russian Communist dictatorship.[72]

Nonetheless, Bevin realized that Great Britain's strategic positions in Egypt and Palestine had become shaky. He conjectured that they might pull back to Kenya. A port in Mombassa would provide a British presence in the Indian Ocean. He even envisaged a route linking Lagos and Kenya. Attlee and Dalton were favorable to the plan.[73] The chiefs of staff, however, were skeptical. For the time being, Bevin was able to win approval to continue the traditional strategy.[74] He knew, as his advisers reminded him, that Great Britain could no longer defend its influence in the Middle East without aid from the United States; but London remained wary of the State Department's inconsistent and occasionally erratic positions.[75]

Kennan's strategic concepts had found their way into the United States administration, where they were now established as incontestable. A State Department memorandum of April 1946 read: "As long as present Soviet policies and attitude in regard to other countries continue unchanged, the U.S. must accept the fact that it is confronted with the threat of an expanding totalitarian state."[76] The Department of State and the Pentagon knew that Great Britain was an essential element in the fight against Soviet imperialism. The Joint Chiefs of Staff suggested that Soviet expansion could be checked by supporting the countries that were its potential victims.[77] Freeman Matthews, head of the Office of Western European Affairs, said that the United States must draw the only logical conclusion

70. CAB 131, n. 3, 18 June.
71. See Lewis, *Changing Direction,* pp. 254–9.
72. Quoted by Bullock, *Ernest Bevin, Foreign Secretary,* p. 242.
73. Ibid., pp. 242–3.
74. Ibid., pp. 244–5.
75. *DBPO,* Series I, vol. 4, document number 62, pp. 208–11.
76. *FRUS 1946,* vol. 1, p. 1167.
77. Ibid., pp. 1165–6.

possible from the USSR's allegations of capitalist encirclement, by which it justified its actions: that the Kremlin's hegemonic tendencies were limitless and would be pursued by direct and indirect measures. The United States government had no other choice but to consolidate its alliance with Great Britain in order to provide it with all the support it needed in political, economic, and even military matters. It would have, in particular, to aid Great Britain in protecting its ties with the Commonwealth. Matthews suggested that the United States should take immediate measures to rebuild its own military capacity. But first, public opinion in the United States must be enlightened on the Soviet threat.[78]

78. Ibid., pp. 1169–71.

6

DEADLOCKS IN EUROPEAN DIPLOMACY

The German Question

It was nearly a year since the Third Reich had been toppled, and Allied troops still occupied Germany, Italy, and Austria. The Red Army was camped in Hungary, Romania, and Bulgaria. It had kept its positions in Poland, situated on its access routes to Germany. The United States and Great Britain were keen to end the peace talks, for both were persuaded that European economic stability and recovery depended on their prompt conclusion. They were anxious for a reply from the Red Army, because, for as long as the armistice continued, the Soviet Union could rightfully occupy the satellite countries. Although there had been little progress in the preparatory negotiations, Byrnes proposed that the foreign ministers meet once again in Paris. Difficulties in drafting the peace treaties for the former satellites made it unlikely that an agreement on Germany, which would be a decisive factor in Europe's future, was close at hand. Soviet determination to maintain absolute control over their sector made the country's economic recovery, and to a further extent, its political reconstruction, impossible. Behind its "iron curtain," the USSR was exacting a complete restructuring of Germany's economy and political activity. On 7 February, the Social Democratic party headed by Otto Grotwohl was forced to merge with the Communist party, the SED. This new political formation engaged in heavy propaganda for a unified, centralized Germany under Communist leadership.

The Kremlin's intentions toward Germany worried the United States and Great Britain. On 24 February, Robert Murphy, a political adviser to General Clay, military commander of the American occupation forces in Germany, said that he was concerned about Soviet ambitions. He feared that the USSR was attempting to spread its hegemony over all of Germany.[1] On 6 March, George Kennan said that the Soviet Union would not give up exclusive control of its sector unless it was in a position to gain ascendancy over the rest of Germany. By allowing the USSR and Poland to appropriate the territory east of the Oder–Neisse line, the United

---

1. R. Murphy to J. Byrnes, 24 February 1946 (*FRUS 1946*, vol. 5, pp. 505–7), quoted by Robert J. Donovan, *Conflict and Crisis. The Presidency of Harry S. Truman, 1945–1948*, New York, Norton, 1982, p. 189.

States had given the USSR its chance to exercise a decisive influence over Germany's economic and political future. It must therefore resolve to bring Germany's division to its logical conclusion by attempting to save the Western sectors, integrating them into Europe and subtracting them from Soviet penetration.[2]

As the Foreign Office saw it, the totalitarian Soviet system had replaced the Nazi system, and was aimed at extending the USSR's influence over all of Germany through the Communist party.[3] Germany was, according to a long Foreign Office memorandum of 24 April 1946, a political "vacuum." It was the pivotal issue in relations among the great powers. From the British viewpoint, the fundamental antagonism was "between the totalitarian and the liberal creeds, both of which claim to represent the true democracy."[4] The military hoped to prevent the USSR from controlling Germany; it even considered restoring Germany's military power if the Soviet threat became serious.[5]

The United States and British governments were now persuaded that European reconstruction necessitated a return to traditional economic exchange and that Germany must be active in this area. Yet the ravages of war, the worst of which were the broken socioeconomic ties between the occupied sectors, in particular between the industrial regions in the west and the Soviet-controlled rural areas; the dismantling of production plant to satisfy reparations claims; and production cuts prescribed by the winners, had created living conditions amounting to destitution. The Germans were going hungry, and the occupation forces were incapable of subsidizing provisions for them. In January 1946, the French military government had asked the United States to deliver foodstuffs so that it might avoid a further reduction of rations, which were already well below the minimum standard; but General Lucius Clay, who was faced with similar shortages of subsistence goods, could not fulfill the request. The situation in the British sector was even worse. In the spring of 1946, a committee charged with examining nutrition in the Western sectors predicted imminent disaster: stunted growth in children, anemia, malnutrition in the entire population, famine in certain urban areas, tuberculosis, and epidemics of all kinds.[6] These dire conditions aggravated economic difficulties. It was a vicious circle: coal production

2. *FRUS 1946*, vol. 5, pp. 518–19.
3. FO 371/55587, 24 April 1946.
4. Ibid.
5. COS (46) 54th Mtg. (6); quoted by Julian Lewis, *Changing Direction. British Military Planning for Post–War Strategic Defence, 1942–1947*, London, Sherwood Press, 1988, p. 263.
6. Ann and John Tusa, *The Berlin Blockade. Berlin in 1948: The Year the Cold War Threatened to Become Hot*, London, Coronet, 1989, pp. 93–4.

was insufficient because the work force was weakened by poverty and hunger. Electric power cuts were frequent, which further slowed reconstruction and industrial development. In April, miners in the Ruhr went on strike. These miserable economic conditions were worsened by the enormous demographic movements that had been predicated by Potsdam. Some ten million people, mostly women, children, and the elderly, had fled the Red Army or been forced to abandon the regions of Pomerania and Silesia that the Soviet Union had taken from Germany with the help of their former allies. The desperate migrations also included the German populations of Czechoslovakia and Hungary, in accordance with the Potsdam agreement.[7] In their exodus, these emigrants brought few belongings. They therefore arrived destitute and often in bad health, which placed an additional burden on the occupation authorities.[8]

German agriculture was also in a pitiable state. Vast regions that had traditionally provided for most of Germany's nutritional needs were now devastated, depopulated, and occupied by Poland. With no central administration to distribute the few agricultural resources available, certain regions, in particular the British sector, suffered from severe shortages. Great quantities of food had to be imported, which taxed the Western occupation forces' budgets heavily at a time when most countries were facing supply problems.[9] Between June 1945 and April 1946, the British sent millions of tons of food stuffs to ensure subsistence in their sector.[10] The United States and Great Britain were plagued by the financial burden of Germany's occupation. The United States budget contained a heading of 200 million dollars to cover occupation costs in the United States sector in the 1946 year.[11] The British budgeted 320 million dollars.[12] Such commitments had become excessive, especially for Great Britain.

The Foreign Office was growing impatient. It had to respond to pressure from the Treasury, which had demanded a cut in foreign spending. Public opinion could not accept such spending in Germany when bread was still rationed in the United Kingdom. The British felt, in the words of Hugh Dalton, that they had been reduced "to paying reparations to the Germans" in the form of food supplies.[13] The reparations policy, which was

7. Alfred de Zayas, *Nemesis at Potsdam. The Anglo–Americans and the Expulsion of the Germans. Background, Execution, Consequences,* London, Routledge and Kegan Paul, 1977.

8. FO 371/55587 (24 April 1946).

9. Ibid.

10. Tusa and Tusa, *The Berlin Blockade,* p. 94; see also p. 208.

11. *FRUS 1946,* vol. 2, p. 849.

12. Ibid., p. 866.

13. Quoted by Allan L. Bullock, *Ernest Bevin, Foreign Secretary, 1945–1951,* Oxford, Oxford University Press, 1985, p. 265.

inseparable from the Potsdam terms concerning German industry, was a source of hardship and poverty in Germany. The USSR was particularly harsh on this matter. On 30 March 1946, after painstaking discussions, the Allied Control Council agreed on a program for industrial production: industry that could serve military ends would be dismantled entirely, while other industries would reduce output to levels corresponding to pre-War production capacity. According to British estimates, the program would limit all German industrial production to a rate of about 50% its pre-War level.

The Foreign Office rejected the arrangement, and it was only after they had introduced an escape clause that the British government accepted the program. London considered that it favored Soviet policy insofar as it mainly affected production in the Western sectors, and the Ruhr area in particular, but especially because it would put Germany on a course toward impoverishment and thus allow for "the extension of Communism." US approval of the program came as a surprise, and there was speculation whether this bespoke a desire to eliminate trade competitors or simply to continue with the plan to "pastoralize" Germany.[14] One thing was certain: the Allied Control Council's 30 March decisions would not help to improve Germany's standard of living. Nonetheless, the United States and Great Britain requested that a common import-export exchange policy be established for all of Germany. In early April, the Soviet Union denied the request, although it was provided for in the Potsdam agreement, demanding that reparations be paid first.[15]

The British and United States sector commanders made incessant demands for central administrations to be set up in accordance with the Potsdam agreement. The French government had been the main obstacle to developing an economic policy that conformed with the agreement's provisions. It did not want Germany to be treated as a single economy and above all, it objected to the establishment of a central administration to manage this economy. In October 1945, it opposed the creation of common transportation, communication, and postal services, blocking any possibility of a common occupation policy for the four sectors with its veto. This was a great source of irritation to the United States and British military, who were managing the occupation of Germany. The French foreign minister continued to press his claim for the detachment of the Ruhr, which he wished to be placed under international control. He asked that the Rhineland be broken up into one or several states, which would be separate from Germany and placed under permanent Allied

---

14. FO 371/55587 (24 April 1946).
15. J.E. Smith (ed.), *The Papers of General Lucius D. Clay, Germany 1945–1949*, Bloomington, University of Indiana Press, 1974, pp. 186–7.

occupation. He made a similar request for the Saarland, but asked that France exercise strong administrative, economic, and military control over this region.

The French position seemed unrealistic, especially given the outlook in the spring of 1946. The British and the Americans dismissed it, for it took no account of US and British economic and political difficulties. It would be absurd to divide Germany further, for dismemberment would facilitate Communist penetration in Western Europe.[16] Furthermore, Bevin refused to conduct negotiations on the British sector alone. He thought that the German question must be examined as a whole, and rejected the idea of separating the Ruhr from the rest of Germany. The Belgian government shared his point of view. The USSR was wary of the French plan, which might lead to its eviction from the Ruhr, the hub of German industrial power.

France's requests had even less chance of endorsement since they were issued by a fragile, divided government with a vacillating foreign policy. Georges Bidault was a weak man on whom Washington and London could not rely, and he lacked solid political support. His claims on Germany aimed to please Gaullist and Communist opinion, but the French Socialists did not favor them, and France was on the eve of a constitutional referendum. Bidault was worried about the results of the coming vote. His greatest fear was that the Communists would gain ground. Furthermore, General de Gaulle's government and its successors had made a commitment to implement a program of economic recovery, which had been largely conceived by Jean Monnet, entailing France's heavy economic dependence on the United States.[17] How could the French lean on the United States if they foiled its plans in Germany? The contradictions became glaringly clear in early 1946, when the French government sent Léon Blum to negotiate a new request for economic aid. In February, Byrnes had made it known discreetly to the French government through his ambassador in Paris that France would be well advised to change its attitude about Germany if it wanted to create an atmosphere in which it might hope to win the economic and financial aid it sought.[18] After lengthy negotiation, France came away disappointed. The United States government had forgiven French debts contracted under Lend–Lease, promised to support France's request to the World Bank, offered a new line of credit to cover imports since the termination

---

16. See the memorandum "Internationalization of the Ruhr" in *The Papers of General Lucius Clay*, pp. 192–202.

17. Irwin M. Wall, *The United States*, p. 36.

18. Anne Deighton, *The Impossible Peace. Britain, the Division of Germany and the Origins of the Cold War*, Oxford, Clarendon Press, 1990, p. 83.

of Lend–Lease, and foregone large US surpluses in France; but the sum of additional moneys from Washington – 650 million dollars – was a sum considerably lower than that which France had requested, and worst of all, it was lower than the United States' loan to Great Britain, which had been approved at the same meeting.[19] The United States was willing to increase its aid, but it wanted first to know if France intended to join the ranks of Western civilization or drift off toward communism.[20]

The French Ministry of Foreign Affairs had no more illusions about the nature of Soviet policy in Europe. On 21 February 1946, as Kennan was addressing his telegram to the Department of State, General Catroux, the French representative in Moscow, wrote to Georges Bidault:

> For a year, the development of Soviet policy has shown that we are dealing not merely with a crisis of distrust or a reaction born of fear, but with a vast program of successive objectives, the aim of which is to ensure the Soviet Union's full security and full freedom of action. If the principal objective of Russian policy in Europe is to maintain a division large enough to prevent European consolidation beyond the Russian buffer zone, in Asia and Africa it is seeking to break the line of force constituted by the British and French Empires. World politics, the USSR's claims to which are voiced by Molotov, does not seem able to accommodate the coexistence of strong and independent nations on the European continent.[21]

The same day, a note was sent to the Eastern section of the French Ministry of Foreign Affairs reading: "Both through the great mass of its territory and its regime's own totalitarian methods, the USSR is currently attacking liberal democratic positions on all points of the globe. Careful to maintain good relations with the United States, the only country they consider to be their equal, the Soviet leaders are going after the Western powers they consider most vulnerable, and whose reinforcement would necessarily curtail their action."[22] In the interview he arranged with the United States secretary of state on 1 May 1946, Bidault referred to the threat of "Cossacks at the Place de la Concorde" several times.[23] Since the beginning of the year, the Foreign Office had been approached by various French figures expressing their desire to revitalize old plans for an alliance of

19. Irwin M. Wall, *The United States*, p. 55.
20. Meeting between Bevin and Byrnes of 5 May (FO 800/513).
21. Z Series, *Europe 1944–1948,* "URSS, politique extérieure," dossier général, November 1945–September 1946, vol. 32.
22. Ibid.
23. *FRUS 1946*, vol. 2, pp. 203–6; see p. 212.

the two countries while soliciting financial aid from Great Britain.[24] At a reception on 17 May, Bidault spoke with Bevin about the possibility of rapprochement of the two countries' imperial policies, adding a nostalgic reference to Winston Churchill's 1940 project for common citizenship.[25]

The Peace Talks Continue

The next session of the Council of Foreign Ministers opened in Paris on 25 April at the Palais de Luxembourg and rose on 16 May. On the agenda were negotiations of the peace treaties for Italy, Romania, Bulgaria, Hungary, and Finland. Molotov agreed to include France in all of the negotiation proceedings on the condition that Bidault's vote would be only consultative in deliberations not concerning Italy. He also approved the French minister's proposal to devote part of the conference to the German problem. It was a gesture of goodwill toward France, which contrasted with his attitude at the conference in London. The vote on the Fourth Republic's new constitution was near, and the Soviet Union had no reason to compromise the French Communist party's stronghold with an unfriendly attitude toward their hosts. The USSR was also counting to some extent on France's support against growing US–British hostility.

The political climate as the council meeting opened was, however, not good. When he met the US secretary of state, Molotov complained bitterly about the stance the United States had taken at the United Nations on the Persian affair.[26] He was fully aware that Churchill's speech at Fulton translated a change in direction in United States diplomacy. The Kremlin was also responsible for this ideological and political confrontation. On 1 May, shortly after the beginning of the Foreign Ministers meeting, Stalin gave general orders to the Red Army that caused disquiet, denouncing "the machinations of international reaction which is hatching plans for new war."[27] The Soviet press was growing increasingly aggressive toward the outside world and toward the United States in particular. Official propaganda spun out variations on the themes of "fascism, a manifestation of capitalist societies in their imperialist phase"; support of fascism by reactionary groups in the capitalist countries; opposition between the imperialist camp versus the democracy embodied by the USSR, and plans by Anglo–American reactionary elements for world domination. Soviet domestic policy was also hardening. Editorials in the 1 May edition of

24. Memorandum by Rumbold of 22 March 1946 (FO 371/59953).
25. FO 371/59954.
26. FO 800/513.
27. *FRUS 1946*, vol. 6, p. 750.

Bolshevik, the Communist party's main theoretical organ, stressed the need to intensify the struggle against the "capitalist survivals" and the influence of hostile ideology on the Soviet people. Shortly after, the same paper denounced the "penetration of alien influences among the youth."[28]

Byrnes was pessimistic about the chances of reaching an agreement with the USSR; he even contemplated separate peace treaties.[29] He did not intend to make any substantial concessions on Italy. United States leadership was resolved to counter Soviet penetration in the Mediterranean, and Byrnes made this clear to Molotov during the interview he managed to schedule with the Soviet minister early in the conference.[30] The secretary of state had taken the precaution of involving the Republicans in the negotiation process, and Senators Tom Connally and Arthur Vandenberg were therefore part of the United States delegation. Vandenberg was in no mind to make concessions to the USSR.[31] He was convinced the Russians had to be shown that the United States was not intending to adopt an "appeasement" policy toward them.[32]

After three weeks of bitter discussions, which often necessitated two sessions a day, the Council of Foreign Ministers had barely advanced. Tired of the lengthy deliberations, the US secretary of state proposed on 8 May that the ministers' proxies draw up a report listing areas of agreement and disagreement, which would then be submitted to the peace conference. The Soviet minister found the proposal unacceptable because his haggling tactic consisted in tying up every aspect of the negotiation procedure, and above all because he had worked hard to limit the influence the other nations would have in negotiating the peace treaties. Molotov would not allow the peace conference to convene until the ministers had resolved their differences.

It was therefore decided to suspend the Council of Foreign Ministers for several weeks. On 20 May, Byrnes exposed publicly and in very clear, precise terms, the divergence that had cropped up among the foreign ministers, pointing out his disagreement with the Soviet position. He made his fears about the USSR's position clear, and vented his frustration that a conclusion to the negotiations had once again been postponed: "The four Allied governments cannot indefinitely delay the making of peace with countries which they have long ceased to fight, simply because they cannot agree among themselves on peace terms. The Council of Foreign Ministers was formed to facilitate and not obstruct the making of peace."[33]

28. Ibid., p. 767.
29. FO 800/513.
30. Ibid.
31. James Edward Miller, *The United States and Italy*, p. 197.
32. Bullock, *Ernest Bevin, Foreign Secretary*, pp. 261–2.
33. *Department of State Bulletin*, 14 (36), June 1946, p. 952.

He added: "Security is the concern of every nation. But the efforts of one nation to increase its security may threaten the security of other nations and cause them in turn to try to increase their own security. The quest for security may lead to less rather then more security in the world. It is in truth extremely difficult to know to what extent the action of any nation may be ascribed to its quest for security or to its desire to expand."[34]

On 4 June, Bevin gave his report on the Council of Foreign Ministers session to the House of Commons. He expressed his regret that Russia had remained on one side while the United States and Great Britain were on the other. The Soviet Union was convinced that it represented the workers, and that it alone practiced democracy. "Their concept of certain other governments is that they are either fascist, crypto-fascist, or something of that kind. This leads to the idea that the security of Russia can only be maintained when every country in the world has adopted the Soviet system. This, I think, is one of their greatest handicaps, and a great handicap to peace."[35] He made a formal appeal to the USSR, stressing the need to regularize the situation with its former enemies.

The Council reconvened on 15 June and rose on 12 July. Again, the discussions were difficult and the Americans were increasingly convinced that Molotov was dragging out the negotiations intentionally. The Soviet minister now asked for an investigation of Italy's domestic situation, saying he was concerned about Fascist activity. He continued to demand agreement on pending major problems before the peace conference met. He would not allow the Council of Foreign Ministers to issue invitations to the conference, for he did not wish to include China among the hosts. Before authorizing the peace conference to convene, he intended to define its rules of procedure so as to make it impossible to reverse decisions taken by the Council of Foreign Ministers. As he imagined it, the enlarged conference would have a purely consultative vote, but it must be prepared to accept the collective opinion of the great powers. This way of thinking was obviously unacceptable, particularly to Great Britain, for it planned to authorize its dominions, which had fought for Europe's liberation, to participate in drafting the peace treaties. Molotov finally accepted a compromise proposed by Georges Bidault: the council would not impose a procedure, but would suggest that proposals issued by the peace conference which had obtained two-thirds of the vote should be retained as "recommendations." This did not close the affair, however, for Molotov made continued objections tending to curtail the right of other countries to take part in the European peace settlement.[36]

34. Ibid.
35. Quoted by Bullock, *Ernest Bevin, Foreign Secretary*, p. 274.
36. *FRUS 1946*, vol. 2, pp. 493–940.

The negotiations were exhausting, for they required sustained attention to burning questions, the discussion of which was made even more tedious by the constraints of interpreting in three languages, as simultaneous translation facilities did not yet exist. The climate was once again abhorrent, dragged down by mutual suspicion, Molotov's procedural tactics, and fundamental disagreement. In addition, the meetings required extensive travel and long stops abroad at a time when transportation was not what it is today. The world was undergoing enormous upheaval, confronting the governments of the great powers with important foreign policy decisions on a daily basis. The ministers and their collaborators negotiating in Paris had to maintain their leadership in these affairs as well. The diary of Bevin's principal private secretary, Dixon, gives an understanding of what working conditions were like for the ministers and their staff, and of their state of exhaustion over the course of that fateful year.[37] In his memoirs, James Byrnes writes: "Many nights I returned to the hotel from the conference depressed as well as exhausted."[38]

Soviet negotiation methods must be taken into account when attempting to understand the dynamic of conflict that emerged between the Western powers and the USSR. These meetings lasted eighty days in the course of 1946, and entailed discussions that could go on for seven to ten hours at a time, occasionally lasting until the early hours of the morning. Molotov's tactic was still the same: to obtain satisfaction of his claims, he would repeat the same arguments endlessly, block negotiations by invoking procedural considerations, refuse to accept solutions for minor problems until his demands were met, pit flagrant bad faith against all other logic but his own, and make tensions mount during the debates with verbal abuse, which was directed against Bevin in particular. Molotov's attitude so irritated Bevin that on occasion, after a drink or two, the British minister looked as if he might punch him. On 23 July, Bevin, who had clearly fallen victim to these Stalinist methods, suffered a heart attack.

At this point, the main stake in the negotiations reduced to protecting and expanding the spheres of influence that the victors had secured for themselves since the hostilities had ended. The USSR began by submitting a draft treaty with Romania that underscored its intention to perpetuate its economic and political control over that country.[39] It expressed plans to maintain armed forces in Romania, Bulgaria, and Hungary, and then obstinately opposed US and British requests to write a clause into the

---

37. Piers Dixon, *Double Diploma. The Life of Sir Pierson Dixon, Don and Diplomat,* London, Hutchinson, 1968, pp. 207 et seq.

38. James Byrnes, *Speaking Frankly,* New York, Harper, 1947, p. 146.

39. *FRUS 1946,* vol. 2, pp. 28–9.

peace treaties guaranteeing free trade and freedom of navigation on the Danube. Molotov accused the Western powers of attempting to install capitalist slavery in these countries. *Izvestia* lashed out against the threat of American capitalism taking hold of the region.[40]

The affair dragged on. To end the stalemate, Bevin proposed a compromise on 25 June: the ministers would settle for a declaration expressing their intention to preserve the right of all countries to navigate freely both the Danube and its tributaries for trade purposes. The declaration would reserve the right of the occupying power – the USSR – to make special dispensations to protect its lines of communication with Austria.[41] Despite this substantial concession, which considerably reduced the initial compass of the liberal principles the Western powers had proposed, Molotov did not accede to the request from the United States and Britain but remained firmly opposed to it.

In fact, the United States, Great Britain, and France had only minor economic and political interests in the East European countries affected by the negotiations, and these held little sway with Western public opinion. As one Eastern European affairs official at the Foreign Office explained it that summer in London:

> With some notable exceptions the newspapers have shown a surprising timidity in commenting on practices being followed in countries of eastern and south-eastern Europe. [...] Attempts by the press to assess the general trends of Russian policy are rare and newspapers are content to record events in colourless unrelated reports from news agencies, without discovering any general pattern of the scene in countries under Russian control or influence.

Few British newspapers had correspondents in these countries. Furthermore, it was clear that journalists feared compromising unity in the former alliance.[42]

Disputes over Italy

Through his obstructive tactics, Molotov was able to divert the talks on Eastern Europe. The fates of Hungary, Romania, and Bulgaria commanded little of the foreign ministers' attention, for the main hurdle at the meetings concerned the peace settlement with Italy, and in particular

40. Redvers Opie, *The Search for Peace Settlements,* Washington, The Brookings Institution, 1951, p. 167.
41. *FRUS 1946,* vol. 2, pp. 629–30.
42. FO 371/56788, 1 August 1946.

the problems of Italy's border with Yugoslavia, the fate of its colonies, and the reparations it would have to pay, all of which affected how East and West would delineate their spheres of influence and where the empires would settle their borders.[43]

In the last weeks of the war, the United States and Great Britain had made it clear that they did not intend to concede Yugoslavia's claims on Trieste and Venezia Giulia. The question was complex, like all matters touching upon the division of ethnic groups and nations in Europe. The city of Trieste's population was three-quarters Italian. Its hinterland was inhabited for the most part by Slovenes, and the population of Istria's western coast was also mixed. Most cities and villages had a majority of Italians, but rural areas had a more composite population. The political and strategic importance of its borders obviously outweighed the cause of the populations affected. Yugoslavia, which was demanding Trieste and all of Istria, had within a few months become a Stalinist Communist state, while Italy, with strong support from the United States, was struggling toward a liberal regime. Yugoslavia's ambitions were defended by the USSR, whose strategic intentions in the Adriatic and the Mediterranean were obvious.

Negotiations on this problem would occupy most of the meetings, and they appeared interminable. Bevin was now convinced, as he explained to the United States secretary of state in a private meeting on 5 May 1946, that the Soviet Union was trying to obtain naval bases on the Adriatic, first in Trieste, but also in Pula and Fiume (Rijeka). If they attained this goal, they could subjugate Italy. He also thought that they would demand a passage to the Aegean for Bulgaria, the intention being to make Turkey a satellite, advancing their penetration of the Middle East. But the secretary did not plan to concede on Trieste. He again considered signing a peace treaty with Italy without the Soviet Union.[44] He refused to discuss the issue when Molotov, after lengthy plenary session negotiations, suggested that he forego Trieste in return for a more flexible Soviet position on the Italian colonies and on Yugoslavia's demands for reparations from Italy.[45]

In June 1946, as the disputes continued, former Soviet people's commissar for foreign affairs Maksim M. Litvinov confided his worry over developments in East–West relations to an American correspondent. Once again, he was pessimistic about the course of Soviet foreign policy. What, asked the American, would happen if the West accepted the Russian demands, in particular those on Trieste and the Italian colonies? The

---

43. Miller, *The United States and Italy*, pp. 193–204.
44. Meeting between Bevin and Byrnes of 5 May (FO 800/513).
45. *FRUS 1946*, vol. 2, pp. 246–9.

climate would improve for a while, Litvinov replied, and then the Soviet Union would formulate new demands. On the question of Germany, he predicted that the country would be divided, each party attempting to unify the country under its own control.[46]

On 21 June, Bidault, playing the middleman between the Soviet side and the side of the US and Great Britain, proposed creating an international zone around Trieste with provisional status under United Nations control. This compromise involving the United Nations might have delayed resolving the problem, but in fact the suggestion brought the negotiations forward because the Soviet side agreed to it. The United States and Great Britain, who recognized France's proposed dividing line between Yugoslavia and the international zone, were forced once again into a stubborn fight to ensure the international zone's effective independence, notably by countering Soviet efforts to place the region under the authority of a Yugoslavian governor.

Another source of dispute underscored conflicting hegemonic ambitions among the great powers. This was the former Italian colonies. Byrnes was now acting on behalf of British strategic concerns in the Mediterranean. He explained clearly to Molotov in a private meeting on 28 April that the United States would not look kindly upon the USSR gaining a toehold in Africa and the Middle East.[47] In the plenary session, Byrnes iterated the proposal he had made in September in London, i.e. to turn the trusteeship of these colonized peoples over to the United Nations. In the post-War environment, this proposal implied a broad transfer of responsibility to the United States in enforcing the mandate, for the United States alone had the resources to implement it. Bevin did not favor this solution. Molotov opposed it, making it clear that he suspected United States hegemony had been the motivation for the proposal. He again requested a Soviet mandate over Tripolitania, all the while stating that he was prepared to confer the administration of Cyrenaica to Italy, as France wished, or to England, as Bevin wished.

The Soviet request ran up against unanimous opposition from the Western ministers. Bevin recalled the British forces' role in taking back the Italian colonies, and the region's strategic importance in controlling communications in the Mediterranean. He supported the motion to recognize Libya's independence immediately, hoping to guarantee with a treaty the presence of British troops in Cyrenaica.[48] He proposed instead to link the former Italian Somalia to British Somaliland, a solution that appeared economically sound to him. Finally, he suggested giving Eritrea

46. *FRUS 1946*, vol. 6, pp. 763–5.
47. FO 800/513, p. 107.
48. Bullock, *Ernest Bevin, Foreign Secretary*, p. 263.

to Ethiopia.

Naturally, Georges Bidault was hostile to the plan for Libya's independence. As he explained in private to the US secretary of state, the decision would set an unfortunate precedent, for it would cause agitation to flare up among the region's peoples. North Africa was of vital importance to France as a source of labor and raw materials. He wished to restore Italy's rights, but was opposed to a United Nations trusteeship and even more so to Molotov's or Bevin's ideas. He vehemently recalled Britain's activity in Syria and Libya, and did not wish to see such intrigue repeated in the neighborhood of Tunisia. During the plenary session, he surprised Bevin by proposing that the colonies be returned to Italy, a proposal that the British minister could not accept under any conditions.[49]

The debate over the Italian colonies gave rise to one of the sharpest altercations in the conference. Molotov charged, not without insight, that Bevin proposed independence for Libya and yet planned to station British troops on its soil – similar to the arrangement in Transjordania. He also upbraided Great Britain for its ambitions of hegemony over Italian Somalia. Bevin protested: "Nineteenth-century imperialism in England is dead. [...] I am driven to suspicion sometimes that our place has been taken by others. But as a Social Democrat, I am not envious." – Molotov retorted, "Nineteenth-century imperialism may be dead in England, but there are now twentieth-century tendencies. When Mr. Churchill calls for a new war and makes militant speeches on two continents, he represents the worst of twentieth-century imperialism, and he evidently approves Mr. Bevin's foreign policies." He went on to point out that Britain had troops and military bases in Greece, Denmark, Egypt, Iraq, Indonesia, and elsewhere. The Soviet Union had no bases beyond its frontiers, and that made the difference between expansion and security. In reply to this dressing down, Bevin simply said, "Now that you have that off your chest, Mr. Molotov, I hope you feel better."[50]

A few days later, Molotov announced that he was accepting the French proposal to transfer one of the United Nations trusteeships to Italy. He justified his about-face by saying that a conversation with A. De Gasperi had convinced him that the Italians did not see these colonies as a burden, but rather as an asset that would give them a market for their goods and an outlet for their overpopulation.[51] He felt therefore that it was legitimate to accept Italy's claims, thus showing a favorable attitude toward the new Italian democracy. Bevin was very uneasy about the solution, especially

49. *FRUS 1946*, vol. 2, pp. 254–6.

50. Arthur H. Vandenberg, Jr. (ed.), *The Private Papers of Senator Vandenberg*, Boston, Houghton Mifflin, 1952, pp. 277–8.

51. *FRUS 1946*, vol. 2, p. 334.

since Byrnes now appeared to support it. He invoked the promises made to the Sanusi during the war, and above all Great Britain's strategic interests in the Middle East, to reinforce his claim for a British trusteeship over Cyrenaica.[52] In the end, the foreign ministers realized that a solution to the problem would have to be postponed. They agreed to ask their representatives to continue the negotiations, set up an investigative committee, and submit the question to the United Nations General Assembly if disagreement still persisted one year after the treaty with Italy came into effect.[53] This meant that Italy would have to renounce its sovereignty over its former colonies, the administration of which was temporarily transferred to the occupying powers and principally to Great Britain.

The reparations negotiations were also difficult. The Soviet side demanded 100 million dollars in reparations for themselves, not including the claims they made on Yugoslavia's behalf. Molotov stated that satisfaction of the Soviet request was the sine qua non condition for a peace treaty with Italy. The United States and Great Britain were wary. The United States, Byrnes recalled, had already offered Italy more than 500 million dollars in aid. It was about to grant it additional credit for economic reconstruction. It did not want to pay out millions of dollars so that Italy or Germany could pay their reparations debts.[54] Byrnes recalled that Italy had sizable assets in Romania, Bulgaria, and Hungary, which could be considered partial payment of the reparations owed to the USSR.[55] If the Soviet Union pursued its claims without taking Italy's economic problems into account, there would indeed be no peace treaty, Byrnes added. Bevin supported the United States position unreservedly.[56] There was every indication that Great Britain and the US intended to encourage Italy's economic reconstruction and keep the country within their political sphere. This position was linked to their desire to restore the Western economies and to prevent the USSR from reigniting social conflict in Italy with its exorbitant claims; also, they intended to demobilize their military forces.

In early July, shortly before the peace conference and after several weeks of dispute, the Soviet side finally won their case in part: their requested figure of 100 million dollars in reparations was accepted. The sum would be levied on Italian assets in Hungary, Bulgaria, and Romania, which would further erode the economies of these Soviet-bloc countries. The USSR would receive reparations from Italy's current production as

52. Ibid., p. 334.
53. Opie, *The Search*, p. 133.
54. *FRUS 1946*, vol. 2, pp. 217–20.
55. *FRUS 1946*, vol. 2, p. 253.
56. *FRUS 1946*, vol. 2, pp. 217–20.

well. The payments would not, however, be automatic. Under the terms of its agreement with the Italian government, the Soviet Union would have to provide the raw materials necessary for the production of goods delivered as reparations. Moreover, given its economic situation, Italy would not be obliged to begin payment immediately. The agreement solved the problem of the USSR's reparation claims on Italy. Now, satisfaction must be given to Yugoslavia, Greece, Ethiopia, and Albania. Negotiations on these issues were to be held in New York, where Yugoslavia, with the USSR's support, would obtain 125 million, Greece 105 million dollars, Ethiopia 25 million, and Albania 5 million.[57]

The Collapse of the Potsdam Agreement

The United States and Great Britain had suggested scheduling a discussion of the peace treaty with Austria on the Council of Foreign Ministers agenda. In principle, the problem was easily resolved. At the Moscow conference in October 1943, the Allies had deemed Austria – albeit incorrectly – to have been the first free country to fall victim to Hitler's aggression. Consequently, they had committed to restore it to its status as a free, independent state. On 13 April 1945, two weeks after the Red Army liberated Vienna, the Soviet Union had authorized an interim Austrian government headed by the Socialist Karl Renner, whose minister of the interior was a Communist. Stalin had renounced his claim to reparations from Austria at the Potsdam conference. The Allied Control Council was established, and the Western Allies finally recognized the Renner government. Elections took place normally, resulting in a coalition government that included Communists, despite their poor showing in the elections.

Bevin and Byrnes had circulated a draft treaty. The Western powers' objective was clear: they intended to re-establish Austria's independence by terminating the occupation of its territory as soon as possible. The presence of Red Army forces in Austria's Soviet sector signed away the future of a country that the Western powers still hoped to remove from the Kremlin's influence. As in Germany, the Soviet Union had begun to dismantle many industries and continued to monopolize Austrian economic resources situated in its sector. As long as the occupation continued, the USSR could legitimate its military presence in Hungary, Romania, and even in Bulgaria on the pretext that these countries lay on its lines of communication with Austria. The Soviet Union attempted to ensure that its occupation of these countries would continue after the

57. Opie, *The Search*, p. 108–12.

peace treaties. It therefore had every reason to drag out negotiations on Austria. This appeared to be what motivated Molotov's obstinate refusal to discuss signing a peace treaty with that country. He accused the British and the Americans of doing nothing to liquidate the vestiges of nazism there. When, in July, Byrnes and Bevin repeated their desire to open the debate on Austria, his opposition was fierce. Before he would examine the draft treaty with Austria, the Western sectors must evacuate hundreds of thousands of "displaced persons" from the troops that had fought alongside Nazi Germany, among whom he said there were "fascist soldiers" from General Wladislaw Anders's Polish army, which had fought on the Italian front.[58]

On 29 April, Byrnes submitted for discussion a four-power draft treaty guaranteeing Germany's demilitarization for twenty-five years. He said in substance:

> The Governments represented on the Council, [showed] a lack of confidence in each other, as was evidenced in their disagreements over little things. At Yalta he had heard Generalissimo Stalin say that twice in twenty-five years Germany had attacked Russia through Poland and Russia had suffered. France had expressed the same fears, and France's experience justified these fears. [...] The views and attitudes of peoples were due to fear of German aggression and to lack of security. [...] [After the First World War] Germany had been permitted to re-arm. That must not happen again. In the hope of contributing to that aim, the United States had, as far back as February of [that] year, submitted a draft of a proposed treaty providing for the demilitarization of Germany in the period following the termination of the occupation.[59]

Although the United States' proposal earned a positive response from Bevin and Bidault, Molotov's reaction was, on the contrary, hardly welcoming: before worrying about the future, one had first to get on with Germany's disarmament. The US program would slow this process. The Soviet minister refused to commence discussions of the treaty until the Allied Control Council had appointed an investigative body to determine whether the Potsdam decisions on disarmament had been carried out in all of the sectors. Molotov's charges were vague, and his request was clearly intended to delay giving a response to the proposal. The existing agreements, as Bevin recalled, made it possible to conduct inspections in all of the sectors. In any case, such an investigation should not hold up discussions of the US program for German disarmament pursuant to

58. *FRUS 1946*, vol. 2, p. 939.
59. *FRUS 1946*, vol. 2, pp. 166–7.

the peace treaty.[60]

Byrnes hoped to find a solution to the German question soon. He felt that the Russians were not respecting their commitment to treat Germany as a single economy, and objected that it had become practically impossible to know what was happening in their sector. The secretary of state confided to his British counterpart that General Clay had just been authorized to stop reparations payments to the USSR until the problem of German economic unity had been settled. It was out of the question to pursue a reparations policy while Germany's imports and exports were still unbalanced. The United States was determined to force the decision.[61] On 3 May, the United States announced that it would suspend reparations payments until Germany was treated as a single economy. The measure affected the French as much as it did the Russians.

In early July, Byrnes again submitted his draft treaty providing for guaranteed German disarmament. This time, Molotov responded formally to the proposal. He considered it to be totally inadequate, for it evaded the issues of armament industry, Germany's reconstruction on democratic bases, and reparations. Once again he accused the Western powers of not proceeding with German disarmament and reproached them for using any and all pretexts to cover up their refusal to enforce the Potsdam agreement.

In the summer of 1946, the United States and Great Britain were staunchly determined to put an end the obstruction of economic recovery in their sectors, and above all to counter the course of Soviet policy in Germany. Now more than ever, the German question was at the heart of the peace settlement; solving it was essential to the establishment of a system of European security. From 9 to 12 July, in a climate of continued mutual acrimony, the Council of Foreign Ministers reopened its debate on Germany. Molotov denounced the US decision to suspend reparations payments to the USSR. Bidault made a lengthy statement reaffirming his former position on the Ruhr and the Rhineland, asking for more coal from the Ruhr, yet at the same time supporting the US secretary of state's four-power draft treaty.[62] Bevin tried to clarify Great Britain's position on Germany. The peace in Europe, he explained, could be envisaged in three ways: as a balance of power between equally strong states; as the predominance of one power or a balance between two blocs; or finally as a cooperative Allied policy to control Germany. Great Britain preferred the last option: it would make it possible to rectify the standard of living in Europe and to further increase the prestige of European cultural influence in the world. The division of Europe must be prevented at all

60. Ibid., p. 167.
61. Meeting between Bevin and Byrnes of 5 May (FO 800/513).
62. Ibid., pp. 860–4.

costs. Bevin recalled that the Potsdam provisions to treat Germany as a single economy had not been put into effect. Germany's division subsequent to the Soviet sector's complete isolation was forcing British taxpayers to subsidize the British sector. The rift between the occupied sectors would ultimately disunite Europe. This created serious difficulties and jeopardized the peace. Bevin said that Great Britain was still prepared to cooperate with the other sectors on a reciprocal basis. If cooperation continued to prove impossible, the British government would be forced to change its economic policy for Germany. In other words, it would increase production levels in the British sector to ensure payment of the imports necessary for the sector's economic activity.[63] Bevin then put the question to Molotov: was the Soviet side agreed that German resources must be distributed equitably, and would it help to draw up an import-export program for all of Germany that would take priority over reparations payments? Molotov immediately answered, "no." Bevin retorted that thereafter the British would organize industry in their sector in such a way that it could produce exports. Great Britain did not intend to spend its dollars to import food to Germany. Byrnes joined in, recalling that the sectors were completely isolated despite the Potsdam agreement, and that there was no longer any exchange of goods, persons, or ideas between them. He proposed therefore that they reestablish free trade and adopt a common policy for all of Germany.[64] Byrnes was also convinced that a new German government structure must be created.

Molotov would have none of this. Despite his colleagues' injunctions, he obstinately refused to contemplate Germany's effective economic unity. He barred the Western powers from conducting investigations – especially into arms production – in the Soviet sector. Above all, he refused to appoint a body that could commence negotiations of the German peace treaty. He repeated his reparations claims, but would not supply the information needed to satisfy his demands, nor would he engage in a cooperative economic policy to facilitate payment. Byrnes announced at this point that pending an agreement among the four powers in accordance with the Potsdam agreement, the United States was prepared to unite its sector with those of the other occupying powers that wished to treat Germany a single economy.[65] This, obviously, was a nod to Bevin's demands. The move to merge the two sectors had begun.

On 6 September, after having obtained the president's assent and heard the counsel of Congressional leaders and his principal political and military advisers, Secretary of State Byrnes made an important speech

63. Ibid., p. 868.
64. Ibid., p. 873.
65. Ibid., p. 897.

in Stuttgart. He repeated his proposal to encourage economic unity between the United States sector and the other occupied sectors and proposed that an interim German government be established. If it proved impossible to unify the country completely, the United States government would strive to encourage the "maximum possible unification." He said, finally, that the United States would not allow Germany to become the satellite of any power whatsoever and that the American forces would remain in the country for as long as the other occupying powers did.[66] Hence, United States leadership seemed to be resigning itself to Germany's division, and in turn to the division of Europe.

In the United States, the "get tough" USSR policy was causing a stir among the liberal community, and even within the administration. Trade Secretary and former United States Vice-President Henry Wallace was still attached to the ideals of the alliance with the USSR. He had taken a firm position against Churchill's speech at Fulton and warned against the risks of a nuclear arms race. He pleaded the USSR's case to President Truman, and held that they must grant it a loan to foster the development of Soviet–US trade relations. On 12 September during the Congressional election campaign, he delivered a foreign policy speech at Madison Square Garden. He argued in favor of spheres of influence, holding that the United States must realize that it should not involve itself in East European affairs, just as Russia should not intervene in Latin American or Western European affairs. Notwithstanding, he defended the principle of trade liberalization world-wide, including Eastern Europe. He also challenged Great Britain's "imperialist" policy, while recommending that the Russians abandon their claim to replace capitalism with communism. Implicitly, he criticized Secretary of State Byrnes's policy, stating that it was impossible to change the direction of Soviet foreign policy by taking a harsher tone with the USSR. His liberal, idealistic rhetoric, which smacked of Midwestern isolationism, was counter to the administration's strategic thinking. It appeared to take the exact opposite position to Byrnes's recent stance on Germany. President Harry Truman finally asked his recalcitrant trade secretary to step down. The outcome of this government skirmish showed that the United States had indeed resolved to get tough in peace treaty negotiations with the USSR.[67]

On 29 July, twenty-one government representatives met in Paris to discuss the draft peace treaties that the Council of Foreign Ministers had drawn up. This conference would rise on 15 October. The debates were

---

66. *Department of State Bulletin,* 15 September 1946, pp. 96–501.
67. John L. Gaddis, *The United States and the Origins of the Cold War, 1941–1947,* New York, Columbia University Press, 1972, pp. 337 et seq.; Donovan, *Conflict and Crisis,* pp. 219 et seq.

public and the arguments intense. As the council had failed to agree on the contents of the peace treaties with Italy, Hungary, Bulgaria, and Romania, the four-power ministers used the new setting to defend their political thinking. This "public" diplomacy exacerbated the effects of propaganda and deepened antagonism. Molotov was even more isolated than usual, although he had the Yugoslav and Czech representatives' support. He brought up the debate over procedure again by returning to the still undecided status of the conference's recommendations. The ministers had spent nearly fifteen days debating this question. He also demanded that separate committees' discussions be submitted to the plenary session, thereby imposing a pointless repetition of the same proceedings and the same votes by the same persons. There were particularly virulent diatribes among Greeks, Bulgarians, and Albanians on the issues of the regions north of Epirus, and Thrace. Molotov took advantage of this exchange to attack the Greek government, challenging its territorial ambitions and its policy of terrorist repression, which it enforced with aid from Great Britain. In early September, Ukraine submitted a new debate of this affair to the Security Council, denouncing Greece's policy toward its northern neighbors as a threat to peace.

The lumbering pace of the peace treaty negotiations, due essentially to Molotov's inflexibility, his support of Yugoslavia's claims in the Adriatic, and the apparently irreducible disagreement between the British and the Americans and the Soviet Union over Germany and Austria, all combined to widen the gap between the United States and the USSR, and tended to confirm the Western leaders' worries about Soviet policy.

7

THE DEVELOPMENT OF THE COLD WAR

The Crystallization of Ideological Antagonism

In the early summer, President Truman instructed Clark Clifford, one of his personal advisers, to draw up a secret report on US–Soviet relations. Clifford, a lawyer with no particular expertise in the matter, took on G. Elsey, a young navy lieutenant, as his assistant. He consulted many government figures, including the secretary of state, the war and navy secretaries, the justice secretary, Admiral Leahy, the Joint Chiefs of Staff, intelligence specialists, and, naturally, George Kennan. His study, submitted to the president in September 1946, reviewed the two countries' diplomatic relations since 1942. It went on to analyze the USSR's ideological foundations, political objectives, and military capacity. Echoing the substance of Kennan's analyses, he recalled that the Soviet leaders believed conflict between the USSR and the capitalist states to be inevitable, and was preparing to meet the challenge. All over the world, but especially in Europe, the Middle East, China, Japan, and Latin America, the USSR was seeking through various means to extend its influence and undermine the US position. For this reason, it sought to increase its military strength as rapidly as possible and to weaken other nations. Soviet propaganda in Latin America aimed to shatter solidarity in the hemisphere so as to stop the flow of raw materials to the United States. Communist parties everywhere were mobilized to serve this policy of hegemony. The Soviet Union was causing delays in the peace treaty negotiations in order to consolidate its influence in Eastern Europe. The USSR was therefore a direct threat to national security, for the United States had become the main target of its aggressive strategy.[1]

The USSR did not yet have the means to engage in heavy military action beyond the "Eurasian landmass." Nevertheless, by acquiring an air force and strategic missiles, increasing its naval forces, building atomic bombs, and developing its biological weapons, the USSR would soon be able to strike any point on the globe, and this was the goal it was pursuing. The operational forces of the Red Army and Soviet aviation were far greater than those of the American units in Germany, Austria,

1. Quoted by Arthur Krock, *Memoirs. Sixty Years on the Firing Line,* New York, Eagle Books, 1968, pp. 393–453.

and Korea. Consequently, the United States must be prepared to use its atomic and biological weapons. A war against the USSR would be total in the most terrifying sense of the term. It was therefore necessary to develop research in offensive and defensive weapons: "The mere fact of preparedness may be the only powerful deterrent to Soviet aggressive action and in this sense the only sure guarantee of peace."[2]

Clifford also proposed that the United States should make it its policy to support "all democratic countries which are in any way menaced or endangered by the USSR." He felt, however, that military aid should be offered only as a last resort. He advocated primarily economic assistance through trade agreements, loans, and technical assistance programs. "The United States can do much to ensure that economic opportunities, personal freedom and social equality are made possible in countries outside the Soviet sphere by generous financial assistance."[3]

The Clifford report translated the extravagant image of the USSR that was coming to the fore among United States leaders, and in particular among the military. It gave a distorted view of Soviet power, notably in underestimating the effects of the recent war. Melvyn P. Leffler writes that at the time, army intelligence reckoned the Soviet Union would need about fifteen years to overcome war casualties, five to ten years to restore long-range military aviation, and fifteen to twenty years to rebuild its navy. There was every indication, however, that the USSR was still too weak in the years immediately following the war to envisage foreign military action: it would have to rebuild its communications network and its industry first.[4] Of course, Clifford acknowledged that the Soviet threat was not imminent, and his report reflected the military's desire to plan an armaments program to meet the new strategic challenges presented by the Kremlin.

As the peace treaty negotiations unfolded, the Foreign Office also became convinced that Soviet foreign policy was a response to revolutionary aims, and the overriding image of the USSR in British diplomatic circles was hardly different from that in Washington. Roberts wrote to Bevin on 4 September 1946 that the Soviet Union was above all an anomalous, abnormal element in the international society. Its ambitions surpassed those of traditional totalitarian powers, for they derived primarily from an ideology. Unless its regime changed, the USSR would not abandon any of its political goals or renounce any of its revolutionary techniques. A weak economy would not discourage it from moving in

2. Ibid., pp. 448–9.
3. Ibid., p. 450.
4. Melvyn P. Leffler, *A Preponderance of Power. National Security, the Truman Administration and the Cold War,* Stanford, Stanford University Press, 1992, pp. 133–4.

this direction, and, contrary to a broadly-shared notion, it would not be appeased by economic aid or a reinforcement of its power. Roberts felt it was futile to hope for a general settlement of the ideological and political conflict: the fact that there were now two separate, coexisting worlds must be faced. It seemed that the USSR would not resort to war and that it would be possible sporadically to find grounds for agreement with the state on specific problems. He recommended diplomacy that was firm, fair, courteous, and prudent, but he suggested that the Foreign Office get used to living in an atmosphere of permanent tension.[5]

In the 1 October 1946 memorandum entitled "The Strategic Aspects of British Foreign Policy," Permanent Under-Secretary at the Foreign Office Sir Orme Sargeant confirmed Roberts's point of view by repeating that as long as the Soviet leaders held the aberrant idea that a confrontation between communism and capitalism was inevitable, they would do all they could to undermine British and US influence in the world. Great Britain would have to join the United States in a concerted effort to define a modus vivendi with the USSR. If this proved unfeasible, however, it would have no option but to put up an efficient resistance buttressed by a strong economy, while it held on to important strategic regions. The United Kingdom should stress the values of freedom and tolerance in its propaganda. He also suggested encouraging the less developed countries to modernize their economies according to the Western model. Poverty among other peoples must be fought with technical aid. Sargeant predicted that the risk of confrontation with the USSR would be greatest in the southern regions, and notably in Turkey, Greece, and northern Persia. In his opinion, the Soviet Union would continue to support Arab nationalists in the Middle East, but would also offer aid to the Jewish immigration movement in Palestine. In Western Europe, the USSR would take a particular interest in Scandinavia, which controlled access to the Baltic. It had also set itself the objective of establishing Communist governments, or at least strong fifth columns, in France, the Netherlands, and Italy. It would stir up a new outburst of civil war in Spain in order to install a Communist government in the country and gain a toehold in the Iberian peninsula. The USSR would consolidate its influence in the Far East by creating a network of satellite states, some of which would be in China. In Korea, Sargeant predicted a direct face-off between the United States and the Soviet Union. He thought that it was hardly possible to help those East European states that were already under Soviet control, but that a love of democratic ideals must be imparted to these countries nevertheless. Poland remained the greatest hope, for the Poles were "born conspirators." Sargeant also thought that Western societies must change their defense

5. FO 371/56835.

systems. The Communists were attempting to exploit popular discontent linked to poverty, social frustrations, and feelings of injustice. They spurred hatred and employed violence. To combat this reactionary strategy one must offer the contrast of a consistent political doctrine including an advanced social program designed to create full employment and extended unemployment insurance and educational opportunities. The Western governments must compel and educate, and create a militant opposition similar to the Communists' to combat the effects in all regions of a dangerous revolutionary ideology.[6]

The USSR continued to isolate itself. The 11 July issue of *Pravda* stated that the Communist party's slackened self-criticism diminished vigilance among its militant members and facilitated the activities of anti-Soviet elements. The new United States ambassador in Moscow, General Bedell Smith, reported a marked, more serious outbreak of repression, notably against persons working at the United States mission.[7] In August, the CPSU Central Committee published a decree on literature and the arts, which clearly aimed to restore Stalinist orthodoxy and purge the elites of Western bourgeois ideas. Andrei A. Zhdanov blamed the intelligentsia, in particular the poet Anna Akhmatova and the literary circle in Leningrad.[8] Through its propaganda, which reeked of anti-Semitism, the Communist party intended to win back control over every aspect of the USSR's economic and social activity, and especially its industry, agriculture, press, and army, in order to counteract the Soviet people's sense of apathy and its low morale. The regime had tolerated a certain measure of liberalization during the war. Ideological repression and the reappearance of articles on the capitalist crisis were bringing an end to this laxness and taking the war-weary people back in hand. The government was confronted with the enormous task of reconstruction, and it appeared that Stalin would not be able to keep the promises he had made early in the year to avoid rationing. The summer harvests had been disastrous. Famine was developing in several regions. In October, the price of subsistence goods, and notably of bread, rose considerably.[9]

On 27 September 1946, shortly after Clifford presented his study, the Soviet ambassador in Washington, Nicolai Novikov, addressed a long dispatch to his foreign minister explaining the gist of United States foreign policy. Molotov himself had suggested the text, apparently in an effort to confirm his intransigent position in the peace treaty negotiations to

---

6. Ibid.
7. *FRUS 1945*, vol. 5, pp. 768–70.
8. Ibid., pp. 774–6.
9. Ibid., report by Dubrow, American chargé d'affaires, of 30 August (pp. 778–80), and telegram of 31 October. See also the report by British Ambassador Peterson, Annual Report on Soviet Union, 1946 (FO 371/66433).

the Kremlin.[10] It was not lacking in formal similarities to Kennan's "Long Telegram":

> The foreign policy of the United States, which reflects the imperialist tendencies of monopolistic American capital, is characterized in the postwar period by a striving for world supremacy. This is the real meaning of the many statements by President Truman and other representatives of American ruling circles: that the United States has the right to lead the world. All the forces of American diplomacy – the army, the air force, the navy, industry, and science – are enlisted in the service of this foreign policy. For this purpose broad plans for expansion have been developed and are being implemented through diplomacy and the establishment of a system of naval and air bases stretching far beyond the boundaries of the United States, through the arms race, and through the creation of ever newer types of weapon.

The Russian diplomat continued his analysis by developing geostrategic conceptions of world politics. In his view, the two great fascist powers of Germany and Japan, which were the United States' main economic and political rivals, had been defeated completely. Great Britain faced enormous difficulties and its Empire had been shaken down to its foundations, as witnessed the situations in India, Palestine, and Egypt. Hence, monopolistic American capitalism was given free rein to strengthen its position by exporting industrial goods and capital to the European and Asian countries which the war had left penniless. However, the USSR was an impediment to US world supremacy. It had fortified its position on the international stage significantly through the heroic victories of its armed forces. It had stationed military forces in Germany and other formerly hostile countries. Therefore, it could influence the democratic reconstruction of the countries it had liberated and rely on their friendship and assistance. The American imperialists saw this state of affairs as a hindrance to their policy of hegemony. With Truman's arrival in office and Byrnes's nomination, the United States government had succumbed to the influence of the Democratic party's most reactionary groups and broken with President Roosevelt's policy, which had incorporated cooperation with the USSR and other peaceful countries. The United States was in the process of increasing its military spending, and was attempting to build a broad network of naval and air force bases in the Atlantic and the Pacific, which manifested its adherence to an offensive strategy. To see its aggressive projects through, it had made an

10. See further, the interesting debate that arose from this document's discovery, in *Diplomatic History*, 15 (4), fall 1991, notably with the participation of George Kennan, pp. 523–63.

agreement with Great Britain to divide the world into spheres of influence. It had thus gained the right to act at will in China and Japan, while Great Britain would maintain its hegemony over a large portion of the rest of Asia and notably over India and Indonesia. The United States and Great Britain were not yet agreed on the Mediterranean and the Near East, and American capital was being used to gain influence in the Near East and to win new oil concessions in the Persian Gulf. This development was reflected, to name one example, in Anglo–American differences over Palestine. Notwithstanding, the United States leaders envisaged a military alliance with Great Britain, and the two countries had coordinated their policies for international conferences. Relations between Great Britain and the United States were, however, compromised by major conflicts, and their partnership could not last. The Near East was potentially the focus of these conflicts. At the time, the United States intended to diminish the USSR's political role in Eastern Europe so as to take its place there. To facilitate capital flows from the United States to the East European countries, it was attempting to block the democratization process. It was seeking to strengthen the influence of reactionary groups in Germany. It would put an end to the country's occupation so as to restore it to imperial power. It would spread a "war psychosis" the world over.[11]

The New Strategy of the United States in the Mediterranean and the Middle East

Essentially a maritime power, the United States had never had the intention nor the strategic means to put up a serious resistance to the Soviet Union's seizure of the East European countries. Along the borders of its empire, the Kremlin had considerable military and police strength at its disposal, but it was also supported by indigenous political forces, the spearhead of which was the Communist party. However, the USSR's policy in Romania and Bulgaria, combined with its constant efforts to pressure Turkey and Persia, the many border clashes between Greece and its northern neighbors of Albania, Yugoslavia, and Bulgaria, and Soviet criticism of British policy before the United Nations, seemed to trace a line of Russian penetration to the Mediterranean and the Middle East, and this movement had prompted United States leadership to revise its strategy. The USSR's threats against Turkey, Greece, and Persia were of eminently greater concern to United States interests than the development

11. Quoted by Kenneth M. Jensen (ed.), *Origins of the Cold War. The Novikov, Kennan, and Roberts's "Long Telegrams" of 1946,* Washington, United States Institute of Peace, 1991, pp. 3–15.

of a Russian sphere of influence in Eastern Europe, for these threats were leveled against strategically important countries in communications among Europe, Asia, and Africa, and in controlling Middle Eastern oil resources. The fact that Great Britain no longer had the economic and military capacity to hold these regions under Western hegemony made such perils even more formidable.

On 7 August, the Soviet government formally restated its request to participate on an equal footing with Turkey in the defense of the Dardanelles and the regulatory administration of the Black Sea straits and the Mediterranean. Edwin Wilson, the United States ambassador in Ankara, interpreted this request as an expression of their desire to control Turkey. In his view, Turkey's defense was essential in protecting United States interests, and especially in preventing the USSR from expanding toward the Persian Gulf and the Suez Canal. Because of these diplomatic and military pressures, Turkey was in a state of emergency, which required mobilizing 500,000 men, and this was a heavy burden on its national budget. The Red Army's movements in Bulgaria were also worrying.[12] Truman, as well as officials from the Departments of State, the Navy, and War, deemed the pressure on Turkey to be inadmissible. Moreover, they had convinced themselves that it constituted a tremendous threat to the eastern Mediterranean, and ultimately to the entire Middle East.

Convinced of this strategic prognosis, which was unusual to say the least if one takes into account the condition of the USSR at the time, the president decided to stand resolutely opposed to Soviet demands on Turkey. He was even prepared to resort to military action. The Turkish government was asked to remain firm. The Department of State sent a memorandum to Moscow repeating that it refused to accept the powers on the Black Sea having sole regulatory authority over the straits, and that it recognized Turkey's right to retain principal responsibility in defending these maritime passages. The United States government planned to harmonize its policy of aid to Turkey and Greece with Britain's.

This reaction manifested United States leadership's will to take over for Great Britain in the Mediterranean. Their determination would become increasingly focused. On 9 September, William Clayton wrote to Byrnes, who was engaged in negotiations in Paris, to inform him that the USSR was attempting to upset stability in Greece and Turkey so as to gain control of the Near East and the Middle East. Soviet ambitions, he said, forced the United States to define a new policy.[13] A few days later, on 19

12. *FRUS 1946*, vol. 7, pp. 836–8. See also Bruce R. Kuniholm, *The Origins of the Cold War in the Near East. Great Power Conflict and Diplomacy in Iran, Turkey, and Greece*, Princeton, Princeton University Press, 1980, p. 360.
13. *FRUS 1946*, vol. 7, pp. 209–13.

September, Loy Henderson publicly aired the new direction of United States strategy. Its objective, he said, was to prevent rivalry and conflicts of interest in the region from leading to a third world war. The Middle East had great strategic value, for it was at the crossroads of East–West communications. It had large mineral resources and a great agricultural potential. Unfortunately, its peoples were in general very poor. Their societies were backward, dissatisfied with their situation, and shaken up by nationalist currents. Their governments were weak and lacked the economic resources to appease national unrest and ensure domestic order. The greatest concern, however, was the fact that they were incapable of coping with threats from abroad. Consequently, Henderson suggested that the United States should aid economic and political progress in the Middle East. He proposed setting up a broad program of cultural, economic, financial, and technical assistance to this end. The United States, he explained, wished to promote its "open doors" policy and eliminate policies that hindered its economic and commercial interests in the region; it also wished to promote its private investments there.[14]

By taking over Great Britain's strategic interests in the Middle East, the United States also became involved in protecting the conservative regime in Greece. In January 1946, it offered Greece a 25-million-dollar loan. This proved quite insufficient, and requests from the Greek government became pressing. In July 1946, the Greek prime minister, Constantine Tsaldaris, took the occasion of a meeting with Byrnes to submit a financial aid request for 6 billion dollars.[15] The request was totally unrealistic. Moreover, it came from a government that had bad press in the United States because it was perceived as reactionary, incompetent, and corrupt. The Department of State was, however, worried about the prevailing economic and social conditions in Greece. In Washington, Soviet ambitions in the Mediterranean and the Middle East were naturally connected with Communist subversion.

In late September, after the Soviet Union had vetoed a Security Council resolution to investigate the Greek border clashes, Navy Secretary James Forrestal announced that the United States intended to maintain a permanent fleet in the Mediterranean. It would soon have an aircraft carrier, three cruisers, and eight destroyers, making it the foremost sea power in the region.[16] The Department of State and the military were

14. "Address delivered before the annual meeting of the National Association of Secretaries of State in Los Angeles, Calif., on 19 Sept. 1946," *Department of State Bulletin*, 29 September 1946, pp. 590–6.
15. Lawrence S. Wittner, *American Intervention in Greece, 1943–1949*, New York, Columbia University Press, 1981, p. 50.
16. Thomas G. Paterson, *On Every Front, The Making of the Cold War*, New York, Norton, 1979, pp. 187–9; Kuniholm, *The Origins of the Cold War*, pp. 373–4.

convinced that Greece was strategically important and that the threats to the country were real. On 15 October 1946, Byrnes met with British Defence Minister A.V. Alexander on the problem. He expressed his desire to see Great Britain continue its military aid to Greece, intimating that the United States also could grant it economic aid.[17]

The request was especially urgent since the USSR was consolidating its sphere of influence in the Balkans. In Bulgaria, the October elections, which, as one might expect, had been fixed, gave 78% of the vote to the National Front, which was a Communist fiefdom, and 22% to the opposition. This made it possible to appoint a government that was entirely favorable to the Kremlin. In Romania, the noncommunist parties' positions continued to deteriorate and their chance of surviving seemed to shrink. It appeared that the opposition, and notably the National Peasant and Liberal parties, would have to drop out of the electoral campaign, for the police was censoring their statements, arresting their activists, breaking up their meetings, and manipulating the voter lists.[18] In mid-October, the Foreign Office sent a note to the Romanian government reminding it of its obligation to hold free, democratic elections. The United States did the same, but their efforts were fruitless. The fixed results of the November ballot gave a majority to the Communists, and the National Democratic Front candidates won a sweeping majority of parliamentary seats. One week later, a huge trial modeled after Stalin's Great Moscow Trials during the purges of the 1930s was held to prosecute the generals and the large opposition party members who had been arrested on 27 May and now stood accused of promoting terrorist organizations.[19]

Washington was coming to the conclusion that Greece was the last state in the Balkans to escape from Soviet hegemony, and that, with Turkey, it formed the sole obstacle to Soviet domination in the eastern Mediterranean. On 21 October, a memorandum from the Office of Near Eastern and African Affairs stated: "Many signs indicate that Greece is becoming a focal point in strained international relations and that its fate during the next few months may be a deciding factor in the future orientation of the Near and Middle East." The document recalled that border clashes between Greece and its neighboring countries of Bulgaria, Yugoslavia, and Albania were on the rise, and that the Communists and extreme right-wing groups had caused another outbreak of the civil war. Defending Greece was a challenge in the enforcement of United Nations principles, and free countries must be able to rely on United States

17. FO 371/58658; quoted by Wittner, *American Intervention,* p. 52.
18. *FRUS 1946,* vol. 6, p. 633.
19. Ibid., pp. 658–62.

support.[20] Without it, the Greek government could not cope successfully with Communist subversion and foreign aggression abetted by the USSR. Consequently, the United States must show its will to preserve Greek independence by acknowledging that it had a strategic interest in this policy. Byrnes approved the memorandum, which clearly declared a strong US commitment to the regime in power in Athens. He recommended that the United States prepare to supply military and economic assistance to Greece in case the British failed. This about-face in US policy gave the Labour government, which had been urging the United States to come to Great Britain's aid in the Mediterranean and the Middle East since the end of the war, every reason to be satisfied.

Persia also remained a source of concern in Washington for strategic reasons. Although Soviet forces had withdrawn from the country in May, the problem of Azerbaijan's secession remained. The central government was feeble and its actions were undermined by the subversive machinations of the Communist party, which had organized an endless string of protest demonstrations in the big cities. Added to this was ethnic unrest in the south. The Soviet Union took advantage of the situation to demand that the oil agreement they had signed with the Persian government be submitted to the parliament.

In September, Loy Henderson pointed out the gravity of the situation, and stated that Persia must be prevented from slipping into the Soviet sphere.[21] Henderson had sounded out the Joint Chiefs of Staff, who had emphasized Persia's strategic importance in the case of a war against the USSR. The country had large oil resources. Because of its geographic situation, it should play an essential role in Near Eastern and Middle Eastern defense. A Soviet sphere of influence in northern Persia must therefore be prevented. If the USSR managed to maintain its control of Azerbaijan or to create and dominate an autonomous Kurdistan, it would be in a good position to spread its influence over southern Persia, Iraq, the Persian Gulf, and Saudi Arabia, and these countries' oil fields were indispensable to United States security.[22]

In mid-October, the Department of State hardened its line with the Persian government, pressing it to take measures to resist renewed pressure from the USSR. It was concerned to learn that Prime Minister Ahmad Qavam was negotiating an aviation agreement with the USSR that would grant it a monopoly on airborne communications, which was inconsistent with the international civil aviation agreement. It had also learned that the Soviet Union knew of internal deliberations in the Persian

20. *FRUS 1946*, vol. 7, pp. 240–5.
21. *FRUS 1946*, vol. 2, p. 524.
22. For the position of the Joint Chiefs of Staff, see *FRUS 1946*, vol. 7, pp. 529–32.

cabinet, and that they had hence taken the liberty of pressuring some of its members.[23] The United States representative in Teheran decided to intervene directly with the shah and appeal to him for a change in government. On 14 October, he suggested that the shah organize a plot against his own government, promising him US military aid. The measure brought results. Shortly after, elections were announced and the prime minister decided to send troops to scout out the rebellion in Azerbaijan. Now that he was sure of United States support, especially in the Security Council, he disregarded Soviet threats. The Persian army arrived in Tabriz late in the year, and partisans of the Communist regime were chased out or massacred. The repression would be terrible.

The Peace Talks Recommence

The peace treaty negotiations were scheduled to reopen in New York among the foreign ministers of the four big powers. If possible they should, based on the results of the Paris conference, conclude the negotiations on the Third Reich's former allied or satellite states, which had been going on since the end of the war. Once again, the talks got off to a bad start. At the United Nations General Assembly on 29 October, Molotov delivered a harsh propaganda speech, stigmatizing the aggressive imperialist groups which were willing to engage in the riskiest military ventures in order to take over the world. Churchill was their "prophet," and these groups had sympathizers in Great Britain and the United States. He also blamed "dollar diplomacy" and "atomic diplomacy." He implicitly condemned the United States by denouncing its policy of exerting pressure on small countries with naval flotillas and air squadrons.

The British and the Americans desired more than ever to bring a rapid end to the negotiations which had been dragging on for so long, in order to tackle the main problem in the European peace settlement, which was Germany. They were fed up with the deliberations. On 30 October, on a ship bound for New York, Bevin collapsed again and had to spend the rest of the crossing in bed. His staff was equally exhausted from "six months of frustration in Paris."[24] In New York, the negotiations were even more tiring than those in Paris, for they took place concurrently with the General Assembly sessions. Bevin also had to cope with problems stemming from the Egyptian and Palestinian affairs. On 20 November,

23. Kuniholm, *The Origins of the Cold War,* p. 387.
24. Piers Dixon, *Double Diploma. The Life of Sir Pierson Dixon, Don and Diplomat,* London, Hutchinson, 1968, p. 234.

he suffered another heart attack. Nevertheless, he delivered a long speech to the General Assembly the next day.[25]

The Council of Foreign Ministers sat from 4 November to 12 December. It began by examining each article of each peace treaty, and especially those of the Italian peace treaty. Molotov challenged the agreement on Trieste. This time, the United States representatives, exasperated by the turn the meeting was taking, made it clear it that they would happily accept its failure. On 25 November, Byrnes explained bluntly to Molotov that he was indifferent to the conference's outcome. The United States would no longer accept humiliation in the name of a pointless negotiation. It had made all the concessions it possibly could, one after the other. Also, it was time to end the sessions of the Council of Foreign Ministers, which increasingly resembled "a farce." The United States would continue the peace negotiations bilaterally if necessary.[26] The Soviet side changed its attitude and became more conciliatory.

The Council of Foreign Ministers reached an agreement at last in mid-December, but Molotov's obstruction tactics paid off in the end. Most of the discussions, during which the Western powers were constantly on the defensive, had been on the Italian treaty and Italy's dispute with Yugoslavia. Under the terms of the agreement, the USSR could maintain its occupation forces in Bulgaria, Romania, and Hungary until the end of Austria's joint occupation. Bevin had attempted to insert a clause in the peace treaties obliging the Soviet Union to withdraw its forces, but was unsuccessful. Moreover, the Western powers had given no support to the government in Hungary, the only country occupied by the Red Army that continued to uphold some liberal values. The US and British negotiators thus failed to reduce the reparations that would be levied on Hungary, yet they knew that the Hungarian economy was in a catastrophic state and that it would be left to the mercy of the USSR.[27] Furthermore, Hungary was to lose Transylvania, the population of which was still part Magyar. Romania was thus rewarded for its docility in following orders from Moscow, though it had once again lost Bessarabia and north Bukovina, which the USSR had taken back into its sphere.

The United States and Great Britain hoped to maintain an economic and political presence in the countries under Soviet domination, notably by obtaining the right of freedom of navigation on the Danube. This principle was far from winning approval, however. The Soviet side had adopted a French proposal, which stipulated that after the treaties were signed, a conference would be called among the four great powers and

25. Ibid., p. 241.
26. FO 800/522, pp. 1–3.
27. FO 800/468.

the riparian states to define an international regulatory code for the Danube. It became obvious, however, that this compromise was simply a stopgap measure to camouflage the USSR's refusal to tolerate free communications and trade in the countries within its sphere.[28]

To bring the peace treaty conference to a close, the Western powers had abandoned many of their principles. Bevin acknowledged this in a telegram to the British ambassador to Greece: "To arrive at this agreement, both Great Britain and the United States have made substantial sacrifices to their interests in Eastern Europe." They had done this, convinced that signing the treaties was the necessary condition for improving the situation in Eastern Europe, and especially for forcing the Soviet forces to withdraw.[29] As Warner suggested in a telegram to the Foreign Office on 23 December, this attitude was clearly the result of Byrnes's impatience to end the negotiations he had started; for the Soviet leaders had used the long duration of the peace talks to consolidate their sphere of influence in the Balkans.[30]

Challenges to Western Hegemony in Asia

As the borders of a huge rift between East and West were hardening in Europe, the Far East was going through a period of political upheaval, the consequences of which were unknown. The unrest was linked to the tragic aftermath of the war, but also to the strength of the political movements opposed to colonial imperial hegemony. In Asia as in Europe, history had taken a leap forward, transforming political and social concepts and changing worldviews. Great Britain's representative in Bangkok commented on the nature of these developments in a dispatch to the Foreign Office:

> We should realize that the world is passing with great travail through a colossal revolution and that, whether we like it or not, politico-economic power is everywhere coming into new hands. We must try and understand the mental processes of these new controlling elements and seek to gain their confidence. I mention this because I detect on occasion in the print a rather sad nostalgia for the disappearance of the nice, gifted people with whom diplomats once used to deal and who everywhere spoke the same language of wealth and privilege.[31]

28. Redvers Opie, *The Search for Peace Settlements,* Washington, The Brookings Institution, 1951, p. 164.
29. FO 800/458, p. 103.
30. FO 371/66379, 23 December 1946.
31. FO 371/56787, 19 July 1946.

At the international level, the move toward liberating colonized peoples was legitimated in liberal and Marxist ideologies, in the US and the USSR, respectively, as well as in the principles of equality and social justice laid down by the Charter of the United Nations. The United States government continued to support this movement, while attempting to control it and make it compatible with the defense of its own strategic interests. Loyal to the anticolonial position it had taken during the war, it made a commitment not to hinder the Philippines in their return to independence, freeing the islands in 1945. The Philippines declared sovereignty on 4 July 1946, but the United States managed to maintain its "unsought trust" over the young republic's economic and political activities. It secured a de facto monopoly of Philippine exports and backed the conservative landowners, who capitalized on US aid to take over when Manuel Roxas was elected president of the republic in April 1946. The United States also kept up its military bases in the Philippines.[32]

The British forces had pulled out of Indonesia, leaving the new republic to seek its sovereignty in a contest against the Dutch government, its malevolent guardian. The Dutch had made many exactions in the waning year, but on 15 November, with the Linggadjati agreement, it seemed at last to recognize the Indonesian republic and its government in Java and Sumatra. The agreement was complicated, and fragile as well. It did not guarantee full independence, and recognized the established rights of foreigners and the suzerainty of the Dutch crown. Its effects were not immediate; rather, they depended on the Dutch governor's goodwill.[33]

In Indochina, General de Gaulle's resignation had not changed the direction of French colonial policy. Its goals were clearly defined, and the program for a French Union laid down in the Fourth Republic's constitution, although it institutionalized new relations of authority, did not challenge the empire's fundamental structure. The French government was determined to maintain its hegemony in North Africa and to restore its power in Indochina. In Tonkin, it was running into resistance from the Vietnamese government under Ho Chi Minh. The agreement of 6 March 1946, which French representative Jean Sainteny signed with the young democratic republic of Vietnam recognizing the new, free state within the French Union, had not been respected by the French military. In addition, the Fontainebleau conference of 6 July to 1 August floundered over France's refusal to accept Vietnam's sovereignty and unity. Haiphong was bombed on 20 November, leaving many dead. On 19 December, the Vietminh attacked Hanoi, which was controlled by the French. In late

32. Philippe Richer, *L'Asie du Sud–Est. Indépendances et communismes*, Paris, Imprimerie nationale, 1981, pp. 147 et seq.
33. Ibid., pp. 147 et seq.

1946, the French government dispatched General Charles Leclerc to assess the military situation. After a brief stay, he recommended army reinforcements and continued warfare. Marius Moutet, the Socialist minister of French territories overseas, who had arrived in Indochina at the same time, supported a tough policy toward the Vietminh, which had Communist leanings. French imperialism aroused a sharp reaction in Asia. The Indian press was indignant and made repeated appeals to youth groups to come to the Vietnam Republic's aid in the fight against Western imperialism.[34]

There was a tendency among the Western ruling classes to suspect the USSR of lurking behind every movement that defied the structures of established order. It was true that the civil war and the national liberation movements in China and Southeast Asia were driven by the Communist party. In the fall, the United States' China policy had suffered serious setbacks. The objective it had set itself – to restore the nation to unity, independence, and democracy by enlarging the Chiang Kai-shek government and integrating Communists – now seemed impossible. The Nationalist leader, relying on the strength of his army, had called a national assembly on 15 November 1946 that excluded the Communist representatives, and thus shut the door on further negotiations with Mao Tse-tung's representative, Chou En-lai. Civil war had broken out again on a vast scale between the Communist forces and Chiang Kai-shek's Nationalist government. Its immediate object was control of Manchuria and northern China. Late in the year, General Marshall returned to the United States, aware that his peace mission had been ineffectual. On 7 January, shortly after he replaced Byrnes as secretary of state, he publicly exposed the reasons for his failure, placing much of the responsibility on the Nationalist government, which was controlled by a "group of reactionaries" who had done everything they could to defeat the creation of a real coalition government. He recommended cutting off United States aid to the dictatorial government.[35]

The Labour government hoped to preserve an "informal empire"[36] in the Middle East by keeping its military bases in Transjordania and Iraq, but the Palestinian affair complicated its task immensely. It needed a solution, for prolonging its mandate was contingent upon maintaining a strong military presence in the Near East, and carried an unbearable

34. Mr. Shone to the Secretary of the Cabinet, 24 January 1947 (FO 371/63451).
35. See Arthur Schlesinger, Jr., *The Dynamics of World Power. A Documentary History of United States Foreign Policy 1945–1973*, vol. 4, *The Far East*, New York, Chelsea House Publishers, 1973, pp. 124–8.
36. This is the term Ernest Bevin used in a speech in November 1945; quoted by Allan N. Bullock, *Ernest Bevin, Foreign Secretary 1945–1951*, Oxford, Oxford University Press, 1985, p. 114.

budgetary expense. Jewish terrorist organizations continued their murderous attacks. In July, Menahem Begin's *Irgun* group bombed the King David Hotel, which was British army headquarters in Jerusalem, leaving nearly one hundred dead and many wounded. London was outraged by the event. In the fall, Zionist terrorist organizations increased their activity in Europe by planting explosives in the British embassy in Rome on 31 October. Bevin tried once again to rally the Arabs to the program for regional autonomy, while carrying on negotiations with the Zionists. His efforts were futile. In late 1946, it seemed that all of London's initiatives to reconcile Great Britain's strategic interests with a policy acceptable to the different communities were bound for failure. The mandate had no future: Great Britain could not maintain its influence in the Middle East without alienating the Arab peoples and governments. The decision to abandon Palestine was not easy, however; for, as pointed out above, the military still hoped to maintain a presence in the Middle East to protect Great Britain's strategic, economic, and political interests.[37]

The Withdrawal of the British Empire

Control of the Mediterranean naturally required a British military presence in Greece, but was the strategy realistic? The defense of Greece was very expensive. Since June, Chancellor of the Exchequer Hugh Dalton had been asking the government to suspend aid to Greece, but the Foreign Office and the military were convinced that they must continue their current policy, and wished to maintain troops in Greece at least throughout the 1947 year.[38] The British ambassador in Athens as well as the commander in chief of the British forces in Greece stated in mid-November 1946 that a premature withdrawal could mean the loss of the country. The British units deterred neighboring countries from attacking and boosted Greek morale. The Foreign Office shared this point of view. "The withdrawal of our troops would be taken both by the Greeks themselves and by the Slav bloc as a marked lessening of our interest, and I think it would be very soon followed by a collapse in Greece which would almost inevitably lead to the domination by the Communists openly backed by the Slavic bloc."[39]

In the Peloponnese, however, the situation was deteriorating rapidly, and on 14 November a group of about 700 people attacked the village of Skra in the north, killing nineteen soldiers and burning most of the village. The Greek government submitted the affair to the Security Council,

37. FO 800/476.
38. Wittner, *American Intervention*, p. 64.
39. FO 800/458, p. 95.

stating, quite correctly, that the guerrillas were receiving aid from Albania, Bulgaria, and Yugoslavia. The new upsurge in civil war brought with it the continued deterioration of economic and social conditions. Greece sunk into chaos. The British now did all they could to engage the United States in supplying economic aid to Greece and Turkey.[40]

In a conversation with Byrnes on 25 November, Bevin mentioned the possibility that the British forces might soon withdraw from Greece.[41] Following the discussion, the Department of State acknowledged that while Great Britain should maintain the primary responsibility for supplying arms to Greece, the United States could arrange to meet the country's additional needs.[42] Concern was growing in Washington, and there was speculation that the USSR was attempting to separate Macedonia from Greece to attach it to the Yugoslav Federation, and to transfer western Thrace to Bulgaria as a prelude to heavier action in Turkey. The precedent of Azerbaijan naturally sprang to mind. The United States government had now resolved to support Great Britain's policy in Greece, and on 11 December Dean G. Acheson announced the envoy of a mission to Greece to study its reconstruction and development requirements. One week later, Prime Minister Constantine Tsaldaris arrived in Washington. Bevin had invited him to Paris in November and suggested that he go to Washington.[43] From 10 to 19 December, a violent argument over Greece's northern border raged among the great powers in the Security Council. An investigation committee was finally appointed. It began work on 30 January, and subsequently eight of its eleven members concluded that the guerrillas were indeed supported by neighboring countries. In late December, the Department of State pressed the British government to send military reinforcements to Greece. The Greek army must be given the means to preserve the country's territorial integrity and independence immediately. But how was the request to be fulfilled?

The British cabinet was increasingly divided over what policy to adopt. Bevin had received sharp criticism from the Labour party, where voices had been raised denouncing his attitude toward the USSR. The prime minister, without withdrawing his confidence in Bevin, was also unsure of British foreign policy and its strategic implications. On 1 December 1946, he wrote to Bevin at the peace conference in New York, to express his doubts. Great Britain had made commitments that it was not in a position to keep. This was especially true with respect to Greece. "I feel

40. Kuniholm, *The Origins of the Cold War*, p. 400.
41. FO 800/458, p. 99.
42. Gallman to Sargeant, 20 December (FO 371/67032).
43. *FRUS 1946*, vol. 7, pp. 286–8; *FRUS 1947*, vol. 5, pp. 2–3.

that we are backing a very lame horse," he wrote. More fundamentally, Attlee again questioned the traditional postulates of British strategy. In his opinion, the Mediterranean had lost its military importance, and Great Britain could not preserve its influence in the Middle East. The Commonwealth's defense depended on Lagos and Kenya. The countries bordering Russia, in particular Greece, Turkey, Iraq and Persia, were too weak to constitute an "effective barrier." He thought that some accommodation must be made with Russia so that, with London, it would recognize these countries' neutrality. Attlee also feared that the United States would use Great Britain to defend its own security interests, without taking any real responsibility in Europe.[44]

Clement Attlee had decided to complete the revision of imperial policy that had been embarked upon during the war, and he wished to hasten India's independence, which would also affect Burma. On 20 December, the prime minister announced to the House of Commons that Aung Sang, a fierce opponent of British imperialism and a wartime ally of Japan, was arriving in London. This gesture signaled the prime minister's determination to turn a page in history by abandoning Great Britain's imperial policy in Asia. Burma's independence heralded that of India, the jewel in the crown. Before the Commons, Churchill expressed his anger by accusing the Labour government of "scuttling" the Empire. Despite Bevin's qualms, the prime minister was preparing to announce a firm deadline for India's rise to full independence. Grave disturbances had flared up in August, leaving some 5,000 dead in Calcutta alone. It was obvious that the British authorities were losing their hopes of reconciling the members of the Muslim League with those of the Congress.

In early January 1947, Attlee elaborated on his strategic considerations, repeating his reservations over the British presence in the Middle East. Maintaining bases in the region seemed to him both too costly and outdated. This strategy required an ability to provide economic and military support to Turkey, Greece, Persia, Lebanon, Syria, Egypt, and Transjordania. It also implied prolonging Britain's mandate in Palestine. Consequently, Great Britain would be dragged into an economic and political confrontation with the USSR in the Middle East and Europe. As in Greece, Great Britain would be accused of supporting indefensible regimes: "We, therefore, endeavouring to keep our influence over this congeries of weak, backward and reactionary States, have to face the USSR." The USSR, the prime minister recalled, was organized with an iron discipline; it was armed with a revolutionary ideology that attracted the masses; from a strategic point of view, it was admirably situated and

44. FO 800/475, 1 December 1946.

could penetrate as far as the Middle East, or attack certain nerve centers. By attempting to preserve its position in the region, Great Britain would have to maintain considerable forces and consent to enormous financial expenditure. "It is a strategy of despair. I have the gravest doubts as to its efficacy. The deterrent does not seem to me to be sufficiently strong." Therefore, Attlee repeated, it was preferable to seek some arrangement with Russia. The mutual fear of another world war might favor rapprochement. Moreover, Europe's economic rehabilitation was the sole means of resisting Soviet pressure, and specifically the pull of communism. The process would take some years. The defense of democracy required economic progress. It also called for a long period of peacetime. In addition, international tensions that reinforced a victim's mentality in the Soviet leaders must not be stirred up.[45]

Bevin was in complete disagreement with his prime minister: "What you propose is a reversal of the whole policy I have been pursuing in the Middle East, with the assent of the Cabinet, since the government took office." He recalled his project: "My whole aim has been to develop the Middle East as a producing area able to help our own economy and take the place of India, which henceforth will absorb her own produce." The policy was based on the hypothesis that Great Britain would play a deciding role in coordinating defense policies in the region, and eventually take responsibility in the projected regional security systems of the United Nations. Bevin was convinced that Great Britain could maintain its influence in the region with limited means, especially after it had resolved the problems of Egypt, Iraq, and Palestine. By abandoning its positions, it would allow Russia to extend its stronghold over a highly important strategic region. "If we disinterest ourselves in the Middle East, they [the Russians] will take it over by infiltration." Bevin criticized Attlee's proposed idea of negotiating with Russia. "It would be Munich over again, only on a world scale, with Greece, Turkey and Persia as the first victims in place of Czechoslovakia." Great Britain had just given up India and Burma. Its retreat from the Middle East would be interpreted as an abdication of its role as a world power. India would be encouraged to meld into the Soviet sphere of influence. It would be impossible to pursue negotiations with Egypt in view of a nonaggression treaty. These countries would rapidly fall under Communist control. Great Britain's position in Sudan would become untenable. The effects of the development would be felt in all of Africa, and notably in North Africa, where Western positions would be shaken. The potential consequences on all of the dominions were incalculable. Bevin also reproached the prime minister for planning to negotiate with the Soviet Union from a weak position.

45. FO 800/476.

Indeed, Great Britain had never been in a worse position. Only when Great Britain had consolidated its economy, Europe had made similar progress, and the USSR had finally accepted that it would not be able to sever the ties between the United Kingdom and the United States, would the Soviet Union be made to listen to reason.[46]

The strategic debate rendered no immediate conclusions. One thing that appeared certain, however, was that Great Britain was not capable of maintaining its influence in the Mediterranean, the Middle East, or even Egypt, without United States support. Consequently, it must channel all of its efforts toward involving Washington in the defense of its interests.[47]

46. Ibid.
47. FO 371/60998.

8

CONTAINMENT

The Division of Europe

In early 1947, Europe's future was still very uncertain. Ideological and political disagreements among the former Allies manifested themselves with growing intensity, giving form to the image of an "iron curtain" that Winston Churchill had made popular. The negotiations on Germany had not advanced since the war, and there was no indication that the Soviet Union would be persuaded to restore it to unity and independence. Austria's fate was equally worrying. In early January, the parliamentary election campaign in Poland took place against a backdrop of fraud and terror. There were a great many arrests, particularly of the more active members of the Peasant party. Police forces exerted heavy pressure on party members to join other political formations and collaborate with the security police. Activists were threatened with losing their jobs; some were assassinated. The police attacked meeting places and the censorship laws were used to ban public distribution of the electoral manifestos.[1] Before the elections were held, Bevin rejected United States proposals to present the Soviet government with a joint protest based on the Yalta agreements. On 5 January, the Department of State acted alone, writing in very firm terms. Shortly after, the Foreign Office in turn sent a warning to Moscow. On the day of the elections, the ballot was cast generally with no guarantee of secrecy, to intimidate those who dared defy the Communists' ascendancy. The results were finally announced on 19 January: 80% of the vote went to the "Democratic bloc," giving it 80% of the parliamentary seats. Mikolajczyk's Peasant party received only 10% of the vote, or twenty-eight seats.[2]

The Sovietization of Poland continued thereafter without significant protest from the rest of Europe. The British government withdrew its support of Mikolajczyk, resigned to his movement's defeat. Western opinion was misinformed, and government officials were absorbed with other priorities. In France, leaders tended to see Polish affairs through the distorting lens of political prejudice born from the war. French

---

1. British embassy reports to the Foreign Office (FO 371/66090 and 66091).
2. John Coutouvidis and Jaime Reynolds, *Poland 1939–1947*, Leicester, Leicester University Press, 1986, p. 299.

Ambassador Roger Garreau, who had resided in Warsaw since 1945, described the strength of the population's Russophile sentiment to President Vincent Auriol on 6 February 1947, shortly after the elections: "It would be a mistake to believe that the parties that emigrated to London have an influence on the population. Today, Poland is quite socially advanced; it is trying to shed its reactionary tradition. [...] The Americans have attempted to support the opposition parties in particular, and have supplied the underground with air drops of arms cargo; but the Poles, even those in the opposition, do not approve of their tactic, which amounts to using Poland to get back at Russia."[3] His report reflected the propaganda of the Communist government in Warsaw, but it also exposed at once inexperience and a vision truncated by the prism of French ideological disputes.

Early in the new year, Communist agitation heated up in Hungary. On 7 January, a plot against the republic was uncovered. Some one hundred persons were arrested. Their wrongdoings were not disclosed precisely, but the conspiracy had indicted members of the Smallholders' party. This gave the Communist ministers and their allies a chance to purge the army and repress elements within the administration and the political forces that were hostile to their control. A short while later, parliament lifted eight deputies' parliamentary immunity. The exploitation of this affair seemed to indicate that the Communists and their Soviet protectors planned to break up the majority party before the peace treaty with Hungary took effect. The Smallholders' party attempted to respond, but the minister of the interior censored its press releases. The justice minister, a Social Democrat, requested that Béla Kovács, the secretary general of the Smallholders' party, have his parliamentary immunity lifted. On 26 February, Kovács was arrested by the Soviet police and charged with spying for a Western power.

The Collapse of British Power

Given the developments in Europe, the Foreign Office tried again to tighten its ties with France. It felt this policy was all the more necessary in anticipation of German and European division. The French ambassador in London proposed to Permanent Under-Secretary at the Foreign Office Sir Orme Sargeant that they hold discussions soon with a view to coordinating Franco–British political and trade relations. The French Ministry of Foreign Affairs was apprehensive about the change of

3. Vincent Auriol, *Journal du septennat, 1947–1954*, vol. 1, Paris, Armand Colin, 1970, p. 61.

Britain's policy for Germany, which resulted in the creation of two zones. The French government was changing its position on Great Britain. After the national assembly was elected on 10 November, subsequent to the adoption of the Fourth Republic's constitution on 13 October, Léon Blum agreed to form an interim cabinet until a president had been elected. He also took charge of France's foreign affairs.[4] Duff Cooper, Great Britain's ambassador in Paris, took advantage of the circumstances to promote the old idea of a treaty between the two countries.

On 13 January 1947, Blum, now prime minister of France, went to London in a politically significant move showing that the French authorities wished to reestablish relations of trust with London and put an end to the vagaries of General de Gaulle's diplomacy. He received a warm welcome, for he enjoyed a certain prestige among Labour party members. He tried, albeit in vain, to obtain concessions for increased shipments of German coal. At Bevin's suggestion, he agreed to reopen negotiations on the Franco–British military alliance treaty, which had been interrupted in 1945 by incidents in the Middle East.[5]

London was also realizing that new measures were needed to reinforce economic cooperation with the Western European countries. Whatever its political or military orientation, Great Britain must improve its economic situation together with continental Europe. Attlee and Bevin agreed to seek rapprochement with Europe. On 18 January, Bevin recalled in a memorandum that Great Britain had committed itself to adopt a free trade policy with the United States in order to encourage world trade expansion, full employment, a general increase in the standard of living, and political stability in the entire international community. He added, however, that it was not impossible that these plans might fail. Great Britain must therefore strengthen its economic ties not only with the Commonwealth but with Western Europe as well. Bevin still hoped to prevent Europe's division into exclusive economic blocs. In early 1947, just before the Moscow conference on Germany and Austria, he doubted that division could be stopped. He even feared that the gap between the regimes would widen, and that the USSR would renew efforts to extend its hegemony over the other Western countries. The only way to check Soviet expansion was to develop very tight economic and political relations with Western Europe. Because of the obstacles created by the Most Favored Nation clause, this might imply accepting to join a customs union, which would inevitably create problems with the Commonwealth countries.[6]

4. Memorandum from Orme Sargeant of 31 December 1946 (FO 371/62389).
5. Pierre Gerbet, *Le relèvement, 1944–1949,* Paris, Imprimerie nationale, 1991.
6. FO 371/62398.

It became clear that Great Britain no longer possessed the resources that had allowed it to dominate the international stage nor the means to conduct an independent foreign policy. In 1946, its economy had started out on a good footing: its exports had risen, industrial investments had picked up, and unemployment was low. The Labour government had passed a series of legislative measures through parliament, including an extensive nationalization program, creation of the National Health Service, which was largely financed by the government, and a broad social security system that followed the Beveridge report of 1942. Nevertheless, progress was fragile and uncertain, especially since coal production was still insufficient.[7]

Early in the new year, all economic indicators sank, and on 20 January 1947 the government had to scale down its estimates of British economic trends. For want of manpower and capital, but especially owing to coal and iron shortages, production could not cover domestic needs, let alone the exports needed to repay the debt. Reserves, which a United States government loan had bailed out, were rapidly being exhausted. The crisis was due to price hikes in the United States, stagnation in the international economy, and the disastrous levels of world agricultural production and raw material supplies. Moreover, Great Britain lacked dollar liquidity, as did all European economies, at a time when the United States was the only country that could provide the investment and consumer goods necessary for reconstruction.[8]

In addition, weather conditions became catastrophic in January and gravely affected economic activity in the United Kingdom. Northern Europe was crippled by the winter. Snow fell almost without end, carried by a bitter wind. It seemed as if the ice age had returned. In late January, the Thames began to freeze. Trains were stopped, and roads and ports were blocked. Coal could not reach the factories. There were electric power outages. Production had to be stopped or slowed, and the government was forced to impose the strictest rationing. In February, there were more than two million unemployed. On 21 February, the government announced drastic cuts for the coming year. In a document submitted to parliament entitled *Economic Analysis for 1947,* the government announced that the failure of the economic recovery plan might mean that the "foundations of national life would never be restored."[9]

In such circumstances, Great Britain could no longer retain its role as

7. Michael J. Hogan, *The Marshall Plan. America, Britain and the Reconstruction of Western Europe,* Cambridge, Cambridge University Press, 1987.

8. Memorandum from the Chancellor of the Exchequer (FO 371/62399).

9. Bruce R. Kuniholm, *The Origins of the Cold War in the Near East. Great Power Conflict and Diplomacy in Iran, Turkey, and Greece,* Princeton, Princeton University Press, 1980, pp. 406–7.

a great power, and the Labour government was forced to repudiate some of its military commitments abroad. A shrinking defense budget was unavoidable. The Treasury had long pleaded for such a policy; it could now demand it. Great Britain still had more than a million soldiers at arms (1,227,000), and with the British pound's progressive devaluation the cost of stationing its troops abroad was rising. This was yet another reason to advance the decolonization process.

On 28 January 1947, the government announced that Burma would soon have an independent government. A few weeks later, after a final effort to win the Zionists' and Arabs' agreement to a partition plan, Bevin announced to the House of Commons on 18 February 1947 that the mandate had failed and the government intended to bring the matter before the United Nations.[10] He still hoped that a solution favorable to Great Britain's political and strategic interests would prevail for Palestine, but clearly the course of events was gaining speed and escaping the powers of the military, as it escaped the United States government, which had done so much to challenge British policy in Palestine. On 20 February, Attlee publicly announced his government's decision to retreat from India before June 1948. It was the end of an era. Great Britain was losing the imperial hegemony that had made it a leader in world affairs.

The Truman Doctrine

It was in these circumstances that the British ambassador in Washington announced to the secretary of state on 21 February that after 31 March 1947, Great Britain would no longer be able to sustain its economic and military responsibilities in guaranteeing independence and security in Greece.[11] Moreover, Great Britain would suspend aid to Turkey, another country threatened by the USSR.[12] The news sounded the alarm in Washington. The British ambassador in Washington wrote to London: "The announcement that His Majesty's government can no longer continue to carry the burden of financial assistance to Greece has come as a tremendous shock to all those interested in external affairs. It is widely realised that the United States is now confronted with a decision which is likely to pre-determine the future course of its history."[13]

In fact, this was hardly surprising. Two weeks earlier, the British

10. Michael J. Cohen, *Palestine and the Great Powers, 1945–1948*, Princeton, Princeton University Press, 1982, p. 223.
11. Robert A. Pollard, *Economic Security and the Origin of the Cold War: 1945–1950*, p. 119.
12. Kuniholm, *The Origins of the Cold War*, pp. 408–9.
13. FO 371/61054.

ambassador had told his American fellow negotiators that the situation in Greece was hopeless. He had suggested that unless there was rapid intervention to improve the country's economic and financial situation, Great Britain's commitments would be in vain, and Greece would be incorporated into the Soviet system. As mentioned above, Loy Henderson, the head official for Middle Eastern affairs, had been attempting for some months to demonstrate Greece's strategic importance as the last of the Balkan countries to hold out against Communist influence. He repeated that losing Greece would eventually mean losing Turkey, and would ultimately lead to Russia gaining control of the entire Middle East. This idea was becoming accepted geostrategic wisdom in the State Department. Under-Secretary of State Dean Acheson was also convinced of this. Dispatches from Ambassador Lincoln MacVeagh, Paul Porter, the head of the United States economic mission, and Mark Etheridge, who was on the United Nations investigating commission, had one overriding tone: alarm. The Greek economic and political situation seemed hopeless to them, and the guerrillas were aggravating the chaos. When consulted by the secretary of state, they agreed that Greece was on the brink of collapse and that the United States must make a clear show of determination to preserve Greek independence and integrity.[14]

The news of the British withdrawal therefore heralded the moment of truth: the United States must take over for Great Britain in Greece, the Middle East, and all of the Mediterranean. In January, George Kennan had spread the concept of "containment" of the USSR in his analysis of the psychological background of Soviet policy for Defense Secretary James Forrestal. He proposed a "firm policy of containment, which would apply vigilant counter force against the Russians and any other place where they manifest their intention to attack the interests of a peaceful and stable world."[15] Kennan, as mentioned earlier, had conducted a painstaking strategic examination of the Soviet threat, enriching his knowledge with readings from Machiavelli and Clausewitz.[16] In the Department of State and the Pentagon, which both lacked a true tradition of doctrine in foreign policy matters, his thoughts had now bridged that gap and received broad support. When the news of the British withdrawal was announced in Washington, Kennan was called upon, together with high officials from the State Department, the War Department, and the military, to define a policy that could answer the new strategic challenge. He held that Greece's "fall" would breed panic and defeatism in the

14. *FRUS 1947*, vol. 5, pp. 15–29.
15. This analysis was reproduced some months later in the famous article signed "X" in *Foreign Affairs*, [25 (4), pp. 566–82].
16. Walter L. Hixson, *George F. Kennan. Cold War Iconoclast*, New York, Columbia University Press, 1989, pp. 34–5.

countries struggling against communism, opening the Near East to Soviet penetration, creating the conditions for Communist dictatorships to emerge in Italy and France, and finally claiming all of Europe.[17] He supported Henderson and Acheson's ideas. A few days earlier, on 17 February, Deputy Director of the Office of European Affairs John Hickerson had sent a memorandum to his chief, Freeman Matthews, stressing the great variety of methods the Soviet Union used to meet its aggressive objectives. "If the right of free men to live out their lives under institutions of their free choice is to be preserved, there must be a vigilant determination on the part of peoples and governments of the USA and the UK to resist Soviet aggression, by force of arms if necessary. [...] If the lessons we learned from efforts to deal with Hitler mean anything, concessions to the Soviet Union would simply whet their appetite for more."[18]

General Marshall, formerly the US chief of staff during the war, had just replaced Byrnes as the head of the State Department. He enjoyed considerable prestige. Unilke his predecessor, he listened to the advice of his department advisers. Immediately, he grasped the strategic implications of the British decision. As he had just ended his mediation mission in China, he knew that the Communists had a strong chance of conquering the immense country. He was worried about Soviet intentions in Korea as well. Marshall saw that Great Britain's decision was tantamount to "a British abdication from the Middle East with obvious implications as to their successor."[19] At once, he transmitted this message to the Pentagon, which was fully convinced that Soviet expansion must be contained and that the United States would be forced to take over for Great Britain in the Mediterranean and the Middle East.[20] Now, the United States must send economic and military aid to Greece, and subsequently to Turkey, to guarantee political and territorial integrity.

The president had every reason to follow Marshall's advice. The British Empire's rapid disintegration and the Attlee government's hasty decision to abandon strategic positions in the Mediterranean worried him deeply. He was aware of the imperatives of classic geostrategy, and feared that Great Britain's economic and political enfeeblement would have a grave effect on the international order. For one year, he had been following the

17. Ibid., pp. 60–1.
18. *FRUS 1947*, vol. 1, pp. 715–16.
19. Quoted by Kuniholm, *The Origins of the Cold War,* p. 409; Walter Millis, *The Forrestal Diaries,* New York, Viking Press, 1952, p. 245; Robert I. Donovan, *Conflict and Crisis, The Presidency of Harry S. Truman, 1945–1948,* New York, Norton, 1982, p. 278.
20. Joseph Marion Jones, *The Fifteen Weeks. An Inside Account of the Genesis of the Marshall Plan,* New York, Harcourt Brace Jovanovich, 1955, p. 130.

counsel of those who recommended resisting Soviet expansion in Europe
and the Middle East. To act in this direction required Congressional
support, however, and the task was not easy. Congress had been
dominated by conservatives since the November elections. The
Republican party had based its electoral campaign on government
spending cuts, and as it had a bicameral majority, it was now trying to
pass drastic spending cuts to lighten the tax burden. These demands
weighed heavily on the army and the navy budgets, and also on the War
Department's ability to restore an acceptable standard of living in
Germany and Japan. President Truman's authority was low, and there was
no indication that he would be able to convince public opinion to support
the political and strategic changes necessitated by the British Empire's
downfall.[21]

On 27 February, the president called a meeting with top Congressional
and White House leaders to inform them that he wanted to aid Greece
and Turkey and to win their endorsement. General Marshall emphasized
the Communist threat to Greece, the risk of that country falling under
Soviet control, and, graver still, the possibility that the USSR could
dominate the entire Middle East to the Indian border, and even all of
Europe.[22] Under-Secretary of State Acheson expounded upon the plea
to redirect strategy, dramatizing the extent of the Soviet menace: in the
past eighteen months, he explained, Soviet pressure on the Black Sea
straits, Persia, and northern Greece had been such that it seemed probable
that the USSR would soon attain a strategic position from which it could
penetrate three continents. The danger was made more serious by the fact
that the Russians were attempting to encircle and attack Germany and
the rest of Western Europe by mobilizing Communist support in France
and Italy. Greece's contamination would spread like an infection to Persia,
and it would sweep toward Africa through Asia Minor and Egypt.[23] The
world was divided between two great antagonistic powers, the United
States and the Soviet Union, a situation the likes of which, in his opinion,
had not been seen since Rome and Carthage. The conflict was ideological:
the United States valued democracy and individual freedom, whereas the
Soviet Union preached totalitarian dictatorship. To protect its security and
freedom, it was imperative that the United States come to the aid of
countries threatened by Soviet aggression and Communist subversion.[24]

Senator Vandenberg, who was attending the meeting as the chairman

21. Ibid., pp. 89 et seq.
22. Donovan, *Conflict and Crisis,* pp. 280–1.
23. Dean Acheson, *Present at the Creation: My Years in the State Department,* New
York, Norton, 1987, p. 219.
24. Howard Jones, *"A New Kind of War." America's Global Strategy and the Truman
Doctrine in Greece,* Oxford, Oxford University Press, 1989.

of the Senate Committee on Foreign Relations, needed no convincing. He had been present at the peace treaty negotiations and had tirelessly warned public opinion about the Soviet menace ever since. He asked the president to appear before Congress to outline the need for renewed strategic resistance to USSR ambitions.[25] To support Greece and Turkey, but more fundamentally, to mobilize the resources for a new global strategy, the government must naturally convince public opinion and rally a majority among American political forces.

The president decided to call a joint session of Congress to present the gravity of the international situation officially and to gain Congressional support in turning around US Mediterranean strategy. In the meanwhile, the Department of State and the White House would brainstorm to find the arguments and the words to win support from Congress and American public opinion. The information campaign was in full force. Commenting on the reaction of the United States press in early March, the British ambassador in Washington wrote: "It is now almost impossible to pick up a newspaper or a general magazine without finding serious articles in which the sorry state of the world is clearly outlined and the implications for this country examined. Most of these articles conclude that America in her own interest cannot shirk the responsibilities resulting from her position as the world's leading Power."[26] Clearly, American public opinion was pondering the consequences of the British Empire's decline and had intuited, more or less consciously, that the United States would have to take over its decadent hegemony.[27]

On 12 March, President Harry Truman made an official speech at the Capitol. His message was rebroadcast on the radio. "The gravity of the situation which confronts the world today necessitates my appearance before a joint session of the Congress. The foreign policy and national security of this country are involved," he explained. He went on to mention the appeals for economic and financial aid he had received from Greece, explaining the drastic economic consequences of the war and the country's occupation, and the imminent dangers it would face. "The very existence of the Greek state is today threatened by the terrorist activities of several thousand armed men, led by Communists, who defy the Government's authority at a number of points, particularly along the northern boundaries. [...] Greece must have assistance if it is to become a self-supporting and self-respecting democracy. The United States must supply that assistance. [...] There is no other country to which democratic

---

25. Donovan, *Conflict and Crisis,* p. 281.
26. "Weekly Political Summary from Washington to Foreign Office," 3 March 1947 (FO 371/61054).
27. Ibid.

Greece can turn." After appealing for aid to Turkey as well so that it could modernize and maintain its national integrity, which was "essential to the preservation of order in the Middle East," Truman recollected that recently, many peoples had fallen under the control of totalitarian regimes. He also recalled the United States government's frequent protests of the coercion and intimidation to which Poland, Romania, and Bulgaria had fallen victim in violation of the Yalta agreements, adding that many other countries had met a similar fate.

> At the present moment in world history nearly every nation must choose between alternative ways of life. The choice is too often not a free one. One way of life is based upon the will of the majority, and is distinguished by free institutions, representative government, free elections, guaranties of individual liberty, freedom of speech and religion, and freedom from political oppression. The second way of life is based upon the will of a minority forcibly imposed upon the majority. It relies upon terror and oppression, a controlled press and radio, fixed elections, and the suppression of personal freedoms. I believe that it must be the policy of the United States to support free peoples who are resisting attempted subjugation by armed minorities or by outside pressure.[28]

His anti-Communist rhetoric, shaped, in particlar, by Joseph Jones, Dean Acheson, and Clark Clifford, helped warm Congress and American opinion to a profound change in the policy and strategy the United States had adopted since the end of the Second World War. From the perspective of United States domestic policy, the speech was shrewd. It did win support from conservative groups, and primarily from the Republicans. By tracing the shadow of communism, clearly linking it to Soviet totalitarianism, and rekindling the flame of American messianism, Truman made a strong bid to rally these voices whilst allowing himself the freedom to conduct a global policy outside of the United Nations, which was now considered incapable of facing the challenge. The funds the president requested were fairly moderate: 400 million dollars. At this point, the main issue was to gain approval for the concept of economic aid as a decisive instrument of foreign policy and United States postwar strategy, to dash the legislative and budgetary impediments to freedom of action in this area, and finally to beat back the resurgence of isolationist tendencies in Congress. The dangers suggested in his speech were,

28. Margaret Carlyle (ed.), *Documents on International Affairs, 1947–1948*, Oxford University Press/Royal Institute of International Affairs, 1952, pp. 2–7.

however, so grave as to give the impression that the request to Congress foreshadowed a far-reaching foreign aid program.

The speech was saluted, and received very broad public support. Senator Vandenberg assured the Republican party's endorsement by immediately backing the presidential message.[29] On the other hand, it gave rise to some concern in France. Vincent Auriol feared that the "aggressive tone of this speech" would have negative repercussions on French Communist attitudes.[30] Truman's declaration also caused a mixture of surprise and expressions of irony in the Foreign Office. His reaction had appeared to be unrehearsed. Officials wondered whether public opinion in the United States had grasped all of its political implications. If the speech were taken literally, wrote G. Gladwyn Jebb, it would mean that there was no limit to the United States' anti-Communist commitment, which had now been extended to all corners of the world. Would aid be provided to the Polish, Romanian, and Bulgarian peoples, not to mention the other countries that had already had totalitarian regimes thrust upon them against their will?[31] A British embassy adviser reported that Washington was considering the idea of massive aid to Korea, which suggested that the United States had in fact abandoned the plan for a four-power trusteeship, and that it intended to fight the Soviet Union's plans to extend its control to the entire country. If the Soviet Union did not withdraw, the United States must be ready to see the combat through to its ultimate conclusion.[32] In a commentary on the reaction of public opinion in the United States, the British ambassador stated:

Comparisons with the Monroe Doctrine are frequent. It is taken for granted that the United States has every justification, including moral reasons, for transforming the basic tenet of its foreign policy into a doctrine which sought to isolate the American sphere from the rest of the world to one which will isolate the rest of the world against encroachment of the Soviet sphere. [...] Americans are congenitally incapable of appreciating that others may not share their unshakable belief in their own righteousness. [...] In this particular instance, the proposed adoption of a frankly anti-Soviet policy is metamorphosed by evangelically-minded Americans into a crusade for democracy. Some of the staunchest supporters of the Administration's policy display a religious fervour which blinds them to the realistic considerations on which the policy is based.[33]

29. Jones, "*A New Kind of War,*" pp. 171 et seq.
30. Vincent Auriol, *Journal,* p. 143.
31. FO 371/76582 A.
32. M.E. Denning, 26 March (FO 371/76582 A).
33. FO 371/61054, 15 March 1947.

The United States must take responsibilities commensurate with its position of global supremacy. The United Nations was no longer in a position to ensure collective security: it could not, in any case, protect Greece and Turkey. It was no secret that the new policy implied interference in the domestic affairs of other countries. This was considered inevitable for US defense, and also for the good of the countries concerned. Since the summer, it had become clear that a confrontation with the USSR could not be avoided. Clearly, an economic and political battle was preferable to a long war in the future.[34] "Fanned by Mr. Truman's conspiratorial tactics over Greece, American public opinion is now swinging rapidly to the conclusion that no time must be lost in plucking the torch of world leadership from our [...] hands," wrote F. Rundall, a British embassy adviser, in his weekly report to the Foreign Office on 11 March. He also noted that there was a growing interest in United States responsibilities in the Middle East.[35] Finally, he observed that the new US foreign policy coincided with a conservative campaign to eliminate "disloyal persons" from the administration, and with a new wave of attacks on the American Communist party.[36]

The Moscow Conference

The Truman doctrine did not create a favorable climate for the German peace treaty negotiations. On 10 March, a new session of the Council of Foreign Ministers opened in Moscow. The German question was the main subject of deliberation, and all involved were aware that Europe's future and the very development of international relations in particular depended on a rapid settlement of the affair, which was a source of great tension among the victorious powers.

Since the end of the war, Great Britain and the United States had changed their positions on the German problem. The occupation policy was a failure. Germany's economic and social situation remained desperate, aggravated by the hardships of the 1947 winter. The temperature had dropped for several weeks to −20° F, and snow lay on the ground until late March, when it melted and caused floods. There was a severe coal shortage. Electricity was cut off for several hours a day. Food rations again had to be reduced. Famine spread throughout the

34. Ibid., 29 March 1947.
35. Ibid., 11 March 1947.
36. Ibid., 5 April 1947.

demolished, under-supplied cities, raising mortality rates among children and the elderly. The populations of Berlin and Hamburg were particularly hard hit. Workers were exhausted from malnutrition, and consequently production rates slowed.

The British government had no intention of continuing an occupation policy that had failed and cost it very dearly, as it was largely responsible for subsidizing the imports the population in its sector needed to survive, and could not raise German industrial production levels. Bevin had spoken confidentially with Byrnes on the matter in New York, outside of the Council of Foreign Ministers negotiations, repeating the principles he had defended in Paris. In late February, he submitted an important document to the British cabinet which coherently defended the aims Great Britain hoped to pursue in Germany and the position he planned to take in Moscow. His objective was to create a German state with federal-type institutions that would guarantee a decentralized structure. He was obviously anxious to counter Soviet ambitions for a centralized state, which might be integrated into the USSR's sphere of influence through German Communist party action. Furthermore, Germany's new borders were supposed to remain the same as before the war, barring some territorial concessions in the east to Poland and Russia and the Saarland's integration into the French economy. Bevin hoped to return to the question of Germany's eastern border, which had been suspended since disagreement over the issue had erupted at Potsdam. He refused to permit Poland to annex de facto a large region of the former Germany with support from the USSR, particularly because the area was rich in the agricultural products the British sector needed urgently. He hoped to persuade the French and especially the Soviet Union to pull down the barriers they had raised between their zones and the other parts of Germany so that the country would finally be treated as a single economy, in conformity with the Potsdam agreement. He intended to propose drafting an economic program covering all German imports and exports. From the British standpoint, industrial production levels must be increased substantially; and, contrary to Soviet demands, no reparations should be levied on current production until the US and Britain had covered the deficits they had accumulated from financing food and subsistence imports for their zones. Until a German federal government was installed, the central administrations planned in the Potsdam agreement must be appointed so that they could draft common regulations for transportation, communication, and the basic areas of the economy, subject to approval by the four powers.

Ernest Bevin was aware that his defense of these principles could end in the failure of the negotiations on Germany, the defeated country's division, and ultimately in Europe's definitive split into two antagonistic camps.[37] As he explained to the House of Commons, he still feared a resurgence of nazism; he hoped therefore that the four occupying powers could agree on how German disarmament was to be monitored and on how the country would progress toward a democratic regime. He maintained, however, that it was absurd to hope that sustaining a destitute population of sixty-six million in the heart of Europe would not affect the economies and living conditions of neighboring nations.[38]

The United States' position was similar to Great Britain's. On 27 February, former president Herbert Hoover, who had been sent to Europe to investigate the nutritional situation, submitted a distressing report on prevailing economic and social conditions in Germany, asking for more emergency aid to respond to immediate needs. Echoing what the American sector's leaders had been saying for so long, he stated that productivity growth in Europe required an economic recovery in Germany.[39] General Lucius Clay, the commander of American occupation forces in Germany, had continually complained of the conditions under which he had to fulfill his mandate. The transfer of industrial resources to the USSR as reparations, combined with the production restrictions that had been stipulated at Potsdam, added to the cost of the United States occupation program and made it impossible to define a coherent economic policy. The War Department in Washington was attempting to obtain orders to authorize German economic recovery, at least in the projected bizonal area. Former President Hoover's report also called for such a measure. The motion had broad support within the administration, especially from Averell Harriman, the new trade secretary, and Navy Secretary James Forrestal.[40] The Department of State was inclined to act accordingly, but it was concerned about how France and the USSR would react. It acknowledged that the policy adopted since the war had failed, and, after seeing the studies by various State Department economists, including C. Kindleberger, Walter Rostow, Harold Cleveland, and Paul Porter, it was sensitive to the European dimension of Germany's economic problems. Germany was a necessary element in European economic reconstruction, and only by integrating the European economies would it be possible both to remedy fractured markets and to overcome old nationalist rifts.[41] It was also conceded that the provisions of the Potsdam

37. CAB 129/16; excerpts from C.P. (47) 68, 20 February 1947, in Anne Deighton, *The Impossible Peace. Britain, the Division of Germany, and the Origins of the Cold War,* Oxford, Clarendon Press, 1990, pp. 224 et seq.

38. Carlyle, *Documents,* pp. 413–17.

39. Ann and John Tusa, *The Berlin Blockade. Berlin in 1948: The Year the Cold War Threatened to Become Hot,* London, Coronet, 1989, p. 108.

40. Roger Morgan, *The United States and West Germany, 1945–1973,* Oxford, Oxford University Press, 1974, pp. 33–4.

41. Ibid., pp. 35 et seq.

agreement concerning reparations had become inoperable. The dismantling of factories, which was intended to reduce Germany's military potential and ensure reparations payments, was prejudicial to the country's recovery, raised the cost of Allied occupation, and made European recovery impossible. The United States government hoped that it could convince the Russians of the need to postpone payment on some reparations, which would be collected later from current production. Washington observed that the USSR had indulged itself abundantly in its sector by dismantling German factories. Its inclination to finance reparations owed to the USSR was weaker than ever.

For the present, the United States government asked that Germany be treated as a single economy, as according to the Potsdam agreement. Consequently, it would expect to dismantle the barriers which had been created by the system of occupied zones. The economic program called for restoring the German political system. The United States naturally wanted to reestablish democratic institutions in the country and was arguing for a highly decentralized, federal structure in which the Länder would be the constituent elements. Moreover, the United States government was not completely in support of the border changes the Soviet Union had imposed to the benefit of Poland. Despite protest from the United States ambassador in Warsaw, the Department of State planned to ask for their partial revision in Germany's favor. Finally, with a view to a global settlement in Moscow, it planned to resubmit its proposal for a four-power treaty on German disarmament and demilitarization.

The secretary of state hoped to solve the problem of Austria soon as well. His predecessor, James Byrnes, had submitted proposals to the Council of Foreign Ministers the year before in an attempt to reach agreement on a peace treaty, but the Soviet Union had blocked discussion of the issue. The United States' objective was still the same: it wanted the Allied troops' withdrawal from the Austrian territory in order to reduce the cost of occupation, to allow for the country's recovery, and especially to force the Red Army to withdraw from Hungary and Romania. Washington feared that the Russians would use their presence in Austria to propagate their political influence and threaten the country's independence.[42]

The United States and Great Britain may have been of like minds about Germany's future and the Austrian peace treaty, but the French and Soviet governments were not. Early in the year, French Prime Minister Léon Blum had seemed willing to redefine France's Germany policy, rallying to the principle of economic unity and renouncing the idea of

42. "Memorandum by the Counselor of the Department of State (Cohen) to the Secretary of State," *FRUS 1947,* vol. 2, pp. 158 et seq.

dismemberment. But when Georges Bidault took over the French Ministry of Foreign Affairs on 22 January, he espoused the concepts General de Gaulle had conceived. Hence, the French government's aims at the Moscow conference were the same as those it had set in 1945: a vengeful peace settlement under which France would annex the Saarland, and the Rhineland and the Ruhr would be detached from Germany, thus affording France maximum exploitation of the mining resources and industry in these regions with a view to securing French predominance in Europe.[43]

This program was above all a response to considerations of domestic policy. The Ramadier government was fragile and it was trying to cope with great economic hardship, high inflation, and an endemic social crisis. Its prickly anti-German nationalism was a unifying factor among its heterogeneous political forces, which were divided over domestic policy problems. It was also used to mask disagreement on colonial policy within the government. There had been a resurgence of violence in Indochina, which destroyed hopes for a peaceful return to French sovereignty in this part of its empire. On 18 March, Marius Moutet announced to the French National Assembly that he dismissed the possibility of negotiating with Ho Chi Minh. The French government had adopted a reform policy in Tunisia and Morocco, while repressing indigenous proindependence demonstrators. The Communist party wavered over what line to follow: it could continue to support its government's actions, or it could resort to a subversive opposition. In March, it voted against military spending, based on its disagreement with France's Indochina policy; this foreshadowed a looming crisis in the government, and the possible resignation of its Communist ministers. On 23 January, the United States ambassador to France sent news to the secretary of state, according to which Moscow had instructed the Communist party to act with moderation but to prepare to ignite a government crisis before the Moscow conference in order to neutralize French foreign policy.[44]

To fulfill its aims in Germany, the French Ministry of Foreign Affairs had made repeated unsuccessful entreaties to Moscow, hoping that the USSR would back its claims on the Saarland, the Rhineland, and the Ruhr in return for France's support of Soviet claims to reparations and Germany's eastern border. The French still believed that they could act as the moderator between the Americans and the British and the Soviet Union. The French leaders' distrust of the Americans was still strong. President Auriol noted in his diary: "General Clay's hostility to our demands and policy does not surprise me. This business-minded General is on excellent terms with the Ruhr magnates, who were the instigators

43. Hogan, *The Marshall Plan*, p. 32.
44. *FRUS 1947*, vol. 3, p. 688.

of the two wars. Hence, the same errors are being repeated and this is the doing of the United States, which is always receptive to capitalist power."[45]

Nevertheless, the French government also had to seek help from Great Britain, which controlled the Ruhr's vast mining resources at the time. "If we do not obtain 500,000 tons of coal per month starting on 1 July 1947 [...] our entire economic and financial development program will be defeated, and with it the nation's standard of living," Pierre-Henri Teitgen reported to Georges Bidault on 14 March 1947.[46] After several weeks of negotiations, the two governments signed a military alliance treaty at Dunkirk on 4 March, which provided for mutual assistance against German aggression. The risk was abstract, but the treaty was more a political gesture to show the emergence of a new climate between Paris and London. The two parties also promised to consult each other closely in economic matters. It grew clear that this treaty, which was signed shortly before the Moscow conference on Germany, intensified Soviet distrust of French intentions.[47]

France's requests for aid from Washington were growing pressing, but appealing to the United States for financial assistance while at the same time frustrating its policy in Germany was a tricky business.[48] Bidault saw the self-contradiction in this, and in early February he confided to Jefferson Caffery, the United States ambassador in Paris: "I am only too well aware that France is a defeated country and our dream of restoring her power and glory at this juncture seems far from reality. While I can admit that privately to you, I cannot admit it either to the French people or to the world at large."[49]

Communist action was of great concern to United States leadership. As early as January, Bidault told the United States ambassador that the Ramadier government would not last if Moscow did not change its orders. The French foreign minister said that he, too, was convinced that the Communists were planning to "destroy Western civilization." The United States ambassador listened attentively, for he had no doubt that the Communist party was a "Soviet Trojan horse." He described Paris as a "veritable hive of Comintern agents with their swarm of followers and dupes, of whom the already large number almost daily increase[d], and

45. Auriol, *Journal,* p. 138.

46. M.A.E. Y 48/I/6, quoted by Catherine de Cuttoli-Uhel in René Girault and Robert Frank, *La Puissance française en question, 1945–1949,* Paris, Publications de la Sorbonne, 1988, p. 98.

47. Georges A. Catroux, *J'ai vu tomber le rideau de fer. Moscou, 1945–1948,* Paris, Hachette, 1952, p. 210–20.

48. *FRUS 1947,* vol. 2, p. 158.

49. Ibid., p. 154.

who [were] endeavoring to 'bore from within' international pacifist and idealist organizations like UNESCO and International United Nations Association."[50]

When the United States secretary of state arrived in Paris en route to Moscow, President Auriol submitted to him that continued rationing in France might create social unrest with grave political consequences. Pierre-Henri Teitgen, the acting foreign minister, went even further. He made it clear that before it would discuss German economic and political issues in Moscow, France demanded satisfaction of its request for coal from the Ruhr. France's economic reconstruction must take precedence over Germany's. With the French Union behind it, France could act as a great power in Europe and the rest of the world.[51] Marshall was sensitive to France's domestic difficulties, but he did not like Teitgen's innuendoes of blackmail in regard to Germany. Nor did he voice any opinion about the French Empire. Now that the United States was working to counter Soviet expansion, he had no interest in weakening France's position in the world.

Prior to the Moscow conference, the Kremlin's intentions for Germany remained, in part, a mystery. In early January, General Smith, the United States ambassador to Russia, suggested that Stalin still espoused Lenin's concepts regarding Germany: the conquest of that country was an essential element in his revolutionary program. The master of the Kremlin would do all he could to prevent Germany from regaining independence and power. He would attempt to integrate it into the Soviet sphere of influence, and was already setting his hooks into the Soviet sector. The Russians would try to expand their control over all of Germany through the Communist party, thwarting economic and political recovery in the Western sectors as well. They would demand a centralized administration and oppose all forms of federalism. They would continue to demand heavy reparations and challenge the formation of a bizonal area. Smith predicted that the Council of Foreign Ministers was embarking upon a long session which would degenerate into endless disputes. Yet he believed that the fate of Germany and ultimately that of Europe were in the balance in these negotiations. He anticipated that the parties would have to resign themselves to a yawning gap between the Western sectors and East Germany.[52]

The Moscow conference's opening deliberations appeared to confirm General Smith's analysis. Once again, the sessions started on a bad footing, blocked by both fundamental disagreement and Soviet

50. *FRUS 1947*, vol. 3, p. 691.
51. *FRUS 1947*, vol. 2, pp. 190–1.
52. Ibid., pp. 139–42.

obstructive tactics. The Soviet side did not appear to be in a hurry to complete negotiations, and Molotov's style was the same as ever. Outside of the plenary sessions, Vyshinskii congested various special committee meetings with his long speeches. Shortly after the Moscow conference opened, the president's speech – the "Truman Doctrine" – came as a public unveiling of the emerging Cold War and manifested US intentions to contain Soviet expansion. What was the effect of the declaration on Russia's position? In reading the record, the historian discerns no change in Molotov's attitude, nor in that of his collaborators. In his report on the conference to the cabinet, however, Bevin said on the contrary that Truman's speech had entirely changed the climate at the conference.[53]

From the very first sessions, Molotov was aggressive toward the British minister, accusing the British of harboring in their sector *Dientsgruppen* commanded by German officers, as well as Yugoslav, Polish, and Hungarian forces, "Ukrainian bandits," and other "allies of Hitler's Germany." He reproached them for not having enforced the de-Nazification and democratization processes vigorously enough. Bevin retorted by disclosing the names of Nazis whom the Soviet Union employed. He denounced their methods for forcing Socialists in their own sector to join the German Communist party, and their efforts to deny various democratic forces representation.[54] The United States secretary of state joined in the quarrel with a lengthy proclamation of democratic faith. Molotov's reaction was predictable: the Soviet Union was not interested in the "generalities of democracy," and in any case, the freedom of the press and the radio to which George Marshall had referred certainly did not include the right to propagandize for the return to a Hitlerite regime. In addition, Molotov fiercely attacked the United States and Great Britain's agreement to create a Germany split into two zones, which he denounced as an instrument of penetration for US and British monopolies in Germany.[55]

It seemed that the question of reparations was still the crux of Soviet concerns. Dismantling German factories had proved inefficient. Russian railway depots and sidings were encumbered by unused German machinery, which was left exposed to the elements.[56] Molotov now asked that reparations be levied from current production, which meant increasing industrial production in the Ruhr. The Soviet Union agreed that industrial output could be stepped up to satisfy Germany's reparations payments, but not to restore its economy. They also asked that there be

53. FO 371/64202.
54. *FRUS 1947,* vol. 2, pp. 249–51. See also FO 371/64206.
55. Forrest C. Pogue, *George C. Marshall: Statesman 1945–1954,* New York, Viking, 1987, pp. 180–1.
56. Walter B. Smith, *My Three Years in Moscow,* New York, Lippincott, 1950, p. 224.

quadripartite control of the Ruhr, yet they refused to open their own sector's economy. Marshall and Bevin could concede the reparations if the Soviet Union agreed to treat Germany as a single economy in accordance with the Potsdam agreement. Great Britain and the US would not, however, allow the Soviet Union to share control of the Ruhr if they themselves were denied the right to conduct inspections in the Russian sector. The economic question was further complicated by the Allies' refusal to accept the Oder–Neisse line. Discussions of the issue in Moscow seemed interminable.

Disagreements over economic and political matters were accompanied by differences over Germany's institutions. The Soviet position seemed paradoxical: Molotov advocated a central, highly powerful government; he was opposed to the federalist conception Great Britain and the United States had put forth, and even more opposed to the French proposal for an extreme form of decentralized government. He pushed for a centralized German political regime and denounced the Western programs, which might encourage centrifugal tendencies, thus making it possible to subtract the Ruhr from Soviet control. He refused, however, to grant the request by the US and Britain to manage Germany as a single economy.

After two weeks of fruitless negotiations, Bevin attempted to circumvent the inflexible Molotov by speaking with Stalin directly. Their meeting was amiable. The two men acknowledged their disagreement on methods of reparations payment. They also went over their differences on the new German state's infrastructure. Bevin nevertheless felt that their positions were not irreconcilable. The Western powers were requesting economic centralization, whereas the Soviet Union was in favor of political centralization and administrative decentralization. Bevin suggested that a compromise could probably be reached. Stalin was equally conciliatory on the Ruhr. He seemed willing to revise his position on the treaty joining the four powers. He said that he had initially believed that this treaty was to include Germany. He was also very understanding on the issues of Persia and India.[57]

Despite the spirit of conciliation, negotiations among the ministers were still floundering. On 31 March, after several weeks of quarrels and vague discussion, Bevin made a long statement explaining the British stance on Germany. The country, he explained, must be rebuilt on democratic foundations and return to its place among the world's peaceful nations as a full member of the European family. The political and economic vacuum it created in the middle of Europe had become intolerable. The German people must take part in the reconstruction effort and rebuild their trust in the future. The first condition of recovery was to treat

57. FO 880/447, p. 40.

Germany as a single economy and adopt a coherent economic policy which defined industrial production levels, reparations, and industrial demilitarization. A single economy in Germany demanded the free circulation of persons and ideas. It called for trade relations to be reestablished. Bevin asked that the cost of occupation be shared equitably. Exports must serve first to cover the cost of imports. The current level of industrial production could no longer be maintained, for it perpetuated poverty and political agitation in the heart of Europe. Bevin refused to continue a reparations policy based on the dismantling of industrial plants.

Hence, the British minister firmly opposed the Soviet Union's demands to share control of the Ruhr, as well as their request to levy reparations on current production. He was convinced that they intended to "loot Germany" at the expense of the British Exchequer. He was convinced that they would use their share of control over the Ruhr to create disorder and extend their sphere. General Marshall elaborated on this:

> The United States is opposed to policies which will continue Germany as a congested slum or an economic poorhouse in the center of Europe. At the same time, we recognize that Germany must pay reparations to the countries who suffered from its aggression. Within these limits, we want Germany to use its resources of skilled manpower, energy and industrial capacity to rebuild the network of trade on which European prosperity depends. Ultimately, it desires to see a peaceful Germany, with strong democratic roots, take its place in the European and world community of nations.[58]

This evidently was a new line of thought, which revealed Washington's current reflections on the need to contain USSR expansion and the urgency of restoring a balance of power.

The French foreign minister opposed the proposals Great Britain and the United States made in Moscow. He refused to accept the agreement on increased German industrial production until France saw its request for coal and its claims on the Ruhr, the Rhineland, and Saarland satisfied. Although he was very hostile to Molotov's proposed idea of political centralization in Germany, some of his positions were quite close to the Soviet Union's, among them, his demand for a share in controlling the Ruhr. He rejected the plan to raise the ceiling on steel production, invoking security reasons, but also because he feared German competition in this sector. On the other hand, he agreed that German coal production should be raised, on the condition that Germany be obliged to export part of this "to its neighbors and victims." He would accept Germany's economic

58. Smith, *My Three Years,* p. 226.

unification; his condition, however, was that Saarland be attached economically to France. In addition, the decision must not cause prejudice to the future status of the Ruhr or the Rhineland.[59] Once again, he showed himself to be intractable. He annoyed his Western colleagues with his claims, his propaganda aimed at the domestic audience, and his confessions of political frailty. He also embarrassed them at receptions by consuming alcohol in quantities that impaired his discernment and decorum.[60] Marshall and Bevin finally consented to France's integrating Saarland. Molotov refused, however, to agree to the request until he had won his case on the Ruhr. This negotiation tactic made agreement on the item impossible and pushed France back into the Western camp.

As the end of the conference was approaching, the United States secretary of state iterated the US proposal for a German disarmament and demilitarization treaty, asking for an agreement of principles on the matter. His Western colleagues supported him, but once again Molotov sidestepped the proposal by adding a series of amendments that rid the treaty of its specificity. The US program, he explained, ignored both the need to de-Nazify and the importance of rebuilding a German state on democratic foundations. It was based on erroneous hypotheses. Molotov restated the Soviet demands: to ensure Germany's demilitarization there must be a quadripartite control of the Ruhr, and any trusts or other monopolies in German industry must be transferred to the central government. A vast agrarian reform must be undertaken in which the Junkers would be forced to convey their land to the farm workers so that agricultural production could be increased to meet supply needs in the cities. Most importantly, all German political activity must be democratized. Clearly, Molotov's proposals amounted to a demand to change Germany's regime. What the Soviet government was requesting, Marshall replied, was the creation of a centralized government that would control most of Germany's industrial and financial enterprises. The United States considered that such a concentration of power would constitute a threat to world peace.[61]

Foreseeing absolutely no hope of an agreement on Germany, the United States secretary attempted to advance in the Austrian treaty negotiation. Again, the question of reparations was at the heart of the talks. The Soviet Union asked for German goods to be seized, including the Austrian assets Germany had taken in 1938. The Western powers did not accept this motion, which could cause the Austrian economy to plummet even

59. Gerbet, *Le relèvement,* p. 263.
60. Private Papers of Orme Sargeant. Letter of 20 March to Warner (FO 800/272).
61. FO 371/64206, p. 141.

further.[62] On 15 April, after over one month of fruitless deliberations, Marshall had his first meeting with Stalin. He stated plainly that the United States was losing patience with the Soviet position. In particular, he objected that he had yet to receive a reply to the requests for a settlement of the nonmilitary aspects of the Lend–Lease Act. He went over his differences with Molotov, stating that he especially regretted that the Soviet Union had not accepted the four-power draft treaty. He made it clear that the United States would give succor to all the countries where democracy was threatened by economic collapse. Stalin attempted to minimize the scope of the disagreements, suggesting that compromise was possible on all of the essential issues, including the questions of demilitarization, reparations, economic unity, and the German political structure. He added that patience was necessary. "He did not think the situation was so tragic. [...] After all, these were only the first skirmishes and brushes of reconnaissance forces on this question. Differences had occurred before on other questions, and as a rule after people had exhausted themselves in dispute they then recognized the necessity of compromise."[63] These military metaphors were not appropriate. At this point, the negotiations had gone on too long, and the United States had indeed lost patience.

On 24 April, after six weeks of deliberations, including forty-three plenary sessions and many unofficial meetings, the Council of Foreign Ministers rose without having made progress on Germany or Austria and, consequently, without the great powers having made progress in reestablishing peace in Europe. Many foreign correspondents had reported on the conference. The United States had insisted on wide coverage of the debates and requested visas for some one hundred journalists. In the end, thirty-six American journalists were allowed in.[64] The press turnout had proved detrimental, as the ministers consequently used the deliberations to serve up domestic propaganda. In debates before the Commons after the conference, Bevin disputed the entire negotiation procedure in the Council of Foreign Ministers, objecting in particular to the publicity surrounding the debates and the role of the American media: a peace settlement could not be made when "every word we say is reported to the press." In negotiation, he explained, one must be able to "think aloud."[65] The media had become a choice instrument in the war of ideologies, which had escalated with the "Truman Doctrine" and the new direction of United States policy.

62. Pogue, *George C. Marshall*, p. 183.
63. *FRUS 1947*, vol. 2, pp. 337–41.
64. Smith, *My Three Years*, p. 215.
65. United Kingdom, *Parliamentary Debates* (Commons), 5th Series, vol. 437 (1947), cols. 1964–5.

Bidault's report on the negotiations in Moscow, as President Auriol relates it in his diary, is revealing:

Seven weeks, for seven to eight hours a day, were characterized by readings of documents prepared in advance. The atmosphere was typical of an international conference: urbanity mixed with reciprocal and absolute imperviousness. Papers are read, then translated, and then it is the next speaker's turn. If you agree, you say: "I have nothing further"; if not, you spin out your commentary with documents. The dialogue and sharp talk are gone, and I sense a growing ossification. [...] in Roosevelt's day, there was discussion, but even that has disappeared. The speeches are handed over to the journalists, and no one budges anymore. Diplomacy is gone. We considered holding smaller conferences with a single delegate, a single adviser, a single interpreter. We tried, and it was worse than all the rest. Another arrangement was conceived of holding private conversations, but it yielded no results; Stalin remained detached and holds himself very high in the Empyrean.[66]

66. Auriol, *Journal,* vol. 1, p. 222.

9

THE CONSOLIDATION OF THE SPHERES OF INFLUENCE

The Development of American Strategy

On 28 April, directly after his return from Moscow, the secretary of state made a speech by radio broadcast to the American people to report on the failed meeting. His tone was moderate, but his statements were firm. He explained the nature of the disagreements that had cropped up among the former Allies over Germany and Austria, recalling that these differences concerned countries whose industrial, mining, and demographic resources were vital for Europe's future. Europe's recovery was taking much longer than expected. "Disintegration forces are becoming evident. The patient is sinking while the doctors deliberate." He suggested that the Soviet government advocated a centralized regime in Germany because it hoped to take control of that country after halting its economic recovery, and that its policy for Austria was the same. Referring to his interview with Stalin, he also implied that the Soviet Union was trying to impose its views by wearing down the Western negotiators' patience.[1]

The former chief of staff was anxious to redirect United States foreign policy in terms of far-reaching strategic planning. Shortly after he took office, he had set up a planning group charged with producing the analyses and data needed to pursue this objective. George Kennan appeared to be the most qualified person to head the Policy Planning Staff, especially in light of Acheson and Forrestal's strong recommendations of him. His appointment began in early May. Kennan did not favor the rhetoric of the Truman Doctrine, although he had contributed largely to the formation of the ideas it expressed. He would have preferred a more circumspect, less ideological message that would limit the nature of the United States' international commitments. The secretary of state shared his reservations, believing that the speech contained "too much flamboyant anti-Communism."[2] Clearly, the scope of the Truman Doctrine had to be delineated.

1. See *Department of State Bulletin,* quoted by Forrest C. Pogue, *George C. Marshall, 1945–1959,* New York, Viking, 1987, p. 200.
2. Wilson Miscamble, *George F. Kennan and the Making of American Foreign Policy, 1947–1950,* Princeton, Princeton University Press, 1992, p. 33.

The general staff and the Department of State had not awaited Marshall's return to Washington to define a new policy for Europe and a framework for their containment strategy. Even before the president's speech, Army Chief of Staff General Eisenhower had requested a coherent analysis of United States objectives, which were then to be translated into strategic terms. War Department Chief Robert Patterson made a similar request to Under-Secretary of State Acheson. By early 1947, United States military conscripts had been sharply reduced. Their forces were for the most part occupation soldiers who were unprepared for combat. Moreover, the 1948 budget contained no provisions for rearmament. The draft had been ended in March 1947, its proposed extension having failed to pass through Congress despite requests from the president and the chiefs of staff.[3] Of course, the United States leaders were well aware that military understaffing was not a major problem. There was no imminent risk of war with the USSR, which was using revolutionary propaganda and subversion to further its expansion. Classical military methods were not a great help in meeting this challenge.

Further to the request, Under-Secretary Acheson asked John H. Hilldring, chairman of the State-War-Navy Coordinating Committee (SWNCC) – a body charged with examining the shared problems of the principal departments affected by United States foreign policy and strategy – to deliver a report on the countries that might require aid similar to what had been earmarked for Greece and Turkey, with a view to building a conceptual framework for US aid programs.[4] The study, which the secretary of state awaited eagerly, was first to examine the countries needing emergency aid and the strategic implications of granting such aid; then, more broadly, it was to extend its examination to any other states that might request longer-term economic, financial, technical, or military aid.

A preliminary report was delivered on 21 April 1947. It stated that aid programs were needed urgently for Persia, Italy, Korea, France, Austria, and Hungary, and possibly for China as well, although the departments consulted did not agree on the last. In the long term, Great Britain, the Benelux countries, the Philippines, Portugal, Czechoslovakia, and Poland should also benefit from United States aid. The United States would export about twice the goods and services it imported from abroad, for its current aid would not suffice and would certainly not offset the imbalance. It had

3. Kenneth W. Condit, *The History of the Joint Chiefs of Staff. The Joint Chiefs of Staff and National Policy,* vol. 2, *1947–1949,* Wilmington, Michael Glazier, 1979, pp. 17–23.
4. *FRUS 1947,* vol. 3, pp. 204–20; Howard Jones, *"A New Kind of War." America's Global Strategy and the Truman Doctrine in Greece,* Oxford, Oxford University Press, 1989, p. 199.

every interest in promoting a stable global economy and rebuilding the international order in accordance with the norms of the United Nations. Consequently, it must fight economic and social conditions that could lead to political extremism, and block any power that was potentially a significant threat to the security and welfare of United States citizens. To this end, it advised increasing foreign aid spending considerably and to distribute the moneys with its strategic priorities in mind. If it failed to assume its role in the defense of free countries, the United States could lose its authority in the rest of the world. It also had to rethink its military collaboration with nations that could be active in United States security defense.[5]

When the Joint Chiefs of Staff were consulted on the new strategy, they agreed that economic aid should be used as an instrument of US strategy, for they realized that the next world war might be "ideological"; but they rejected the idea of granting economic assistance to countries under Soviet influence or control. In their view, Great Britain and France should be called upon to play a decisive role in the defense of United States interests. They considered economic, political, and military recovery in Germany necessary for safety in Europe, which could not resist the Red Army without German support. In Asia, they recommended looking to Japan for support. Yet the Middle East, northwestern Africa, Latin America, and the Far East were also key strategic points. In Latin America, the Communist party was gaining influence. "In consequence, anything less than complete rapprochement between the United States and every one of her neighbors to the south is entirely unacceptable from the viewpoint of United States security. To stand by and watch a fifth column grow stronger and stronger to the south of us is to invite disaster. The United States is, by reason of its strength and political enlightenment, the natural leader of the hemisphere." The Joint Chiefs of Staff proposed to expand and complete the Chapultepec defense treaty and to advocate standards for armaments and weapons transfers in Latin America; also, they planned to aid the military, on whom all Latin American governments were now reliant.[6]

Since the elaboration of the Truman Doctrine, the president's staff had begun to study the chances of revising the Japan occupation policy.[7] Halford Mackinder's geopolitics had Kennan persuaded that certain countries or regions were of vital strategic importance, and that their potential industrial capacity and military forces could start another world

5. *FRUS 1947*, vol. 3, "Report of the Special 'Ad Hoc' Committee of the State-War-Navy Coordinating Committee," pp. 204–19.

6. "Memorandum by the Joint Chiefs of Staff to the State-War-Navy Coordinating Committee, May 12, 1947" (*FRUS 1947*, vol. 1, pp. 734–50).

7. Walter Millis (ed.), *The Forrestal Diaries*, New York, Viking, 1952, pp. 256.

war. These countries must be prevented from entering the Soviet sphere. USSR containment meant defining a defense perimeter and ensuring that "certain strong points" were protected within a peripheral strategy. In this perspective, Japan was a necessary link in containment strategy. In April 1947, the Joint Chiefs of Staff approved a financial aid grant to Japan to restore its industrial capacity and its economic independence.[8] They feared that the Communists would take advantage of Japan's economic and social disintegration. Moreover, occupation was costly, requiring bottomless financial resources. Japanese economic recovery would benefit all of Asia, and notably the Southeast Asian countries.[9] Hence, United States policy for Japan was on the brink of radical change, and Washington already envisioned turning that country into a bastion against the USSR.[10]

Japan's defense gained in urgency as China sank into civil war and the United States administration lost hopes of securing a victory for Chiang Kai-shek. China's economic and political situation had deteriorated further, and after late April inflation reached catastrophic proportions. The Nationalist government's military position was weakening. Its forces were greater in number and materiél than the Communists', but they were unable to cope with the adversary's revolutionary strategy. In Shantung and Manchuria, Mao Tse-tung's army had won back the advantage over the Nationalist troops. It held the rural areas and gained a massive constituency among farm workers. The student agitation started in early May in Shanghai was spreading to the principal Nationalist-controlled cities. The future of the Chiang Kai-shek regime, which, with its corruption, incompetence, and police overlords, seemed more fragile than ever to United States diplomats. The United States had placed an embargo on arms shipments to China in 1946 to force the Nationalist government to change direction and negotiate a rapid solution to the civil war, but could this policy be continued with the growing threat of a Communist takeover in China? On 5 May, the United States government decided to lift the arms embargo against the nationalists. How it would respond to Chiang Kai-shek's massive economic aid appeals was another question. The Communist advance toward Manchuria and northern China worried the United States leadership, especially since the Republicans were increasing pressure on Congress to support the Nationalist government and a new program of United States aid to Europe was being planned. The administration's

8. J.L. Gaddis, *The United States and the Origins of the Cold War, 1941–1947,* New York, Columbia University Press, 1972, pp. 55 et seq.
9. Michael Schaller, *The United States Crusade in China: 1938–1945,* New York, Columbia University Press, 1979, pp. 76 et seq.
10. Ibid., p. 104.

military arm hoped for a new economic and military aid grant to Chiang Kai-shek, but Secretary of State Marshall was familiar with prevailing conditions in China, and had no illusions about the nature of the Chiang Kai-shek government.

The Implementation of the Marshall Plan

The situation in Western Europe continued to deteriorate. In late March, Hugh Dalton, the chancellor of the Exchequer, informed the cabinet that Great Britain's monetary reserves, which had been given a partial boost in 1946 by loans from the United States and Canada, were rapidly running out, notably because of the constant price rises in US imports, the cost of occupying Germany, and the energy crisis occasioned by the harsh winter. On 12 May, he warned the United States ambassador that Great Britain might be unable to restore the pound's convertibility or to dismantle its System of Imperial Preferences as it had undertaken to do in accepting the United States' loan.[11]

Moreover, eroding economic and social conditions in France and Italy, and the advance of Communist influence in these countries, were matters of extreme concern in Washington. The French government continued to draw the United States government's attention to its difficulties in meeting grain supply needs and asked for an increase in United States shipments. The situation had become so harsh, the United States ambassador in Paris reported, that the government would have to ration bread until the end of May at levels below those reached during the Nazi occupation.[12] General de Gaulle tried to take advantage of the crisis by launching attacks on the government's policy, which, for that matter, was also a source of deep apprehension among the MRP (Mouvement républicain populaire) and the Rassemblement des gauches.[13] Moreover, colonial affairs continued to shake the government coalition. Rioting had broken out in Madagascar in late March and was repressed violently. The Communists opposed the arrest of Madagascan deputies on charges that they had stirred up the unrest.[14] On 25 April, Jefferson Caffery wrote to the secretary of state: "Qualified observers here of the world Communist movement, especially those formerly connected with the Comintern, are increasingly inclined to believe that the French Communists are being directed to accelerate their agitation in the French colonies to the extent

---

11. Allan N. Bullock, *Ernest Bevin, Foreign Secretary 1945–1951*, Oxford, Oxford University Press, 1985, p. 400.
12. *FRUS 1947*, vol. 3, pp. 696–7.
13. Ibid., pp. 696–9.
14. Ibid., pp. 699 et seq.

even that they may not be able to remain in the government."[15] Caffery also reported on debates within the Communist party and the CGT (Confédération générale du travail, the association of French trade unions) on their prospects for remaining in the government.

The failure of the Moscow conference also intensified the split between Communist ministers and other government members. When Georges Bidault reported the results of the peace talks to the French cabinet, the Communist leader Maurice Thorez took him aside to reproach him for banding together with the British and the Americans over "a bit of coal" and failing to support the Soviet position.[16] On 25 April, a strike broke out at the Renault factories. Although the CGT had not called the strike, the Communists wished to show their solidarity. By supporting the picketers, they also undermined the government's economic policy. Paul Ramadier then opted for a power play: on 4 May, he asked the National Assembly for a vote of confidence. The Communist ministers and deputies voted no confidence, thinking that this would force the prime minister to step down. But he held on and removed the Communists. By voting against their own government in the National Assembly and marking a growing hostility toward French foreign or colonial policy, the Communists had placed themselves in a position that led to their expulsion from power, thus creating the conditions for firmer ties between the United States and British governments.[17]

The French government seemed to have no other solution than rapprochement with Great Britain and the United States, which controlled the resources of the Ruhr, and German coal production in particular. The Soviet Union had not supported France's claim to Saarland in Moscow. Bidault had counted on Molotov's support in this. In many respects, he returned from Moscow "empty-handed."[18] At his meeting with Paul-Henri Spaak on 8 June in the Ardennes, his pique was obvious when he characterized the Soviet leaders as "simple-minded, obstinate, and in bad faith."[19] The French minister was beginning to face the facts: collaboration with the Kremlin was no longer possible. From then on, his anti-Soviet sentiment was commensurate with his disillusionment. The United States and Great Britain, on the other hand, had promised to ship

15. Ibid., pp. 702–3.
16. Pierre Gerbet, *Le relèvement, 1944–1949*, Paris, Imprimerie nationale, 1991, pp. 267–8.
17. Ibid.
18. René Massigli, *Une comédie des erreurs: 1943–1946. Souvenirs et réflexions sur une étape de la construction européenne*, Paris, Plon, 1978.
19. Paul-Henri Spaak, *Combats inachevés*, vol. 1, Paris, Fayard, 1969, p. 172, quoted by Massigli, *Une comédie des erreurs*, p. 98.

more German coal to France at the Moscow conference.[20] Georges Bidault knew that they were determined to organize the area comprising the British and American zones and raise its level of industrial production; he now saw that France could no longer make it alone. He must be able to rely on the United States for economic support,[21] for without foreign aid, he would not survive politically. On 2 June, Vincent Auriol noted in his diary:

> The outlook for the 1947–1948 campaign is very bad. Only 45 million quintals are forecast, and 18–25 million of these will go to trade. We will have to import 24 million quintals, a 250 million dollar expenditure, in order to keep rations at 250 grams. But we do not have the currency to do it. [...] For we have had rather pessimistic news about our balance of trade, which will be running a deficit of nearly 5 billion francs. To offset this, we should develop exports, but French prices are too high. We are circled by difficult problems. Also, the persistent smears and immorality in the country have us submerged by wild self-importance and moral anarchy.[22]

France seemed to be stuck in a desperate economic situation: price rises were gaining speed and largely exceeded wage increases. In early June, wheat supplies were so low that bread rations had to be lowered to 200 grams a day.[23] The ensuing turmoil shook the government's authority and its policies.

Italy, too, was becoming a matter of grave concern in Washington. Political and social instability had increased steadily in Italy, aggravated by the shortage of subsistence goods. The lira's value was plummeting. From December 1946 to March 1947, the cost of living had risen almost 20%. It was, therefore, hardly surprising that protest demonstrations and clashes with the police occurred almost every day.[24] The Italian premier, Alcide De Gasperi, went to the United States in January in an attempt to obtain support from the Italo–American community and the Roman Catholic Church. Truman promised more economic aid. Yet despite relief from the United States, the Italian government, in which the Communists had a good showing, remained fragile. On 11 March, the secretary-general of the Italian Communist party took an ominous tone, implying that he

20. John W. Young, *Britain, France and the Unity of Europe, 1945–1951*, Leicester, Leicester University Press, 1984, p. 58.
21. Ibid., p. 63.
22. Vincent Auriol, *Journal du septennat, 1947–1954*, vol. 1, Paris, Armand Colin, 1970, p. 251.
23. Irwin M. Wall, *The United States*, p. 80.
24. John Lamberton Harper, *America and the Reconstruction of Italy, 1945–1948*, Cambridge, Cambridge University Press, 1986, p. 122.

might proceed with "direct action."[25] The United States and British forces stationed in Italy could still contain the threat of subversion, but the peace treaty stipulated their imminent departure, and the impending date was cause for worry. Great Britain made efforts to reinforce Italian military aviation. The United States supplied weapons.[26] There was pressure on the British government to limit its foreign commitments, however, and the Americans did not have enough conscripts to keep up a military presence in Italy.[27]

Deteriorating economic conditions broadened the Communist party's influence. This, at least, was the belief the secretary of state shared with James Dunn, the United States ambassador in Rome. Dunn believed that the Communist party was doing everything it could to aggravate inflation and economic chaos. As hunger and unemployment created a hotbed for communism, it was time for the United States to grant economic and political aid to the Italian democratic forces: the population was dispirited and businesses did not dare make investments. Dunn recommended that the president take a firm stand on the matter. De Gasperi also tried to warn Truman, as he repeated requests for economic aid. Dunn made it clear that it would be very difficult for him to win support from Congress and the United States people until the Italians had taken steps to "put their house in order," which was another way of suggesting that they exclude the Communists.[28] On 12 May, De Gasperi resigned. At the end of the month, he formed a new minority government, without Communists.[29] Secretary of State Marshall took an open position in favor of the new De Gasperi government.

On 8 May, Under-Secretary of State Acheson took the opportunity of a speaking engagement in the Midwest to prepare American public opinion for the demands of a large aid program, which was the core element of the new US strategy. He stressed the imperatives of economic reconstruction in Europe, and the grievous problems posed by shortages of food, clothing, coal, steel, and machinery, which were aggravated by the European countries' enormous dollar deficits. He painted a very bleak picture of the economic and social slump brought about in Europe and Asia by wartime destruction, relating the crisis to the disappearance of Germany and Japan as industrial hubs. The slow pace of negotiating the

25. *FRUS 1947*, vol. 3, p. 877.
26. *FRUS 1947*, vol. 3, pp. 887–8.
27. Cf. memorandum from the war secretary (Patterson) to the acting secretary of state (Acheson), 23 April 1947 (*FRUS 1947*, vol. 3, pp. 884–5).
28. *FRUS 1947*, vol. 3, pp. 889–94.
29. See also James E. Miller, *The United States and Italy, 1940–1950, The Politics and Diplomacy of Stabilization,* London, University of North Carolina Press, 1986, pp. 227 et seq.

peace treaties kept the disastrous economic situation going and led to serious political instability. The United States had already done much to finance humanitarian relief and economic reconstruction programs, but its national interest commanded it to do still more. As long as other countries had not regained their economic independence, the world would remain politically unstable and Americans would not live in peace and prosperity. Hopeless, famine-ridden peoples, he continued emphatically, often chose the road of despair, compromising their democratic institutions and their independence. This was not only a question of politics but an economic affair. It was in the United States' interest to give other nations the means to buy US goods and services. There was every advantage in maintaining and expanding the trade channels which fostered national production.

Admittedly, he said, the United States did not have the resources to rebuild the world economy. It would therefore have to make choices, giving priority for aid to the regions that might effectively contribute to global political and economic stability. It must support free democratic nations that helped to raise the principles of the United Nations. Most of all, it must aid Germany and Japan in putting their industries back on their feet. Acheson emphasized the fact that restoring the European economy would be impossible without rebuilding Germany. German reconstruction must start immediately, even if the four occupying powers were not in agreement. The European economy formed a whole, and its integration was one of the fundamental objectives of United States policy.[30]

After his return from Moscow, the secretary of state asked George Kennan and his new Policy Planning Staff to carry on with the SWNCC study in order, notably, to define Europe's economic needs more precisely. On 16 May, Kennan described some of the principles that might guide the United States in the distribution of resources to the old world. First, there should be an agreement with the British government to include US aid in a plan to resolve Great Britain's problems. Economic assistance to European countries would complement these countries' own efforts. It would be part of a broad, four- to five-year program, after which the states that had benefited from US aid would become autonomous again. The program would encourage some sort of political integration among the Western European countries. The Western sectors in Germany and Austria would contribute fully to economic recovery. Czechoslovakia and the other countries in the Soviet sphere would have to be allowed some constructive participation in the program, but the Communists must be

---

30. *Department of State Bulletin*, 18 May 1947, pp. 991–4.

prevented from sabotaging United States assistance or misappropriating it.[31]

In the days that followed, Kennan again defined the European recovery program's political direction, and in particular its relationship with the anti-Soviet strategy being developed in Washington. Communist activity, Kennan stated, was not the source of current difficulties in Western Europe. These were largely the effect of the war's economic, political, and social consequences, and of the European peoples' physical and psychological exhaustion. They also resulted from Europe's division subsequent to the split between East and West. The Communists were exploiting this crisis, which might be a danger to United States security. The US aid program must not, however, be directed against communism; rather, its primary objective must be to fight the factors that were making European societies vulnerable to the totalitarian-type movements exploited by the Soviet Union. The program must be conceived to succor all of Europe, but in such a way as to force the "Russian satellites" either to change the direction of their economy, or to turn down US aid. Kennan also recommended a rapid clarification of the Truman Doctrine's implications, which gave the impression that the United States was prepared to fight Communists the world over: this was like signing over a blank check to all of the countries that could potentially come under United States protection. The European recovery program must be thought out based on "economic policy," in the literal sense of the term, and dispensed based on essentially strategic calculations.[32]

Since the fall of 1946, Under-Secretary of State for Economic Affairs W. Clayton had been involved in negotiations to create the International Trade Organization, the function of which would be to liberalize international trade. On 27 May, after long months of talks in London and Geneva, he sent an alarming memorandum on the "European crisis":

It is now obvious that we grossly underestimated the destruction to the European economy by the war. [...] Europe is steadily deteriorating. The political position reflects the economic. One political crisis after another merely denotes the existence of grave economic distress. Millions of people in the cities are slowly starving. [...] Without further prompt and substantial aid from the United States, economic, social and political disintegration will overwhelm Europe. Aside from the awful implications which this would have for the future peace and security of the world, the immediate effects on our domestic

31. *FRUS 1947,* vol. 3, pp. 221–2.
32. Ibid., pp. 223–30.

economy would be disastrous: markets for our surplus production gone, unemployment, depression, a heavily unbalanced budget on the background of a mountainous war debt.[33]

Clayton thought that, short of a resounding appeal from the government to the American people to accept the sacrifices needed to prevent famine and chaos in Europe, the problem could not be resolved. He proposed a coordinated, rigorous recovery program in which the leading European nations would participate, steered by Great Britain, France, and Italy. By his reckoning, 6, or even 7 billion dollars in annual aid was needed over three years, and aid should be based on European economic federation.[34]

On 5 June, Secretary of State Marshall delivered his famous speech on a European recovery program at Harvard University, where he was receiving an honorary degree.[35] His address included a very pessimistic analysis of the European economy. It was meant to impress, to explain the consequences of the war in Europe to the American people, and to underscore the collapse of the basic framework of European economic and social activity. It also revealed the danger this grievous situation posed for world peace and prosperity in the United States. His statements were precise, coherent, and irrefutable: without foreign aid to help it meet its needs for food and other staple goods, Europe would sink even farther. The United States must be the provider, for it had a duty to help restore the world economy, without which there would be neither stability nor peace. "Our policy is directed not against any country or doctrine, he added, but against hunger, poverty, desperation and chaos. Its purpose should be the revival of a working economy in the world so as to permit the emergence of the political and social conditions in which free institutions can exist." Economic aid could not be extended piecemeal, but must be part of a comprehensive program drawn up by the participating European governments. Marshall also stated that all governments that agreed to cooperate with the program's implementation would benefit from United States aid. He warned, however, that the United States would oppose any government, party, or group that sought to perpetuate human hardship for political ends.[36]

33. "Memorandum by the Under Secretary for Economic Affairs (Clayton)" (Ibid., pp. 230–2).
34. Ibid., p. 233.
35. Ibid., pp. 237–9.
36. Ibid., pp. 237–8.

The Soviet Reply

British reaction to Marshall's speech was very positive. The French government was equally favorable.[37] In his speech on 13 June to the foreign press association, Bevin said that the secretary of state's speech might "well rank as one of the greatest in the world's history." The British minister clearly hoped that with US aid, the United Kingdom would be able to preserve its role as a great power that enjoyed privileged relations with the United States: "We are more than ever linked with the destinies of Europe. We are in fact, whether we like it or not, a European nation and must act as such. But we are not just a little island on the West of Europe. We are Great Britain, a link and bridge between Europe and the rest of the world."[38] There was a great temptation to use the Marshall Plan as a quick way of gaining credit sought within the framework of bilateral relations. But the United States leaders had taken the initiative of creating a global aid program because they wished to avoid this kind of haggling. The United States ambassador in London, Lewis Douglas, advised René Massigli to act soon: if he delayed to make his thoughts known, he would risk being presented with an Anglo–American agreement, whereas now he could direct views in Washington provided he moved fast![39] Bevin, although anxious for immediate aid to finance the massive imports needed for grain resupply, understood the necessity of cooperative action. He therefore proposed a bilateral discussion with the French government to examine the United States' proposals. On 17 June, he went to Paris to draft a joint reply with Bidault.

The Kremlin's first reaction to the Marshall Plan was, however, negative. Shortly after the secretary of state's speech, the 11 June issue of *Pravda* denounced the US aid program as an extension of the Truman Doctrine and a new display of imperialism against the forces of progress and democracy. Rather than buying each country separately, the United States leaders had thought up a plan by which they could appropriate Europe bodily by subjecting it to dollar colonialism. Moscow had no doubts that this initiative would create a "Western bloc" under the United States' absolute domination.[40] After the talks between Bidault and Bevin, TASS insinuated that France and Great Britain were attempting to expand at the expense of the USSR and other European countries.[41]

On 22 June, however, after its initial salvo, the Soviet government

37. FO 371/62399.
38. Ibid.
39. Massigli, *Une comédie des erreurs,* pp. 99–100.
40. Telegram from Ambassador Smith to the secretary of state (*FRUS 1947,* vol. 3, pp. 294–5).
41. FO 371/62400.

accepted a Franco–British invitation to discuss the US secretary of state's proposals in Paris. But from the outset of the Paris conference, Molotov made it clear that he was not prepared to accept the principles in Marshall's speech. He asked to know the exact sum total of resources involved in the program; he also expected a guarantee that the United States Congress would approve the plan.[42] After making this preposterous demand, he announced that he was opposed to all forms of planning requiring investigations of existing resources in European countries. Any request to investigate national requirements in terms of the Marshall Plan would be an attack on the sovereignty of the states concerned.[43]

On 28 June, Molotov publicly denounced the Marshall Plan in Paris. It was common knowledge, he said, that the United States was seeking to increase credit abroad to expand its own markets, yet the capitalist system was facing imminent crisis. The Soviet government had replied to *Monsieur* Marshall's proposal, he explained, despite the fact that its own socialist-style economy was sheltered from the crises and upheaval described in the secretary of state's speech. Notwithstanding, the USSR could not accept the idea of a comprehensive program for the European economies. It was in the process of rebuilding its own economy based on a five-year plan and would not stand for interference in domestic economic affairs; for this was a matter of the Soviet people's sovereign rights.[44] In the days that followed, it appeared that Molotov was again trying to drag out the negotiations in order to sap them of their substance.[45] Having adopted a policy of political isolation and economic autarky since the war, the USSR could not bend to the conditions of an aid program to revive the liberal economy in Europe. Furthermore, the Kremlin considered the statistical data which the United States authorities had requested to implement the recovery program to be state secrets. Indeed, as some Western observers suggested, it was not impossible that the Soviet leaders truly believed their own propaganda about an imminent economic crisis in the United States, an aggravated capitalist conflict between the US and British economies, and consequently the Marshall Plan's inevitable failure.[46]

The Western ministers refused to delay by yielding to these dilatory tactics and hence, the tripartite negotiations were a failure. Molotov denounced Bevin and Bidault's positions in vigorous terms. He warned them against the danger of dividing Europe. Immediately after this altercation, Bevin and Bidault invited all of the European countries (with

42. *FRUS 1947,* vol. 3, p. 298.
43. Jefferson Caffery to the secretary of state, 28 June and 29 June (Ibid., p. 299).
44. FO 371/62404.
45. Jefferson Caffery to the secretary of state, 29 June (*FRUS 1947,* vol. 3, p. 301).
46. Peterson to Bevin, 18 July 1947 (FO 371/66433).

the exception of the USSR and Spain) to confer in Paris on the United States aid proposal and to create a committee for its implementation.

The Soviet refusal to participate in the Marshall Plan was good from the Western perspective; for, in the summer of 1947, it was inconceivable that United States public opinion and Congress would accept the granting of economic aid to the USSR. Even before Molotov arrived in Paris, Bevin and Bidault had separately related their hopes that the USSR would refuse to participate in the Plan to the United States ambassador.[47] However, no one was blind to the fact that the Marshall Plan would intensify the Cold War, and the prospect was troublesome. Bevin laid out his views on the matter before the House of Commons in late June, stating that Russia was entirely responsible for what had happened:

> May I remind the Hon. Member with emphasis that the beginning of all that trouble was Russia. It was not Great Britain, it was not the United States. The proposal that special arrangements should be made for neighbouring countries in the discussion of the treaties was made by Soviet Russia. I pleaded with them, and urged them in the interest of the reconstruction of the world that that policy should not be followed.

In an address to members of the British far Left, Bevin added: "May I suggest that, before they [admonish] me on the division of Europe, they should ask their own [Soviet] friends why they have been dividing Europe." Bevin recalled that he had sat for six weeks in Moscow, attempting to obtain economic unity for Germany in order to secure that of Europe and to advance reconstruction on the continent. He said he was convinced that by accepting the United States' offer, he was seizing the first chance since the end of the war to see economic unity restored in Europe as a whole.[48]

French President Vincent Auriol would have liked to see the Soviet Union participate in the Marshall Plan to avoid splitting Europe into two hostile camps. On 29 June, however, after a meeting with Molotov, he noted in his diary: "I have the impression that the Soviet Union plans to keep its authority over all of the satellite states and build a vast empire, which it will dominate." To his mind, this European split was "catastrophic." He said as much to Molotov: "If you create blocs, there will be a war one day or another, especially if you intend to make them ideological blocs."[49] Bidault voiced agreement with Bevin, and their

47. *FRUS 1947*, vol. 3, p. 260.
48. United Kingdom, *Parliamentary Debates*, (Commons), 5th Series, vol. 438 (1947), col. 2338.
49. Auriol, *Journal*, vol. 1, pp. 312–13.

compact marked the beginning of the "Western bloc" that the Kremlin had apparently feared since the end of the war. The French foreign minister was resolved to confront the Soviet threats. He was convinced that the European nations must coordinate their economic recovery. His attitude, however, was not easy to defend. The political and social climate in France was bad. General de Gaulle was digging in against the republic's institutions and government action. Attacks by the French Communist party, although of another nature, had the same unsettling effect. Molotov had arrived in Paris with an enormous delegation, one of whose functions was to mobilize the French Communist party against the Marshall Plan.[50]

The aid program was a great hindrance to Stalin's East European policy. Fearless in its military and political hegemony, the Kremlin had imposed a series of trade agreements on the East European countries starting in 1945 in order to integrate them into its economic orbit. It also encouraged bilateral trade agreements among these states. In its liberalism, the Marshall Plan constituted a frontal attack on the USSR's imperial conceptions, especially because it was of the greatest interest to the governments and peoples of the states that the USSR had incorporated into its sphere and was turning into its satellites.

Hence, despite the preponderant influence of Communist members, the Czechoslovakian government accepted an invitation to the Paris conference. Its economy was still dependent on trade with Western countries. Yet, shortly after, it recanted. Foreign Minister Jan Masaryk, Communist Prime Minister Klement Gottwald, and Trade Minister Dritna had gone to Moscow and met with Stalin, who told them he was opposed to the Marshall Plan. Masaryk saw that it was futile to counter his menacing determination. "We have been reduced to vassals," he is said to have stated on returning.[51] The Western powers were aware of the Moscow dealings between Stalin and the Czechoslovak ministers.[52] What had most struck Masaryk, Auriol wrote in his diary, recalling his minister Maurice Dejean's account, was Stalin's insistence on the danger that US credit might allow Germany to recover as it had after the First World War, and his assertions that the Marshall Plan was an attempt to isolate the USSR.[53]

The Polish government also wished to send a delegation to Paris. It announced to the United States ambassador that it would be attending

50. Ambassador of the United Kingdom to the US secretary of state, 4 July (*FRUS 1947*, vol. 3, pp. 310–12).
51. Quoted by François Fejtö, *Histoire des démocraties populaires*, vol. 1, Paris, Le Seuil, 1969, p. 183.
52. Steinhardt to the US secretary of state (*FRUS 1947*, vol. 3, p. 319).
53. Auriol, *Journal*, vol. 1, p. 351.

the upcoming Paris conference.[54] Radio Moscow announced, however, that Poland had declined the Franco–British invitation.[55] In Hungary, all parties immediately declared themselves in favor of the Marshall Plan, and the program won broad support from the public. The Sovietization process had picked up speed after the conference in Moscow, however. Even before the Marshall Plan was launched, Hungarian Prime Minister Imre Nagy had gone to Switzerland for rest. Shortly after his arrival there, he received intelligence from Budapest that he risked arrest if he returned, for the Soviet authorities claimed that their interrogation of Béla Kovács, whom they had arrested in February and tortured, had produced evidence that the prime minister was involved in a plot against the republic. Imre Nagy resigned on 30 May. The Communists further enforced their position in the new Hungarian government under Lajos Dinnyés, also a Peasant party member, and continued their assaults to break up the majority in power.[56] By refusing to attend the Paris conference, the Hungarian government was clearly acting on outside orders, and the press made no mystery of it.[57]

The Marshall Plan therefore spurred the satellization process in the countries occupied by the Red Army. Poland and Hungary signed a new economic agreement with the USSR in mid-July, and Hungary and Yugoslavia signed yet another two weeks later. These were all bartering pacts under which each party agreed to deliver raw materials or industrial goods in consideration for quantities of products deemed equivalent or similar within a planned economy system based on the Soviet model. The USSR, which was lacking in everything, planned to use these agreements to help it implement its new five-year plan. Most important, it planned thus to turn these states into satellites, for the integration of their economies was an indispensable element in its political plan.[58]

The Communist parties were tightening their clamp on liberal forces in the Balkans. By ratifying the peace treaties, the United States had lost all means of pressuring the governments of the countries in the Soviet sphere. On 5 June, after the United States Senate ratified the peace treaty with Bulgaria, Petkov, the courageous leader of the Agrarian party, was arrested. He was sentenced to death in August and hanged the following month, despite Western protest. One week after the tragic event, the

54. Krystyna Kersten, *The Establishment of Communist Rule in Poland, 1943–1948,* Berkeley, University of California Press, 1991.

55. Fejtö, *Histoire,* p. 182.

56. Jörg K. Hoensch, *A History of Modern Hungary, 1867–1986,* London, Longman, 1988, pp. 180–1; Joseph Rothschild, *Return to Diversity. A Political History of East Central Europe since World War II,* Oxford, Oxford University Press, 1989.

57. Helm to the Foreign Office, 11 July 1947 (FO 371/62411).

58. Roberts to Bevin, 16 August 1947 (FO 371/66433).

United States recognized the Bulgarian government. In Romania, government repression of the opposition parties was even harsher. On 15 July, Iuliu Maniu, the head of the National Peasant party, was arrested along with other figures from his party. They were accused of conspiring with United States espionage to organize the overthrow of the government and set up a United States base in Romania. In August, the Liberal and Peasant parties were banned. One month later, the Social Democratic party was forced to merge with the Romanian Communist party.[59] Over the summer, the Hungarian liberal forces' room for maneuver grew increasingly narrow. Their parties were infiltrated, their leaders neutralized in various ways. In late August, the Communists called for new parliamentary elections. Despite fraud and coercion, they remained firmly in the minority, winning only 22% of the vote. Nonetheless, they managed to control the course of Hungarian political activity with repression tactics and by nibbling away at the opposition.[60]

The Development of American Hegemony

The division of Europe seemed complete, and this fracture left its mark on international politics as a whole. "These [were], in short, two worlds instead of one," Bohlen observed in a memorandum on 30 August 1947. This fact called for a broad revision of the postulates on which United States foreign policy previously had rested. The USSR was totally opposed to the idea of a united international society. It was consolidating its hegemony over the states it controlled in Europe and the Far East. Consequently, Bohlen wrote, the free world must do all it could to strengthen not only its political, economic, and financial union, but its military union as well. Charles Bohlen was convinced that a major political crisis between the United States and the USSR was close at hand, and feared that this might go as far as open warfare. The confrontation could not be avoided unless there was a fundamental change in Soviet policy. Meanwhile, the United States must secure the political support of the countries that were not yet in the Soviet sphere. By consolidating its power, the US could prevent the looming crisis from leading to war. Recovery and greater unity in Western Europe must be given absolute priority in United States policy.[61] The military, and Chief of Staff General

59. Barbara Jelavich, *History of the Balkans,* vol. 2, *Twentieth Century,* Cambridge, Cambridge University Press, 1984, p. 291. See also Auriol, *Journal,* vol. 1, p. 781.
60. See Miklós Molnár, *De Bela Kun à Janos Kadar. Soixante-dix ans de communisme hongrois,* Paris, Presses de la fondation nationale des sciences politiques, 1987, p. 355.
61. *FRUS 1947,* vol. 1, pp. 763–5.

Eisenhower in particular, shared this opinion.[62]

Under the circumstances, Washington had set to work consolidating its own sphere of influence and security system in Latin America. For some years, the Pentagon had advocated a coordinated arms program for Latin America, notably by pressuring Great Britain to stop shipping aircraft to Argentina. Naturally, this was a great economic and strategic gambit. On a continent jeopardized by large social fractures, the United States was supporting the established order and its traditional prop, the military. Most Latin American governments played up the Communist threat to justify their authoritarian regimes and demand arms shipments and increased economic aid. At this point, overt opposition of Colonel Perón's regime was out of the question.

On 2 September 1947, at the end of the Rio de Janeiro conference, the United States won approval for the inter-American treaty of reciprocal assistance. Article 3 stipulated that an attack against one of the states party to the agreement would be considered an attack against all American states. The defense treaty did not define aggression, but it was clearly understood that it could be invoked against possible threats of Communist subversion. In Latin America, as in Europe, containment strategy consisted in transforming economic structures and making financial aid grants. In Rio de Janeiro, there was heavy pressure on Secretary of State Marshall to support a new economic aid program. This was, however, out of the question, for the United States government's resources were not infinite and Europe was now an absolute priority for the Truman administration. Washington liked to believe that the recovery of European economies would aid development in Latin America.

The secretary of state made a formal statement that the Europeans must play an essential role in defining and implementing the US aid program. The same principle was endorsed in the State Department's internal deliberations. In this interpretation, the European governments would take a decisive part in drafting the program, whereas United States experts would be satisfied with offering them "friendly advice." It was inconceivable, however, for the Truman administration to raise the massive financial resources to aid foreign economies without imposing conditions on the capital's use. Congress and American business would not stand for it. In reality, United States leadership was determined to pursue the liberal objectives it had upheld since the war, and the Marshall Plan was meant to serve this purpose. It was the United States government's wish to promote European economic recovery by bolstering German reconstruction, lifting all restrictions on free trade, reestablishing currency convertibility, and creating a market large enough to revive

62. Ibid., pp. 762–3.

anemic production capacity. Eventually, the project would lead to Western Europe's economic and political integration;[63] but, as its momentum came from overseas, the movement would necessarily force the Western European countries to change their political tack and might interfere with traditional notions of national sovereignty.

It appeared inevitable that the French government would relinquish its claims on Germany. In early July, it had voiced a desire to merge its own sector with the Anglo–American bizonal area;[64] yet, at the Paris conference to define the European recovery program, it returned to its former position on Germany. It opposed the Anglo–American proposal to raise production in steel mills, coal mines, and industry in the bizonal area. To be efficient, aid under the Marshall Plan required an immediate increase in German industrial output. This, at least, was the thesis Washington and London supported.[65] The US and Britain were counting on Germany's political collaboration as well.

On 16 July, shortly after the Paris conference began, Bidault was informed of the Anglo–American decision to raise steel production in the Ruhr. He reacted harshly, panicked at the prospect of French opinion's predictable response. He feared that this policy would reduce France's share of reparations from Germany and interfere with the economic objectives of the Monnet Plan. He was especially worried about Communist party demagoguery, whose current anti-German campaign was aimed at undermining the Marshall Plan and destabilizing government action.[66] The French reaction was unfortunate, and might have blocked the negotiations. It was in direct opposition to Bevin's policy, which was firmly aimed at stopping aid that was going to Germany at the British taxpayer's expense. It crossed the policies of other European countries as well, in particular those of the Benelux countries and Italy. Yet the French government was vulnerable, and, if it fell, the decisions of the Paris conference would be gravely compromised. The possibility worried Bevin.[67]

The ongoing talks on Germany in London were of no comfort to the French Ministry of Foreign Affairs, which, regardless, had to resign itself to the industrial production rises already approved by Generals Robertson and Clay. In exchange, Prime Minister Paul Ramadier requested a new

63. Michael J. Hogan, *The Marshall Plan, America, Britain and the Reconstruction of Western Europe,* Cambridge, Cambridge University Press, 1987, p. 54.
64. FO 371/64204, 6 July 1947.
65. Hogan, *The Marshall Plan,* pp. 60–3.
66. Irwin M. Wall, *The United States,* p. 78.
67. CAB 1 29/20, C.P. (47) 209, 22 July 1947.

line of credit, promising to implement a comprehensive program for economic and monetary equilibrium, and espoused the United States' conception of European economic integration, acknowledging that the French sector must join the Anglo–American zone.[68] He added, however, that Germany's economic and political recovery should occur within the framework of a broader security system comprising a very strict control of the country.[69]

France's concessions notwithstanding, the Paris deliberations on the nature and meaning of the Marshall Plan did not meet the United States' expectations. Each of the governments represented on the Committee on European Economic Cooperation (CEEC), established to draft a reply to the US aid proposal, tended to present the financial requirements of its own country, surrendering nothing to the imperatives of multilateral cooperation and integration. Furthermore, Great Britain was not prepared to sacrifice its ties with the Commonwealth and its privileged relations with the United States to satisfy the demands of economic cooperation with the other European countries. By late summer, the Americans had grown impatient; they were disappointed by the extravagance of the European claims, but especially by the lack of real progress in defining a coordinated aid program. Time was running out, for the European economies were on a steady downhill course.

In early September, France was forced to admit that its monetary reserves would soon be exhausted. The French government was faced with suspending its raw material imports. Great Britain's situation was even more catastrophic. In July, the British government had reestablished the pound's convertibility to respect the commitments it had made as consideration for a United States loan in 1946. This was the worst possible time for it to fulfill its obligation. After the harsh winter and the droughts in summer, Great Britain was running shortages in oil, foodstuffs, and coal. It counted heavily on imports, particularly from the United States. Its social commitments were a further drain on its budget. Its dollar reserves were dissipating rapidly. It must negotiate more US aid immediately.[70]

In the meantime, it continued to reduce its foreign commitments. Since March, it had withdrawn 9,000 men from its forces in Greece. On 3 July, the Foreign Office informed the United States government that Great Britain would have to repatriate the rest of its troops – some 5,000 men – to respond to economic imperatives. The United States ambassador in Greece saw the prospect of their withdrawal as "catastrophic," for in his

68. Irwin M. Wall, *The United States*, p. 89.
69. John Young, *Britain, France*, pp. 66–7.
70. Hogan, *The Marshall Plan*, p. 68.

view the British forces were the last remaining deterrent against the "Slavic invasion" attempting to occupy the north of the country.[71] Secretary of State Marshall reacted strongly to the news, refusing to allow the British government to abandon its strategic responsibilities in Europe.[72] The Communist guerrillas were gaining ground and the Greek army was unable to cope. Marshall therefore insisted that Great Britain keep up its forces in Greece.[73] Given the circumstances in the summer of 1947, as the United Kingdom grew increasingly dependent on the United States, it was difficult to resist his pressure.[74]

In early September, Kennan commented on the "indescribable" situation with mixed feelings of compassion and disdain: the British people and government seemed to him "deeply sick," but "this sickness" appeared to be "endemic" to all of the governments participating in the Paris negotiations. He recommended aiding Europe "in spite of itself."[75] The United States administration began to put heavy pressure on the European governments to submit their proposals.

At the time, the political situation in Italy was continuing to fall apart. The Communist party had taken an even harder position, supporting strikes and acts of violence. Palmiro Togliatti threatened to overthrow the government by force.[76] Italy's ambassador in Washington, Alberto Tarchiani, told Under-Secretary of State Robert Lovett that he feared the Communist party would resort to insurrection in order to establish a government in the north with help from Yugoslavia.[77] Prophesies of this danger were brandished to prop up further requests for financial aid; they were not, however, absurd, for US and British forces were to leave Italy before the year's end. In early August, Marshall asked the British government to postpone the decision to withdraw its military force from Italy.[78] The United States ambassador informed the secretary of state that Italy had exhausted its dollar resources, and this would force it to further curtail economic activity. He anticipated a rise in unemployment and inflation, as well as social unrest of unprecedented proportions. He also

71. Lawrence S. Wittner, *American Intervention in Greece, 1943–1949*, New York, Columbia University Press, 1981, p. 228.

72. Allan N. Bullock, *Ernest Bevin, Foreign Secretary, 1945–1951*, Oxford, Oxford University Press, 1985, pp. 469–70.

73. CAB 129/5, C.P. (47) 228, 4 August 1947.

74. In fact, the last British forces pulled out of Greece in 1954 (see Wittner, *American Intervention*, p. 230).

75. *FRUS 1947*, vol. 3, pp. 401–3.

76. Memorandum of a conversation between ambassador Tarchiani and Norman Armou, Assistant Secretary of State for Political Affairs (*FRUS 1947*, vol. 3, p. 967).

77. Memorandum of a conversation between Ambassador Tarchiani and Robert Lovett, Acting Secretary (*FRUS 1947*, vol. 3, pp. 969–70).

78. FO 800/451, pp. 116–69.

feared Communist insurrection.[79] On 24 September, as the Policy Planning Staff reviewed the demonstrations and strikes organized in Italy, it saw in them the Communist party's intent to subject Italy to Soviet control. It acknowledged that the party might attempt to seize power by force.[80]

The Creation of the Cominform

The USSR was isolating itself by degrees. Since the beginning of the year, anti-American propaganda had taken on wild forms. It echoed Leninist themes of imperialism, economic crisis in the capitalist regime, and the inexorable movement of history, while exalting "Soviet man" and glorifying Stalin. Foreigners, and diplomats in particular, saw their movement circumscribed by security measures, which also prohibited contact with Soviet citizens.[81] The Soviet press was unleashed against the Marshall Plan and United States policy. On 18 September, shortly after the second session of the United Nations General Assembly convened, Vyshinskii, the USSR deputy foreign minister, made a scathing indictment of the United States and its Western allies, Great Britain in particular. He attacked the Marshall Plan as an instrument of United States imperialism that was forcing the European countries to sacrifice their sovereignty to satisfy the interests of United States monopolies. He read in it an attempt to divide Europe into two camps and to form a block opposed to the interests of democratic East European states – especially those of the Soviet Union – with aid from the United Kingdom and France. According to the Soviet minister, the United States meant to transform West Germany and the heavy industry of the Ruhr into a major economic base of American expansion in Europe. He also denounced the pro-war propaganda that was cropping up in the United States media, and the capitalist monopolies' role in these bellicose schemes. He pointed a finger at Churchill, whom he compared to Hitler. He also stigmatized the Netherlands' policy of aggression against the Indonesian people, the continued presence of British troops in Egypt, and the racial discrimination suffered by Indians in South Africa.

The USSR called a secret meeting of the principal European Communist party leaders, from 22 to 27 September in Szklarska Poreba, Poland, near Wroclaw, the former Prussian city of Breslau. The meeting's main objective was to change Communist party strategy, taking into

79. *FRUS 1947*, vol. 3, pp. 973–5.
80. Ibid., pp. 976–81.
81. *FRUS 1947*, vol. 4, pp. 562 et seq.

account the political circumstances the Marshall Plan had created in Europe. Moscow intended, among other things, to increase its sway with the regimes of these countries, and also to use the East European parties to mobilize the populace against the Marshall Plan in the West. The USSR ordered a revival of revolutionary tradition within the Communist parties. At the meeting, the Yugoslav delegates, Milovan Djilas and Edvard Kardelj, and Stalin's representative, Andrei Zhdanov, delivered harsh criticism of French and Italian Communist policy. Zhdanov envisaged abandoning the tactic of allying with other parties, which had made it possible to form government coalitions in Italy and France and patriotic "fronts" in the Eastern countries. Deputy Prime Minister Malenkov, a Politburo member, proclaimed that the struggle between the socialist and capitalist regimes had begun. The USSR, the embodiment of the cause of peace, must surround itself with antiimperialist democratic forces to shield the Socialist camp's conquests.[82] The meeting culminated in the creation of the Cominform, the successor to the Comintern, and, shortly afterward, began publishing *For a Lasting Peace, for a Popular Democracy,* a periodical of rabid Stalinist propaganda.

As Polish historian Krystyna Kersten points out, the Cold War was entering a new phase that would affect all of the countries in the Soviet sphere, further limiting the autonomy of national political forces and of the Communist parties in particular, which now followed orders from Moscow.[83] On 21 October, with the aid of the United States and British missions, Mikolajczyk fled Poland after he was informed that his parliamentary immunity was about to be lifted and that he would be tried and sentenced. The event brought an end to his efforts since 1945 to safeguard Polish freedom and independence. Several Peasant party leaders also followed the road to exile. As in all other noncommunist parties, subversive action and repression by the Soviet-appointed regime had rotted this group from the inside. It could no longer make itself heard or act independently. The government was extending its stronghold to cultural and artistic groups, which had previously enjoyed a certain freedom, and was intensifying its propaganda against the Roman Catholic Church.[84] In Romania, Iuliu Maniu and other opposition leaders were tried in the fall. The former head of the National Peasant party was sentenced to life imprisonment in early November. Ana Pauker and Vasile Luca, the most fanatical agents of the Kremlin, entered the government, the former as its foreign minister. The royal family was losing its room

82. François Fejtö, *Le coup de Prague,* 1948, Paris, Le Seuil, 1976, pp. 92 et seq.
83. Kersten, *Communist Rule in Poland,* p. 406.
84. Ibid., pp. 408 et seq.

for maneuver, and at the end of the year, it was forced to exile itself.[85] Bulgaria was also completing its transformation into a Stalinist regime, and repression of former parties and opposition forces grew sharper. Hungary, which had enjoyed some measure of freedom at home, was rapidly becoming a satellite. The Communists controlled Lajos Dinnyés's government, formed after the 23 September elections, for they held the main posts in the ministry and could count on support from ministers who had formerly belonged to other parties. In late November, the government nationalized banks and some 270 industrial and commercial businesses.[86]

Strategic Rapprochement in Europe and the Middle East

These events heightened the British and French governments' desire to tighten their economic and political ties, in an extension of the rapprochement that had led to their signing of the Treaty of Dunkirk. On 22 September, Bevin met with Prime Minister Paul Ramadier. The climate of their discussion was very cordial.[87] At a dinner in Paris on 6 October 1947, Bidault told the British minister that he had for long believed he would be able to cultivate a position as middleman between East and West. He saw now that his hope had been an illusion. The Russians' recent initiatives had convinced him of their determination to divide the international society artificially into two distinct worlds. Bidault reproached General Marshall for being overly conciliatory with the Soviet Union. He also lashed out against the United Nations Organization, which had done nothing save to recruit staff and had shown itself incapable of settling the Palestine question. Bevin, reporting the conversation to the Foreign Office, was now certain that the French minister had "completely burnt his bridges as regards the Russians."[88]

The French government was equally eager to establish military cooperation with London. In separate interviews with Sargeant and Bevin on 21 October in London, Ambassador Jean Chauvel mentioned the prospect of failure in the negotiations with the Soviet Union on Germany. France would join the area combining the Anglo–American zones, and the decision would cause its relations with the USSR to deteriorate further. New threats to security in the Western European countries would follow. Before taking this path, said Chauvel, France must improve its defense

85. *FRUS 1947*, vol. 4, pp. 492 et seq.

86. Jörg K. Hoensch, *A History of Modern Hungary*, p. 182. Cf. also Minister Selden Chapin's telegrams to the secretary of state (*FRUS 1947*, vol. 4, pp. 340–8 and pp. 384–92).

87. Young, *Britain, France*, p. 70.

88. FO 371/64207.

system and also be able to rely on support from England and the United States. Sargeant mentioned the Byrnes plan for a treaty with Germany, but this solution was no longer adequate, for the real threat to peace in Europe came from the USSR. Bevin was similarly vague. However, he touched upon the need for military cooperation between Great Britain and France, with the possible addition of Italy and the Benelux countries. He also suggested creating a vast political region encompassing Western Europe and Africa.[89] Chauvel proposed that the military chiefs of staff meet to prepare Western Europe's defense against Russia.[90] British military leadership was reticent to force cooperation, however, for it still feared Communist influence within the Defence Ministry.

In reality, to implement its strategic objectives, British leadership relied essentially on the privileged ties it had made with the United States during the war. Yet problems stemming from Middle East defense were still a source of discord between London and Washington. On 15 August, India's independence was proclaimed, while the Labour government remained deeply divided on the issue of continued military presence in the Middle East. Clearly, United States support was needed in this region. It had yet to be offered, however.

On 14 May 1947, the Soviet delegate astounded the United Nations General Assembly by announcing that he was in favor of the Palestine partition plan. Andrei Gromyko recalled that no Western state had been capable of defending the Jews against Hitler, and therefore it seemed appropriate that the Zionists should have their own state in Palestine, a country with which they had ancient historical ties. The proper solution, he added, would be for each of the two communities to have its own state with equal rights. If this proved impossible, however, they must resolve to share the territory. This change in position was surprising, for the Soviet Union had never lent support to the Zionist cause and had no reason to cut themselves off from the Arabs. But their top priority was to push the British out of Palestine while creating an inextinguishable forum for agitation in a region considered strategically important for the West.

In late August, the United Nations Special Committee on Palestine issued its report in Geneva. It recommended unanimously that the British mandate be terminated at the earliest possible date and that Palestine be granted independence. It had not, however, reached unanimous agreement on a policy to resolve the dire conflict. The majority had adopted a report recommending a partition of the territory into three distinct entities: a Jewish state, an Arab state, and a special entity in Jerusalem. The British mandate would continue for two years under United Nations supervision.

89. FO 371/67674.
90. Young, *Britain, France*, pp. 74–5.

The Jewish part would have the right to grant asylum to 150,000 immigrants. Before they became independent, the two states would sign a treaty of economic union, and their respective constitutions would contain provisions guaranteeing protection for minorities. Jerusalem would remain under United Nations trusteeship. The minority report, which was adopted by the Indian, Persian, and Yugoslav representatives, recommended the creation of a federal state after a period of three years, during which Palestine would be governed by a UN-appointed authority.

At this juncture, Bevin had a long meeting with the United States ambassador in London to discuss the problems of the Middle East. Great Britain intended to maintain its influence in the region. To this end, it planned to reinforce its military presence in Transjordania, keep its bases in Iraq, and pursue its protectorate in Kuwait. It also intended to remain in Sudan and Cyrenaica. Bevin was well aware that he could not ensure British predominance in this part of the world without United States aid, especially as his policy required substantial resources to guarantee economic and social development, which would counter nationalist or Communist influence. The United States constantly gave the impression that it was trying to undermine British policy in this region. Bevin was visibly bitter. The United States had supported the entry of 100,000 Jews in to Palestine. It had kept up regular shipments of equipment to Zionist terrorist groups. In the Security Council, the United States delegate supported Egypt's views.

On 18 September, in a memorandum to the cabinet, Bevin commented on the proposals of the United Nations Special Committee on Palestine. These motions, or at least those of the majority, seemed to him "so manifestly unjust to the Arabs" that Great Britain could not support them. He predicted an Arab uprising in Palestine, which would have the moral support of the entire Muslim world and active backing from the Arab states. Bevin also thought that the Zionists, who were trying to cope with demographic expansion and pressure from ultranationalist parties, would not accept the partition plan. They would attempt to enlarge Palestine's borders by stirring up the Arab irredentists. Great Britain could not increase its military force in Palestine, nor could it distance itself from the Arab states whose cooperation it needed to defend its strategic interests in the Middle East.[91] The Palestinian affair sparked an upsurge in anti-Western nationalism all over the Arab world; and, when negotiations with the Egyptian government on Sudan broke off, it was clear that Great Britain had lost control of current political developments in the region.

The United States was worried, especially because Great Britain clearly intended to reduce its commitments in the eastern Mediterranean. For

91. CAB 129, C.P. (47) 259, 18 September 1947.

this reason, Secretary Marshall accepted Bevin's request for secret deliberations on Western strategic defense in the Middle East. The talks were held in Washington in October. They confirmed the United States' intention to continue its containment of the USSR in the Middle East, and more generally, the Pentagon's desire to maintain Western influence there. The British and the Americans agreed to a cooperative defense of security and economic development in the region. They also resolved to preserve the territorial independence and sovereignty of Italy, Greece, Turkey, and Persia. The White House continued to advocate the Zionist program, but the State Department and the military were well aware of this irresponsible policy's predictable consequences. They feared that nationalist forces would erupt in the Arab world, and knew that the USSR might some day take advantage of the West's weakened positions in the Middle East. It was clear to them that it behooved the United States to take over Great Britain's traditional policies in the Mediterranean and the Middle East.[92]

92. FO 800/444.

10

THE DEFENSE OF EUROPE

The Division of Germany

By promoting the Marshall Plan, the United States leadership had shown its determination to defend Western Europe. But its support was slow in materializing, for negotiations of the Committee on European Economic Co-operation in Paris were complex and laborious, and a precise request for funding had yet to be submitted to the United States Congress. Considering the social and political difficulties the French and Italian governments were facing, rapid action was in order. On 24 October, President Harry Truman made a formal announcement that Italy and France would receive emergency aid to prevent their economies from collapsing. He invoked the looming threat of totalitarianism in these countries to defend the measure. In conjunction with the military and the CIA, the National Security Council – a new body created in July 1947 bringing together the main US foreign policy and strategy leaders under the president's authority – prepared an intervention program in Italy to prevent a Communist regime from forming. Italy's defense was henceforth a matter of priority for the United States.[1]

Was another war brewing in Europe? Charles Bohlen had mentioned the possibility in the summer, but George Kennan did not believe it. In early November, Kennan said that the Soviet government neither wished for nor anticipated war. He did, however, predict an upsurge of Communist agitation in France and Italy, arguing that the Kremlin sought to push the two countries into civil war. He also anticipated a new swell of insurgent movements in Greece. He submitted that the Soviet Union would move to integrate Czechoslovakia into its camp definitively, so that it could not serve as a spearhead for the East European democratic forces. In the long term, of course, the Russians would have trouble maintaining hegemony over 90 million Europeans, but they would strive nevertheless to impose their ascendancy over the Eurasian landmass.[2]

In November, the French Communists, apparently on Moscow's

---

1. Kenneth W. Condit, *The History of the Joint Chiefs of Staff. The Joint Chiefs of Staff and National Policy*, vol. 2, *1947–1949*, Wilmington, Glazier, 1979, pp. 65–81.
2. "Report of the Policy Planning Staff, 6 November 1947," *FRUS 1947*, vol. 1, pp. 770–7.

initiative, set off on a rampage of strikes and wrecking. The political tendency of these disturbances was obvious. By the end of November, 80,000 men had to be drafted to keep order and allow public services to function.[3] The Paris–Tourcoing was derailed on 3 December, claiming twenty-one victims.

These events coincided with the next sessions of the Council of Foreign Ministers, which sat in London from 25 November to 16 December to debate the future of Germany and Austria. Before the conference was convened, the Western powers were pessimistic about the outlook, for they expected no change in attitude from the USSR. They planned to reexamine the problems of German economic unity and reparations payments, as they had in Moscow. There were still hopes that obstacles preventing the movement of persons, ideas, and goods from zone to zone would be eliminated; there was also hope that German industrial production would be stepped up, and a monetary reform implemented. They were well aware that the Kremlin was not prepared to satisfy these requests. In early June, shortly after the United States and Great Britain decided to establish a German economic council, the Soviet Union had created a similar organization in their sector. Moreover, on 6 December, shortly after the Council of Foreign Ministers opened, the Soviet side called a Congress of German People for Unity and a Just Peace, which was to assemble representatives from all of the German antifascist parties and organizations. The Social Democratic Party (SPD) and the Christian Democratic Union (CDU) refused to join. The congress nevertheless appointed a delegation to plead the cause of German unity in London. The Western ministers refused to receive the delegation, and the British government denied its members entry visas.

Marshall and Bevin were willing to explore every avenue for quadripartite agreement on Germany, but they did not plan to carry on with a hopeless negotiation or to be interminably subjected to Molotov's procedural maneuvers and propaganda speeches. The secretary of state had clearly defined United States policy on the German problem. His position had hardened: unity must be brought about in accordance with the United States' conditions. It was out of the question for the Russians to take up a position in the Ruhr solely in the interest of hindering Germany's economic recovery. If the negotiations on this issue failed, as one could predict they would, the United States deemed an immediate monetary reform necessary in West Germany, followed by the creation of a German government body with real executive powers. The US did not wish to give up the rights and privileges it enjoyed in Berlin. The

---

3. René Massigli, *Une Comédie des erreurs: 1943–1956. Souvenirs et réflexions sur une étape de la construction européenne,* Paris, Plon, 1978, p. 105.

United States and Great Britain feared that the Soviet minister's tactic would be to compromise with the sole intention of hampering the implementation of the Marshall Plan. General Clay confided to the British ambassador in Washington that if the Russians suddenly conceded to their demands, the United States would be in a difficult position, for the economy of the area composed of the American and British zones was on the road to recovery and full German economic unity might break its momentum. Moreover, it was no longer certain that German unity would be compatible with the United States' European aid program.[4]

Bidault was still wavering, yet it was clear that Communist influence had been seriously diminished by the insurgent strikes in the previous weeks. The government had stood firm, and public opinion had followed. Admittedly, de Gaulle and his supporters had not come around on the German question: they still defended the idea of several independent German states, although they acknowledged that France could profit from German economic revival.[5] The French government's position on the matter had hardly changed since the Moscow conference and was especially inflexible on the issues of Germany's political regime and international control of the Ruhr. Yet at this point, Bidault's room for maneuver was negligible, considering France's economic dependence on the United States. Moreover, he saw that the French sector would have to be united with the Anglo–American combined zones.[6] On 28 November, he assured the secretary of state that he would remain in close contact with the US and British delegations throughout the conference and that he would present them with the positions he planned to defend in the plenary sessions. At a dinner the next day, Georges Bidault said he was convinced that the Russians were making no effort to reach agreement on Germany. "We must strengthen our collaboration and together confront a situation that threatens us all," he added. He did not want France to be invaded again; nor did he wish to resume his post as head of the French Resistance. Time was short, and action was in order. Bevin shared this view: he spoke of Western Europe's great resources, to which he attached those of the African colonies. Africa had a wealth of raw materials, he recalled, and in a few years, when the problems of communication among the continent's countries and regions were overcome, Great Britain could fully exploit these riches. If African resources were developed correctly, they would surpass those of the United States and the USSR combined;

4. Ibid.
5. See the 5 November 1947 telegram from Ambassador Jefferson Caffery to Secretary of State Marshall, which reports conversations with persons near to General de Gaulle's staff (*FRUS 1947*, vol. 2, pp. 699–700).
6. Bidault–Marshall meetings of 18 September and 8 October 1947 (*FRUS 1947*, vol. 2, pp. 680–4).

Western Europe could then adopt a policy independent from the two great powers. Bidault approved, but also stressed the need for close military collaboration between France and Great Britain. He was convinced that France must integrate with the Western camp and that the United States and Great Britain had an essential peacekeeping role to play in Europe.[7]

The Council of Foreign Ministers sessions unfolded as predicted. Molotov was completely isolated in the negotiations. He clamped onto his positions and was even more aggressive than usual. He accused the United States of trying to reduce Germany to slavery through its economic recovery program, and denounced American desire to turn Germany into a strategic base facing Europe's democratic states.[8] He repeated the positions he had adopted in Moscow, and blocked the discussion of Austria by refusing to allow a definition of the "German assets" that might be transferred to the USSR as reparations. At this point, agreement on the procedure for a peace treaty with Germany seemed impossible. Rapidly, Marshall grew convinced that the USSR was banking on the conference's failure.[9]

Immediately after the disappointing conference broke up, Bevin told Bidault that Europe now stood divided from Greece to the Baltic, from the Oder to Trieste, and that it would be difficult, if not impossible, to penetrate beyond these lines. Now, all efforts must be focused on saving Western civilization. He mentioned the idea of a European federation, and hoped that its military collaboration with the United States would be possible. Yet he feared that the United States would never enter an alliance under which it was bound to defend Europe.[10] The same day, he outlined a plan for a "Western democratic system," comprising the United States, Great Britain, France, Italy, the Netherlands, Belgium, Luxembourg, and the dominions, to Secretary Marshall. On 17 December, he brought up the plan again with Marshall, stating his conviction that Western civilization could be joined in spirit, and that France could rise again to great power. Marshall's reaction was positive, though he wanted to see a more concrete plan for the alliance. Bevin informed him that the French army chief of staff was due in London, and that he was hoping to reinforce France's military capacity. Western Europe's military must be restored to its former strength, he added. Clearly, he was sounding Marshall out on the possibility of support from the United States.[11]

United States leadership was resolved to recreate a "balance of power" in Europe, and it counted on the Marshall Plan and the European

7. FO 800/447.
8. *FRUS 1947*, vol. 2, p. 767.
9. Conversation between Bevin and Marshall of 2 December 1947 (FO 800/447).
10. Conversation between Bevin and Bidault (Ibid.).
11. Ibid.

integration movement to accomplish this. In his address reporting that the London conference had been a disappointment, Marshall stressed that the "political vacuum" that had been created in Europe after the war must be filled "by the restoration of a healthy European community."[12] During the London Conference, the secretary of state had proposed a merger of the German-occupied sectors to Georges Bidault. Bidault seemed to agree, though he hoped for international control of the Ruhr and military support from the United States and Great Britain in return. This had been his position at the Council's 19 December session.[13] Bevin and Marshall had met with Generals Lucius Clay and Brian Robertson shortly before the session: all had acknowledged that the Economic Council's powers must be extended progressively to include governmental responsibilities. The possibility of monetary reform was also mentioned, but the Berlin question, which remained unanswered, was still a source of concern.[14]

On 7 and 8 January 1948, Clay and Robertson met in Frankfurt with the premiers of the *Länder* in the Anglo–American combined zones and put forth a series of proposals reflecting their intention to restore some form of German government. Membership of the Anglo–American area's Economic Council, on which the *Länder* representatives sat, was to be expanded from 52 to 104. It would have the power to lay down customs duties and levy taxes. A legislative branch was to be established, with two representatives from each.

Länd; it would have the power to pass laws and would enjoy control over the Economic Council. Furthermore, the powers of the executive would be expanded to cover full management of the Anglo–American area's economic and financial affairs. The US and Britain also intended to create a central bank and a high court of justice.[15]

The proposals were publicized, and met with vehement Soviet protest. The French government, which had not been consulted, also reacted with surprise and hostility. It felt, in particular, that decisions made within the framework of the Anglo–American area were leading to the de facto establishment of a German government. It feared that this would give the Soviet Union an excuse to create its own German government in Berlin. It also disliked the fact that it had been excluded from negotiations which would necessarily determine Germany's future. Though it hoped

12. United States Department of State, *Documents on Germany, 1944–1985,* 1985, p. 139.
13. Pierre Gerbet, *Le relèvement, 1944–1949,* Paris, Imprimerie nationale, 1991, p. 282.
14. J.E. Smith (ed.), *The Papers of General Lucius D. Clay, Germany 1945–1949,* Bloomington, Indiana University Press, 1974, vol. 1, p. 514.
15. Ann and John Tusa, *The Berlin Blockade. Berlin in 1948: The Year the Cold War Threatened to Become Hot,* London, Coronet, 1989, p. 127.

that more power would accrue to the *Länder*,[16] it was in a poor position to influence US–British policy in the "bizonal area," as a high-ranking European Affairs official in the State Department pointed out on 16 January: "Public opinion in France on the German problem has not been allowed to evolve with the times. The armed truce by the political parties on this subject has frozen French thought on Germany as it was in 1944 when it differed hardly at all from 1919."[17] The United States government was not about to slow the program's implementation. The British government was more anxious than ever to reconstruct a stable, peaceful, democratic Germany. Bevin knew that the German people were going hungry, and he feared that prevailing conditions of poverty would lead to Communist, and eventually Soviet, domination.[18] In late January, even as the idea of a European security system was taking shape, the British chiefs of staff sensed that German rearmament was inevitable.[19] On 9 February, despite protest from the French, the political regime provided for under the Clay–Robertson agreement came to power.

The Bevin Initiative

The failure of the London conference, the problems surrounding German reconstruction, the USSR's expansionist policy in Europe, and subversive activity by the French and Italian Communist parties had convinced Bevin that Great Britain must increase its part in countering the Soviet threat. On 8 January, he submitted a long memorandum to the Cabinet proposing a European coalition of Western democratic countries, stronger ties with the Commonwealth, and an assembly of nations to defend the values of democracy, social justice, and freedom. Great Britain would steer the movement, guiding its spiritual, moral, and political direction.[20]

Bevin was convinced that the Soviet government was counting on economic "chaos" in Europe. On 13 January, he sent a memorandum to the Department of State proposing a union of Western countries:

> The Soviet Government, has formed a solid economic and political block. There is no prospect in the immediate future that we shall be able to re-establish and maintain normal relations with European countries behind their line. [...] Indeed we shall be hard put to it to stem the further encroachment of the Soviet

16. *FRUS 1948,* vol. 2, p. 20, p. 34.
17. Ibid., p. 28.
18. Ernest Bevin and George Marshall (Ibid., p. 24).
19. Chiefs of Staff Committee, 27 January 1948 (FO 800/452).
20. Allan N. Bullock, *Ernest Bevin, Foreign Secretary, 1945–1951,* Oxford, Oxford University Press, 1985, pp. 513 et seq.

tide. It is not enough to reinforce the physical barriers which still guard our Western civilisation. We must also organise and consolidate the ethical and spiritual forces inherent in this Western civilisation of which we are the chief protagonists. This in my view can only be done by creating some form of union in Western Europe, whether of a formal or informal character, backed by the Americas and the Dominions.[21]

Bevin planned initially to invite the Belgian, Dutch, and Luxembourg governments to join a defense system similar to that described in the Treaty of Dunkirk. In the long term, the alliance he imagined would include Greece, and possibly Portugal and the Scandinavian countries. Later, it could be extended to Spain and Germany, countries "without whom no Western system [would] be complete."[22] He was relying on the Marshall Plan to accelerate European economic revival, but also on French cooperation in starting a development plan for Africa.[23]

Two weeks later, on 22 January, he delivered a momentous speech on foreign policy to the House of Commons. The Soviet Union, he declared, had not respected the commitments it had made during the war, notably at the Yalta conference. It had used every available means to impose Communist regimes on the East European countries. Referring to the brutal Sovietization of Poland, Bulgaria, Hungary, and Romania, and the complete eradication of democratic opposition in East Germany through police coercion, he pointed out the extreme aberration of these totalitarian regimes, when one considered the objectives of the Second World War and the blood spilt in the struggle against nazism and fascism. He implied that a new advance of Soviet hegemony was in the working, apparently alluding to Czechoslovakia, and perhaps Italy. In an implicit reference to Churchill's famous speech at Fulton, he recalled that the Soviet Union's European border had advanced from Stettin (i.e. Szczecin) to Trieste. He also mentioned the unsolved problems of Trieste, the Communist threat in Greece, and the USSR's attempts to exploit international crises to its own ends through a "war of nerves" and propaganda speeches. Invariably, the Soviet Union had blocked negotiations at international conferences, it had used the United Nations as a platform from which to rain insults on its Western opponents. Finally, he pointed out Moscow's reaction to the Marshall Plan, its creation of the Cominform, and the methods used by the Soviet Union and its Communist allies to prevent US aid from

21. *FRUS 1948,* vol. 3, pp. 4–5.
22. Ibid., p. 5.
23. Note from British Ambassador Lord Inverchapel to the United States secretary of state, 13 January 1948 (Ibid., pp. 3–4). British memorandum presenting Bevin's consideration of the formation of a Western European union (Ibid., pp. 4–6).

being implemented.

To cope with the threats, the Soviet Union's expansion, and the further development of the police state, Bevin proposed a consolidation of Western European countries that shared "a hatred of injustice and oppression," "parliamentary democracy," the desire to achieve "economic and social rights," and "a conception and love of liberty common among us all." His plan was imprecise, but he mentioned that the Treaty of Dunkirk with France could be extended to the Benelux countries and Italy. He also envisioned a larger consolidated political space comprising the European empires. In his view, South Africa, France, Belgium, Portugal, and the Netherlands had a shared responsibility to their colonies, which were regions rich in raw materials. He suggested stronger collaboration among these states and the British Commonwealth to improve the quality of life of the indigenous populations and to plan their economic, social, and cultural development. In this context, he pointed out Great Britain's influence in the Middle East and the region's strategic importance for the Commonwealth. He also underscored the role of the United States and the Americas in the common defense of Western civilization. A way of integrating Germany into the family of democratic nations must be found, he submitted.[24]

Bevin's speech was welcomed by public opinion in Great Britain and the United States.[25] The British minister naturally counted on political and military support from Washington. On 27 January, he proposed an Anglo–American military conference with the Department of State, similar to the recent talks on the Middle East, to examine how the United States might reinforce the European defense system. Although reaction to Bevin's plan was positive, the State Department was preoccupied with the coming debate in Congress on the European recovery program. At this point, therefore, it could not openly support a draft alliance that might harden isolationist opposition to the Marshall Plan.[26] It was, however, gratified to see that a European initiative to strengthen defense of the Old World was developing. John Hickerson, the State Department's head of European affairs, and George Kennan even mentioned the possibility that a European organization might one day be strong enough to constitute a third power able to match the USSR or the United States.[27] In the

---

24. See Margaret Carlyle, *Documents on International Affairs, 1947–1948,* Oxford, Oxford University Press/Royal Institute of International Affairs, 1952, pp. 201–21.

25. Bullock, *Ernest Bevin, Foreign Secretary,* pp. 520–2.

26. *FRUS 1948,* vol. 3, p. 22.

27. See memorandum from the director of the Policy Planning Staff (Kennan) to the secretary of state, and especially the memorandum of a conversation between the director of the European Affairs Bureau (Hickerson) and British Ambassador Lord Inverchapel of 21 January 1948 (*FRUS 1948,* vol. 3, pp. 7–12).

American view, Europe's economic recovery was primarily contingent upon Germany's recovery and the development of an economic and political integration movement in Western Europe. This policy would entail a new military security system, for one thing to assuage French public opinion's qualms about Germany, but also, more crucially, to offset Soviet power. For this reason, the plan for a European alliance modeled on the Treaty of Dunkirk – which was pointed against Germany – met with some skepticism in Washington. On the other hand, the Department of State approved the idea of the United States being in some way associated with a European defense system. The treaty of Rio de Janeiro, which bound the Americas to come to each other's defense against outside aggression, was suggested as a model.[28]

The Cold War was escalating, and the United States faced unavoidable strategic choices. European defense remained, as in the Second World War, a priority in US security policy, but strategy implementation was controversial. On 24 February 1948, in a long memorandum to the secretary of state, George Kennan denounced the universalistic inspiration behind the United Nations Organization. It seemed to him neither possible nor desirable to resolve all international problems on the basis of identical legal norms and procedures. Adhering to abstract principles of international law and intergovernmental institutions was no guarantee of peace. The international society embraced a great diversity of ideologies and cultures, and it would be a dangerous illusion to believe that the United States government could shrug off national differences when drafting its containment strategy. The United States certainly could not fight every Communist threat that cropped up the world over. It must not commit its armed forces to fighting resistance movements overseas that enjoyed large popular support. According to Kennan, "power politics" was a reality. For the United States, this meant ensuring security by promoting regional equilibrium, and possibly by entering limited alliances based on real common interests. Consequently, he conceived of a defense strategy based on his knowledge of classical geopolitics, which would entail, notably, military bases in Libya, Crete, and even Italy to counter Soviet pressures in the Mediterranean and force the Kremlin to curtail its support of national Communist forces. For this reason, the plan to create a Western European union, an alliance at once political, economic, and military, appeared to him an excellent one. He believed that West Germany would soon be able to join such a union. Yet he was not convinced that the United States should have a formal association with this security system. Finally, he approved of a joint undertaking by

28. See meeting between Lord Inverchapel and the director of the European Affairs Bureau (Hickerson) of 21 January 1948 (Ibid., pp. 9–12).

the Western European nations to develop and promote the African continent.[29]

As it prepared to defend Western Europe, the United States could not ignore its economic and political interests in the rest of the world. The situation in Korea had hardly advanced, and socioeconomic conditions in China were deteriorating steadily. After completing his mission, General Albert Wedemeyer submitted a report to the secretary of state that he saw little hope for the Chiang Kai-shek regime. The Communists controlled Manchuria and northern China; they had a good chance of moving farther. Could they be stopped? Marshall was familiar with the problem, and he knew that the United States could hardly expect to change the course of events in China. Early that year, Kennan had suggested redefining United States strategy in the Pacific. Liberal political philosophy did not seem to him to apply to Asia's civilizations. The United States could not presume to lead the peoples of the Asian continent, whose poverty was appalling, and whose agricultural production could not keep up with demographic growth. He was convinced that it would be difficult for the Asian population to adapt to conditions of modern living. The process of development would be brutal for them, and many would fall under Moscow's influence by succumbing to the lure of communism. The United States must keep its opinions to itself: it would gain nothing from propagating its vague, abstract concepts of human rights, democracy, and economic and social welfare the world over. Kennan proposed that the US should leave Korea and, more urgently, China. In addition, however, it should completely revise its occupation policy in Japan to foster the recovering Japanese economy and consolidate Japan's power to resist the Soviet threat and Communist penetration. He recommended that the United States keep up its bases in the Philippines, for, as he saw it, the islands were crucial to United States defense in the region.

The chief of the Policy Planning Staff left for Japan in February 1948 to examine the measures that would replace General MacArthur's policy of control and reparations and to study conditions for a peace treaty.[30] The secretary of state joined Kennan in acknowledging that the United States had strategic choices to make, and that China was a poor and backward country. Yet the military did not accept their resignation, nor did the Chinese lobby, which was powerful in the United States Congress. If it did not receive some satisfaction, the lobby could become a further obstacle in the European recovery program. In February, Marshall proposed a program of 570 million dollars in economic aid for the Chiang

---

29. *FRUS 1948*, vol. 1, pp. 510–29.

30. Michael Schaller, *The United States Crusade in China: 1938–1945*, New York, Columbia University Press, 1979, pp. 122 et seq.

Kai-shek government. Soon after, Congress added 125 million dollars in military aid to the figure.[31]

The Western European Union

Bevin's speech had a great influence on Europe's capital cities, and on Brussels in particular, where Paul-Henri Spaak immediately sensed the historical significance of Bevin's initiative. On 23 January, Spaak published a communiqué underlining Belgium's interest in the British foreign minister's remarks, and its will to collaborate with its colleagues from the Netherlands and Luxembourg. One week later, the foreign ministers of the Benelux countries gave their full support to the initiative and announced they were prepared to enter negotiations, suggesting that "the main lines of a common position inspired by a Western European sense of solidarity and the consciousness of the role their countries might play in [Western Europe's] consolidation" be defined.[32]

The reaction of French leaders and public opinion was more mixed. Of course, European construction as a theme enjoyed an broad following, especially among those who were concerned about the Soviet threat and Communist subversion. This idea's development helped make palatable the idea of Germany's inevitable recovery, while legitimating a new political order that would conform with economic integration as defined in the Marshall Plan. Moreover, the strikes in the fall of 1947 had once again made it obvious that the national defense was inadequate.[33] In diary entries starting early that year, Vincent Auriol had often raised questions of security. These he connected with threats of subversion and plotting by the Communists and the Gaullists. He wrote on 5 February 1948 to General Koenig, "If war breaks out abroad, the commander of the French forces in Germany, there will be no escaping civil war, and we shall have to fight on two fronts, one at home, and one abroad."[34] The vulnerability of France and Europe seem to have plagued him. Yet President Auriol still cherished the idea of a "third power": with support from other European countries – Britain, Belgium, and the Netherlands in particular

31. Melvyn P. Leffler, *A Preponderance of Power. National Security, the Truman Administration and the Cold War,* Stanford, Stanford University Press, 1992, pp. 246–51.

32. Paul-Henri Spaak, *Combats inachevés,* vol. 1, *De l'indépendance à l'alliance,* Paris, Fayard, 1969, p. 255.

33. Ibid., pp. 256–7; Massigli, *Une Comédie des erreurs,* pp. 106 et seq. The latter were reticent, as was the United States. See US secretary of state to the French ambassador (*FRUS 1948,* vol. 3, pp. 33–4).

34. Vincent Auriol, *Journal du septennat, 1947–1954,* Paris, Armand Colin, 1970, vol. 1, p. 67.

– France would seek its role as moderator between "Russia and the United States."[35] He was wary of the US–British policy in Germany, for the dangers it posed to France were troubling, and, furthermore, it meant cutting Europe in two. He was particularly worried that the policy would lead West Germany to look to the USSR for help in unification, or even that it might drive the Soviet Union to declare war. Despite its misgivings over the developments in Kremlin policy, the French Ministry of Foreign Affairs was equally concerned by the British initiative's anti-Soviet tone, and Georges Bidault predicted that this would deepen the rift between the two European camps beyond repair. Robert Schumann's government, however, was aware that French security in Europe was precarious. He knew that he could not do without support from Great Britain and the United States, and he hoped that they would indeed commit themselves to protecting Western Europe from the USSR.[36]

Events brewing in Prague would soon precipitate the European integration movement and steel the British and French governments in their determination to join, with the United States, in a defense alliance against the USSR. The crisis had been smoldering since the fall; it was brought to a head when the Communists decided to take action to secure control of the state apparatus before the elections scheduled for May. Since early in the year, they had been aggravating social conflict, and their ascendancy now encompassed the army and police forces. Poorly organized and subverted by fellow-travelers, the moderate parties appeared incapable of offering any real resistance. On 20 February, they handed in their collective resignation to protest the infiltration of the police by the Ministry of the Interior. President of the Republic Edvard Benes was the democratic forces' last hope, but he was elderly, ill, and had always been indecisive. He gave in to organized insurgent agitation, and accepted the constitution of a government that was entirely under the heel of Stalinist Prime Minister Klement Gottwald. Events sped on, and within a few days censorship, arrests, and intimidation tactics completed Czechoslovakia's transformation into a Communist state.

On 26 February, French, US, and British government representatives meeting in London condemned in very severe terms the methods used to suspend parliamentary procedure and establish a Communist party dictatorship in Czechoslovakia. In reality, the United States and Great Britain had already resigned themselves to surrendering Czechoslovakia to Stalin's sphere of influence. Weakness and vacillation in Czechoslovakian

35. Ibid., p. 66.

36. See further the conversation of 29 January among, on one side, American General Harold Bull, personal representative of the Chief of Staff, US Army (Eisenhower), and, on the other, Georges Bidault and Minister of the French Armed Forces Pierre-Henri Teitgen (*FRUS 1948*, vol. 3, pp. 617–22).

foreign policy since 1945, and its alignment with Soviet positions in the United Nations, had not prompted Washington and London to act sooner. After the "coup d'état," Lawrence Steinhardt, the United States ambassador in Prague, requested that the United States sector in Germany be temporarily closed to Czechoslovakian export goods so as to pressure the Prague authorities. The Department of State had, however, refused.[37] Clearly, the United States could do nothing to change the course of events, especially since the Czechoslovakian people and its elites had made no sign of resistance when their liberties were jeopardized. Czechoslovakia was now a Communist state. On 10 March, the foreign minister, Jan Masaryk, son of the founder of the republic, Tomas, was found dead on the cobbled courtyard of the Cernín palace. His tragic death symbolized the end of freedom in Czechoslovakia.

These events accelerated the negotiations on West Germany, which had been in session in London since 23 February. The Netherlands, Belgium, and Luxembourg had been invited to the conference. The United States planned to end its occupation of Germany, and this policy inevitably had a dramatic effect on the discussions as they unfolded. On 20 February, the secretary of state summarized the US position clearly: Germany, exhausted since its defeat, was no longer a military threat; within the new geostrategic balance, it could no longer attain the same political position it had in the past, at least not in the foreseeable future. Yet its foreign policy would be as dependent on its domestic regime as on its international position. The Soviet sector, like the other East European satellites, was fashioned after a totalitarian model. Its economy was now incorporated in the Communist bloc. Consequently, the Western powers must prevent Germany from being pulled as a body into the Soviet orbit. It was their responsibility to guarantee Germany's economic recovery, which would in turn contribute to Europe's recovery. Germany must therefore be incorporated in the Western European community. Bevin was in agreement with this and with the idea of creating a German government.[38]

The French government still opposed restoring Germany's sovereignty, and did not want the occupation to end. It still maintained that the Länder should be considered the principal components of power and thus envisaged a federal structure of no great importance. France's strongest recommendation was for continued Allied control of the Ruhr.[39] In the face of Anglo–American determination, however, its room for maneuver grew increasingly slim. The Prague coup further weakened its ability to conduct an independent policy. Hervé Alphand, who was with the French

37. *FRUS 1948*, vol. 4, p. 742.
38. *FRUS 1948*, vol. 2, pp. 71–3.
39. Ibid., pp. 98 et seq.

delegation in London, noted in his diary on 24 February: "The Soviet menace seems imminent. Western solidarity is about to be transformed. It would appear that nothing at this point is more urgent than to cope with this new danger."[40]

After an initial phase of difficult negotiations, which ended on 6 March, the French accepted the principle of economic and political recovery in West Germany. They gave up their request for the Rhineland to be detached. They also relaxed their position on international control of the Ruhr, and allowed that their sector should benefit from the Marshall Plan and merge with the combined Anglo–American zones. This first agreement provided for a democratic Germany, which would participate in "the community of free peoples." The move to install a German government based on a federal constitution had begun. Secretary George Marshall had taken France's security concerns into account, however, and promised to support the creation of a tripartite body to monitor German disarmament and demilitarization.[41] Evidently, it was impossible to formulate a European security system that could thoroughly dispel French worries over a resurgence of the threat from Germany.

President Vincent Auriol saw the Prague coup as the sign that the USSR would not back down at the possibility of war. This was at least his interpretation of the dispatches the French ambassadors in Prague and Moscow sent him.[42] The Kremlin seemed to be gambling on Western democracy's weakness, pacifism, and division.[43] Shortly after the event, Stalin invited the Finnish president, Juho Paasikivi, to Moscow to sign a treaty of friendship and military alliance. Western chancelleries interpreted the proposal as a portent of Finland's imminent incorporation into the Soviet sphere. Norway was especially worried by this threat, as the Norwegian foreign minister informed the British government.[44]

On 4 March, Bidault sent an important message to the United States secretary of state on the consequences of the Prague coup and the division of Europe. The iron curtain, he recalled, had already descended upon Hungary, Bulgaria, Romania, and Poland. Czechoslovakia was the latest victim of the Soviet *Gleichschaltung*. He was apprehensive that similar events would occur in Austria, Italy, or elsewhere. France hoped to participate in the defense of liberty. Unfortunately, it did not have the means to match "what fate had thrust upon it."[45] The United States' efforts

40. Hervé Alphand, *L'étonnement d'être. Journal (1939–1973)*, Paris, Fayard, 1973, p. 206.
41. *FRUS 1948*, vol. 2, pp. 122–3.
42. Auriol, *Journal*, p. 111, p. 119, pp. 131–2.
43. Ibid., p. 119.
44. Bullock, *Ernest Bevin, Foreign Secretary*, p. 532.
45. Quoted by Irwin M. Wall, *The United States*, p. 133.

in European economic reconstruction must be extended to the political and military levels. The French minister therefore proposed to the secretary of state that Great Britain, the United States, and France confer on the subject soon.[46] Marshall was clearly pleased with this move: "We share your views as to the seriousness of the developments in Europe and as to the urgency of determining the best course to be adopted to prevent the expansion of the area of Communist dictatorship. We appreciate fully, I think, the dangers facing France and the other free countries of Europe." He stressed that the consolidation of a European defense system was a precondition to US participation in creating a broader system.[47] The Department of State sent a similar message to Bevin.

When Bevin arrived in Paris in mid-March to attend the Conference on European Economic Cooperation, he found Georges Bidault and Maurice Couve de Murville visibly fearful that Russia would soon declare war. The Western world was beginning to take shape, but it was still weak. The Soviet Union would be crazy not to seize this moment to deal a heavy blow, said Bidault.[48] On 11 March, Bevin used the Soviet threat as a rationale to repeat and further define his proposal to the US government to create one or more security systems for Europe, the Atlantic, and the Mediterranean.[49]

At the time, relations between the Western powers and the Soviet Union were deteriorating rapidly in Germany. In March, the German people's congress held its second meeting, where it decided to create a people's council of four hundred deputies, and a twenty-nine member presidium. It also announced its request for a nationwide plebiscite on the questions of "unity and a just peace."[50] Hence, the Soviet Union was preparing to implement its own political structures in its sector. Moreover, the periodic meetings among Berlin's leaders – the Allied commanders – were crippled by the Soviet representative's invective. Robert Murphy, General Clay's political adviser, believed that this was a tactic to set the stage for the Soviet withdrawal from the Allied control bodies.[51] On 5 March, General Clay sent a telegram to Washington to say he sensed that war was nearing. "For many months, based on logical analysis, I have felt and held that war was unlikely for at least ten years. Within the last few weeks, I have felt a subtle change in Soviet attitude which I cannot define but

46. *FRUS 1948*, vol. 3, p. 38.
47. Ibid., p. 50.
48. Conversations of Bevin, Bidault, and Couve de Murville (FO 800/447).
49. *FRUS 1948*, vol. 3, pp. 46–8.
50. Peter Calvocaressi, *Survey of International Affairs 1947–1948*, Oxford, Oxford University Press, 1952, pp. 258–9.
51. Murphy to the secretary of state, 3 March (*FRUS 1948*, vol. 2, pp. 87–9).

which now gives me a feeling that it may come with dramatic suddenness."[52]

The Department of State grew alarmed as well. On 8 March, John Hickerson, the head of the European Affairs Bureau, sent a memorandum to Secretary Marshall suggesting he consult with the congressional leaders on measures to contain the further expansion of Communist dictatorship in Europe. The USSR government might take risks if it underestimated the United States' will to defend Western Europe. Furthermore, if the United States did not show its determination conspicuously, populations would resign themselves to integration in the USSR's orbit. Hickerson held that the United States must make a public commitment to take all necessary measures, including the use of armed force, to beat back further Communist expansion; its determination was a matter of national security. Hickerson therefore suggested that the United States enter an agreement for the defense of the Atlantic and the Mediterranean.[53]

These projects were not unrelated to the fear of a further Communist advance in Italy. Reports from the United States ambassador in Rome indicated that the Communists were now imposing themselves by force in northern Italy. Parliamentary elections were scheduled for 17 April, and there was no indication that the Christian Democrats and their allies would win. Pietro Nenni's Socialist party was campaigning against the Marshall Plan and denouncing austerity measures taken by the De Gasperi government. The United States was determined to intervene, militarily if necessary, to prevent the forces of the far left from taking power. Meanwhile, the CIA was lending financial support to the Christian Democrats, the Vatican was mobilized against the Left, and a vast propaganda campaign was launched to coax voters to choose the Western camp. On 15 March, the Department of State announced that Italy would not benefit from aid under the Marshall Plan if the election results allowed the Communists to enter a coalition government.[54]

Negotiations on a multilateral defense system had opened in Brussels. They ended on 17 March in the signing of the Brussels pact by the United Kingdom, Belgium, France, Luxembourg, and the Netherlands. The five countries party to the treaty promised mutual assistance if any party was the victim of armed aggression in Europe. The agreement's preamble recalls the parties' "faith in fundamental human rights, in the dignity and worth of the human person," their intent "to fortify and preserve the principles of democracy, personal freedom and political liberty, the

52. Walter Millis (ed.), *The Forrestal Diaries*, New York, Viking, 1952, p. 387.

53. *FRUS 1948*, vol. 3, pp. 40–2.

54. James A. Miller, *The United States and Italy 1940–1950. The Politics and Diplomacy of Stabilization*, London, University of North Carolina Press, 1986, pp. 243 et seq. See also Leffler, *A Preponderance of Power*, p. 206.

constitutional traditions and the rule of law, which are their common heritage." In the first articles, the parties also laid down their desire to jointly promote European economic recovery, and their will to harmonize their economic and social policies and foster cultural exchange.

The day the Brussels pact was signed, Harry Truman announced to the Senate that he wished the United States to take part in European defense, breaking definitively with traditional American isolationism. The next week, on 22 March, a series of security meetings of the utmost secrecy began in Washington among State and Defense Department representatives and their British and Canadian counterparts. France had no representative at the talks, the subject matter of which was the possibility of a military assistance agreement joining the United States, Canada, and the states party to the Brussels pact. France's position on Germany remained equivocal, and in the eyes of the United States, this justified excluding it from the exploratory talks on European defense. Military circles in the United States and Great Britain were still wary of involving French representatives in their secret strategy negotiations for fear that the Communist party had infiltrated the French army and administration. This was a wise precaution! Donald MacLean, a first secretary at the British embassy in Washington, was a Soviet spy. In his position, he had access to the most sensitive documents concerning diplomatic and strategic relations between London and Washington. He followed the entire negotiations, the purpose of which was to join the United States with Western European security and which produced the North Atlantic Treaty one year later.[55]

In January 1948, Bevin had spoken of a Western defense program to protect the colonial empires. The Brussels pact had a more limited scope, as did the draft treaties being drawn up in Washington. Yet for the United States, Western European defense was part of a worldwide security strategy to contain the threat of the USSR and its Communist proponents. It was therefore not surprising that United States leadership was changing its views of the European empires. Admittedly, it did not approve of renewed military action in Indochina: it thought that France should end its colonial regime and progressively hand over control to the moderate nationalists, accepting the establishment of an autonomous Indochinese government. It hoped nevertheless that France would honor its responsibilities in Indochina, and that it would fight off communism or "already apparent anti-Western or Pan-Asian tendencies" in that country.[56] On 22 March 1948, the Policy Planning Staff issued a memorandum on

55. *FRUS 1948*, vol. 3, pp. 59 et seq.
56. George Marshall to Ambassador Jefferson Caffery, 13 May 1947 (*FRUS 1947*, vol. 6, pp. 95–7).

the importance of preventing North Africa "from falling into the hands of elements hostile to [the United States] or vulnerable to penetration by political forces outside the Atlantic community." Indeed, the Department of State and the Pentagon lent great strategic importance to North Africa, which lay on US and British maritime routes to the eastern Mediterranean and the Middle East. Nationalist agitation was particularly rampant in Morocco. During the war, the United States had encouraged it. The Department of State considered the Moroccans to be unprepared for independence, since they had neither the right persons nor the technical know-how to lead the country without foreign aid; yet it feared the possibility of a North African nationalist-Communist alliance. Therefore, the Department planned to support France politically, while encouraging it to develop a policy in favor of its mandates and colonies progressively evolving into independent regimes.[57]

Protection of the Middle East was now considered vitally important to United States security.[58] The war was raging in Palestine, and Washington feared that the conflict would have dire consequences. The United States was growing increasingly dependent on oil from the Middle East, and the Marshall Plan would fail if supplies were cut.[59] By supporting Israel, the United States government risked cutting itself off from the Arab world. The Department of State and the military were aware of this, and the prospect worried them. The Middle East was becoming Secretary of Defense James Forrestal's bête noire. In his view, the impossibility of the partition plan was a fact that must be faced. Furthermore, he was convinced that the United States did not have the military means to honor its heavy political and strategic commitments in the Middle East. Great Britain still had some 60,000 men in Palestine, and if the United States were to intervene in the region, it would lack adequate resources. Military forces were insufficient everywhere.[60] In late February, Marshall tried to convince Truman to reconsider his support of the partition plan for Palestine, and the president wavered. On 19 March, the United States representative to the United Nations requested a cease-fire, suggesting that the United States might rethink its position on a United Nations trusteeship. In late March, the president asked Great Britain to continue its military presence in Palestine. He also contemplated an envoy of US forces to the war-ridden country. In April, as the situation in Palestine continued to deteriorate, the United States asked the French and British governments to plan dispatching armed forces to Palestine

57. *FRUS 1947*, vol. 3, pp. 682–8.
58. *FRUS 1948*, vol. 1, pp. 510–29.
59. Millis, *The Forrestal Diaries*, p. 358.
60. Ibid., p. 375.

to reinstate a mandate under the aegis of the three powers. The request was denied: the French and the British were still too bitter over US policy in the Near East to approve continued service in the region.[61] Shortly before, on 17 March, Bidault had told Bevin he was sorry that France had voted for the partition at the United Nations General Assembly in November, suggesting that the decision had been taken in his absence and without his assent. Moreover, Forrestal was very reticent to send United States troops to Palestine. The president did not have a coherent policy, and had to consider the Jewish lobby, whose repudiation could be fatal to him in this, an electoral year. When the Zionist leaders declared Israel's independence on 14 May, President Harry Truman quickly recognized the new state.[62]

The Berlin Blockade

The Soviet Union did not delay its riposte to the Brussels pact and the London decisions on Germany. On 20 March, General Vasilii D. Sokolovskii, who was presiding the Allied Control Council meeting in Berlin, harshly attacked the Western powers' policy for Germany, accused them of breaking their commitments, and then closed the session without hearing a response to his accusations. His reaction was worrying, especially as it coincided with Soviet measures to impede Western surface traffic to the Soviet sector in Berlin.[63] On 31 March, road and rail traffic to the city was halted. The move had been anticipated. General Clay and the director of the CIA had been expecting it as early as the fall. In the beginning of the year, the German Communist press had started rumors about the imminent departure of the British, the Americans and the French from Berlin.

What could be done? Could the Western powers remain in Berlin? In Washington, Army Chief of Staff General Omar Bradley was unsure. In contrast, Lucius Clay, the US commander of forces in Germany, advocated military measures to deter the Soviet Union from further harassing Western positions in Berlin. The crisis had a symbolic value for him. If the United States quit Berlin, he said, its policy in Germany would be compromised, and its desire to stop the Communist advance in

---

61. See the conversation between Georges Bidault and Ernest Bevin at the Quai d'Orsay of 17 April 1948 (FO 800/447).

62. Leffler, *A Preponderance of Power,* p. 240.

63. See Avi Shlaim, *The United States and the Berlin Blockade, 1948–1949. A Study in Crisis Decision Making,* Berkeley, University of California Press, 1983, pp. 110 et seq.

Western Europe would appear to be wavering.[64] In confidential meetings
with the United States ambassador in London, Winston Churchill openly
advocated giving the USSR some form of ultimatum, demanding its
withdrawal from Berlin and East Germany, and threatening to flatten its
cities with an atomic attack. He was convinced that the Soviet Union
would resort to war once they possessed the weapon and that a policy of
appeasement would prove a disappointment. His solitary opinion differed
broadly with the Labour government's position.[65]

With the prime minister's consent, Bevin continued to push the United
States to support a North Atlantic defense system which, according to
him, was capable of changing Soviet policy. A firm commitment from
the United States would boost European confidence, encouraging
economic recovery and heightening resistance to Communist infiltration.
It was also the only way to settle the German problem with France, by
offering it the security guarantees it was seeking.[66] In reality, there was
hardly any doubt that this commitment would come: the United States
Congress had passed the Economic Co-operation Act (Title 1 of the
Foreign Assistance Act) endorsing the Marshall Plan, and President Harry
Truman had signed it on 3 April, thus authorizing 5 billion dollars in aid
to support the first twelve months of the European Recovery Program.
Shortly afterward, the Organization for European Economic Cooperation
was established in Paris as the vital instrument of European economic
recovery.

The London conference on Germany reopened on 20 April, amidst
increased Soviet pressure on Berlin. The French government was
concerned about this new crisis. Paris doubted that an Allied presence
could be maintained in the Third Reich's former capital, which was at
the heart of the Soviet sector. Although Georges Bidault acknowledged
the city's symbolic value in the confrontation with the Soviet Union over
control of Germany,[67] President Vincent Auriol was plagued by doubts.
He was tremendously apprehensive about the consequences of United
States policy in Germany. The Soviet Union might provoke an incident
that would lead to war, and nothing could stop their divisions from fanning
out over Western Europe. The United States was likely to intervene, but
the final victory would be meaningless for the defense of European
civilization and values. He also feared that the desire of the US and Britain
to hasten German political recovery would consummate the division of
Europe. "It will give the entire world a case of insomnia," he stated on

64. Smith, *The Papers of General Lucius D. Clay*, vol. 2, pp. 621–3. See also Shlaim,
The United States and the Berlin Blockade, p. 137.
65. *FRUS 1948*, vol. 3, p. 895.
66. Telegram from Ernest Bevin, 9 April (*FRUS 1948*, vol. 4, pp. 79–80).
67. Meeting of 17 April between Bevin and Bidault (FO 800/447).

21 April 1948 to the French cabinet.[68]

In London, Ernest Bevin was more calm. Strengthened economic and military cooperation among the European countries, the implementation of the Marshall Plan, the United States' growing desire to participate in European defense, and the spectacular defeat of the Communists in the Italian elections on 18 April were all encouraging signs of the Western world's ability to match the Soviet threat. He recognized that the USSR was a permanent danger to peace; he did not, however, believe that it wanted war. He planned to resist the pressure of the Soviet blockade of Berlin, exercising restraint and patience in managing the crisis.[69] The United States government shared his assessment of the situation, but feared that the USSR might spark a war by underestimating the United States' desire to remain in Berlin.[70] Moreover, United States intelligence specialists posted in Moscow reckoned at the time that the Red Army and the Soviet air force were capable of taking continental Europe and the principal Asian regions within a few months. The authors of that 1 April report also believed, however, that the USSR would not deliberately resort to military action, at least not in the immediate future, and that it would pursue its objectives through other means.[71] The National Security Council held that "the ultimate objective of Soviet-directed world communism is the domination of the world." It also held that the USSR was intent on using "aggressive pressure from without and militant revolutionary subversion from within."[72]

Western European security must therefore be consolidated. On 17 April, after the Brussels pact consultative council session, Bevin and Bidault sent a joint message to the secretary of state formally requesting US military assistance and asking the United States to join a new Western European defense system.[73] The French government also requested the United States' commitment, while the United States and Britain were pressing France to accept a new German government. On 2 June, the London agreements called for the rapid summoning of a constituent assembly to found the base of a federal, liberal Germany. An agreement was also made on control of the Ruhr, which would remain attached to Germany, though its mines and industry would contribute to the European economic recovery program under the Marshall Plan. The three powers would keep up their forces in Germany until peace was reestablished in

68. Auriol, *Journal*, vol. 2, p. 191.
69. *FRUS 1948*, vol. 4, pp. 842–4.
70. Ibid., p. 858.
71. *FRUS 1948*, vol. 1, p. 551.
72. National Security Council Report (Ibid., p. 546).
73. *FRUS 1948*, vol. 3, p. 91.

Europe. They would consult each other before withdrawing.[74] To advance the negotiations on Germany, Bevin and Bidault had put incessant pressure on the United States to commit formally to the North Atlantic defense agreement. The Department of State now fully supported the idea. It needed the Republican party's backing to act, however, for the alliance plan ran counter to American political and constitutional tradition. Republican support was particularly important for the coming presidential election.

On 11 June, the Senate almost unanimously accepted Senator Vandenberg's famous motion to authorize the alliance. On 18 June, the London agreement was passed by the French National Assembly with a narrow margin (300 votes to 286). The United States' promise to participate in European defense had helped win the vote.[75] Thus, the road to a new West German government and the North Atlantic pact was open.

On 23 June, the USSR called Poland, Hungary, Romania, Czechoslovakia, Bulgaria, and Yugoslavia to an East European conference in Warsaw to protest the London agreement. This move did not deter the Western powers from carrying out their monetary reform program for Berlin as the USSR attempted to impose its own currency in the city. The Soviet Union retaliated by blockading all ground access to Berlin. The United States and British air forces responded with the most gigantic air lift in contemporary history. Some time later, the United States moved a fleet of B-29 bombers to England, which were able to transport atomic weapons. This was the beginning of a long power struggle that marked a new stage in Cold War confrontation and the division of Europe.

---

74. United States Department of State, *Documents on Germany, 1944–1985,* 1985, pp. 143 et seq.

75. Timothy P. Ireland, *Creating the Entangling Alliance. The Origins of the North Atlantic Treaty Organization,* Boulder, Westview, 1981, pp. 96 et seq.

CONCLUSION

With the Berlin blockade, one of the most critical phases of the Cold War in Europe began. By deciding to remain in the former capital of the Reich and to use nuclear deterrents against the USSR for the first time, the United States, with Great Britain's aid, showed firm resolve to restore West Germany, protect its democratic regime, and incorporate it in the process of European integration fueled by the Marshall Plan. The Berlin crisis hastened the birth in 1949 of the Federal Republic of Germany and the creation of the North Atlantic Treaty Organization. It also precipitated the constitution of the German Democratic Republic, a USSR satellite that braced the "iron curtain" and for which even Tito's dissidence was no match. Stalin finally lifted the Berlin blockade when he saw that the US–British airlift was working in spite of it. Yet Berlin remained a symbol of the Cold War, a place where the tragic drama of European division would be acted out time and again, and upon which threats of nuclear terror converged, notably in the late 1950s. The construction of the Berlin Wall in 1961 marked the peak of the Cold War in Europe. Its destruction in 1989 heralded German reunification and the end of the conflict.

The Berlin blockade and Germany's ensuing division into two hostile states also indicated a turning point in the Cold War. Once they had delineated their spheres of influence and consolidated their respective defense systems in Europe, the great powers gave truly global dimensions to the ideological and political conflict. Indeed, this was a new phase in the Cold War, which had begun when Chiang Kai-shek's forces were defeated and the People's Republic of China was established on 1 October 1949. Asia was becoming the principal theater of operations in the East–West confrontation. In June 1950, Kim Il Sung's North Korean army crossed the 38th. parallel with help from Stalin and Mao Tse-tung, provoking the United States to act immediately by sending in its troops under the UN flag. Korea descended into a cruel war, and the tragedy gave new intensity to the Cold War, sparking a rise of far Rightist currents in the United States and spurring on the nuclear arms race among the great powers. The containment policy was applied to Asia. In 1954, after the French defeat in Dien Bien Phu, the United States gave its support to Ngo Dinh Diem's pro-Western regime south of the 17th. parallel. This was the start of a new United States commitment in Asia that soon led to

261

the long and merciless war in Vietnam. Elsewhere, the East–West confrontation influenced the nature and meaning of the Israeli–Arab conflict, for the USSR and the United States became increasingly involved in the Middle East and played an essential hand in the outbreak of war in 1967 and 1973. In Latin America, military and conservative sections of society used United States support to remain in power, spinning out doctrines of "national security" to legitimate their repressive policies. Africa, too, became a battlefield for the great powers.

Hence, for more than forty years the Cold War affected the dynamics of international relations, dividing Europe into two hostile camps, dictating ideological and political rifts within Western countries, and finally leaving its mark on the international society as a whole. Naturally, its written history is substantial, principally in the United States and Great Britain. It is based on frequently consulted archival references. One day, when the Soviet archives are opened, it will be completed.

The literature is largely focused on the study of the factors leading to the outbreak of the Cold War. Before the conflict was written down in history, various journalists and politicians speculated whether the United States and Great Britain might have avoided the breakdown of the "grand alliance" by recognizing the Soviet sphere of influence in Eastern Europe. This was the thesis of the famous American journalist Walter Lippman, who coined the expression the "Cold War."[1] As mentioned above, Henry Wallace, the United States trade secretary, developed similar arguments in his September 1947 speech. A number of historians adopted this position later, either reproaching Truman for having destroyed the privileged relations Roosevelt had worked so hard to establish with Stalin or complaining that he should have recognized the validity of the Soviet security programs.[2]

At the end of the war, George Kennan, who played such an important role in conceptualizing containment, favored recognizing spheres of influence; he strongly criticized Roosevelt's universalism, which was based on traditional postulates of geopolitics and "realism." The dispatches and memoranda that he and his British counterpart Frank Roberts wrote, however, tended to prescribe that Stalin must not be appeased by nodding to his preponderance in Eastern Europe. In their view, the USSR's foreign policy was inherent to its totalitarian regime and essential to its survival. In retrospect, and especially in light of the events ensuing the

---

1. See Walter Lippmann, *The Cold War. A Study in U.S. Foreign Policy,* New York, Harper, 1947.

2. See notably Denna Frank Fleming, *The Cold War and its Origins, 1917–1960,* 2 vols., New York, Doubleday, 1961. On the historiographical debate, see Jerald A. Combs, *American Diplomatic History, Two Centuries of Changing Interpretations,* Berkeley, University of California Press, 1983, pp. 220–346.

Soviet empire's collapse, it seems difficult to challenge the validity of this opinion. The Kremlin leaders would not have systematically created the conditions of conflict – in Germany in particular – with Great Britain and the United States if there had not been some domestic advantage to be gained from the revival of the "Western bloc" which they had denounced since 1945. Yet, as discussed above, the Western leaders were willing to concede the USSR's sphere of influence in the East European countries, especially since they themselves were defending their own imperial structures or consolidating their hegemony in Latin America, the Middle East, and Asia. They could not, however, allow the Soviet stronghold in Central Europe and the Balkans to coincide with an expansion of Communist totalitarianism so soon after the war against fascist tyranny. Incontestably, Stalin and his regime account for the origins, and particularly the specific nature, of the Cold War.

If one accepts this thesis, it is natural to wonder at the policy and strategy the United States and Great Britain adopted during the Second World War and in the months following the end of the conflict. In a commentary dated 30 April on the consequences of the "Prague coup," the United States ambassador to Czechoslovakia said in diplomatic style that the United States should have lent a greater emphasis to the war's political aspects. If it had not halted its forces in May 1945, it could easily have secured control of Central Europe.[3] Churchill, one recalls, had done his best to urge the United States and British armies to act thus. As the war came to an end, London and Washington began to comprehend that Stalin did not share his allies' war aims and that they could not rely on him to help advance the spread of pluralistic political regimes and the principles of a market economy in liberated Europe. His attitude toward the Polish resistance, notably during the Warsaw uprising, the harshness of his territorial demands on Poland at the Yalta talks, and his fierce defense of the Lublin regime should have sufficed to awaken doubts over his interest in the principles of the United Nations, and in the Declaration on Liberated Europe especially. Admittedly, however, at the time of the Yalta and Potsdam conferences, as in the months following the end of the war, the United States and Britain had hardly a strategic or political trump to play; and there is no knowing whether a firmer, steadier, diplomacy would have reversed Stalin's intent to impose his regime on the countries he wanted in the Soviet sphere.

This question, which in turn raises the question of Anglo–American strategy during the Second World War, is also the subject of broad historical debate. The British postponed opening a second front in Europe, and wagered on a strategy on the periphery in hopes of minimizing their

3. *FRUS 1948*, vol. 4, pp. 748–9.

losses and protecting their empire. Moreover, the strategy of massive bombing on German cities had proved militarily ineffective. Yet there is no proof that a landing in the Balkans, which Churchill long advocated, would have made a significant contribution to the collapse of the Third Reich. Czechoslovakia, on the other hand, might have met a different fate if Patton's tanks had liberated Prague. It is doubtful, however, that Berlin's liberation by the Western Allies would have changed the course of the Cold War, because the USSR, having essentially led the war against the Third Reich, had an irrevocable part in Germany's occupation. In May 1945, as the world celebrated the collapse of the German regime, public opinion basked in the atmosphere of the "grand alliance," and the USSR's aid was secured in the war against Japan, it would have been very difficult to engage a contest against the great victorious power.

Many American historians – the so-called revisionists – have ascribed the origins of the Cold War to the United States' imperialistic ambitions and the internal contradictions of its capitalist regime.[4] This current of thought was widespread in the sixties, when United States leadership invoked the "defense of the free world" to justify the endless growth of its "military-industrial complex" and the "imperial Republic's" ventures, notably in Central America and Vietnam. These opinions also fit in to the ancient American tradition of idealism, which bases its simplistic and in some cases black-and-white vision of international realities on a new reading of Marxist tenets. Drawing upon the Soviet propaganda that dates from after the Potsdam conference, this tradition holds that Byrnes applied "atomic diplomacy," but it ignores the fact that the State Department and the Pentagon waited until late 1946 to draft their containment strategy, the military dimensions of which were limited. The "revisionists" focus on the United States leaders' economic programs, whose liberal inspiration they interpret as a sign of imperialist intent. They ignore the aspects of the Cold War that can be traced back to Europe, neglect Stalin's role in the development of the conflict, and overlook the repercussions of the USSR's political ambitions on the East European governments and peoples. Too often, American authors write as if the entire history of the period was dictated from Washington and thus lose sight of Great Britain's fundamental role in resisting Soviet expansion in Europe and the Middle East and in creating a European defense system. Of course, the United

---

4. See notably William Appleman Williams, *The Tragedy of American Diplomacy*, Cleveland, World Publ., 1959; Gabriel and Joyce Kolko, *The Limits of Power. The World and United States Foreign Policy, 1945–1954*, New York, Harper and Row, 1972; Gar Alperovitz, *Atomic Diplomacy. Hiroshima and Potsdam*, New York, Simon and Schuster, 1965; Lloyd C. Gardner, *Architects of Illusion. Men, Ideas and American Foreign Policy, 1941–1949*, Chicago, Quadrangle Books, 1972.

States' principles and policy of free trade, its campaign for bases abroad, its will to maintain economic and strategic preponderance in Latin America, its refusal to include the Soviet Union in the occupation of Japan, and even its opposition to European imperialist structures were not without ambitions of hegemony; on the contrary. Obviously, it would be absurd to deny that the United States, or any great power over the course of history, had its own interests in mind as it sought to propagate ideological and political values. The Cold War was not, however, merely a typical confrontation between great powers, but a conflict stemming from antagonistic conceptions of history and politics. Its historiography is also a reflection of such opposing conceptions.

PRIMARY SOURCES

Unpublished Sources

Bevin's papers, which are kept in the Public Record Office at Kew, London, in the FO 800 series, are also available on microfilm.

Also found in the Public Record Office are: the minutes of the British Cabinet's discussions, decisions, and annexes, under CAB 128 and CAB 129; the minutes of international conferences under CAB 133; the minutes and documents of the Cabinet Defence Committee under CAB 131/1–131/11. Last, and most importantly, the vast collection of diplomatic papers, notably the dispatches between the Foreign Office and the British embassies, is found in the FO 371 series.

The French government's diplomatic archives at its Quai d'Orsay seat in Paris comprise two important series for the period 1945–1948:

1. The Y series, which is composed of international treaties and treaties signed by France; general issues of world politics; Allied relations; the conferences of Potsdam, Moscow, and Paris; the Marshall Plan, and Allied policy in Germany.

2. The Z series for Europe 1944–1948, which covers the creation of NATO; the Eastern bloc; the issue of the Balkans.

Diplomatic Papers

1. Collection of American Documents:

Foreign Relations of the United States
    1945: 11 volumes published in Washington from 1960–1969.
    1946: 11 volumes published from 1969–1972.
    1947: 8 volumes published from 1971–1973.
    1948: 9 volumes published from 1972–1975.

The Papers of General Lucius D. Clay, Germany 1945–1949, 2 vol., (J.E. Smith, ed.) Bloomington, 1974.

2. Collection of British Documents:

Documents on British Policy Overseas: Series I (1945–1950)
Vol. I: *The Conference at Potsdam.*
Vol. II: *Conferences and Conversations 1945.*
Vol. III: *Britain and America: Negotiation of the United States Loan, August–December 1945.*
Vol. IV: *Britain and America: Atomic Energy, Peace and Food, 12 December 1945–31 July 1946.*
Vol. V: *Germany and Western Europe, August–December 1945.*
Vol. VI: *Eastern Europe, August–December 1945.*

Edited Documents

Bernstein (Barton J.), Matusow (Allen J.), eds, *The Truman Administration: A Documentary History*, New York, Harper and Row, 1968.

Black (J.L.), *Origins, Evolution, and Nature of the Cold War. An Annotated Bibliographic Guide*, Santa Barbara (Cal.), Oxford, ABC–Clio, 1986.

Etzold (Thomas H.), Gaddis (John Lewis), eds, *Containment. Documents on American Policy and Strategy, 1945–1950*, New York, Columbia University Press, 1978.

Ferrel (Robert H.), ed., *Off the Record: The Private Papers of Harry S. Truman*, New York, Harper and Row, 1980.

Görtemaker (Manfred), Wettig (Gerhard), *USA-USSR: Dokumente zur Sicherheitspolitik*, Hanovre, Niedersächschische Landeszentrale für politische Bildung, 1986.

Iatrides (John O.), ed., *Ambassador MacVeagh Reports: Greece, 1933–1947*, Princeton (N.J.), Princeton University Press, 1980.

Kimball (Warren F.), ed., *Churchill and Roosevelt. The Complete Correspondence*, 3 vol., Princeton (N.J.), Princeton University Press, 1984.

Lafeber (Walter), *The Origins of the Cold War, 1941–1947. A Historical Problem with Interpretations and Documents*, New York, John Wiley and Sons, 1971.

Loewenheim (Francis), ed., *Roosevelt and Churchill. Their Secret Wartime Correspondence*, New York, Saturday Review Press, 1975.

Molotov (V.M.), *Problems of Foreign Policy, Speeches and Statements, April 1945-November 1948*, Moscow, Foreign Language Publ. House, 1949.

Roosevelt (Franklin D.), Bullit (William C.), *For the President. Personal and Secret Correspondence between F.D. Roosevelt and W.C. Bullit*, London, André Deutsch, 1972.

Ross (Graham), ed., *The Foreign Office and the Kremlin. British Documents on Anglo-Soviet Relations, 1941–1945*, Cambridge, Cambridge University Press, 1984.

Smith (J.E.), ed., *The Papers of General Lucius D. Clay: Germany 1945–1949*, 2 vol., Bloomington, Indiana University Press, 1974.

Vandenberg (Arthur H., Jr.), *The Private Papers of Senator Vandenberg*, Boston, Houghton Mifflin, 1952.

SECONDARY SOURCES

Memoirs

Acheson (Dean), *Present at the Creation: My Years in the State Department*, London, Hamish Hamilton, 1970, 798 p.

Adenauer (Konrad), *Memoirs 1945–1953*, London, Weidenfield & Nicholson, 1966.

Alphand (Hervé), *L'étonnement d'être. Journal (1939–1973)*, Paris, Fayard, 1973.

Auriol (Vincent), *Journal du septennat, 1947–1954*, 2 vol., Paris, Armand Colin, 1970, 1974.

Bérard (A.), *Un ambassadeur se souvient, 1945–1955*, Paris, 1978.

Bohlen (Charles), *Witness to History, 1929–1969*, New York, Norton, 1973.

Bullitt (Orville H.), ed., *For the President, Personal and Secret Correspondence between Franklin D. Roosevelt and William C. Bullitt*, London, A. Deutsch, 1973.

Byrnes (James F.), *All in One Lifetime*, New York, Harper & Brothers, 1948.

Byrnes (James F.), *Speaking Frankly*, London, W. Heinmann, 1947.

Campbell (Thomas A.), Herring (George), eds, *The Diaries of Edward R. Stettinius, Jr.*, New York, New Viewpoints, 1975.

Catroux (Georges), *J'ai vu tomber le rideau de fer. Moscou, 1945–1948*, Paris, Hachette, 1952.

Chauvel (Jean), *Commentaire. D'Alger à Berne (1944–1952)*, Paris, Fayard, 1972.

Churchill (Winston S.), *The Second World War*, 6 vol., London, Cassel and Houghton, 1948–1954.

Clays (Lucius D.), *Decision in Germany*, London, W. Heinmann, 1950.

Deane (John R.), *The Strange Alliance. The Story of our Efforts at Wartime Cooperation with Russia*, New York, Viking, 1947.

Djilas (Milovan), *Conversations with Stalin*, New York, Harcourt Bruce & World, 1962.

Dumaine (Jacques), *Quai d'Orsay, 1945–1952*, Paris, Julliard, 1955.

Eden (Anthony), *Full Circle. The Memoirs of Anthony Eden*, Boston, Houghton Mifflin, 1962.

Gaulle (Charles de), *Mémoires de guerre, 1940–1946*, 3 vol., Paris, Plon, 1954–1959.

Gromyko (Andrei), *Memoirs*, New York, Doubleday, 1989.

Harriman (Averell W.), Abel (Elie), *Special Envoy to Churchill and Stalin, 1941–1946*, New York, Random House, 1975.

Hull (Cordell), *Memoirs*, 2 vol., New York, Macmillan, 1948.

Jones (Joseph M.), *The Fifteen Weeks. An Inside Account of the Genesis of the Marshall Plan*, New York, Viking, 1955.

Kennan (George), *Memoirs, 1925–1950*, London, Hutchinson, 1968.

Leahy (William), *I Was There*, New York, Whittlesey House, 1950.

Massigli (René), *Une comédie des erreurs: 1943–1956. Souvenirs et réflexions sur une étape de la construction européenne*, Paris, Plon, 1978.

Millis (Walter), ed., *The Forrestal Diaries*, New York, Viking Press, 1952.

Murphy (Robert), *Diplomat Among Warriors*, London, Collins, 1964.

Nagy (Imre), *The Struggle behind the Iron Curtain*, New York, Macmillan, 1948.

Nitze (Paul H.), *From Hiroshima to Glasnost. At the Center of Decision. A Memoir*, New York, Grove Wiedenfeld, 1989.

Smith (Walter B.), *My Three Years in Moscow*, Philadelphia, J.B. Lippincott, 1955.

Stettinius (Edward R., Jr.), *Roosevelt and the Russians: The Yalta Conference*, London, J. Cape, 1950.

Truman (Harry S.), *Memoirs*, vol. 1, *Years of Decisions*, Garden City, N.Y. Doubleday, 1955; *Memoirs*, vol. 2, *Years of Trial and Hope*, Garden City, N.Y. Doubleday, 1956.

Books

Ageron (Charles-Robert), *Les chemins de la décolonisation*, Paris, Institut d'histoire du temps présent/CNRS, 1986.

Alexander (G.M.), *The Prelude to the Truman Doctrine. British Policy in Greece, 1944–1947*, Oxford, Clarendon Press, 1982.

Alperovitz (Gar), *Atomic Diplomacy. Hiroshima and Potsdam*, New York, Simon and Schuster, 1965.

Ambrose (Stephen E.), *Rise to Globalism: American Foreign Policy Since 1938*, London, Allen Lane, Penguin Press, 1971.

Amen (Michael Mark), *American Foreign Policy in Greece, 1944–1949*, Bern, P. Lang, 1978.

Anderson (Terry H.), *The United States, Great Britain, and the Cold War, 1944–1947*, Columbia, University of Missouri Press, 1981.

Arcidiacono (Bruno), *Le "précédent italien" et les origines de la guerre froide. Les alliés et l'occupation de l'Italie, 1943–1944*, Brussels, Bruylant, 1984.

Arkes (Hadley), *Bureaucracy, the Marshall Plan and the National Interest*, Princeton (N.J.), Princeton University Press, 1972.

Aron (Raymond), *Les articles du Figaro*, tome 1, *La guerre froide, 1947–1955*, Paris, de Fallois, 1990.

Barral (Pierre), *Il y a trente ans la guerre froide*, Paris, Armand Colin, 1984.

Baylis (John), *Anglo–American Defense Relations, 1939–1984*, 2nd edition, London, Macmillan, 1984.

Beloff (Nora), *Tito's Flawed Legacy, Yugoslavia and the West, 1939–1984*, London, Victor Gollancs, 1984.

Best (Richard A.), *Cooperation with like-minded People. British Influences on American Security Policy, 1945–1949*, New York, Greenwood Press, 1986.

Betts (R.R.), ed., *Central and South East Europe*, London, Royal Institute of International Affairs, 1950.

Blum (Robert M.), *Drawing the Line. The Origins of the American Containment Policy in East Asia*, New York, Norton, 1982.

Brands (H.W.), *Inside the Cold War. Loy Henderson and the Rise of the American Empire, 1918–1961*, Oxford, Oxford University Press, 1991.

Buhite (Russel D.), *Soviet-American Relations in Asia, 1945–1954*, Norman, University of Oklahoma Press, 1981.

Bullock (Allan L.), *Ernest Bevin, Foreign Secretary, 1945–1951*, Oxford, Oxford University Press, 1985.

Burns (James McGregor), *Roosevelt, The Soldier of Freedom*, New York, Harcourt, Brace Jovanovich, 1970.

Calvocoressi (Peter), *Survey of International Affairs, 1947–1948*, Oxford, Oxford University Press, 1952.

Cho (Soon Sung), *Korea in World Politics, 1945–1950. An Evaluation of American Responsibility*, Berkeley, University of California Press, 1967.

Chotard (Jean-René), *La politique américaine en Europe, 1944–1948. Etudes des archives officielles*, Paris, Messidor/Editions sociales, 1991.

Clemens (Diane Shaver), *Yalta*, Oxford, Oxford University Press, 1970.

Cohen (Michael J.), *Palestine, Retreat from the Mandate*, New York, Holmes & Meier, 1978.

Cohen (Michael J.), *Palestine and the Great Powers, 1945–1948*, Princeton, Princeton University Press, 1982.

Combs (Jerald A.), *American Diplomatic History. Two Centuries of Changing Interpretations*, Berkeley, University of California Press, 1983.

Condit (Kenneth W.), *The History of the Joint Chiefs of Staff. The Joint Chiefs of Staff and National Policy*, vol. 2, 1947–1949, Wilmington, Glazier, 1979.

Coutouvidis (John), Reynolds (Jaime), *Poland, 1939–1947*, Leicester, Leicester University Press, 1986.

Dallek (Robert), *Franklin D. Roosevelt and American Foreign Policy, 1932–1945*, Oxford, Oxford University Press, 1974.

Dalloz (Jacques), *La guerre d'Indochine*, Paris, Le Seuil, 1987.

Davis (Lynn Etheridge), *The Cold War Begins. Soviet-American Conflict over Eastern Europe*, Princeton, Princeton University Press, 1974.

Davison (W. Philips), *The Berlin Blockade*, Princeton, Princeton University Press, 1958.

Deighton (Anne), *The Impossible Peace. Britain, the Division of Germany, and the Origins of the Cold War*, Oxford, Clarendon Press, 1990.

DePorte (A.V.), *De Gaulle's Foreign Policy, 1944–1948*, Cambridge, Harvard

University Press, 1968.

Devillers (Philippe), *Paris, Saïgon, Hanoï*, Paris, Galimard/Julliard, 1988 (coll. "Archives").

Divine (Robert), *Roosevelt and World War II*, Baltimore, The Johns Hopkins University Press, 1969.

Donovan (Robert J.), *Conflict and Crisis. The Presidency of Harry S. Truman, 1945–1948*, New York, Norton, 1982.

Douglas (Roy), *From War to Cold War, 1942–1948*, London, Macmillan, 1987.

Durand (Yves), *Naissance de la guerre froide: 1944–1949*, Paris, Messidor/Temps actuels, 1984.

Edmonds (Robin), *Setting the Mould. The United States and Britain, 1945–1950*, Oxford, Clarendon Press, 1986.

Feis (Herbert), *From Trust to Terror. The Onset of the Cold War, 1945–1950*, New York, Norton, 1970.

Feis (Herbert), *Le marchandage de la paix. Potsdam, juillet 1945*, Paris, Arthaud, 1963.

Feis (Herbert), *Churchill-Roosevelt-Stalin*, Princeton, Princeton University Press, 1967.

Feis (Herbert), *The Atomic Bomb and the End of World War II*, Princeton, Princeton University Press, 1966.

Fejtö (François), *Histoire des démocraties populaires*, 2 vol., Paris, Le Seuil, 1969.

Fleming (D.F.), *The Cold War and its Origins, 1917–1960*, 2 vol., Garden City, Doubleday, 1961.

Fontaine (André), *Histoire de la guerre froide*, 2 vol., Paris, Fayard, 1966–1967.

Fonvielle-Alquier (François), *La grande peur de l'après-guerre, 1946–1953*, Paris, Robert Laffont, 1973.

Freeland (Richard M.), *The Truman Doctrine and the Origins of McCarthyism. Foreign Policy, Domestic Policy and International Security (1946–1948)*, New York, New York University Press, 1985.

Fritsch-Bournazel (Renata), *L'Union soviétique et les Allemagnes*, Paris, Presses de la Fondation nationale des sciences politiques, 1979.

Funk (Arthur), *De Yalta à Potsdam: des illusions à la guerre froide*, Brussels, Complexe, 1982.

Gaddis (John L.), *The United States and the Origins of the Cold War, 1941–1947*, New York, Columbia University Press, 1972.

Gaddis (John L.), *The Long Peace. Inquiries into the History of the Cold War*, New York, Columbia University Press, 1987.

Gaddis (John L.), *Strategies of Containment. A Critical Appraisal of Postwar American National Security Policy*, Oxford, Oxford University Press, 1982.

Gardner (Lloyd C.), *Economic Aspects of New Deal Diplomacy*, Madison, Wisconsin University Press, 1964.

Gardner (Lloyd C.), *Architects of Illusion. Men, Ideas in American Foreign Policy, 1941–1949*, Chicago, Quadrangle Books, 1972.

Gardner (Richard N.), *Sterling-Dollar Diplomacy, The Origins and the Prospects of our International Economic Order*, New York, McGraw Hill, 1969.

Gerbet (Pierre), *Le relèvement, 1944–1949*, Paris, Imprimerie nationale, 1991.

Gilbert (Martin), *Winston S. Churchill, 1874–1945*, 7 vol., Boston, Houghton Mifflin, Heinemann, 1966–1986.

Gillingham (John), *Coal, Steel and the Rebirth of Europe, 1945–1955. The German and French from Ruhr Conflict to Economic Community*, Cambridge, Cambridge University Press, 1991.

Gimbel (John), *The Origins of the Marshall Plan*, Stanford, Stanford University Press, 1976, 344 p.

Gimbel (John), *The American Occupation of Germany. Politics and the Military, 1945–1949*, Stanford, Stanford University Press, 1968.

Girault (René), Frank (Robert), dir., *La puissance française en question, 1945–1949*, Paris, Publications de la Sorbonne, 1988.

Goldman (Eric F.), *The Crucial Decade and After: America, 1945–1960*, 2nd edition, New York, A. Knopf, 1960.

Gormly (James L.), *The Collapse of the Grand Alliance, 1945–1948*, Baton Rouge, Louisiana State University Press, 1987.

Gowing (Margaret), *Independence and Deterrence. Britain and Atomic Energy, 1945–1952*, London, Macmillan, 1974.

Grosser (Alfred), *Affaires extérieures. La politique de la France, 1944–1984*, Paris, Flammarion, 1984.

Hahn (Werner G.), *Postwar Soviet Politics. The Fall of Zhdanov and the Defeat of Moderation*, Ithaca, Cornell University Press, 1982.

Harbutt (Fraser J.), *The Iron Curtain. Churchill, America and the Origins of the Cold War*, Oxford, Oxford University Press, 1986.

Harper (John L.), *America and the Reconstruction of Italy, 1945–1948*, Cambridge, Cambridge University Press, 1988.

Harris (Kenneth), *Attlee*, London, Weidenfeld & Nicholson, 1984.

Hathaway (Robert), *Ambiguous Partnership. Britain and America, 1944–1947*, New York, Columbia University Press, 1981.

Herken (Gregg), *The Winning Weapon. The Atomic Bomb in the Cold War: 1945–1950*, New York, Vintage Books, 1982.

Herring (George C., Jr.), *Aid to Russia, 1941–1946. Strategy, Diplomacy and the Origins of the Cold War*, New York, Columbia University Press, 1973.

Heuser (Beatrice), *Wester « Containment » Policies in the Cold War. The Yugoslav Case, 1948–1953*, London, Routledge, 1989.

Hixson (Walter L.), *George F. Kennan. Cold War Iconoclast*, New York, Columbia University Press, 1989.

Hogan (Michael J.), *The Marshall Plan. America, Britain and the Reconstruction of Western Europe*, Cambridge, Cambridge University Press, 1987.

Iatrides (John), *Revolt in Athens. The Greek Communist "Second Round" 1944–1945*, Princeton, Princeton University Press, 1972.

Ireland (Timothy), *Creating the Entangling Alliance. The Origins of the North Atlantic Treaty Organization*, Westview, Boulder, 1981.

Iriye (Akira), *The Cold War in Asia: A Historical Introduction*, Englewood Cliffs,

Prentice Hall, 1974.

Iriye (Akira), Nagai (Yonosuke), eds, *The Origins of The Cold War in Asia*, New York, Columbia University Press, 1977.

Jelavich (Barbara), *History of the Balkans*, vol. 2, *Twentieth Century*, Cambridge, Cambridge University Press, 1984.

Jones (Howard), *"A New Kind of War". America's Global Strategy and the Truman Doctrine in Greece*, Oxford, Oxford University Press, 1989.

Kardelj (Edvard), *Reminiscences: The Struggle for Recognition and Independence. The New Yugoslavia, 1944–1957*, London, Bond & Briggs, 1982.

Kersaudy (François), *Churchill & De Gaulle*, London, Fontana Press, 1990.

Kersten (Krystyna), *The Establishment of Communist Rule in Poland, 1943–1948*, Berkeley, University of California Press, 1991.

Kertesz (Stephen D.), *Between Russia and the West. Hungary and the Illusion of Peacemaking, 1945–1947*, Notre Dame, University of Notre Dame Press, 1984.

Kindelberger (Charles P.), *Marshall Plan Days*, Boston, Allen & Unwin, 1982.

Knapp (Wilfried), *A History of War and Peace, 1939–1965*, London, Oxford University Press, 1967.

Kolko (Gabriel), *The Politics of War. The World and United States Foreign Policy, 1943–1945*, New York, Harper and Row, 1968.

Kolko (Gabriel et Joyce), *The Limits of Power. The World and United States Foreign Policy, 1945–1954*, New York, Harper and Row, 1972.

Kovrig (Bennett), *The Myth of Liberation. East-Central Europe in United States Diplomacy and Politics since 1941*, Baltimore, The Johns Hopkins University Press, 1973.

Kuklick (Bruce), *American Policy and the Division of Germany. The Clash with Russia Over Reparations*, Ithaca, Cornell University Press, 1972.

Kuniholm (Bruce Robillet), *The Origins of the Cold War in the Near East. Great Power Conflict and Diplomacy in Iran, Turkey, and Greece*, Princeton, Princeton University Press, 1980.

Lacouture (Jean), *De Gaulle*, 3 vol., Paris, Le Seuil, 1985.

Lafeber (Walter), *America, Russia and the Cold War, 1945–1975*, New York, John Wiley and Sons, 1976.

Lafeber (Walter), *The Origins of the Cold War, 1941–1947. A Historical Problem with Interpretations and Documents*, New York, John Wiley and Sons, 1971.

Laloy (Jean), *Yalta, hier, aujourd'hui, demain*, Paris, Robert Laffont, 1988.

Leffler (Melwyn P.), *A Preponderance of Power. National Security, the Truman Administration and the Cold War*, Stanford, Stanford University Press, 1992.

Levine (Stephen I.), *Anvil of Victory. The Communist Revolution in Manchuria, 1945–1948*, New York, Columbia University Press, 1987.

Lewis (Julian), *Changing Direction. British Military Planning for Postwar Strategic Defense, 1942–1947*, London, The Sherwood Press, 1988.

Lippman (Walter), *The Cold War. A Study in U.S. Foreign Policy*, New York, Harper & Brothers, 1947.

Louis (William Roger), *Imperialism at Bay*, Oxford, Oxford University Press, 1978.

Lundestad (Geir), *The American Non-Policy towards Eastern Europe, 1943–1947. Universalism in an Area not of Essential Interest to the United States*, New York, Humanities Press, 1975.

Maddox (Robert James), *The New Left and the Origins of the Cold War*, Princeton (N.J.), Princeton University Press, 1973.

Marcou (Lilly), *La guerre froide: l'engrenage*, Brussels, Complexe, 1987.

Mastny (Vojtech), *Russia's Road to the Cold War. Diplomacy, Warfare, and the Politics of Communism, 1941–1945*, New York, Columbia University Press, 1979.

Max (Stanley M.), *The United States, Great Britain and the Sovietization of Hungary, 1945–1948*, New York, Columbia University Press, 1985.

Mayers (David A.), *George Kennan and the Dilemmas of US Foreign Policy*, Oxford, Oxford University Press, 1989.

McMahon (Robert J.), *Colonialism and Cold War. The United States and the Struggle for Indonesian Independence*, Ithaca, Cornell University Press, 1981.

Mee (Charles), *Meeting at Potsdam*, New York, Evans and Co., 1975.

Mee (Charles), *The Marshall Plan. The Launching of Pax Americana*, New York, Simon & Shuster, 1984.

Mélandri (Pierre), *Les Etats-Unis face à l'unification de l'Europe, 1945–1954*, Paris, A. Pédone, 1980.

Messer (Rober L.), *The End of Alliance. James F. Byrnes, Roosevelt, Truman and the Origins of the Cold War*, Chapel Hill, University of North Carolina Press, 1982.

Miller (Aaron), *Search for Security. Saudi Arabian Oil and American Foreign Policy, 1939–1949*, Chapel Hill, University of North Carolina Press, 1980.

Milward (Alan S.), *The Reconstruction of Western Europe, 1945–1951*, Berkeley, University of California Press, 1984.

Miscamble (Wilson D.), *George F. Kennan and the Making of American Foreign Policy, 1947–1950*, Princeton (N.J.), Princeton University Press, 1992.

Morgan (Kenneth O.), *Labour in Power, 1945–1951*, Oxford, Oxford University Press, 1984.

Morgan (Roger), *The United States and West Germany, 1945–1973*, Oxford, Oxford University Press, 1974.

Notter (Harley), ed., *Postwar Foreign Policy Preparation, 1939–1945*, Washington, Government Printing Office, 1950.

Oran (Nissan), *Revolution Administred. Agrarianism and Communism in Bulgaria*, Baltimore, The Johns Hopkins University Press, 1973.

Page (Bruce) et al., *Philby: The Spy Who Betrayed a Generation*, London, Penguin, 1969.

Paterson (Thomas G.), *Soviet American Confrontation. Postwar Reconstruction and the Origins of the Cold War*, Baltimore, Johns Hopkins University Press, 1973.

Paterson (Thomas G.), *On Every Front. The Making of the Cold War*, New York,

W.W. Norton, 1979.

Pogue (Forrest C.), *George C. Marshall, 1945–1959*, New York, Viking Press, 1987.

Pollard (Robert), *Economic Security and the Origin of the Cold War: 1945–1950*, New York, Columbia University Press, 1985.

Polvinen (Tuomo), *Between East and West: Finland in International Politics 1944–1947*, Minneapolis, University of Minnesota Press, 1986.

Richer (Philippe), *L'Asie du Sud-Est. Indépendances et communismes*, Paris, Imprimerie nationale, 1981.

Rogow (Arnold A.), *James Forrestal. A Study in Personality, Politics and Policy*, New York, Macmillan, 1963.

Rothschild (Joseph), *Return to Diversity. A Political History of East Central Europe since World War II*, Oxford, Oxford University Press, 1989.

Rothwell (Victor), *Britain and the Cold War, 1941–1947*, London, J. Cape, 1982.

Senarclens (Pierre de), *Yalta*, Paris, PUF, 1984 (coll. "Que sais-je?").

Seton-Watson (Hugh), *The East European Revolution*, London, Methuen, 1956.

Sherwood (Robert E.), *Roosevelt and Hopkins: an Intimate History*, New York, Harper & Brothers, 1948.

Shlaim (Avi), *The United States and the Berlin Blockade, 1948–1949. A Study in Crisis Decision Making*, Berkeley, University of California Press, 1989.

Shulman (Marshall), *Stalin's Foreign Policy Reappraised*, Cambridge, Harvard University Press, 1963.

Smith (Gaddis), *Dean Acheson*, New York, Cooper Square Publ., 1972.

Stoff (Michael B.), *Oil, War, and American Security. The Search for a National Policy on Foreign Oil, 1941–1947*, New Haven, Yale University Press, 1980.

Stoler (Mark A.), *The Politics of the Second Front. American Military Planning and Diplomacy in Coalition Warfare, 1941–1943*, Westport, Greenwood Press, 1977.

Stueck (William W.), ed., *The Road to Confrontation. American Policy toward China and Korea, 1947–1950*, Chapel Hill, University of North Carolina Press, 1982.

Thomas (Hugh), *Armed Truth, The Beginnings of the Cold War, 1945–1946*, London, Hamish Hamilton, 1986.

Thorne (Christopher), *Allies of a Kind*, Oxford, Oxford University Press, 1979.

Tsou (Tang), *America's Failure in China, 1941–1950*, Chicago, The University of Chicago Press, 1963.

Tucker (R.W.), *The Radical Left and American Foreign Policy*, Baltimore, The Johns Hopkins University Press, 1971.

Tusa (Ann et John), *The Berlin Blockade. Berlin in 1948: The Year the Cold War Threatened to Become Hot*, London, Coronet, 1989.

Ulam (Adam), *The Rivals. America and Russia since World War II*, New York, Viking Press, 1971.

Ulam (Adam), *Expansion and Co-existence. Soviet Foreign Policy, 1917–1967*, New York, Praeger, 1974.

Ulam (Adam), *Stalin, the Man and his Era*, New York, Viking Press, 1973.

Urban (G.R.), *Stalinism, Its Impact on Russia and the World*, London, Wildwood House, 1985.

Wall (Irwin M.), *The United States and the Making of Postwar France, 1945–1954*, Cambridge, Cambridge University Press, 1991.

Wexler (Imanuel), *The Marshall Plan Revisited. The European Recovery Program in Economic Perspective*, Westport, Greenwood Press, 1983.

Wheeler-Bennett (John W.), *The Semblance of Peace. The Political Settlement after the Second World War*, London, Macmillan, 1972.

Williams (William A.), *The Tragedy of American Diplomacy*, Cleveland, World Publ., 1959.

Wittner (Lawrence S.), *American Intervention in Greece, 1943–1949*, New York, Columbia University Press, 1981.

Wolfe (Thomas W.) *Soviet Power and Europe, 1945–1970*, Baltimore, Johns Hopkins University Press, 1970.

Wolff (Robert L.), *The Balkans in Our Time*, Cambridge, Harvard University Press, 1974.

Wood (Robert E.), *From Marshall Plan to Depth Crisis. Foreign Aid and Development Choices in the World Economy*, Berkeley, University of California Press, 1986.

Woodhouse (C.M.), *The Struggle for Greece, 1941–1949*, Brooklin Heights, Beekman-Esanu, 1979.

Yergin (Daniel), *Shattered Peace: The Origins of the Cold War and the National Security State*, Boston, Houghton Mifflin, 1977.

Young (John), *Britain, France and the Unity of Europe, 1945–1951*, Leicester, Leicester University Press, 1984.

INDEX